SEVEN CENTURIES
OF POETRY

SEVEN CENTURIES OF POETRY

CHAUCER TO DYLAN THOMAS

Edited by

A. N. JEFFARES

BOOKS FOR LIBRARIES PRESS
PLAINVIEW, NEW YORK

LONGMANS, GREEN AND CO LTD
6 & 7 CLIFFORD STREET, LONDON WI

THIBAULT HOUSE, THIBAULT SQUARE CAPE TOWN
605-611 LONSDALE STREET, MELBOURNE CI
433 LOCKHART ROAD, HONG KONG
ACCRA, AUCKLAND, IBADAN
KINGSTON (JAMAICA), KUALA LUMPUR
LAHORE, NAIROBI, SALISBURY (RHODESIA)

LONGMANS, GREEN AND CO INC
119 WEST 40TH STREET, NEW YORK 18

LONGMANS, GREEN AND CO
20 CRANFIELD ROAD, TORONTO 16

ORIENT LONGMANS PRIVATE LTD
CALCUTTA, BOMBAY, MADRAS
DELHI, HYDERABAD, DACCA

PRINTED IN THE UNITED STATES OF AMERICA

To Jeanne

ACKNOWLEDGMENTS

For permission to include copyright material we are indebted to:—

The Cresset Press Ltd. for 'The stockdove' by Ruth Pitter from *The Spirit Watches* and *Urania*; Messrs. Martin Secker & Warburg Ltd. for 'White Christmas' by W. R. Rodgers, and 'Saadabad' by James Elroy Flecker; Mr. Hugh MacDiarmid for 'Deep-sea fishing', 'De profundis' and 'Antenora'; Mrs. Ida M. Flower for 'Troy' by Robin Flower; The Clarendon Press, Oxford, for 'Triolet', 'London snow' and 'Cheddar pinks' from *The Poetical Works of Robert Bridges*; Mrs. Harold Monro for 'Living' and 'Week-end' by Harold Monro; Mr. Sydney Goodsir Smith for 'Can I forget?'; The Trustees of the George Meredith Estate for 'Love dies', 'A dusty answer' and 'Juggling Jerry' by George Meredith; the Executors of the late Dr. Douglas Hyde for 'The Red man's wife' and 'I am Raftery'; Messrs. Burns Oates & Washbourne Ltd. for 'Anti-Christ' by G. K. Chesterton; Mr. A. S. J. Tessimond for 'Daydream'; Mr. Robert Graves for 'Ogres and Pygmies', 'The bards' and 'In the wilderness' from *Collected Poems 1914-1947*; Dr. John Masefield, O.M., The Society of Authors and The Macmillan Company, New York, for 'Sonnet'; Editions Poetry London for 'On the Grand Canal' by David Gascoyne; Mr. Robert Farren for 'The cool gold wines of Paradise'; Messrs. Percy Dobell & Son for 'Wonder' by Thomas Traherne; Messrs. Sidgwick & Jackson for 'Menelaus and Helen' by Rupert Brooke, 'The barn' by Edmund Blunden and 'Poetry and science' by W. J. Turner; Messrs. John Murray Ltd. for 'Before the Anaesthetic' from *Selected Poems* by John Betjeman; Messrs. J. M. Dent & Sons Ltd. for 'And death shall have no dominion', 'The hand that signed the paper', 'A refusal to mourn the Death, by Fire, of a child in London', 'Light breaks where no sun shines', 'Poem in October' and 'When all my five and country senses see' by Dylan Thomas; Mandeville Publications for 'Proserpine at Enna' by Ronald Bottrall; the Oxford University Press for 'Moonrise', 'Life death does end', extracts from 'The wreck of the Deutschland' and 'Six Epigrams' from *Poems of Gerard Manley Hopkins*, and 'A correct compassion' by James Kirkup; the owners of the copyright for 'The threshing machine' and 'The wind is blind' by Alice Meynell, 'To a snowflake' and 'The hound of Heaven' by Francis Thompson; Messrs. Allen & Unwin for 'Evening' by Richard Aldington, 'The fair at Windgap' by Austin Clarke and 'In hospital: Poona' by Alun Lewis; Mr. Douglas Young for 'Ice-flumes owregie their lades' and 'Last lauch'; the Executor of the late Norman Cameron for 'The verdict'; The Society of Authors as the Literary Representative of the Trustees of the Estate of the late A. E. Housman and Messrs. Jonathan Cape Ltd. for 'Yon far country', 'Wenlock' and 'Friends' from *Collected Poems* by A. E. Housman; Messrs. Jonathan Cape Ltd. for 'On the sea wall' from *Poems* 1943-47 by C. Day Lewis, and 'Naming of parts' from *A Map of Verona* by Henry Reed; Mrs. H. M. Davies for 'The wind' and 'Leisure' from *The Collected Poems of W. H. Davies* and the author for 'In December' and 'The round barrow' from *The Collected Poems of Andrew Young*, all published by Messrs. Jonathan Cape Ltd.; Messrs. Gerald Duckworth & Co. Ltd. for 'On the coast of Coromandel' by Osbert Sitwell, and 'The Rio Grande' by Sacheverell Sitwell; Messrs. Wm. Heinemann Ltd. for 'The garden of Proserpine' by A. C. Swinburne from *Swinburne's Collected Poetical Works;* Mrs. Frieda Lawrence for 'Humming-bird' and 'Giorno

viii   ACKNOWLEDGMENTS

dei Morti' by D. H. Lawrence, published by Messrs. Wm. Heinemann Ltd.;
Messrs. Routledge & Kegan Paul Ltd. for 'Autumn' and 'Fantasia of a fallen
Gentleman' by T. E. Hulme, 'The Magazine Fort' by William Wilkins from
Nineteenth Century Poetry, 'Poem', 'The atoll in the mind' and 'Notes for my
son' by Alex Comfort, 'William Wordsworth' and 'Time will not grant' by Sidney
Keyes; The Hogarth Press Ltd. for 'September Evening 1938' by William Plomer,
'Consider these for we have condemned them' by C. Day Lewis, and 'January
1940' by Roy Fuller; Mrs. Stephens and Messrs. Macmillan & Co. Ltd. for 'A
glass of beer' and 'Egan O Rahilly' from *Collected Poems* by James Stephens;
The Trustees of the Hardy Estate and Messrs. Macmillan & Co. Ltd. for 'When
I set out for Lyonesse', 'In Tenebris' and 'Weathers' from *Collected Poems* by
Thomas Hardy; Mrs. Sturge Moore for 'The dying swan' from Vol. II p. 7 and
'Shells' from Vol. IV p. 43 of *The Poems of T. Sturge Moore Collected Edition*,
Mr. Diarmuid Russell for 'Ancient' and 'Dark rapture' from *Collected Poems*
by Æ, Mrs. W. B. Yeats for 'The curse of Cromwell', 'No second Troy', 'The
Second Coming', 'Sailing to Byzantium', 'Byzantium' and an extract from 'The
wanderings of Oisin' from *Collected Poems of W. B. Yeats*, and Mrs. George
Bambridge for 'Harp song of the Dane women' from Rudyard Kipling's *Puck
of Pook's Hill* all published by Messrs. Macmillan & Co. Ltd.; Mrs. George
Bambridge and Messrs. Methuen & Co. Ltd. for 'Danny Deever' from *The
Craftsman* by Rudyard Kipling; Mr. Walter de la Mare and Messrs. Faber &
Faber Ltd. for 'Breughel's Winter', 'Slim cunning hands' and 'The last coachload';
Messrs. Faber & Faber Ltd. for 'Childhood' and 'Horses' from *Collected Poems
1921-1951* and 'The Interrogation' from *Collected Poems of Edwin Muir*, 'Pre-
ludes' and 'Gerontion' from *Collected Poems 1909-1935*, and 'The Dry Salvages',
by T. S. Eliot, 'At last the secret is out', 'Musee des beaux arts' and 'Lay your
sleeping head' from *Collected Shorter Poems 1930-1944* by W. H. Auden, 'The
British Museum Reading Room', 'Among these turf-stacks' and 'Bagpipe music'
from *Collected Poems 1925-1948* by Louis MacNeice, 'Ultima ratio regum' from
The Still Centre and 'Ice' from *The Edge of Being* by Stephen Spender, 'The
island' by Sean Jennett from *The Cloth of Flesh*, 'Sonnet to my Mother' from
Eros in Dogma and 'Munich Elegy No. 1' from *Lament and Triumph* by George
Barker, 'For a child expected' from *The Nine Bright Shiners* and 'O Love, answer'
from *The Golden Bird* by Anne Ridler; 'The burning bush' by Norman Nicholson
from *Five Rivers*, and 'The Expanding Universe' from *Pot Geranium*; 'A northern
legion' and 'The seven sleepers' by Sir Herbert Read from *Collected Poems*; Mrs.
Helen Thomas for 'Haymaking' and 'Health' by Edward Thomas and Mr. Roy
Campbell for 'Horses on the Camargue' from *Adamastor*, all published by Messrs.
Faber & Faber Ltd.; Mr. Maurice Craig for 'Ballad to a traditional refrain';
Messrs. Chatto & Windus for 'Break of day in the trenches' by Isaac Rosenberg,
'Anthem for doomed youth' and 'Futility' by Wilfred Owen, and 'This last pain'
by William Empson, and 'Speak with the sun' by David Campbell from *Speak
with the Sun*; Dame Edith Sitwell for 'Hornpipe', 'Still falls the Rain', and 'Dirge
for the New Sunrise' from *The Canticle of the Rose* (*Selected Poems 1920-1947*)
published by Messrs. Macmillan & Co. Ltd.; Mr. Ruthven Todd for 'Various
ends'; Messrs. Angus & Robertson Ltd. for 'The Builders' and 'Night and the
child' by Judith Wright from *Woman to Man*, 'Rock carving' by Douglas Stewart
from *The Dosser in Springtime* and 'Mahony's Mountain' by Douglas Stewart
from *Sun Orchids and Other Poems*, 'Five bells' by Kenneth Slessor from *One
Hundred Poems* and 'Two chronometers' by Kenneth Slessor from *Five Visions
of Captain Cook*; Mr. David Campbell for 'The end of exploring' published by
The Bulletin; Miss Judith Wright and *The Bulletin* for 'Bullocky' from *The Moving
Image*.

CONTENTS

CONTENTS

CONTENTS

CONTENTS

xiv   CONTENTS

CONTENTS

CONTENTS

CONTENTS

xviii CONTENTS

CONTENTS

INTRODUCTION

In many schools throughout the world where English Literature is studied the history of that literature is not taught. This may be due to a reaction against those textbooks which offered their readers a readymade and often illfitting critical comment on the authors whom they surveyed in chronological sequence. We now have an emphasis upon the value of examining several writers in some detail. A greater depth of knowledge and a more original power of criticism are meant to be aroused in the pupil because of this concentration. So far, so good. These isolated blocks of literature are meant to be related to each other and to the general development of the literature by the efforts of the schoolteacher, the independent reading of the pupil. The good teacher does his or her best to indicate some of the gaps, and the pupil who is interested in poetry often explores them.

Many people, brought up on this system of a deep knowledge of a few writers, regret that they have not been given a larger view of the whole scope of English Literature during their last years at school. The danger of setting a few writers upon a course is that some teachers, faced with a need to pass as many pupils as possible through their examinations, are tempted to grind in a knowledge of the set texts and neglect the general picture. There are some syllabuses which do not include a history of English Literature as a set book, much less a general anthology of English poetry. Even among undergraduates studying English seriously I have noticed a distressing lack of chronological knowledge of their subject, and hence a lack of feeling for the development of the literature. Ask a first, second, and even third year University student of English if he knows in which quarter of the eighteenth century Gray or Thompson or Akenside or Crabbe wrote, and you may be surprised at the answers you get. If the answers are as I anticipate then perhaps you will agree with me if I query whether the reaction against those authoritarian guide books which mixed history with criticism has not gone too far. We have got rid of the compressed criticism but in doing so we may have destroyed ideas of the inter-relationships of literature, recognitions both of its accretive growth and its constant rebirth. An insistence upon an historical attitude as distinct from a critical would provide a better basis for the appreciation and understanding of English literature, particularly in its social relationship, not only for the people whose past and present life is interpreted by its writers, but for those who inherit this rich and complex culture. To develop this historical attitude it is necessary to have some literary history set upon the syllabuses and used.

In an expanding period of universal education, when many schoolchildren and university students come from homes which have a meagre supply of books, where no habit of extensive reading, let alone book-buying, has existed, it is well to supply an anthology. This will serve to supplement the poets studied in detail (though that detail is not often impressive); to hint at the gaps to be filled; and to help in the civilising process of education in general.

Further, such an anthology must offer what we might call a skeletal perception of its subject: the tree-like growth of English poetry from its gnarled roots in the dark Anglo-saxon soil to the modern blossom, the *anthos*. This particular blossom may seem to many to be unsatisfactory. It is disgruntling to the old because it often expresses the contradiction of what they believed themselves, because life before and after the first world war is so changed, 'changed utterly'—

'Things thought too long can be no longer thought.'

It is disappointing because of its sadness or satire, its self-mockery, to the young, who still believe, an unconscionable number of them, in an inevitable Wellsian 'progress' of scientific man. Unsatisfactory it may well be because we live in a social age, a levelling age, and many of our poets are writing either metaphysical poetry or romantic poetry: the one over-ripe, the other an *omphax*, an unripe grape for our occasionally bitter harvesting. But none the less it is a bloom, more varied than is sometimes thought, and it must be seen for any of the past meanings and ramifications of poetry to achieve their full effect upon a nascent mind.

Without a sight of it, the wood is dead, the individual tree a ring-barked gum passed with sadness, meaningless to those who have their lives to live in the future, a mere liability from the once gloriously living past. To read poetry creatively should be the aim of anyone; it is most natural to want to know what one's contemporaries say, to share their preoccupations, their sensitivities, their disgusts and delights. Contemporary poets however are generally a little older than oneself when young: and youth does not trust youth quite as much as in the roaring twenties and marching thirties of the youth movements. Age it has never completely trusted. Nevertheless, to find the index blocking the way where modern poetry might be expected in an anthology is exasperating to the young who are being given a chronological introduction to English poetry. But the exasperation may well not last long enough for contemporary poetry to be sought out by themselves—there is so much competition for attention, the radio, the cinema, television, that private reading now needs watering and weeding incessantly, in its crucial transplantation from youth to adulthood.

Excellent though such anthologies as the Golden Treasury and the Oxford Book of English Verse are, yet they do not entirely answer the needs of our time, an age which is less sure of the value of poetry, one in which, shall we say, the readers of Eliot and Yeats, of Auden and MacNeice, of Dylan Thomas and Roy Campbell, will be stamped as 'intellectuals'. These are the readers who have gone on and made their own prospect of poetry unaided: but there are many who stop at Wordsworth or Tennyson or Masefield still, and think of poetry in Keatsian terms, who consider poetry to be solely the production of inspiration, of the poet who is an impractical dreamer. These are the readers who need an anthology reaching right into our contemporary literary scene.

It is strange that such ideas about poets and poetry should prevail into an age when British poets transfer themselves with a Chaucerian ease and mastery of affairs from one patronage to another in their search for bread and pensions: from the B.B.C. to the British Council according to which side the axe is sharpened, from the fecklessness of an advanced publishing house to the anonymous privacy of a public service. They are not seen by the majority as heirs to the long tradition of an old demanding craft, workers who as often open up old workings with modern mechanism as they mine fresh shafts in a geiger-counter age. To link them with their predecessors is essential, even at the risk of the anthologist's own preferences and dislikes, joyful or grudging admissions and rejections failing to accord with later climates of opinion: but no anthology has ever been made without incurring risks.

Anthologies should be made reasonably often, just as fresh critical estimations and new historical surveys are desirable. Taste changes, estimates alter, just as spelling and syntax and style vary. Literature is not static. While informed opinion in most English schools in the universities of today has reached a truer perspective of the eighteenth century than in the past, that perspective has not yet passed into the schools. There should, therefore, be an attempt on the part of the anthologist to give a more balanced view of that period within which so much sensible and amusing poetry was written, when satire was used in a way which could be useful now, a period when many members of an upsurging population had to be taught their manners, as now their cultural deficiencies.

The eighteenth century offers us much which we can appreciate if only we have the inkling what is there. Few people realise its riches until they have themselves passed from the romantic subjectivity of adolescence into what may be some degree of rationality, some greater social consciousness. Some, however, will never desire to leave Wordsworthian raptures, perhaps because they neither know nor care who now reads Pope.

Again, new light is being thrown on the nineteenth century. After a period of denigration the Victorians are being re-valued, and new emphasis should, accordingly, appear in an anthology.

There is an increasing interest in the medieval element in British civilisation, and this too must be represented. The Honours student, the specialist, will naturally turn to the original manuscripts, the texts of the first editions, to get as near as possible to the original, even though we cannot completely rely, for instance, upon our ability to read an Elizabethan poem or even a Jacobean as the poet's contemporaries read them. We can best serve the general reader and the first year student by providing a text that is easy to read without the distractions of old spelling, punctuation, and occasionally syntax and vocabulary, though in the last two there can be less editorial freedom. I subscribe to the opinions expressed by the late Mr. Norman Ault, in the prefaces to his collections of 16th and 17th century lyrics; but with the reservation that modernised texts commence in this anthology with the Tudor period.

There is one plea which must be made in an age when the art of private speech and conversation is wilting under the impact of mass media which encourage passivity rather than participation, an age which threatens us with a vast new illiteracy, where children will 'think' in a series of balloons containing the most meagre vocabulary reinforced by the crudest of visual stimuli, a time of primitive pictorialism within which abstract ideas and clear thinking languish for want of good (which implies disciplined) linguistic teaching. The plea is simple. Read poetry aloud. Poetry is a princely thing, not made to lie in the prison of the printed word, but intended to voice the human spirit in all its aspects.

In compiling this anthology I have chosen poems which I consider suited to the general texture of poetry with which I would like a first year student to be acquainted. I have made it because none of the available anthologies served the purposes I have in mind. Some of the selections are orthodox, some unorthodox: some are based on personal preference, other things being equal; others because of conviction that they should be known by anyone wishing to use this book as a means of obtaining a brief chronological view of English poetry. Inevitably, there will be omissions and inclusions that seem capricious, for this is the human factor of poetry: that everyone reads a poem differently, so that each poem is an unique poem and has a life of its own, independent of its author, its age, its original format—and its anthologist.

I have had many discussions with members of the English department in the University of Adelaide, to whom I am deeply grateful for the interest they showed, the help they gave: in particular to Mr. M. Bryn Davies, Mr. G. P. H. Dutton, Mr. H. W. Piper, Mr. D. C. Muecke and Mr. B. R. Elliott. Mr. J. A. Annand also aided me greatly as did Miss Jean Whyte of the Public Library of South Australia, Mr. W. A. Cowan, Barr Smith Librarian of the University of Adelaide, and Professor Milgate of the University of Sydney.

Like so many other books, this owes much to the encouragement and inevitable kindness of Professor D. Nichol Smith.

A. Norman Jeffares.

Adelaide, 1955.

For help in preparing a new edition of this anthology I am deeply grateful to my colleagues in the University of Leeds, Professor H. Orton, Head of the Department of English Language and Medieval Literature, and Miss A. C. Stead, Research Archivist. in the Department of English Literature. I am also indebted to Professor R. Quirk, of University College, London.

A. Norman Jeffares.

Leeds, 1960.

ANONYMOUS

Sumer is icumen in

Sumer is icumen in,
Lhude sing cuccu!
Groweth sed and bloweth med
And springth the wude nu.
Sing cuccu!

Awe bleteth after lomb,
Lhouth[1] after calve cu,
Bulluc sterteth, bucke verteth.
Murie sing cuccu!
Cuccu, cuccu,
Wel singes thu cuccu,
Ne swik[2] thu naver nu.

Sing cuccu nu, sing cuccu!
Sing cuccu, sing cuccu nu!

1. *lhouth* = loweth.   2. *swik* = cease.

ANONYMOUS

Now comes the blast of winter

Mirie it is while sumer ilast
With fugheles[1] song,
Oc[2] nu necheth[3] windes blast
And weder strong
Ei, ei, what this night is long,
And ich with wel michel wrong
Soregh and murne and fast.

1. *fugheles* = fowls.   2. *oc* = but.   3. *necheth* = approaches.

A

ANONYMOUS

When the turuf is thi tuur

Wen the turuf is thi tuur,
And thi put[1] is thi bour,
Thi wel[2] and thi wite throte
Ssulen wormes to note.
Wat helpit the thenne
Al the worilde wnne?

1. *put*=pit.   2. *wel*=skin.

ANONYMOUS

Christ's prayer in Gethsemane

A sory beuerech it is and sore it is abouth;
Nou in this sarpe time this brewing hath me brouth.
Fader, if it mowe ben don als I haue besouth,
Do awey this beuerich, that I ne drink et nouth.

And if it mowe no betre ben, for alle mannis gilth,
That it ne muste nede that my blod be spilth,
Suete fader, I am thi sone, thi wil be fulfilt.
I am her thin owen child, I wil don as thu wilt.

ANONYMOUS

Wynter wakeneth al my care

Wynter wakeneth al my care;
Nou this leves waxeth bare;
Ofte I sike and mourne sare,
When hit cometh in my thoght
Of this worldes ioie, hou hit geth al to noht.

Nou hit is, and nou hit nys,
Also hit ner nere ywys.
That moni man seith, soth[1] hit is,
Al goth bote Godes wille.
Alle we shule deye, thah[2] us like ylle.

Al that gren me greveth grene,
Now hit faleueth[3] al by dene[4].
Jesu, help that hit be sene,
Ant shild us from helle,
For I not whider I shal, ne hou longe her duelle.

1. *soth*=truth.   2. *thah*=though.   3. *falueth*=fades.   4. *by dene*=at once.

ANONYMOUS

The Irish dancer

Ich am of Irlaunde,
Ant of the holy londe
Of Irlaunde.

Gode sire, pray Ich the,
For of saynte charite
Come ant daunce wyt me
In Irlaunde.

ANONYMOUS

A forsaken maiden's lament

Were it undo that is y-do
I wolde be-war

Y lovede a child of this cuntre,
And so y wende he had do me;
Now myself the sothe y see,
That he is far.

Were it undo that is y-do
I wolde be-war

He seyde to me he wolde be trewe,
And change me for non othur newe;
Now y sykke and am pale of hewe,
For he is far.

ANONYMOUS

Were it undo that is y-do
I wolde be-war

He seide his sawus he wolde fulfille,
Therfore y lat him have al his wille;
Now y sykke and morne stille,
For he is far.

Were it undo that is y-do
I wolde be-war

ANONYMOUS

Bring good ale

Bryng us in good ale, and bryng us in good ale;
For our blyssyd lady sake, bryng us in good ale.

Bryng us in no browne bred, for that is mad of brane;
Nor bryng us in no whyt bred, for therin is no game,
But bryng us in good ale.

Bryng us in no befe, for there is many bonys;
But bryng us in good ale, for that goth downe at onys
And bryng us in good ale.

Bryng us in no bacon, for that is passyng fate;
But bryng us in good ale, and gyfe us I-nought of that,
And bryng us in good ale.

Bryng us in no mutton, for that is ofte lene;
Nor bryng us in no trypys, for thei be syldom clene,
But bryng us in good ale.

Bryng us in no eggys, for there are many schelles;
But bryng us in good ale, and gyfe us nothing ellys,
And bryng us in good ale.

Bryng us in no butter, for ther-in ar many herys;
Nor bryng us in no pygges flesch, for that wyl mak us borys,
But bryng us in good ale.

Bryng us in no podynges, for ther-in is al gotes blod;
Nor bryng us in no veneson, for that is not for owr good,
But bryng us in good ale.

Bryng us in no capons flesch, for that is ofte der;
Nor bryng us in no dokes flesch, for thei slober in the mer,
But bryng us in good ale.

GEOFFREY CHAUCER (1343-4?—1400)

Now welcome, somer

'Now welcome, somer, with thy sonne softe,
That hast this wintres wedres overshake,
And driven away the longe nyghtes blake!

'Saynt Valentyn, that art ful hy on-lofte,
Thus syngen smale foules for thy sake:
    Now welcome, somer, with thy sonne softe,
    That hast this wintres wedres overshake.

'Wel han they cause for to gladen ofte,
Sith ech of hem recovered hath hys make,
Ful blissful mowe they synge when they wake:
Now welcome, somer, with thy sonne softe,
That hast this wintres wedres overshake,
And driven away the longe nyghtes blake!'

From *The Parlement of Foules*

At the gate

Tyl it was noon, they stoden for to se
Who that ther come; and every maner wight
That com fro fer, they seyden it was she,
Til that thei koude knowen hym aright.
Now was his herte dul, now was it light.
And thus byjaped stonden for to stare
Aboute naught this Troilus and Pandare.

GEOFFREY CHAUCER

To Pandarus this Troilus tho seyde,
'For aught I woot, byfor noon, sikirly[1],
Into this town ne comth nat here Criseyde.
She hath ynough to doone, hardyly,
To wynnen from hire fader, so trowe I.
Hire olde fader wol yet make hire dyne
Er that she go; God yeve hys herte pyne!'

Pandare answerede, 'It may wel be, certeyn.
And forthi lat us dyne, I the byseche,
And after noon than maystow come ayeyn.'
And hom they go; withoute more speche,
And comen ayeyn; but longe may they seche
Er that they fynde that they after gape.
Fortune hem bothe thenketh for to jape!

Quod Troilus, 'I se wel now that she
Is taried with hire olde fader so,
That er she come, it wol neigh even be.
Com forth, I wole unto the yate go.
Thise porters ben unkonnyng evere mo,
And I wol don hem holden up the yate
As naught ne were, although she come late.'

The day goth faste, and after that com eve,
And yet com nought to Troilus Criseyde.
He loketh forth by hegge[2], by tre, by greve,
And fer his hed over the wal he leyde,
And at the laste he torned hym and seyde,
'By God, I woot hire menyng now, Pandare!
Almoost, ywys, al newe was my care.

'Now douteles, this lady kan hire good;
I woot, she meneth riden pryvely.
I comende hire wisdom, by myn hood!
She wol nat maken peple nycely
Gaure on hire when she comth; but softely
By nyghte into the town she thenketh ride.
And, deere brother, thynk not longe t'-abide.

'We han naught elles for to don, ywis.
And Pandarus, now woltow trowen me?
Have here my trouthe, I se hire! yond she is!
Heve up thyn eyen, man! maistow nat se?'
Pandare answerede, 'Nay, so mote I the!
Al wrong, by God! What saistow man, where arte?
That I se yond nys but a fare-carte³.'

'Allas! thow seyst right soth,' quod Troilus.
'But, hardily, it is naught al for nought
That in myn herte I now rejoysse thus.
It is ayeyns som good I have a thought.
Not I nat how, but syn that I was wrought,
Ne felte I swich a comfort, dar I seye;
She comth to-nyght, my lif that dorste I leye!'

Pandare answerde, 'It may be, wel ynough,'
And held with hym of al that evere he seyde.
But in his herte he thoughte, and softe lough,
And to hymself ful sobreliche he seyde,
'From haselwode, there joly Robyn pleyde,
Shal come al that that thow abidest heere.
Ye, fare wel at the snow of ferne yere!'

The warden of the yates gan to calle
The folk which that withoute the yates were,
And bad hem dryven in hire bestes alle,
Or al the nyght they most bleven there.
And fer withinne the nyght, with many a teere,
This Troilus gan homward for to ride;
For wel he seth it helpeth naught t'abide.

From *Troilus and Criseyde*

1. *sikirly*=certainly.   2. *hegge*=hedge.
3. *fare-cart*=travelling cart.

This fresshe flour

And doun on knes anoon-ryght I me sette,
And, as I koude, this fresshe flour I grette,
Knelyng alwey, til it unclosed was,
Upon the smale, softe, swote gras,
That was with floures swote enbrouded al,

Of swich swetnesse and swich odour overal,
That, for to speke of gomme, or herbe, or tree,
Comparisoun may noon ymaked bee;
For yt surmounteth pleynly alle odoures,
And of riche beaute alle floures.

From *The Legend of Good Women*

ANONYMOUS

Gracius and gay

Gracius and gay,
　　on hyr lyyt all my thogth;
Butt sche rew on me to-day,
　　to deth sche hatt me broth.

Hyr feyngerys bytt long and small,
　　Hyr harmus byth rown[1] and toth[2]
Hyr mowth as sweth as lycory,
　　Vn hyr lyytt all my toth.

Hyr eyne bytt feyr and gray,
　　Hyr bruys[3] bytt well y-benth,
Hyr rode[4] as rede as roose yn may,
　　Hyr medyll ys small and gent.

Sche ys swett under schett;
　　I low hyr and no mo.
Sche hatt myne harth to kepe,
　　In londes wher sche go.

Sodenly tell, y pray,
To the my low ys lend;
Kysse me yn my way,
　　Onys ar y wend.

rown=round.　2. *toth*=firm.　3. *bruys*=eyebrows.　4. *rode*=complexion.

A song to the Virgin

Of on that is so fayr and briht,
velut maris stella,
Brighter than the dayis liht,
parens et puella

Ic crie to the, thou se to me,
Levedy preye thi sone for me,
tam pia,
That ic mote come to the,
Maria.

Of kare conseil[1] thou ert best,
felix fecundata,
Of alie wery thou ert rest,
mater honorata,
Bisek[2] him wiz milde mod,
That for ous alle sad is blod,
in cruce,
That we moten comen til him,
in luce.

Al this world was forlore,
Eva peccatrice,
Tyl our lord was y-bore,
de te genetrice,
With Ave it went away,
Thuster[3] nyth and comet the day
salutis
The welle springet hut of the,
virtutis.

Levedi, flour of alle thing,
rosa sine spina,
Thu bere Jhesu, hevene king,
gratia divina,
Of alle thu berst the pris,
Levedi, quene of parays,
electa,
Mayde milde, Moder, *es*
effecta.

Wel he wot he is thi sone,
ventre quem portasti,
He wyl nout werne[4] the thi bone,
parvum quem lactasti,

So hende[5] and so god he his,
He havet brout ous to blis,
superni,
That havez hidut[6] the foule put,
inferni.

1. *conseil*=consolation.   2. *bisek*=beseech.   3. *thuster*=dark.
4. *werne*=refuse.   5. *hende*=kindly.   6. *hidut*=closed.

KING JAMES I (1394—1437)

Walking under the tour

And therewith cast I doun mine eye again,
   Whereas I saw, walking under the tour,
Full secretly new cummyn her to pleyne,
   The fairest and the freshest younge flour
   That ever I saw, methought, before that hour;
For which sudden abate[1] anon astert
The blood of all my body to my hert.

And though I stood abased tho a lyte[2]
   No wonder was; for-why my wittis all
Were so owre-come with pleasance and delight,
   Only through latting of mine eyen fall,
   That suddenly my heart became her thrall
For ever, of free will; for of manace
There was no token in her sweete face.

And in my head I drew right hastily,
   And eft-soones I leant it forth again,
And saw her walk, that very womanly,
   With no wight mo, but only women twain.
   Than gan I study in myself and seyne,
'Ah sweet! are ye a warldly creature,
Or heavenly thing in likeness of nature?'

From *The Kingis Quair*

1. *abate*=casting down.   2. *lyte*=little.

ROBERT HENRYSON (1425?—1506)

Cressida's leprosy

Thus chydand with her drery desteny,
Weiping, sho woik the nicht fra end to end,
But all in vane; hir dule, hir cairfull cry
Micht nocht remeid, nor yit hir murning mend.'
Ane lipper-lady rais, and till hir wend,
And said, 'Quhy spurns thou aganis the wall,
To sla thyself, and mend na-thing at all?

'Sen[1] that thy weiping dowbillis bot thy wo,
I counsall thee mak vertew of ane neid,
To leir[2] to clap thy clapper to and fro,
And live efter the law of lipper-leid[3].'
Thair was na buit[4], bot forth with thame sho yeid[5]
Fra place to place, quhill cauld and hounger sair
Compellit hir to be ane rank beggair.

That samin tyme, of Troy the garnisoun,
Quhilk had to chiftane worthy Troilus,
Throw jeopardy of weir had strikkin doun
Knichtis of Greece in number mervellous.
With greit triumph and laud victorious
Agane to Troy richt royally thay raid
The way quhair Cresseid with the lipper baid.

Seing that company thai come, all with ane stevin[6]
They gaif ane cry, and shuik coppis gude speid;
Said, 'Worthy lordis, for goddis lufe of hevin,
To us lipper part of your almous-deid.'
Than to thair cry nobill Troilus tuik heid;
Having pity, neir by the place can[7] pas
Quhair Cresseid sat, not witting quhat sho was.

Than upon him sho kest up baith her ene,
And with ane blenk it com into his thocht
That he sum-tyme hir face befoir had sene;
But sho was in sic ply[8] he knew hir nocht.
Yit than hir luik into his mind it brocht
The sweit visage and amorous blenking
Of fair Cresseid, sumtyme his awin darling.

11

Na wonder was, suppois in mynd that he
Tuik her figure sa sone, and lo! now, quhy;
The idole of ane thing in cace may be
Sa deip imprentit in the fantasy,
That it deludis the wittis outwardly,
And sa appeiris in forme and lyke estait
Within the mynd as it was figurait.

Ane spark of lufe than till his hart coud spring,
And kendlit all his body in ane fyre;
With hait fevir ane sweit and trimbilling
Him tuik, quhill he was redy to expyre;
To beir his sheild his breist began to tyre;
Within ane whyle he changit mony hew,
And nevertheles not ane aneuther knew.

For knichtly pity and memoriall
Of fair Cresseid, ane girdill can he tak,
Ane purs of gold, and mony gay jowall,
And in the skirt of Cresseid doun can swak[9]
Than raid away, and not ane word he spak,
Pensive in hart, quhill he com to the toun,
And for greit cair oft-syis almaist fell doun.

The lipper-folk to Cresseid than can draw,
To see the equall distribucioun
Of the almous; but quhan the gold they saw,
Ilk ane to uther prevely can roun[10],
And said, 'Yon lord hes mair affectioun,
However it be, unto yon lazarous
Than to us all; we knaw be his almous.'

'Quhat lord is yon?' quod sho, 'have ye na feill[11],
Hes don to us so greit humanitie?'
'Yes,' quod a lipper-man, 'I knaw him weill;
Shir Troilus it is, gentill and free.'
Quhen Cresseid understude that it was he,
Stiffer than steill thair stert ane bitter stound
Throwout hir hart, and fell doun to the ground.

Quhen sho ourcome[12] with syching sair and sad,
With mony cairfull cry and cald—'Ochane!
Now is my breist with stormy stoundis stad,
Wrappit in wo, ane wretch full will of wane[13].'
Than swounit sho oft or sho coud refrane,
And ever in hir swouning cryit sho thus:
'O fals Cresseid, and trew knicht Troilus!

'Thy luf, thy lawtee[14], and thy gentilnes
I countit small in my prosperitie;
Sa elevait I was in wantones,
And clam upon the fickill quheill sa hie;
All faith and lufe, I promissit to thee,
Was in the self fickill and frivolous;
O fals Cresseid, and trew knicht Troilus!

'For lufe of me thou keipt gude continence,
Honest and chaste in conversatioun;
Of all wemen protectour and defence
Thou was, and helpit thair opinioun.
My mynd, in fleshly foull affectioun,
Was inclynit to lustis lecherous;
Fy! fals Cresseid! O, trew knicht Troilus!

'Lovers, be war, and tak gude heid about
Quhom that ye lufe, for quhom ye suffer paine;
I lat yow wit, thair is richt few thairout
Quhom ye may traist, to have trew lufe againe;
Preif quhen ye will, your labour is in vaine.
Thairfoir I reid ye tak thame as ye find;
For they ar sad[15] as widdercock in wind.

'Becaus I knaw the greit unstabilnes
Brukkil as glas, into my-self I say,
Traisting in uther als greit unfaithfulnes,
Als unconstant, and als untrew of fay[16].
Thocht sum be trew, I wait richt few ar thay.
Quha findis treuth, lat him his lady ruse[17];
Nane but myself, as now, I will accuse.'

ROBERT HENRYSON

Quhen this was said, with paper sho sat doun,
And on this maneir maid hir TESTAMENT:—
'Heir I beteich[18] my corps and carioun
With wormis and with taidis to be rent;
My cop and clapper, and myne ornament,
And all my gold, the lipper-folk sall have,
Quhen I am deid, to bury me in grave.

'This royall ring, set with this ruby reid,
Quhilk Troilus in drowry[19] to me send,
To him agane I leif it quhan I am deid,
To mak my cairfull deid unto him kend.
Thus I conclude shortly, and mak ane end.
My spreit I leif to Diane, quhair sho dwellis,
To walk with hir in waist woddis and wellis.

'O Diomeid! thow hes baith broche and belt
Quhilk Troilus gave me in takinning
Of his trew lufe!' And with that word sho swelt[20],
And sone ane lipper-man tuik of the ring,
Syne buryit hir withoutin tarying.
To Troilus furthwith the ring he bair,
And of Cresseid the deith he can declair.

Quhen he had hard hir greit infirmitie,
Hir legacy and lamentatioun,
And how sho endit in sic povertie,
He swelt for wo, and fell doun in ane swoun;
For greit sorrow his hart to birst was boun.
Syching full sadly, said, 'I can no moir;
Sho was untrew, and wo is me thairfor!'

Sum said, he maid ane tomb of merbell gray,
And wrait hir name and superscriptioun,
And laid it on hir grave, quhair that sho lay,
In goldin letteris, conteining this ressoun[21]:—
'Lo! Fair ladyis, Cresseid of Troyis toun,
Sumtyme countit the flour of womanheid,
Under this stane, lait lipper, lyis deid!'

Now, worthy wemen, in this ballet short,
Made for your worship and instructioun,
Of cheritie I monish and exhort,
Ming[22] not your luf with fals deceptioun.
Beir in your mynd this short conclusioun
Of fair Cresseid, as I have said befoir;
Sen sho is deid, I speik of hir no moir.

From *The Testament of Cresseid*

1. *sen*=since. 2. *leir*=learn. 3. *lipper-leid*=leper-folk. 4. *buit*=boot, help.
5. *yeid*=went.   6. *stevin*=voice.   7. *can*=did.   8. *ply*=plight.
9. *swak*=throw.   10. *roun*=whisper.   11. *feill*=knowledge.
12. *ourcome*=revived.   13. *will of wane*=at a loss.   14. *lawtee*=loyalty.
15. *sad*=settled.   16. *fay*=faith.   17. *ruse*=praise.   18. *beteich*=bequeath.
19. *drowry*=love-token.   20. *swelt*=fainted.   21. *ressoun*=sentence.
                       22. *ming*=mingle.

JOHN SKELTON (1460?—1529)

Upon a dead man's head

*Sent to him from an honourable gentlewoman for a token, he devised
this ghostly meditation in English covenable, in sentence commen-
dable, lamentable, lacrimable, profitable for a soul.*

Your ugly token
My mind hath broken
From worldly lust:
For I have discust
We are but dust,
And die we must.
  It is general
To be mortal:
I have well espied
No man may him hide
From Death hollow-eyed,
With sinews withered,
With bones shivered,
With his worm-eaten maw,
And his ghastly jaw
Gasping aside,
Naked of hide,

Neither flesh nor fell.
  Then, by my counsell,
Look that ye spell
Well this gospell:
For whereso we dwell
Death will us quell,
And with us mell.
  For all our pampered paunches
There may no fraunchis,
Nor worldly bliss,
Redeem us from this:
Our days be dated
To be check-mated
With draughtes of death
Stopping our breath:
Our eyen sinking,
Our gummes grinning,
Our soules brinning[1].
To whom, then, shall we sue,
For to have rescue,
But to sweet Jesu
On us then for to rue?
  O goodly Child
Of Mary mild,
Then be our shield!
That we be not exiled
To the dun dale
Of bootless bale[2],
Nor to the lake
Of fiendes blake[3].
  But grant us grace
To see thy Face,
And to purchase
Thine heavenly place,
And thy palace
Full of solace
Above the sky
That is so high,
Eternally
To behold and see
The Trinitie!
  Amen.

1. *brinning* = burning.   2. *bale* = sorrow.   3. *blake* = black.

Philip Sparrow

When I remember again
How my Philip was slain,
Never half the pain
Was between you twain,
Pyramus and Thisbe,
As then befell to me:
I wept and I wailed,
The teares down hailed,
But nothing it availed
To call Philip again,
Whom Gib, our cat, hath slain.

Gib, I say, our cat
Worrowed her on that
Which I loved best.
It cannot be exprest
My sorrowful heaviness,
But all without redress!
For within that stound[1],
Half slumb'ring in a sound[2]
I fell down to the ground.
Unneth[3] I cast mine eyes
Toward the cloudy skies!
But when I did behold
My sparrow dead and cold
No creature but that wold
Have rued upon me,
To behold and see
What heaviness did me pang:
Wherewith my hands I wrang,
That my sinews cracked,
As though I had been racked,
So pained and so strained
That no life wellnigh remained.

I sighed and I sobbed,
For that I was robbed
Of my sparrow's life.
O maiden, widow, and wife,
Of what estate ye be,

Of high or low degree,
Great sorrow then ye might see,
And learn to weep at me!
Such pains did me fret
That mine heart did beat,
My visage pale and dead,
Wan, and blue as lead!
The pangs of hateful death
Wellnigh had stopped my breath!

1. *stound*=moment.   2. *sound*⇌swoon.   3. *unneth*=hardly.

WILLIAM DUNBAR (1465?—1530?)

Meditatioun in Wyntir

In to thir dirk and drublie dayis,
Quhone sabill all the hevin arrayis
With mystie vapouris, cluddis, and skyis,
Nature all curage me denyis
Off sangis, ballattis, and of playis.

Quhone that the nycht dois lenthin houris,
With wind, with haill, and havy schouris,
My dule spreit dois lurk for schoir,
My hairt for languor dois forloir
For laik of symmer with his flouris.

I walk, I turne, sleip may I nocht,
I vexit am with havie thocht;
This warld all ouir I cast about,
And ay the mair I am in dout,
The mair that I remeid have socht.

I am assayit on everie syde:
Dispair sayis ay, 'In tyme provyde
And get sum thing quhairon to leif,
Or with grit trouble and mischief
Thow sall in to this court abyd.'

Then Patience sayis, 'Be not agast:
Hald Hoip and Treuthe within the fast,
And lat Fortoun wirk furthe hir rage,
Quhome that no rasoun may assuage,
Quhill that hir glas be run and past.'

And Prudence in my eir sayis ay,
'Quhy wald thow hald that will away?
Or craif that thow may have no space,
Thow tending to ane uther place,
A journay going everie day?'

And than sayis Age, 'My freind, cum neir,
And be not strange, I the requeir:
Cum, brodir, by the hand me tak,
Remember thow hes compt to mak
Off all thi tyme thow spendit heir.'

Syne Deid castis upe his yettis wyd,
Saying, 'Their oppin sall the abyd;
Albeid that thow were never sa stout,
Undir this lyntall sall thow lowt:
Thair is nane uther way besyde.'

For feir of this all day I drowp;
No gold in kist, nor wyne in cowp,
No ladeis bewtie, nor luiffis blys,
May lat me to remember this,
How glaid that ever I dyne or sowp.

Yit, quhone the nycht begynnis to schort,
It dois my spreit sum pairt confort,
Off thocht oppressit with the schowris.
Cum, lustie symmer! with thi flowris,
That I may leif in sum disport.

ANONYMOUS

The Twa Corbies

As I was walking all alane,
I heard twa corbies[1] making a mane;
The tane unto the t'other say,
'Where sall we gang and dine to-day?'

'In behint yon auld fail[2] dyke
I wot there lies a new-slain knight;
And naebody kens that he lies there
But his hawk, his hound, and lady fair.

'His hound is to the hunting gane,
His hawk to fetch the wild-fowl hame,
His lady's ta'en another mate,
So we may mak our dinner sweet.

'Ye'll sit on his white hause-bane[3],
And I'll pike out his bonny blue een:
Wi' ae lock o' his gowden hair
We'll theek[4] our nest when it grows bare.

'Mony a one for him makes mane,
But nane sall ken where he is gane:
O'er his white banes, when they are bare,
The wind sall blaw for evermair.'

1. *corbies*=ravens.   2. *fail*=turf.   3. *hause*=neck.   4. *theek*=thatch.

ANONYMOUS

Baby Lon, or The bonnie banks o' Fordie

There were three ladies lived in a bower,
  Eh, wow, bonnie!
And they went out to pull a flower
  On the bonnie banks o' Fordie.

They hadna pu'ed a flower but ane,
When up started to them a banisht man.

He's ta'en the first sister by her hand,
And he's turn'd her round and made her stand.

'It's whether will ye be a rank[1] robber's wife,
Or will ye die by my wee pen-knife?'

'It's I'll not be a rank robber's wife,
But I'll rather die by your wee pen-knife.'

He's killed this may[2], and he's laid her by,
For to bear the red rose company.

He's taken the second ane by the hand,
And he's turn'd her round and made her stand.

'It's whether will ye be a rank robber's wife,
Or will ye die by my wee pen-knife?'

'It's I'll not be a rank robber's wife,
But I'll rather die by your wee pen-knife.'

He's killed this may, and he's laid her by,
For to bear the red rose company.

He's taken the youngest ane by the hand,
And he's turn'd her round and made her stand.

Says, 'Will ye be a rank robber's wife,
Or will ye die by my wee pen-knife?'

It's I'll not be a rank robber's wife,
Nor will I die by your wee pen-knife.

'For in this wood a brother I hae,
And gin ye kill me, it's he'll kill thee.'

'What's thy brother's name? come tell to me.'
'My brother's name is Baby Lon.'

'O sister, sister, what have I done!
O have I done this ill to thee!

'O since I've done this evil deed,
Good sall never be seen o' me.'

He's taken out his wee pen-knife,
   Eh, wow, bonnie!
And he's twyn'd himself o' his ain sweet life
   On the bonnie banks o' Fordie.

1. *rank*=violent.   2. *may*=maid.

ANONYMOUS

I have a gentil cok

I have a gentil cok,
Crowyt me day;
He doth me rysyn erly,
My matyins for to say.

I have a gentil cok,
Comyn he is of gret;
His comb is of red corel,
His tayil is of get.

I have a gentil cok,
Comyn he is of kynde;
His comb is of red corel,
His tayl is of inde[1].

His legges ben of asor,
So gentil and so smale;
His spores arn of syluer qwyt,
Into the worte-wale[2].
His eynyn arn of cristal,
Lokyn[3] al in aumbyr;
And euery nyght he perchit hym
In myn ladyis chaumbyr.

1. *inde* = indigo.   2. *worte-whale* = skin of the claws.   3. *lokyn* = locked, set.

GAVIN DOUGLAS (1474?—1522)

Winter

The soil ysowpit[1] into water wak,
The firmament ourcast with rokis black,
The ground fadit, and fauch[2] wox all the fieldis,
Mountain toppis sleikit[3] with snaw ourheildis[4];
On ragged rockis of hard harsk[5] whin stane,
With frosen frontis cauld clynty[6] clewis[7] shane;
Beautie was lost, and barrand shew the landis,
With frostis hair ourfret the fieldis standis.
Sour bitter bubbis[8], and the showris snell,
Seemit on the sward ane similitude of hell,

Reducing to our mind, in every steid,
Ghostly shadowis of eild and grisly deid,
Thick drumly skuggis[9] derknit so the heaven;
Dim skyis oft furth warpit fearful levin,
Flaggis of fire, and mony felloun flaw[10],
Sharp soppis of sleet, and of the snipand snaw.
The dowie ditches were all donk and wait,
The law valley flodderit[11] all with spate,
The plain streetis and every hie way
Full of flushis[12], dubbis[13], mire and clay.
Laggerit[14] leas wallowit[15] fernis shew,
Broun muiris kithit their wisnit[16] mossy hue,
Bank, brae, and boddum blanchit wox and bare;
For gurll[17] weather growit beastis hair;
The wind made wave the reid weed on the dyke;
Bedovin[18] in donkis deep was every syk[19];
Owre craggis, and the front of rockis seir,
Hang great ice-schoklis lang as ony spear;
The grund stude barrand, widderit, dosk and grey,
Herbis, flouris, and grasses wallowit away;
Woddis, forestis, with naked bewis blout[20],
Stude strippit of their weid in every hout[21],
So busteously Boreas his bugle blew.

1. *ysowpit*=sodden. 2. *fauch*=discoloured. 3. *sleikit*=smooth.
4. *ourheildis*=are covered. 5. *harsk*=harsh. 6. *clynty*=rocky.
7. *clewis*=cliffs. 8. *bubbis*=squalls. 9. *skuggis*=rain-clouds.
10. *flaw*=blasts. 11. *flodderit*=flooded. 12. *flushis*=pools.
13. *dubbis*=puddles. 14. *Laggerit*=muddied. 15. *wallowit*=withered.
16. *wisnit*=withered. 17. *gurll*=rough. 18. *Bedovin*=plunged.
19. *syk*=ditch. 20. *blout*=bare. 21. *hout*=wood.

SIR DAVID LINDSAY (1490—1555)

So young ane King

To you, my lordis, that standis by,
I shall you show the causis why.
Gif ye list tarry, I sall tell,
How my infortune first befell.
I prayit daily, on my knee,
My young maister that I mycht see
Of eild, in his estate royal,

Havand power imperial,
Then traistit[1] I, without demand,
To be promovit to some land.
Bot my asking I gat owre soon,
Because ane clipse[2] fell in the moon,
The whilk all Scotland made asteir,
Then did my purpose rin arreir,
The whilk were longsome to declare,
And als my heart is wonder sair,
When I have in remembrance
The sudden change, to my mischance.
The King was bot twelf yearis of age,
When new ruleris come, in their rage,
For common weill makand no care,
Bot for their profit singulair.
   Imprudently, like witless fulis,
They took the young Prince from the sculis,
Where he, under obedience,
Was lernand virtue and science,
And hastily plat in his hand
The governance of all Scotland;
As who wald in ane stormy blast,
When marineris bene all aghast
Through danger of the seis rage,
Wald tak ane child of tender age,
Whilk never had bene on the sea,
And to his bidding all obey,
Giving him haill the governall
Of ship, marchand, and marinall.
For dreid of rockis and foreland,
To put the rudder in his hand.
Without Goddis grace is no refuge:
Gif there be danger, ye may judge.
I give them to the Devil of Hell,
Whilk first devisit that counsell.
I will nocht say that it was treason,
Bot I dar swear, it was no reason.
I pray God let me never see ryng
Into this realm so young ane King.

1. *traistit*=trusted.   2. *clipse*=eclipse.

ANONYMOUS

Song

Westròn wynde when wyll thou blow,
The smalle rayne downe can rayne,
Cryst yf my love wer in my armys
And I yn my bed agayne.

SIR THOMAS WYATT (1503?—1542)

In Spain

Tagus, farewell, that westward with thy streams
Turns up the grains of gold already tried;
For I with spur and sail go seek the Thames,
Gainward[1] the sun that showeth her wealthy pride,
And to the town that Brutus sought by dreams,
Like bended moon, doth lean her lusty side.
My king, my country, alone for whom I live,
Of mighty love the wings for this me give.

1. *gainward*=flowing against.

How like you this?

They flee from me, that sometime did me seek
With naked foot, stalking in my chamber.
I have seen them gentle, tame, and meek,
That now are wild, and do not remember
That sometime they put themselves in danger[1]
To take bread at my hand; and now they range
Busily seeking with a continual change.

Thanked be fortune it hath been otherwise
Twenty times better; but once, in special,
In thin array, after a pleasant guise,
When her loose gown from her shoulders did fall,
And she me caught in her arms long and small[2],
Therewithall sweetly did me kiss
And softly said, 'Dear heart, how like you this?'

It was no dream; I lay broad waking;
But all is turned, now thorough my gentleness,
Into a strange fashion of forsaking;

And I have leave to go, of her goodness,
And she also to use newfangleness.
    But since that I so kindly am served,
    I would fain know what she hath deserved.

    1. *danger*=subjection.   2. *small*=slim.

To his Lady

Madam, withouten many words,
    Once, I am sure, ye will or no.
And if ye will, then leave your bourds[1]
    And use your wit and show it so.

And with a beck ye shall me call;
    And if of one, that burneth alway,
Ye have any pity at all,
    Answer him fair with yea, or nay.

If it be yea, I shall be fain;
    If it be nay, friends as before;
Ye shall another man obtain,
    And I mine own and yours no more.

    1. *bourds*=jests.

HENRY HOWARD, EARL OF SURREY (1517?—1547)

In Windsor Castle

So cruel prison how could betide, alas,
As proud Windsor, where I in lust and joy
With a king's son my childish years did pass
In greater feast than Priam's sons of Troy?
Where each sweet place returns a taste full sour;
The large green courts where we were wont to hove
With eyes cast up unto the maidens' tower,
And easy sighs, such as folk draw in love;
The stately seats, the ladies bright of hue,
The dances short, long tales of great delight,
With words and looks that tigers could but rue,
Where each of us did plead the other's right;

The palm-play where, despoiled for the game,
With dazed eyes oft we by gleams of love
Have missed the ball and got sight of our dame,
To bait her eyes, which kept the leads above; ·
The gravelled ground, with sleeves tied on the helm,
On foaming horse, with swords and friendly hearts,
With cheer, as though the one should overwhelm,
Where we have fought and chased oft with darts;
With silver drops the meads yet spread for ruth,
In active games of nimbleness and strength,
Where we did strain, trailed by swarms of youth,
Our tender limbs that yet shot up in length;
The secret groves which oft we made resound
Of pleasant plaint and of our ladies' praise,
Recording soft what grace each one had found,
What hope of speed, what dread of long delays;
The wild forest, the clothed holts with green,
With reins avaled[1], and swift ybreathed horse,
With cry of hounds and merry blasts between,
Where we did chase the fearful hart a force;
The void walls eke that harboured us each night,
Wherewith, alas, reviveth within my breast
The sweet accord, such sleeps as yet delight,
The pleasant dreams, the quiet bed of rest,
The secret thoughts imparted with such trust,
The wanton talk, the divers change of play,
The friendship sworn, each promise kept so just,
Wherewith we passed the winter nights away.
And with this thought the blood foresakes my face,
The tears berain my cheeks of deadly hue,
The which as soon as sobbing sighs, alas,
Upsupped have, thus I my plaint renew:
O place of bliss, renewer of my woes,
Give me account where is my noble fere[2],
Whom in thy walls thou didst each night enclose;
To other lief[3], but unto me most dear.'
Echo, alas! that doth my sorrow rue,
Returns thereto a hollow sound of plaint.
Thus I alone, where all my freedom grew,
In prison pine with bondage and restraint;
And with remembrance of the greater grief
To banish the less, I find my chief relief.

1. *avaled*=lowered.   2. *fere*=comrades.   3. *lief*=beloved.

Description of Spring, wherein each thing renews, save only the lover

The soote season, that bud and bloom forth brings,
With green hath clad the hill and eke the vale:
The nightingale with feathers new she sings;
The turtle to her make hath told her tale.
Summer is come, for every spray now springs:
The hart hath hung his old head on the pale;
The buck in brake his winter coat he flings;
The fishes float with new repaired scale;
The adder all her slough away she slings;
The swift swallow pursueth the flies smale;
The busy bee her honey now she mings;
Winter is worn that was the flowers' bale.
And thus I see among these pleasant things
Each care decays; and yet my sorrow springs.

THOMAS SACKVILLE, EARL OF DORSET (1536—1608)

Winter

The wrathful winter, 'proaching on apace,
  With blust'ring blasts had all ybared the treen:
And old Saturnus, with his frosty face,
  With chilling cold had pierced the tender green,
  The mantles rent, wherein enwrapped been
    The gladsome groves that now lay overthrown,
    The tapets torn, and every bloom down blown.

The soil, that erst so seemly was to seen,
  Was all despoiled of her beauty's hue;
And soote fresh flowers, wherewith the summer's queen
  Had clad the earth, now Boreas' blasts down blew:
  And small fowls flocking, in their song did rue
    The winter's wrath, wherewith each thing defaced
    In woeful wise bewailed the summer past.

Hawthorn had lost his motley livery,
  The naked twigs were shivering all for cold,
And dropping down the tears abundantly.
  Each thing, methought, with weeping eye me told
  The cruel season, bidding me withhold
    Myself within; for I was gotten out
    Into the fields, whereas I walked about. . . .

And sorrowing I, to see the summer flowers,
  The lively green, the lusty leas, forlorn;
The sturdy trees so shattered with the showers,
  The fields so fade, that flourished so beforne:
  It taught me well, all earthly things be born
     To die the death; for nought long time may last:
     The summer's beauty yields to winter's blast.

From *The Induction*, *A Mirror for Magistrates*

Troy

But Troy, alas, methought above them all,
It made mine eyes in very tears consume,
When I beheld the woeful word befall,
That by the wrathful will of gods was come;
And Jove's unmoved sentence and foredoom
  On Priam king, and on his town so bent,
  I could not lin[1], but I must there lament.

And that the more, sith destiny was so stern
As, force perforce, there might no force avail,
But she must fall, and by her fall we learn
That cities, towers, wealth, world, and all shall quail;
No manhood, might, nor nothing mought prevail;
  All were there prest, full many a prince and peer,
  And many a knight that sold his death full dear.

Not worthy Hector, worthiest of them all,
Her hope, her joy; his force is now for nought.
O Troy, Troy, Troy, there is no boot but bale;
The hugy horse within thy walls is brought;
Thy turrets fall, thy knights, that whilom fought
  In arms amid the field, are slain in bed,
  Thy gods defiled and all thy honor dead.

The flames upspring and cruelly they creep
From wall to roof till all to cinders waste;
Some fire the houses where the wretches sleep,
Some rush in here, some run in there as fast;
In everywhere or sword or fire they taste;
  The walls are torn, the towers whirled to the ground;
  There is no mischief but may there be found.

Cassandra yet there saw I how they haled
From Pallas' house, with spercled tress undone,
Her wrists fast bound and with Greeks' rout empaled;
And Priam eke, in vain how did he run
To arms, whom Pyrrhus with despite hath done
    To cruel death, and bathed him in the baign
    Of his son's blood, before the altar slain.

But how can I describe the doleful sight
That in the shield so livelike fair did shine?
Sith in this world I think was never wight
Could have set forth the half, not half so fine;
I can no more but tell how there is seen
    Fair Ilium fall in burning red gledes down,
    And from the soil great Troy, Neptunus' town.

1. *lin*=cease .

From *The Induction, A Mirror for Magistrates*

GEORGE GASCOIGNE (1525?—1577)

The looks of a lover enamoured

Thou, with thy looks, on whom I look full oft,
And find therein great cause of deep delight,
Thy face is fair, thy skin is smooth and soft,
Thy lips are sweet, thine eyes are clear and bright,
And every part seems pleasant in my sight;
Yet wote thou well, those looks have wrought my woe,
Because I love to look upon them so.

For first those looks allured mine eye to look,
And straight mine eye stirred up my heart to love;
And cruel love, with deep deceitful hook,
Choked up my mind, whom fancy cannot move,
Nor hope relieve, nor other help behoove
But still to look; and though I look too much,
Needs must I look because I see none such.

Thus in thy looks my love and life have hold;
And with such life my death draws on apace:
And for such death no med'cine can be told
But looking still upon thy lovely face,
Wherein are painted pity, peace, and grace.
Then though thy looks should cause me for to die,
Needs must I look, because I live thereby.

Since then thy looks my life have so in thrall
As I can like none other looks but thine,
Lo, here I yield my life, my love, and all
Into thy hands, and all things else resign
But liberty to gaze upon thine eyen:
Which when I do, then think it were thy part
To look again, and link with me in heart.

ANONYMOUS

The Bailey beareth the bell away

Alone walking
And oft musing
all by a riverside.
of whence be they
I pray you say
what craftsmen
trust you they be?
Name them now let see.
There came that time
and many mo
what merchants also
both fresh and gay
for the morrow
was the market day.
From every village
there beside
at that market time
bullocks
fat swine and sheep,
oats big
both rye and wheat
pigs yet
and capons
fat butter cheese
nuts crabs and eggs
with leeks both
green and great
and cherries from Denton
from Meduslye
that cometh among
and harrowes strong

spades shovels and goads
right long.
Nor for to presume for to sell
until they have hung the corn bell
tynkell tong tynkell tong
tynkell tong ty to
tynkell tong.
[Some go] to ask a mare
and other gear
O yet O yet O yet O yet
Lo a great bay mare,
she is slit in the right ear.
Maybe a month she came
from white barn
on the path towards the fields
of Kimblesworth, of Kimblesworth.
'Tell us let see for gladly would we
where to' quoth he
'I am here
say what you will.'
'It is Saint Cuthbert's day.'
'If it so be
I'll go' quoth he.

Not far from the
city woods and meadows
great and fair
and wholesome of air
In all of this realm
none such truly
a strong palace
a goodly moat
But on one place
to enter save only
with a boat
upon a craggy rock
it stands pleasantly.
Now we will go
the Bailey to,
there of something
now for to sing.
In lusty May

here they met
in the North Bailey
and at Elvett.
There was disguising,
Piping and dancing,
and as we came near [we heard a song]
which thus began 'Robin
Robin Robin.
And many [a] man
hath a fair wife
who does him little good
Robin Robin Robin
and jolly Robin lend you
me the bow.'
Through every street
thus they did go,
and every man
his horn did blow,
tro tro tro
ro ro . . . . .
The maidens came [too and sang]
'When I was in my mother's bower
I had all that I would
The Bailey beareth the bell away
The lily the rose the rose I lay
The silver is white red is the gold.
The robes they lay in fold.
The Bailey beareth the bell away,
The lily the rose the rose I lay.
And through the glass window
shines the sun.
How should I love and I so young.
The Bailey beareth the bell away
The lily the rose the rose I lay.'
The Bailey beareth the bell away
For to report it were now tedious,
we will therefore now sing no more
Of the games joyous
right mighty and famous
Elizabeth our Queen and princess,
prepotent and eke victorious
vertuous and benign.

B

Let us pray all
To Christ Eternal
which is the heavenly King.
After their life grant them
a place eternally to sing
Amen.

NICHOLAS BRETON (1545?—1626?)

A report song

Shall we go dance the hay, the hay?
Never pipe could ever play
Better shepherd's roundelay.

Shall we go sing the song, the song?
Never Love did ever wrong.
Fair maids, hold hands all along.

Shall we go learn to woo, to woo?
Never thought came ever to,
Better deed could better do.

Shall we go learn to kiss, to kiss?
Never heart could ever miss
Comfort. where true meaning is.

Thus at base they run, they run,
When the sport was scarce begun.
But I waked, and all was done.

Phyllida and Corydon

In the merry month of May,
In a morn by break of day,
Forth I walked by the woodside,
Whenas May was in his pride.
There I spied all alone
Phyllida and Corydon.
Much ado there was, God wot,
He would love and she would not.
She said, never man was true;
He said, none was false to you.

He said, he had loved her long;
She said, love should have no wrong.
Corydon would kiss her then;
She said, maids must kiss no men
Till they did for good and all.
Then she made the shepherd call
All the heavens to witness truth,
Never loved a truer youth.
Thus with many a pretty oath,
Yea and nay, and faith and troth,
Such as silly shepherds use
When they will not love abuse;
Love, which had been long deluded,
Was with kisses sweet concluded.
And Phyllida with garlands gay
Was made the Lady of the May.

SIR WALTER RALEIGH (1552?—1618)

The passionate man's pilgrimage

Give me my scallop-shell of quiet;
My staff of faith to walk upon;
My scrip of joy, immortal diet;
My bottle of salvation;
My gown of glory, hope's true gage;
And thus I'll take my pilgrimage.
Blood must be my body's balmer—
No other balm will there be given—
Whilst my soul, like a white palmer,
Travels to the land of heaven,
Over the silver mountains,
Where spring the nectar fountains;
And there I'll kiss
The bowl of bliss,
And drink my eternal fill
On every milken hill.
My soul will be a-dry before,
But after it will ne'er thirst more.

And by the happy blissful way,
More peaceful pilgrims I shall see,
That have shook off their gowns of clay,
And go apparalled fresh like me:
I'll bring them first
To slake their thirst,
And then to taste those nectar suckets,
At the clear wells
Where sweetness dwells,
Drawn up by saints in crystal buckets.
And when our bottles and all we
Are filled with immortality,
Then the holy paths we'll travel,
Strewed with rubies thick as gravel.
Ceilings of diamonds, sapphire floors,
High walls of coral, and pearl bowers.
From thence to heaven's bribeless hall,
Where no corrupted voices brawl;
No conscience molten into gold;
Nor forged accusers bought and sold;
No cause deferred; nor vain-spent journey;
For there Christ is the King's Attorney,
Who pleads for all without degrees,
And he hath angels, but no fees.
When the grand twelve million jury
Of our sins and sinful fury,
'Gainst our souls black verdicts give,
Christ pleads his death, and then we live.
Be thou my speaker, taintless pleader,
Unblotted lawyer, true proceeder!
Thou movest salvation even for alms,
Not with a bribed lawyer's palms.
And this is my eternal plea
To him that made heaven, earth, and sea,
Seeing my flesh must die so soon,
And want a head to dine next noon,
Just at the stroke, when my veins start and spread,
Set on my soul an everlasting head:
Then am I ready, like a palmer fit,
To tread those blest paths which before I writ.

The Nymph's reply to the Shepherd

An answer to Marlowe's The Passionate Shepherd to his Love[1]

If all the world and love were young,
And truth in every shepherd's tongue,
These pretty pleasures might me move
To live with thee and be thy love.

Time drives the flocks from field to fold,
When rivers rage and rocks grow cold;
And Philomel becometh dumb;
The rest complains of cares to come.

The flowers do fade, and wanton fields
To wayward winter reckoning yields:
A honey tongue, a heart of gall,
Is fancy's spring, but sorrow's fall.

Thy gowns, thy shoes, thy beds of roses,
Thy cap, thy kirtle, and thy posies
Soon break, soon wither, soon forgotten,
In folly ripe, in reason rotten.

Thy belt of straw and ivy buds,
Thy coral clasps and amber studs,
All these in me no means can move
To come to thee and be thy love.

But could youth last, and love still breed,
Had joys no date, nor age no need,
Then these delights my mind might move
To live with thee and be thy love.

My body in the walls captived

My body in the walls captived
Feels not the wound of spiteful envy
But my thralled mind, of liberty deprived,
Fast fettered in her ancient memory,
Doth nought behold but sorrow's dying face,
Such prison erst was so delightful
As it desired no other dwelling place;

1. See page 69.

But time's effects and destinies despiteful
Have changed both my keeper and my fare;
Love's fire and beauty's light I then had store,
But now close kept, as captives wonted are:
That food, that heat, that light I find no more;
Despair bolts up my doors, and I alone
Speak to dead walls, but those hear not my moan.

EDMUND SPENSER (1552?—1599)

Prothalamion

Calm was the day, and through the trembling air
Sweet-breathing Zephyrus did softly play,
A gentle spirit, that lightly did delay
Hot Titan's beams, which then did glister fair;
When I, whom sullen care,
Through discontent of my long fruitless stay
In prince's court, and expectation vain
Of idle hopes, which still do fly away
Like empty shadows, did afflict my brain,
Walked forth to ease my pain
Along the shore of silver-streaming Thames;
Whose rutty bank, the which his river hems,
Was painted all with variable flowers,
And all the meads adorned with dainty gems
Fit to deck maidens' bowers,
And crown their paramours
Against the bridal day, which is not long:
  Sweet Thames! run softly, till I end my song.

There in a meadow by the river's side
A flock of nymphs I chanced to espy,
All lovely daughters of the flood thereby,
With goodly greenish locks all loose untied
As each had been a bride;
And each one had a little wicker basket
Made of fine twigs entrailed curiously,
In which they gathered flowers to fill their flasket,
And with fine fingers cropped full feateously
The tender stalks on high.
Of every sort which in that meadow grew
They gathered some; the violet, pallid blue,

The little daisy that at evening closes,
The virgin lily and the primrose true,
With store of vermeil roses,
To deck their bridegrooms' posies
Against the bridal day, which was not long:
   Sweet Thames! run softly, till I end my song.

With that I saw two swans of goodly hue
Come softly swimming down along the Lee;
Two fairer birds I yet did never see;
The snow which doth the top of Pindus strew
Did never whiter shew,
Nor Jove himself, when he a swan would be
For love of Leda, whiter did appear;
Yet Leda was, they say, as white as he,
Yet not so white as these, nor nothing near;
So purely white they were
That even the gentle stream, the which them bare,
Seemed foul to them, and bade his billows spare
To wet their silken feathers, lest they might
Soil their fair plumes with water not so fair,
And mar their beauties bright,
That shone as heaven's light,
Against their bridal day, which was not long;
   Sweet Thames! run softly, till I end my song

Eftsoons the nymphs, which now had flowers their fill,
Ran all in haste to see that silver brood
As they came floating on the crystal flood;
Whom when they saw, they stood amazed still
Their wondering eyes to fill;
Them seemed they never saw a sight so fair,
Of fowls so lovely that they sure did deem
Them heavenly born, or to be that same pair
Which through the sky draw Venus' silver team;
For sure they did not seem
To be begot of any earthly seed,
But rather angels, or of angels' breed;
Yet were they bred of Somers-heat, they say,
In sweetest season, when each flower and weed
The earth did fresh array;

So fresh they seemed as day,
Even as their bridal day, which was not long:
   Sweet Thames! run softly, till I end my song.

Then forth they all out of their baskets drew
Great store of flowers, the honour of the field,
That to the sense did fragrant odours yield,
All which upon those goodly birds they threw,
And all the waves did strew,
That like old Peneus' waters they did seem
When down along by pleasant Tempe's shore,
Scattered with flowers, through Thessaly they stream,
That they appear, through lilies' plenteous store,
Like a bride's chamber-floor.
Two of those nymphs meanwhile two garlands bound
Of freshest flowers which in that mead they found,
The which presenting all in trim array,
Their snowy foreheads therewithal they crowned,
Whilst one did sing this lay
Prepared against that day,
Against their bridal day, which was not long:
   Sweet Thames! run softly, till I end my song.

'Ye gentle birds! the world's fair ornament,
And heaven's glory, whom this happy hour
Doth lead unto your lovers' blissful bower,
Joy may you have, and gentle heart's content
Of your love's couplement;
And let fair Venus, that is queen of love,
With her heart-quelling son upon you smile,
Whose smile, they say, hath virtue to remove
All love's dislike, and friendship's faulty guile
For ever to assoil.
Let endless peace your steadfast hearts accord,
And blessed plenty wait upon your board;
And let your bed with pleasure chaste abound,
That fruitful issue may to you afford,
Which may your foes confound,
And make your joys redound
Upon your bridal day, which is not long:
   Sweet Thames! run softly, till I end my song.'

So ended she; and all the rest around
To her redoubled that her undersong,
Which said their bridal day should not be long:
And gentle Echo from the neighbour ground
Their accents did resound.
So forth those joyous birds did pass along,
Adown the Lee, that to them murmured low,
As he would speak but that he lacked a tongue,
Yet did by signs his glad affection show,
Making his stream run slow.
And all the fowl which in his flood did dwell
'Gan flock about these twain, that did excel
The rest, so far as Cynthia doth shend[1]
The lesser stars. So they, enranged well,
Did on those two attend,
And their best service lend
Against their wedding day, which was not long:
    Sweet Thames! run softly, till I end my song.

At length they all to merry London came,
To merry London, my most kindly nurse,
That to me gave this life's first native source,
Though from another place I take my name,
An house of ancient fame:
There when they came whereas those bricky towers
The which on Thames' broad aged back do ride,
Where now the studious lawyers have their bowers,
There whilom wont the Templar knights to bide,
Till they decayed through pride:
Next whereunto there stands a stately place,
Where oft I gained gifts and goodly grace
Of that great Lord, which therein wont to dwell,
Whose want too well now feels my friendless case;
But ah! here fits not well
Old woes, but joys to tell
Against the bridal day, which is not long:
    Sweet Thames! run softly, till I end my song.

Yet therein now doth lodge a noble peer,
Great England's glory and the world's wide wonder,
Whose dreadful name late through all Spain did thunder,

And Hercules' two pillars standing near
Did make to quake and fear:
Fair branch of honour, flower of chivalry!
That fillest England with thy triumphs' fame,
Joy have thou of thy noble victory,
And endless happiness of thine own name
That promiseth the same;
That through thy prowess and victorious arms
Thy country may be freed from foreign harms,
And great Eliza's glorious name may ring
Through all the world, filled with thy wide alarms,
Which some brave Muse may sing
To ages following,
Upon the bridal day, which is not long:
    Sweet Thames! run softly, till I end my song.

From those high towers this noble lord issuing,
Like radiant Hesper when his golden hair
In the ocean billows he hath bathed fair,
Descended to the river's open viewing,
With a great train ensuing.
Above the rest were goodly to be seen
Two gentle knights of lovely face and feature,
Beseeming well the bower of any queen,
With gifts of wit and ornaments of nature
Fit for so goodly stature,
That like the twins of Jove they seemed in sight
Which deck the baldric of the heavens bright;
They two, forth pacing to the river's side,
Received those two fair brides, their love's delight;
Which, at the appointed tide,
Each one did make his bride
Against their bridal day, which is not long:
    Sweet Thames! run softly, till I end my song.

1. *shend*=shame.

Like as a huntsman

Like as a huntsman after weary chase,
Seeing the game from him escaped away,
Sits down to rest him in some shady place,
With panting hounds beguiled of their prey:
So after long pursuit and vain assay,
When I all weary had the chase forsook,
The gentle dear returned the selfsame way,
Thinking to quench her thirst at the next brook.
There she beholding me with milder look,
Sought not to fly, but fearless still did bide:
Till I in hand her yet half-trembling took,
And with her own goodwill her firmly tied.
Strange thing, me seemed, to see a beast so wild,
So goodly wonne with her own will beguiled.

Her name upon the strand

One day I wrote her name upon the strand,
But came the waves and washed it away:
Again I wrote it with a second hand,
But came the tide and made my pains his prey.
Vain man, said she, that dost in vain assay
A mortal thing so to immortalise,
For I myself shall like to this decay,
And eke my name be wiped out likewise.
Not so, quoth I, let baser things devise
To die in dust, but you shall live by fame:
My verse your virtues rare shall eternise,
And in the heavens write your glorious name.
Where whenas death shall all the world subdue
Our love shall live and later life renew.

The Dragon

His flaggy wings when forth he did display,
   Were like two sails, in which the hollow wind
Is gathered full, and worketh speedy way:
   And eke the pennes, that did his pinions bind,
   Were like main-yards, with flying canvas lined,
With which whenas him list the air to beat,
   And there by force unwonted passage find,
The clouds before him fled for terror great,
And all the heavens stood still amazed with his threat.

His huge long tail wound up in hundred folds,
    Does overspread his long brass-scaly back,
Whose wreathed boughts[1] when ever he unfolds,
    And thick entangled knots adown does slack,
    Bespotted as with shields of red and black,
It sweepeth all the land behind him far,
    And of three furlongs does but little lack;
And at the point two stings in-fixed are,
Both deadly sharp, that sharpest steel exceeden far.

But stings and sharpest steel did far exceed
    The sharpness of his cruel rending claws;
Dead was it sure, as sure as death indeed,
    Whatever thing does touch his ravenous paws,
    Or what within his reach he ever draws.
But his most hideous head my tongue to tell
    Does tremble: for his deep devouring jaws
Wide gaped, like the griesly mouth of hell,
Through which into his dark abyss all ravin fell.

And that more wondrous was, in either jaw
    Three ranks of iron teeth enranged were
In which yet trickling blood and gobbets raw
    Of late devoured bodies did appear,
    That sight thereof bred cold congealed fear:
Which to increase, and all at once to kill;
    A cloud of smoothering smoke and sulphur sere
Out of his stinking gorge forth steamed still,
That all the air about with smoke and stench did fill.

His blazing eyes, like two bright shining shields,
    Did burn with wrath, and sparkled living fire;
As two broad beacons, set in open fields,
    Send forth their flames far off to every shire,
    And warning give, that enemies conspire,
With fire and sword the region to invade;
    So flamed his eyne with rage and rancorous ire:
But far within, as in a hollow glade,
Those glaring lamps were set, that made a dreadful shade.

From *The Faerie Queene*

1. *boughts*=coils.

Despair

Who travels by the weary wandering way,
    To come unto his wished home in haste,
And meets a flood, that doth his passage stay,
    Is not great grace to help him over past,
    Or free his feet, that in the mire stick fast?
Most envious man, that grieves at neighbours' good,
    And fond, that joyest in the woe thou hast,
Why wilt not let him pass, that long hath stood
Upon the bank, yet wilt thyself not pass the flood?

He there does now enjoy eternal rest
    And happy ease, which thou doest want and crave,
And further from it daily wanderest:
    What if some little pain the passage have,
    That makes frail flesh to fear the bitter wave?
Is not short pain well borne, that brings long ease,
    And lays the soul to sleep in quiet grave?
Sleep after toil, port after stormy seas,
Ease after war, death after life does greatly please.

From *The Faerie Queene*

FULKE GREVILLE, LORD BROOKE (1554—1628)

Chorus sacerdotum

Oh wearisome condition of humanity!
Born under one Law, to another bound:
Vainly begot, and yet forbidden vanity,
Created sick, commanded to be sound:
What meaneth Nature by these diverse laws?
Passion and Reason, self-division cause:
Is it the mark or majesty of power
To make offences that it may forgive?
Nature herself, doth her own self deflower,
To hate those errors she herself doth give.
For how should man think that, he may not do
If Nature did not fail, and punish too?
Tyrant to others, to herself unjust,
Only commands things difficult and hard.
Forbids us all things, which it knows is lust,
Makes easy pains, unpossible reward.

If Nature did not take delight in blood,
She would have made more easy ways to good.
We that are bound by vows, and by promotion,
With pomp of holy sacrifice and rites,
To teach belief in good and still devotion,
To preach of Heaven's wonders, and delights:
Yet when each of us, in his own heart looks,
He finds the God there, far unlike his books.

From *Mustapha*

JOHN LYLY (*c.* 1554—1606)

Song

It is all one in Venus' wanton school,
Who highest sits, the wise man or the fool.
    Fools in Love's college
    Have far more knowledge,
    To read a woman over,
    Than a neat prating lover.
      Nay, 'tis confessed
    That fools please women best.

Syrinx

Pan's Syrinx was a girl indeed,
Though now she's turned into a reed;
From that dear reed Pan's pipe does come,
A pipe that strikes Apollo dumb;
Nor flute, nor lute, nor gittern can
So chant it, as the pipe of Pan;
Cross-gartered swains, and dairy girls,
With faces smug, and round as pearls,
When Pan's shrill pipe begins to play,
With dancing wear out night and day;
The bagpipe's drone his hum lays by,
When Pan sounds up his minstrelsy;
His minstrelsy! O base! This quill,
Which at my mouth with wind I fill,
Puts me in mind, though her I miss,
That still my Syrinx' lips I kiss.

SIR PHILIP SIDNEY (1554—1586)

Leave me, O Love!

Leave me, O Love, which reachest but to dust,
And thou, my mind, aspire to higher things;
Grow rich in that which never taketh rust:
Whatever fades but fading pleasures brings.
Draw in thy beams, and humble all thy might
To that sweet yoke where lasting freedoms be,
Which breaks the clouds and opens forth the light
That doth both shine and give us sight to see.
O, take fast hold; let that light be thy guide
In this small course which birth draws out to death,
And thinketh how evil becometh him to slide
Who seeketh heaven, and comes of heavenly breath.
   Then, farewell, world! thy uttermost I see.
   Eternal Love, maintain thy life in me!

Underneath my window

'Who is it that this dark night
   Underneath my window plaineth?'
It is one who from thy sight
   Being, ah! exiled, disdaineth
Every other vulgar light.

'Why, alas! and are you he?
   Be not yet those fancies changed?'
Dear, when you find change in me,
   Though from me you be estranged,
Let my change to ruin be.

'Well, in absence this will die;
   Leave to see and leave to wonder.'
Absence sure will help, if I
   Can learn how much myself to sunder
From what in my heart doth lie.

'But time will these thoughts remove;
   Time doth work what no man knoweth.'
Time doth as the subject prove;
   With time still the affection groweth
In the faithful turtle dove.

47

'What if you new beauties see,
    Will not they stir new affection?'
I will think they pictures be,
    Image-like of saints' perfection,
Poorly counterfeiting thee.

'But your reason's purest light
    Bids you leave such minds to nourish.'
Dear, do reason no such spite;
    Never doth thy beauty flourish
More than in my reason's sight.

'But the wrongs love bears will make
    Love at length leave undertaking.'
No, the more fools it do shake,
    In a ground of so firm making
Deeper still they drive the stake.

'Peace, I think that some give ear;
    Come no more lest I get anger.'
Bliss, I will my bliss forbear,
    Fearing, sweet, you to endanger;
But my soul shall harbour there.

'Well, begone, begone, I say,
    Lest that Argus' eyes perceive you.'
Oh, unjust is Fortune's sway,
    Which can make me thus to leave you,
And from lowts[1] to run away.

1. *lowts* = servants.

Loving in truth

Loving in truth, and fain in verse my love to show,
    That she, dear she, might take some pleasure of my pain,
Pleasure might cause her read, reading might make her know,
    Knowledge might pity win, and pity grace obtain,
I sought fit words to paint the blackest face of woe;
    Studying inventions fine, her wits to entertain,
Oft turning others' leaves to see if thence would flow
    Some fresh and fruitful showers upon my sun-burned brain.

But words came halting forth, wanting Invention's stay;
  Invention, Nature's child, fled step-dame Study's blows,
And others' feet still seemed but strangers in my way.
  Thus, great with child to speak, and helpless in my throes,
    Biting my truant pen, beating myself for spite,
      'Fool,' said my Muse to me, 'look in thy heart and write.'

GEORGE PEELE (c. 1557—1596)

When as the rye

When as the rye reach to the chin,
  And chopcherry, chopcherry ripe within,
Strawberries swimming in the cream,
And school-boys playing in the stream;
  Then O, then O, then O my true love said,
    Till that time come again,
  She could not live a maid.

From *The Old Wife's Tale*

What thing is love

What thing is love? for sure love is a thing.
It is a prick, it is a sting,
It is a pretty, pretty thing;
It is a fire, it is a coal,
Whose flame creeps in at every hole;
And as my wit doth best devise,
Love's dwelling is in ladies' eyes,
From whence do glance love's piercing darts,
That make such holes into our hearts;
And all the world herein accord,
Love is a great and mighty lord;
And when he list to mount so high,
With Venus he in heaven doth lie,
And evermore hath been a god,
Since Mars and she played even and odd.

THOMAS LODGE (*c.* 1557—1625)

Rosalind's madrigal

Love in my bosom like a bee
   Doth suck his sweet;
Now with his wings he plays with me,
   Now with his feet.
Within mine eyes he makes his nest,
His bed amidst my tender breast;
My kisses are his daily feast,
And yet he robs me of my rest.
   Ah, wanton, will ye?

And if I sleep, then percheth he
   With pretty flight,
And makes his pillow of my knee
   The livelong night.
Strike I my lute, he tunes the string;
He music plays if so I sing;
He lends me every lovely thing;
Yet cruel he my heart doth sting.
   Whist, wanton, still ye!

Else I with roses every day
   Will whip you hence,
And bind you, when you long to play,
   For your offence.
I'll shut mine eyes to keep you in,
I'll make you fast it for your sin,
I'll count your power not worth a pin.
Alas! what hereby shall I win
   If he gainsay me?

What if I beat the wanton boy
   With many a rod?
He will repay me with annoy,
   Because a god.
Then sit thou safely on my knee,
And let thy bower my bosom be;
Lurk in mine eyes, I like of thee.
O Cupid, so thou pity me,
   Spare not, but play thee!

GEORGE CHAPMAN (1559?—1634)

Love and Philosophy

Muses that sing Love's sensual empery,
  And lovers kindling your enraged fires
At Cupid's bonfires burning in the eye,
  Blown with the empty breath of vain desires;
You that prefer the painted cabinet
  Before the wealthy jewels it doth store ye,
That all your joys in dying figures set,
  And stain the living substance of your glory:
Abjure those joys, abhor their memory,
  And let my love the honoured subject be
  Of love, and honour's complete history;
Your eyes were never yet let in to see
  The majesty and riches of the mind,
  But dwell in darkness; for your God is blind.

Rich mine of knowledge

Rich mine of knowledge, O that my strange muse
Without this body's nourishment could use
Her zealous faculties, only t' aspire
Instructive light from your whole sphere of fire:
But woe is me, what zeal or power soever
My free soul hath, my body will be never
Able t'attend: never shall I enjoy
Th'end of my hapless birth: never employ
That smothered fervour that in loathed embers
Lies swept from light, and no clear hour remembers:
O had your eye perfect organs to pierce
Into that chaos whence this stifled verse
By violence breaks, where glowworm-like doth shine
In nights of sorrow this hid soul of mine,
And how her genuine forms struggle for birth,
Under the claws of this foul panther earth;
Then under all those forms you should discern
My love to you in my desire to learn.

From *To my admired and soul-loved friend, M. Hariots.*

51

Learning

But this is learning; to have skill to throw
Reins on your body's powers that nothing know,
And fill the soul's powers, so with act and art,
That she can curb the body's angry part;
All pertubations, all affects that stray
From their one object, which is to obey
Her sovereign empire, as herself should force
Their functions only to serve her discourse;
And that, to beat the straight path of one end,
Which is, to make her substance still contend
To be God's image; in informing it
With knowledge; holy thoughts, and all forms fit
For that eternity ye seek in way
Of his sole imitation; and to sway
Your life's love so that he may still be centre
To all your pleasures; and you, here, may enter
The next life's peace; in governing so well
Your sensual parts, that you, as free may dwell
Of vulgar raptures, here, as when calm death
Dissolves that learned empire with your breath.
To teach and live thus is the only use
And end of Learning.

From *Euthymiae Raptus: or The Tears of Peace*

ROBERT SOUTHWELL (c. 1561—1595)

The burning Babe

As I in hoary winter's night stood shivering in the snow,
Surprised I was with sudden heat which made my heart to glow:
And lifting up a fearful eye to view what fire was near,
A pretty Babe all burning bright did in the air appear;
Who, scorched with excessive heat, such floods of tears did shed,
As though his floods should quench his flames which with his tears
    were fed.
'Alas!' quoth he, 'but newly born in fiery heats I fry,
Yet none approach to warm their hearts or feel my fire but I.
My faultless breast the furnace is, the fuel wounding thorns;
Love is the fire, and sighs the smoke, the ashes shame and scorns;

The fuel justice layeth on, and mercy blows the coals;
The metal in this furnace wrought are men's defiled souls:
For which, as now on fire I am to work them to their good,
So will I melt into a bath to wash them in my blood.'
With this he vanished out of sight and swiftly shrunk away,
And straight I called unto mind that it was Christmas day.

SIR JOHN HARINGTON (1561—1612)

Fair, rich, and young

Fair, rich, and young: how rare is her perfection,
Were it not mingled with one foul infection!
I mean, so proud a heart, so curst a tongue,
As makes her seem nor fair, nor rich, nor young.

HENRY CONSTABLE (1562—1613)

To Sir Philip Sidney's soul

Give pardon, blessed soul, to my bold cries
If they, importune, interrupt thy song,
Which now with joyful notes thou sing'st among
The angel-quiristers of heavenly skies.
Give pardon eke, sweet soul, to my slow eyes,
That since I saw thee now it is so long,
And yet the tears that unto thee belong
To thee as yet they did not sacrifice.
I did not know that thou wert dead before;
I did not feel the grief I did sustain;
The greater stroke astonisheth the more;
Astonishment takes from us sense of pain.
    I stood amazed when others' tears begun,
    And now begin to weep when they have done.

SAMUEL DANIEL (1562?—1619)
The half-blown rose

Look, Delia, how we esteem the half-blown rose,
The image of thy blush and summer's honour.
Whilst yet her tender bud doth undisclose
That full of beauty Time bestows upon her.
No sooner spreads her glory in the air,
But straight her wide-blown pomp comes to decline;
She then is scorned, that late adorned the fair:
So fade the roses of those cheeks of thine.
No April can revive thy withered flowers,
Whose springing grace adorns thy glory now:
Swift speedy Time, feathered with flying hours,
Dissolves the beauty of the fairest brow.
    Then do not thou such treasure waste in vain,
    But love now, whilst thou may'st be loved again.

The most unloving one

My spotless love hovers with purest wings
About the temple of the proudest frame;
Where blaze those lights, fairest of earthly things,
Which clear our clouded world with brightest flame.
My ambitious thoughts, confined in her face,
Affect no honour, but what she can give;
My hopes do rest in limits of her grace;
I weigh no comfort unless she relieve.
For she that can my heart imparadise
Holds in her fairest hand what dearest is;
My fortune's wheel's the circle of her eyes,
Whose rolling grace deign once a turn of bliss.
All my life's sweet consists in her alone,
So much I love the most unloving one.

MICHAEL DRAYTON (1563—1631)
Since there's no help

Since there's no help, come let us kiss and part.
Nay, I have done; you get no more of me,
And I am glad, yea, glad with all my heart,
That thus so cleanly I myself can free;
Shake hands for ever, cancel all our vows,

And when we meet at any time again,
Be it not seen in either of our brows
That we one jot of former love retain.
Now at the last gasp of Love's latest breath,
When, his pulse failing, Passion speechless lies,
When Faith is kneeling by his bed of death,
And Innocence is closing up his eyes,
Now if thou wouldst, when all have given him over,
From death to life thou mightst him yet recover.

To the Virginian voyage

You brave heroic minds
   Worthy your country's name,
     That honour still pursue;
     Go and subdue!
Whilst loitering hinds
   Lurk here at home with shame.

Britons, you stay too long:
   Quickly aboard bestow you,
     And with a merry gale
     Swell your stretched sail
With vows as strong
   As the winds that blow you.

Your course securely steer,
   West and by south forth keep!
     Rocks, lee-shores, nor shoals
     When Eolus scowls
You need not fear;
   So absolute the deep.

And cheerfully at sea
   Success you still entice
     To get the pearl and gold,
     And ours to hold
Virginia,
   Earth's only paradise.

Where nature hath in store
   Fowl, venison, and fish,
      And the fruitfull'st soil
      Without your toil
Three harvests more,
   All greater than your wish.

And the ambitious vine
   Crowns with his purple mass
      The cedar reaching high
      To kiss the sky,
The cypress, pine,
   And useful sassafras.

To whom the Golden Age
   Still nature's laws doth give,
      No other cares attend,
      But them to defend
From winter's rage,
   That long there doth not live.

When as the luscious smell
   Of that delicious land
      Above the seas that flows
      The clear wind throws,
Your hearts to swell
   Approaching the dear strand;

In kenning of the shore
   (Thanks to God first given)
      O you the happiest men,
      Be frolic then!
Let cannons roar,
   Frighting the wide heaven.

And in regions far,
   Such heroes bring ye forth
      As those from whom we came;
      And plant our name
Under that star
   Not known unto our North.

And as there plenty grows
  Of laurel everywhere—
    Apollo's sacred tree—
    You it may see
A poet's brows
  To crown, that may sing there.

The *Voyages* attend,
  Industrious Hakluyt,
    Whose reading shall inflame
    Men to seek fame,
And much commend
  To after times thy wit.

The thirteenth song

The forest so much fallen from what she was before,
That to her former height Fate could not her restore;
Though oft in her behalf, the Genius of the land
Importuned the Heavens with an auspicious hand.
Yet granted at the last (the aged Nymph to grace)
They by a lady's birth would more renown that place
Than if her woods their heads above the hills should seat;
And for that purpose, first made Coventry so great
(A poor thatched village then, or scarcely none at all,
That could not once have dreamed of her now stately wall)
And thither wisely brought that goodly virgin-band,
Th'eleven thousand maids, chaste Ursula's command,
Whom then the Britain Kings gave her full power to press,
For matches to their friends in Britany the less.
At whose departure thence, each by her just bequest
Some special virtue gave, ordaining it to rest
With one of their own sex, that there her birth should have,
Till fullness of the time which Fate did choicely save;
Until the Saxons' reign, when Coventry at length,
From her small, mean regard, recovered state and strength,
By Leofric her Lord yet in base bondage held,
The people from her marts by tollage who expelled:
Whose Dutchess, which desired this tribute to release,
Their freedom often begged. The Duke, to make her cease,

Told her that if she would his loss so far enforce,
His will was, she should ride stark naked upon a horse
By daylight through the street: which certainly he thought,
In her heroic breast so deeply would have wrought,
That in her former suit she would have left to deal.
But that most princely dame, as one devoured with zeal,
Went on, and by that mean the city clearly freed.

From *Polyolbion*

WILLIAM SHAKESPEARE (1564—1616)

The Phoenix and the Turtle

Let the bird of loudest lay,
    On the sole Arabian tree,
    Herald sad and trumpet be,
To whose sound chaste wings obey.

But thou shrieking harbinger,
    Foul precurrer of the fiend,
    Augur of the fever's end,
To this troop come thou not near.

From this cession interdict
    Every fowl of tyrant wing,
    Save the eagle, feathered king;
Keep the obsequy so strict.

Let the priest in surplice white
    That defunctive music can,
    Be the death-divining swan,
Lest the requiem lack his right.

And thou treble-dated crow,
    That thy sable gender makest
    With the breath thou givest and takest,
'Mongst our mourners shalt thou go.

Here the anthem doth commence:
   Love and constancy is dead;
   Phoenix and the turtle fled
In a mutual flame from hence.

So they loved, as love in twain
   Had the essence but in one;
   Two distincts, division none;
Number there in love was slain.

Hearts remote, yet not asunder;
   Distance, and no space was seen
   'Twixt the turtle and his queen;
But in them it were a wonder.

So between them love did shine,
   That the turtle saw his right
   Flaming in the Phoenix' sight;
Either was the other's mine.

Property was thus appalled,
   That the self was not the same;
   Single nature's double name
Neither two nor one was called.

Reason, in itself confounded,
   Saw division grow together,
   To themselves yet either neither,
Simple were so well compounded:

That it cried, 'How true a twain
   Seemeth this concordant one!
   Love hath reason, reason none,
If what parts can so remain.'

Whereupon it made this threne
   To the phoenix and the dove,
   Co-supremes and stars of love,
As chorus to their tragic scene.

Threnos

Beauty, truth, and rarity,
Grace in all simplicity,
Here enclosed in cinders lie.

Death is now the phoenix' nest;
And the turtle's loyal breast
To eternity doth rest,

Leaving no posterity:
'Twas not their infirmity,
It was married chastity.

Truth may seem, but cannot be;
Beauty brag, but 'tis not she;
Truth and beauty buried be.

To this urn let those repair
That are either true or fair;
For these dead birds sigh a prayer.

Sonnets

xviii

Shall I compare thee to a summer's day?
  Thou art more lovely and more temperate:
Rough winds do shake the darling buds of May,
  And summer's lease hath all too short a date:
Sometime too hot the eye of heaven shines,
  And often is his gold complexion dimmed;
And every fair from fair sometime declines,
  By chance, or nature's changing course untrimmed;
But thy eternal summer shall not fade,
  Nor lose possession of that fair thou owest,
Nor shall death brag thou wander'st in his shade,
  When in eternal lines to time thou growest;
    So long as men can breathe, or eyes can see,
    So long lives this, and this gives life to thee.

xxxiii

Full many a glorious morning have I seen
  Flatter the mountain-tops with sovereign eye,
Kissing with golden face the meadows green,
  Gilding pale streams with heavenly alchemy;
Anon permit the basest clouds to ride
  With ugly rack on his celestial face,
And from the forlorn world his visage hide,
  Stealing unseen to west with this disgrace:
Even so my sun one early morn did shine,
  With all-triumphant splendour on my brow;
But, out! alack! he was but one hour mine,
  The region cloud hath masked him from me now.
    Yet him for this my love no whit disdaineth;
    Suns of the world may stain when heaven's sun staineth.

cxix

Let me not to the marriage of true minds
  Admit impediments. Love is not love
Which alters when it alteration finds,
  Or bends with the remover to remove.
O, no! it is an ever-fixed mark,
  That looks on tempests and is never shaken;
It is the star to every wandering bark,
  Whose worth's unknown, although his height be taken.
Love's not Time's fool, though rosy lips and cheeks
  Within his bending sickle's compass come;
Love alters not with his brief hours and weeks,
  But bears it out even to the edge of doom.
    If this be error, and upon me proved,
    I never writ, nor no man ever loved.

cxxix

The expense of spirit in a waste of shame
  Is lust in action; and till action, lust
Is perjured, murderous, bloody, full of blame,
  Savage, extreme, rude, cruel, not to trust;
Enjoyed, no sooner but despised straight;
  Past reason hunted; and no sooner had,
Past reason hated, as a swallowed bait,
  On purpose laid to make the taker mad:

Mad in pursuit, and in possession so;
   Had, having, and in quest to have, extreme;
A bliss in proof, and proved, a very woe;
   Before, a joy proposed; behind, a dream.
All this the world well knows; yet none knows well
To shun the heaven that leads men to this hell.

Spring

When daisies pied and violets blue
   And lady-smocks all silver-white
And cuckoo-buds of yellow hue
   Do paint the meadows with delight,
The cuckoo then, on every tree,
Mocks married men; for thus sings he,
     Cuckoo!
Cuckoo, cuckoo! O, word of fear,
Unpleasing to a married ear!

When shepherds pipe on oaten straws,
   And merry larks are ploughmen's clocks
When turtles tread, and rooks, and daws,
   And maidens bleach their summer smocks,
The cuckoo then, on every tree,
Mocks married men; for thus sings he,
     Cuckoo!
Cuckoo, cuckoo! O, word of fear
Unpleasing to a married ear!

Winter

When icicles hang by the wall,
   And Dick the shepherd blows his nail,
And Tom bears logs into the hall,
   And milk comes frozen home in pail;
When blood is nipped, and ways be foul,
Then nightly sings the staring owl,
Tu-whit, tu-who! a merry note,
While greasy Joan doth keel the pot.

When all aloud the wind doth blow,
   And coughing drowns the parson's saw,
And birds sit brooding in the snow,
   And Marian's nose looks red and raw,

When roasted crabs hiss in the bowl,
Then nightly sings the staring owl,
Tu-whit, tu-who! a merry note,
While greasy Joan doth keel the pot.

From *Love's Labour Lost*

The pages' song

It was a lover and his lass,
With a hey, and a ho, and a hey nonino,
That o'er the green corn-field did pass,
In spring time, the only pretty ring time,
When birds do sing, hey ding a ding, ding;
Sweet lovers love the spring.

Between the acres of the rye,
With a hey, and a ho, and a hey nonino,
Those pretty country folks would lie,
In spring time, the only pretty ring time,
When birds do sing, hey ding a ding, ding;
Sweet lovers love the spring.

This carol they began that hour,
With a hey, and a ho, and a hey nonino,
How that a life was but a flower
In spring time, the only pretty ring time,
When birds do sing, hey ding a ding, ding;
Sweet lovers love the spring.

And therefore take the present time,
With a hey, and a ho, and a hey nonino;
For love is crowned with the prime
In spring time, the only pretty ring time,
When birds do sing, hey ding a ding, ding;
Sweet lovers love the spring.

From *As You Like It*

Ariel's song

Full fathom five thy father lies;
  Of his bones are coral made;
Those are pearls that were his eyes:
  Nothing of him that doth fade,
But doth suffer a sea-change
Into something rich and strange:
Sea nymphs hourly ring his knell.
    Ding-dong!
  Hark! now I hear them,
    Ding-dong, bell!

From *The Tempest*

CHRISTOPHER MARLOWE (1564—1593)

Perfect bliss and sole felicity

Nature, that framed us of four elements
Warring within our breasts for regiment,
Doth teach us all to have aspiring minds:
Our souls, whose faculties can comprehend
The wondrous architecture of the world,
And measure every wandering planet's course,
Still climbing after knowledge infinite,
And always moving as the restless spheres,
Will us to wear ourselves, and never rest,
Until we reach the ripest fruit of all,
That perfect bliss and sole felicity,
The sweet fruition of an earthly crown.

From *Tamburlaine*

Hero and Leander

On Hellespont, guilty of true love's blood,
In view, and opposite, two cities stood,
Sea borderers, disjoined by Neptune's might;
The one Abydos, the other Sestos hight.
At Sestos, Hero dwelt; Hero the fair,
Whom young Apollo courted for her hair,
And offered as a dower his burning throne,
Where she should sit for men to gaze upon.

The outside of her garments were of lawn,
The lining purple silk, with gilt stars drawn;
Her wide sleeves green, and bordered with a grove,
Where Venus in her naked glory strove
To please the careless and disdainful eyes
Of proud Adonis, that before her lies;
Her kirtle blue, whereon was many a stain,
Made with the blood of wretched lovers slain.
Upon her head she ware a myrtle wreath,
From whence her veil reached to the ground beneath.
Her veil was artificial flowers and leaves,
Whose workmanship both man and beast deceives.
Many would praise the sweet smell as she passed,
When 'twas the odour which her breath forth cast;
And there for honey, bees have sought in vain,
And, beat from thence, have lighted there again.
About her neck hung chains of pebble-stone,
Which, lightened by her neck, like diamonds shone.
She ware no gloves, for neither sun nor wind
Would burn or parch her hands, but to her mind
Or warm or cool them, for they took delight
To play upon those hands, they were so white.
Buskins of shells all silvered used she,
And branched with blushing coral to the knee,
Where sparrows perched, of hollow pearl and gold,
Such as the world would wonder to behold:
Those with sweet water oft her handmaid fills,
Which, as she went, would chirrup through the bills.
Some say, for her the fairest Cupid pined,
And, looking in her face, was strooken blind.
But this is true, so like was one the other,
As he imagined Hero was his mother;
And oftentimes into her bosom flew,
About her naked neck his bare arms threw,
And laid his childish head upon her breast,
And with still panting rocked, there took his rest.
So lovely fair was Hero, Venus' nun,
As Nature wept, thinking she was undone,
Because she took more from her than she left,
And of such wondrous beauty her bereft;
Therefore, in sign her treasure suffered wrack,

Since Hero's time hath half the world been black.
Amorous Leander, beautiful and young,
(Whose tragedy divine Musaeus sung)
Dwelt at Abydos; since him dwelt there none
For whom succeeding times make greater moan.
His dangling tresses that were never shorn,
Had they been cut and unto Colchos borne,
Would have allured the venturous youth of Greece
To hazard more than for the Golden Fleece.
Fair Cynthia wished his arms might be her sphere;
Grief makes her pale, because she moves not there.
His body was as straight as Circe's wand;
Jove might have sipped out nectar from his hand.
Even as delicious meat is to the taste,
So was his neck in touching, and surpassed
The white of Pelop's shoulder. I could tell ye
How smooth his breast was, and how white his belly,
And whose immortal fingers did imprint
That heavenly path, with many a curious dint,
That runs along his back; but my rude pen
Can hardly blazon forth the loves of men,
Much less of powerful gods; let it suffice
That my slack muse sings of Leander's eyes
Those orient cheeks and lips, exceeding his
That leapt into the water for a kiss
Of his own shadow, and despising many,
Died ere he could enjoy the love of any.
Had wild Hippolytus Leander seen,
Enamoured of his beauty had he been;
His presence made the rudest peasant melt,
That in the vast uplandish country dwelt;
The barbarous Thracian soldier, moved with nought,
Was moved with him, and for his favour sought.
Some swore he was a maid in man's attire,
For in his looks were all that men desire,
A pleasant smiling cheek, a speaking eye,
A brow for love to banquet royally;
And such as knew he was a man, would say,
'Leander, thou art made for amorous play;
Why art thou not in love, and loved of all?
Though thou be fair, yet be not thine own thrall.'

CHRISTOPHER MARLOWE

The men of wealthy Sestos, every year,
For his sake whom their goddess held so dear,
Rose-cheeked Adonis, kept a solemn feast.
Thither resorted many a wandering guest
To meet their loves; such as had none at all,
Came lovers home from this great festival.
For every street, like to a firmament,
Glistered with breathing stars, who, where they went,
Frighted the melancholy earth, which deemed
Eternal heaven to burn, for so it seemed
As if another Phaeton had got
The guidance of the sun's rich chariot.
But, far above the loveliest, Hero shined,
And stole away th'enchanted gazer's mind;
For like sea-nymphs' inveigling harmony,
So was her beauty to the standers by.
Nor that night-wandering pale and watery star
(When yawning dragons draw her thirling car
From Latmos' mount up to the gloomy sky,
Where, crowned with blazing light and majesty,
She proudly sits) more over-rules the flood,
Than she the hearts of those that near her stood.
Even as, when gaudy nymphs pursue the chase,
Wretched Ixion's shaggy-footed race,
Incensed with savage heat, gallop amain
From steep pine-bearing mountains to the plain;
So ran the people forth to gaze upon her,
And all that viewed her were enamoured on her.
And as in fury of a dreadful fight,
Their fellows being slain or put to flight,
Poor soldiers stand with fear of death dead strooken,
So at her presence all, surprised and tooken,
Await the sentence of her scornful eyes;
He whom she favours lives, the other dies.
There might you see one sigh, another rage,
And some, their violent passions to assuage,
Compile sharp satires; but alas! too late,
For faithful love will never turn to hate.
And many, seeing great princes were denied,
Pined as they went, and thinking on her, died.
On this feast day, O cursed day and hour,

Went Hero thorough Sestos, from her tower
To Venus' temple, where unhappily,
As after chanced, they did each other spy.
So fair a church as this had Venus none;
The walls were of discoloured jasper stone,
Wherein was Proteus carved, and o'erhead
A lively vine of green sea-agate spread,
Where by one hand light-headed Bacchus hung,
And with the other wine from grapes out-wrung.
Of crystal shining fair the pavement was;
The town of Sestos called it Venus' glass.
There might you see the gods in sundry shapes,
Committing heady riots, incest, rapes:
For know that underneath this radiant floor
Was Danae's statue in a brazen tower;
Jove slyly stealing from his sister's bed
To dally with Idalian Ganymede,
And for his love Europa bellowing loud,
And tumbling with the rainbow in a cloud;
Blood-quaffing Mars heaving the iron net
Which limping Vulcan and his Cyclops set;
Love kindling fire to burn such towns as Troy;
Silvanus weeping for the lovely boy
That now is turned into a cypress tree,
Under whose shade the wood-gods love to be.
And in the midst a silver altar stood;
There Hero sacrificing turtle's blood,
Vailed to the ground, vailing her eyelids close,
And modestly they opened as she rose:
Thence flew love's arrow with the golden head,
And thus Leander was enamoured.
Stone-still he stood, and evermore he gazed,
Till with the fire that from his countenance blazed
Relenting Hero's gentle heart was strook;
Such force and virtue hath an amorous look.
    It lies not in our power to love or hate,
For will in us is over-ruled by fate.
When two are stripped, long ere the course begin,
We wish that one should lose, the other win;
And one especially do we affect
Of two gold ingots, like in each respect.

The reason no man knows; let it suffice,
What we behold is censured by our eyes.
Where both deliberate, the love is slight;
Who ever loved, that loved not at first sight?
  He kneeled, but unto her devoutly prayed;
Chaste Hero to herself thus softly said:
'Were I the saint he worships, I would hear him';
And as she spake these words, came somewhat near him
He started up; she blushed as one ashamed;
Wherewith Leander much more was inflamed.
He touched her hand; in touching it she trembled;
Love deeply grounded hardly is dissembled.

These lovers parled by the touch of hands;
True love is mute, and oft amazed stands.
Thus while dumb signs their yielding hearts entangled,
The air with sparks of living fire was spangled.
And night, deep drenched in misty Acheron,
Heaved up her head, and half the world upon
Breathed darkness forth (dark night is Cupid's day).

The passionate shepherd to his love

Come live with me and be my love,
And we will all the pleasures prove,
That hills and valleys, dales and fields,
And all the craggy mountains yields.

There we will sit upon the rocks,
And see the shepherds feed their flocks,
By shallow rivers to whose falls
Melodious birds sing madrigals.

And I will make thee beds of roses
With a thousand fragrant posies,
A cap of flowers, and a kirtle
Embroidered all with leaves of myrtle;

A gown made of the finest wool
Which from our pretty lambs we pull;
Fair lined slippers for the cold,
With buckles of the purest gold;

A belt of straw and ivy buds,
With coral clasps and amber studs:
And if these pleasures may thee move,
Come live with me and be my love.

The shepherds' swains shall dance and sing
For thy delight each May morning:
If these delights thy mind may move,
Then live with me and be my love.

KING JAMES I (1566—1625)

Sonnet

The azured vault, the crystal circles bright,
The gleaming fiery torches powdered there;
The changing round, the shining beamy light,
The sad and bearded fires, the monsters fair;
The prodigies appearing in the air;
The rearding[1] thunders and the blustering winds;
The fowls in hue and shape and nature rare,
The pretty notes that winged musicians finds;
In earth, the savoury flowers, the metalled minds,
The wholesome herbs, the hautie pleasant trees,
The silver streams, the beasts of sundry kinds,
The bounded roars and fishes of the seas,
    All these, for teaching man, the Lord did frame
    To do his will whose glory shines in thame.

1. *rearding*=roaring.

THOMAS CAMPION (1567—1620)

Laura

Rose-cheeked Laura, come;
Sing thou smoothly with thy beauty's
Silent music, either other
    Sweetly gracing.

Lovely forms do flow
From concent divinely framed;
Heaven is music, and thy beauty's
    Birth is heavenly.

These dull notes we sing
Discords need for helps to grace them;
Only beauty purely loving
    Knows no discord;

But still moves delight,
Like clear springs renewed by flowing,
Ever perfect, ever in them-
    selves eternal.

Now winter nights enlarge

Now winter nights enlarge
    The number of their hours,
And clouds their storms discharge
    Upon the airy towers.
Let now the chimneys blaze,
    And cups o'erflow with wine;
Let well-tuned words amaze
    With harmony divine.
Now yellow waxen lights
    Shall wait on honey Love,
While youthful revels, masks, and courtly sights
    Sleep's leaden spells remove.

This time doth well dispense
    With lovers' long discourse.
Much speech hath some defence
    Though beauty no remorse.
All do not all things well:
    Some measures comely tread,
Some knotted riddles tell,
    Some poems smoothly read.
The Summer hath his joys,
    And Winter his delights.
Though Love and all his pleasures are but toys,
    They shorten tedious nights.

Follow your saint

Follow your saint, follow with accents sweet;
Haste you, sad notes, fall at her flying feet.
There, wrapped in cloud of sorrow, pity move,
And tell the ravisher of my soul I perish for her love.
But if she scorns my never-ceasing pain,
Then burst with sighing in her sight, and ne'er return again.

All that I sung still to her praise did tend.
Still she was first, still she my songs did end.
Yet she my love and music both doth fly,
The music that her echo is, and beauty's sympathy.
Then let my notes pursue her scornful flight;
It shall suffice that they were breathed, and died for her delight.

THOMAS NASHE (1567—c.1601)

Dust hath closed Helen's eye

In time of Pestilence 1593.

Adieu, farewell earth's bliss,
This world uncertain is;
Fond are life's lustful joys,
Death proves them all but toys,
None from his darts can fly.
I am sick, I must die.
    Lord, have mercy on us!

Rich men, trust not in wealth,
Gold cannot buy you health;
Physic himself must fade,
All things to end are made.
The plague full swift goes by.
I am sick, I must die.
    Lord, have mercy on us!

Beauty is but a flower
Which wrinkles will devour;
Brightness falls from the air,
Queens have died young and fair,
Dust hath closed Helen's eye.
I am sick, I must die.
    Lord, have mercy on us!

Strength stoops unto the grave,
Worms feed on Hector brave,
Swords may not fight with fate,
Earth still holds ope her gate.
Come! come! the bells do cry.
I am sick, I must die.
    Lord, have mercy on us!

Wit with his wantonness
Tasteth death's bitterness;
Hell's executioner
Hath no ears for to hear
What vain art can reply.
I am sick, I must die.
    Lord, have mercy on us!

Haste, therefore, each degree,
To welcome destiny.
Heaven is our heritage,
Earth but a player's stage;
Mount we unto the sky.
I am sick, I must die.
    Lord, have mercy on us!

ROBERT GREENE (1558?—1592)

Weep not, my wanton

Weep not, my wanton, smile upon my knee;
When thou art old there's grief enough for thee.
        Mother's wag, pretty boy,
        Father's sorrow, father's joy,
        When thy father first did see
        Such a boy by him and me,
        He was glad, I was woe:
        Fortune changed made him so,
        When he left his pretty boy
        Last his sorrow, first his joy.

Weep not, my wanton, smile upon my knee;
When thou art old there's grief enough for thee.
    Streaming tears that never stint,
    Like pearl drops from a flint,
    Fell by course from his eyes,
    That one another's place supplies:
    Thus he grieved in every part,
    Tears of blood fell from his heart,
    When he left his pretty boy,
    Father's sorrow, father's joy.

Weep not, my wanton, smile upon my knee;
When thou are old there's grief enough for thee.
    The wanton smiled, father wept;
    Mother cried, baby leapt;
    More he crowed, more we cried;
    Nature could not sorrow hide.
    He must go, he must kiss
    Child and mother, baby bliss;
    For he left his pretty boy,
    Father's sorrow, father's joy.

Weep not, my wanton, smile upon my knee;
When thou art old there's grief enough for thee.

SIR JOHN DAVIES (1569—1626)

The dance of Love

This is true Love, by that true Cupid got,
Which danceth galliards in your amorous eyes,
But to your frozen heart approacheth not;
Only your heart he dares not enterprize,
And yet through every other part he flies,
   And everywhere he nimbly danceth now,
   That in yourself, yourself perceive not how.

For your sweet beauty, daintily transfused
With due proportion throughout every part,
What is it but a dance where Love hath used

His finer cunning and more curious art;
Where all the elements themselves impart,
    And turn, and wind, and mingle with such measure,
    That th' eye that sees it, surfeits with the pleasure?

Love in the twinkling of your eyelids danceth;
Love danceth in your pulses, and your veins;
Love, when you sew, your needle's point advanceth,
And makes it dance a thousand curious strains
Of winding rounds, whereof the form remains,
    To show that your fair hands can dance the *Hay*,
    Which your fine feet would learn as well as they.

And when your ivory fingers touch the strings
Of any silver-sounding instrument,
Love makes them dance to those sweet murmurings,
With busy skill and cunning excellent.
Oh, that your feet those tunes would represent
    With artificial motions to and fro,
    That Love, this art in every part might show.

        From *Orchestra, or a Poem of Dancing*

ANONYMOUS

The bellman's song

Maids to bed and cover coal;
Let the mouse out of her hole;
Crickets in the chimney sing
Whilst the little bell doth ring:
If fast asleep, who can tell
When the clapper hits the bell?

SIR ROBERT AYTON (1570—1638)

To his forsaken mistress

I do confess thou'rt smooth and fair,
    And I might have gone near to love thee,
Had I not found the slightest prayer
    That lips could move, had power to move thee;
        But I can let thee now alone,
        As worthy to be loved by none.

I do confess thou'rt sweet, yet find
  Thee such an unthrift of thy sweets,
Thy favours are but like the wind
  Which kisseth everything it meets;
    And since thou canst with more than one,
    Thou'rt worthy to be kissed by none.

The morning rose, that untouched stands
  Armed with her briars, how sweet she smells!
But plucked and strained through ruder hands,
  Her sweets no longer with her dwells,
    But scent and beauty both are gone,
    And leaves fall from her, one by one.

Such fate, ere long, will thee betide
  When thou hast handled been a while,
With sere flowers to be thrown aside;
  And I shall sigh, when some will smile,
    To see thy love to every one
    Hath brought thee to be loved by none.

THOMAS MIDDLETON (1570?—1627)

Midnight

Midnight's bell goes ting, ting, ting, ting, ting,
Then dogs do howl, and not a bird does sing
But the nightingale, and she cries, twit, twit, twit:
Owls then on every bough do sit;
Ravens croak on chimneys' tops;
The cricket in the chamber hops,
  And the cats cry mew, mew, mew.
The nibbling mouse is not asleep,
But he goes peep, peep, peep, peep, peep,
  And the cats cry mew, mew, mew,
  And still the cats cry mew, mew, mew.

CYRIL TOURNEUR (1570?80—1626)

A soldier's death

He lay in's armour; as if that had been
His coffin, and the weeping sea (like one
Whose milder temper doth lament the death
Of him whom in his rage he slew) runs up
The shore; embraces him; kisses his cheek,
Goes back again and forces up the sands
To bury him; and every time it parts,
Sheds tears upon him; till at last (as if
It could no longer endure to see the man
Whom it had slain, yet loath to leave him) with
A kind of unresolved unwilling pace,
Winding her waves one in another, like
A man that folds his arms, or wrings his hands
For grief; ebbed from the body and descends,
As if it would sink down into the earth
And hide itself for shame of such a deed.

From *The Atheist's Tragedy*

THOMAS DEKKER (*c.*1570—*c.*1632)

Hey derry derry

Cold's the wind, and wet's the rain,
   Saint Hugh be our good speed!
Ill is the weather that bringeth no gain,
   Nor helps good hearts in need.

Troll the bowl, the jolly nut-brown bowl,
   And here, kind mate, to thee!
Let's sing a dirge for Saint Hugh's soul,
   And down it merrily.

Down-a-down, hey, down-a-down,
   Hey derry derry down-a-down!
Ho! well done, to me let come,
   Ring compass, gentle joy!

From *The Shoemaker's Holiday*

BEN JONSON (1573?—1736)

Still to be neat

Still to be neat, still to be dressed,
As you were going to a feast;
Still to be powdered, still perfumed:
Lady, it is to be presumed,
Though art's hid causes are not found,
All is not sweet, all is not sound.

Give me a look, give me a face
That makes simplicity a grace;
Robes loosely flowing, hair as free:
Such sweet neglect more taketh me
Than all th' adulteries of art;
They strike mine eyes, but not my heart.

Hymn to Cynthia

Queen and huntress, chaste and fair,
Now the sun is laid to sleep,
Seated in thy silver chair,
State in wonted manner keep:
Hesperus entreats thy light,
Goddess excellently bright.

Earth, let not thy envious shade
Dare itself to interpose;
Cynthia's shining orb was made
Heaven to clear when day did close:
Bless us then with wished sight,
Goddess excellently bright.

Lay thy bow of pearl apart,
And thy crystal-shining quiver;
Give unto the flying hart
Space to breathe, how short soever:
Thou that mak'st a day of night—
Goddess excellently bright.

An ode to himself

Where do'st thou careless lie
Buried in ease and sloth?
Knowledge that sleeps, doth die;
And this security,
It is the common moth,
That eats on wits, and arts, and destroys them both.

Are all th' Aonian springs
Dried up? Lies Thespia waste?
Doth Clarius' harp want strings,
That not a nymph now sings!
Or droop they as disgraced,
To see their seats and bowers by chattering pies defaced?

If hence thy silence be,
As 'tis too just a cause;
Let this thought quicken thee,
Minds that are great and free,
Should not on fortune pause,
'Tis crown enough to virtue still, her own applause.

What though the greedy fry
Be taken with false baits
Of worded balladry,
And think it poesy?
They die with their conceits,
And only piteous scorn upon their folly waits.

Then take in hand thy lyre,
Strike in thy proper strain,
With Iaphet's line, aspire
Sol's chariot for new fire,
To give the world again:
Who aided him, will thee, the issue of Jove's brain.

And since our dainty age
Cannot endure reproof,
Make not thyself a page
To that strumpet the stage,
But sing high and aloof,
Safe from the wolf's black jaw, and the dull ass's hoof.

BEN JONSON

Hymn to the Belly

Room! room! make room for the bouncing Belly,
First father of sauce and deviser of jelly;
Prime master of arts and the giver of wit,
That found out the excellent engine, the spit,
The plough and the flail, the mill and the hopper,
The hutch and the boulter, the furnace and copper,
The oven, the bavin, the mawkin, the peel,
The hearth and the range, the dog and the wheel.
He, he first invented the hogshead and tun,
The gimlet and vice too, and taught 'em to run;
And since, with the funnel and hippocras bag,
He's made of himself that he now cries swag;
Which shows, though the pleasure be but of four inches,
Yet he is a weasel, the gullet that pinches
Of any delight, and not spares from his back
Whatever to make of the belly a sack.
Hail, hail, plump paunch! O the founder of taste,
For fresh meats or powdered, or pickle or paste!
Devourer of broiled, baked, roasted or sod!
And emptier of cups, be they even or odd!
All which have now made thee so wide i' the waist,
As scarce with no pudding thou art to be laced;
But eating and drinking until thou dost nod,
Thou break'st all thy girdles and break'st forth a god.

JOHN DONNE (1573—1631)

The Sun rising

Busy old fool, unruly Sun,
Why dost thou thus,
Through windows and through curtains call on us?
Must to thy motions lovers' seasons run?
Saucy pedantic wretch, go chide
Late schoolboys and sour prentices,
Go tell court-huntsmen that the King will ride,
Call country ants to harvest offices;
Love, all alike, no season knows, nor clime,
Nor hours, days, months, which are the rags of time.

Thy beams, so reverend and strong
Why should'st thou think?
I could eclipse and cloud them with a wink,
But that I would not lose her sight so long:
If her eyes have not blinded thine,
Look, and to-morrow late, tell me,
Whether both the Indias of spice and mine
Be where thou left'st them, or lie here with me.
Ask for those kings whom thou saw'st yesterday,
And thou shalt hear, all here in one bed lay.

She is all states, and all princes, I,
Nothing else is.
Princes do but play us; compared to this,
All honour's mimique; all wealth alchemy.
Thou Sun art half as happy as we,
In that the world's contracted thus;
Thine age asks ease, and since thy duties be
To warm the world, that's done in warming us.
Shine here to us, and thou art everywhere;
This bed thy centre is, these walls thy sphere.

The canonisation

For God's sake hold your tongue, and let me love,
Or chide my palsy, or my gout,
My five gray hairs, or ruined fortune flout;
With wealth your state, your mind with arts improve,
Take you a course, get you a place,
Observe his honour, or his grace,
Or the King's real, or his stamped face
Contemplate, what you will, approve,
So you will let me love.

Alas! alas! who's injured by my love?
What merchant's ships have my sighs drowned?
Who says my tears have overflowed his ground?
When did my colds a forward spring remove?
When did the heats which my veins fill
Add one more to the plaguy bill?
Soldiers find wars, and lawyers find out still
Litigious men, which quarrels move,
Though she and I do love.

Call us what you will, we are made such by love;
Call her one, me another fly,
We are tapers too, and at our own cost die,
And we in us find the eagle and the dove,
The phoenix riddle hath more wit
By us, we two being one, are it.
So, to one neutral thing both sexes fit,
We die and rise the same, and prove
Mysterious by this love.

We can die by it, if not live by love,
And if unfit for tombs and hearse
Our legend be, it will be fit for verse;
And if no piece of chronicle we prove,
We'll build in sonnets pretty rooms;
As well a well-wrought urn becomes
The greatest ashes, as half-acre tombs,
And by these hymns, all shall approve
Us canonised for love;

And thus invoke us 'You, whom reverend love
Made one another's hermitage;
You, to whom love was peace, that now is rage;
Who did the whole world's soul contract, and drove
Into the glasses of your eyes—
So made such mirrors, and such spies,
That they did all to you epitomise—
Countries, towns, courts: beg from above
A pattern of your love.'

The ecstacy

Where, like a pillow on a bed,
    A pregnant bank swelled up, to rest
The violet's reclining head,
    Sat we two, one another's best.
Our hands were firmly cemented
    With a fast balm, which thence did spring,
Our eye-beams twisted, and did thread
    Our eyes upon one double string;
So to intergraft our hands, as yet,
    Was all the means to make us one,
And pictures in our eyes to get
    Was all our propagation.

As 'twixt two equal armies, fate
   Suspends uncertain victory,
Our souls, which to advance their state,
   Were gone out, hung 'twixt her and me.
And whil'st our souls negotiate there,
   We like sepulchral statues lay;
All day, the same our postures were,
   And we said nothing, all the day.
If any, so by love refined,
   That he soul's language understood,
And by good love were grown all mind,
   Within convenient distance stood,
He, though he knew not which soul spake,
   Because both meant, both spake the same,
Might thence a new concoction take,
   And part far purer than he came.
This ecstacy doth unperplex,
   We said, and tell us what we love;
We see by this, it was not sex;
   We see, we saw not what did move:
But, as all several souls contain
   Mixture of things, they know not what,
Love, these mixed souls, doth mix again,
   And makes both one, each this and that.
A single violet transplant,
   The strength, the colour, and the size,
(All which before was poor and scant)
   Redoubles still, and multiplies.
When love, with one another so
   Interinanimates two souls,
That abler soul, which thence doth flow,
   Defects of loneliness controls.
We then, who are this new soul, know,
   Of what we are composed and made;
For, th'atomies of which we grow,
   Are souls, whom no change can invade.
But O alas, so long, so far
   Our bodies why do we forbear?
They are ours, though they are not we; We are
   The intelligences, they the spheres.
We owe them thanks, because they thus,

Did us, to us, at first convey,
Yielded their forces, sense, to us,
  Nor are dross to us, but allay.
On man heaven's influence works not so,
  But that it first imprints the air,
So soul into the soul may flow,
  Though it to body first repair.
As our blood labours to beget
  Spirits, as like souls as it can,
Because such fingers need to knit
  That subtle knot, which makes us man:
So must pure lovers' souls descend
  T'affections, and to faculties,
Which sense may reach and apprehend,
  Else a great prince in prison lies.
To our bodies turn we then, that so
  Weak men on love revealed may look;
Love's mysteries in souls do grow,
  But yet the body is his book.
And if some lover, such as we,
  Have heard this dialogue of one,
Let him still mark us, he shall see
  Small change, when we are to bodies gone.

Love's deity

I long to talk with some old lover's ghost,
Who died before the god of love was born:
I cannot think that he, who then loved most,
Sunk so low as to love one which did scorn.
But since this god produced a destiny,
And that vice-nature, custom, lets it be,
I must love her, that loves not me.

Sure, they which made him god, meant not so much
Nor he in his young godhead practised it;
But when an even flame two hearts did touch,
His office was indulgently to fit
Actives to passives. Correspondency
Only his subject was; it cannot be
Love, till I love her that loves me.

But every modern god will now extend
His vast prerogative as far as Jove.
To rage, to lust, to write to, to commend,
All is the purlieu of the god of love.
Oh! were we wakened by this tyranny
To ungod this child again, it could not be
I should love her, who loves not me.

Rebel and atheist too, why murmur I,
As though I felt the worst that love could do?
Love may make me leave loving, or might try
A deeper plague, to make her love me too;
Which, since she loves before, I am loath to see.
Falsehood is worse than hate; and that must be,
If she, whom I love, should love me.

Truth

Seek true religion. Oh, where? Mirreus,
Thinking her unhoused here and fled from us,
Seeks her at Rome; there, because he doth know
That she was there a thousand years ago;
He loves her rags so, as we here obey
The statecloth where the prince sat yesterday.
Crantz to such brave loves will not be enthralled,
But loves her only, who at Geneva is called
Religion, plain, simple, sullen, young,
Contemptuous, yet unhandsome; as among
Lecherous humours, there is one that judges
No wenches wholesome, but coarse country drudges.
Graius stays still at home here, and because
Some preachers, vile ambitious bawds, and laws
Still new like fashions, bid him think that she
Which dwells with us, is only perfect, he
Embraceth her, whom his godfathers will
Tender to him, being tender, as wards still
Take such wives as their guardians offer, or
Pay values. Careless Phrygius doth abhor
All, because all cannot be good, as one
Knowing some women whores, dares marry none.
Gracchus loves all as one, and thinks that so
As women do in divers countries go

In divers habits, yet are still one kind,
So doth, so is religion; and this blind-
Ness too much light breeds; but unmoved thou
Of force must one, and forced but one allow,
And the right; ask thy father which is she,
Let him ask his; though truth and falsehood be
Near twins, yet truth a little elder is;
Be busy to seek her, believe me this,
He's not of none, nor worst, that seeks the best.
To adore, or scorn an image, or protest,
May all be bad. Doubt wisely; in strange way
To stand inquiring right, is not to stray;
To sleep, or run wrong, is. On a huge hill,
Cragged, and steep, Truth stands, and he that will
Reach her, about must, and about must go;
And what the hill's suddenness resists, win so;
Yet strive so, that before age, death's twilight,
Thy soul rest, for none can work in that night.
To will implies delay, therefore now do:
Hard deeds, the body's pains; hard knowledge too
The mind's endeavours reach, and mysteries
Are like the sun, dazzling, yet plain to all eyes.

From *Satire Three*

Batter my heart

Batter my heart, three-personed God; for you
As yet but knock, breathe, shine, and seek to mend;
That I may rise and stand, o'erthrow me, and bend
Your force, to break, blow, burn and make me new.
I, like an usurped town, to another due,
Labour to admit you, but Oh, to no end,
Reason your viceroy in me, me should defend,
But is captived, and proves weak or untrue.
Yet dearly I love you, and would be loved fain,
But am bethrothed unto your enemy:
Divorce me, untie, or break that knot again,
Take me to you, imprison me, for I
Except you enthrall me, never shall be free,
Nor ever chaste, except you ravish me.

Devout fits

Oh, to vex me, contraries meet in one:
Inconstancy unnaturally hath begot
A constant habit; that when I would not
I change in vows, and in devotion.
As humorous is my contrition
As my profane Love, and as soon forgot:
As ridlingly distempered, cold and hot,
As praying, as mute; as infinite, as none.
I durst not view heaven yesterday; and to day
In prayers, and flattering speeches I court God;
To morrow I quake with true fear of his rod.
So my devout fits come and go away
Like a fantastic Ague: save that here
Those are my best days, when I shake with fear.

JOHN FLETCHER (1579—1625)

Into slumbers

Care charming sleep, thou easer of all woes,
Brother to death, sweetly thyself dispose
On this afflicted Prince, fall like a cloud
In gentle showers, give nothing that is loud,
Or painful to his slumbers; easy, sweet,
And as a purling stream, thou son of night,
Pass by his troubled senses; sing his pain
Like hollow murmuring wind, or silver rain,
Into this Prince gently, Oh gently slide,
And kiss him into slumbers like a bride.

From *The Tragedy of Valentinian*

JOHN WEBSTER (1580?—1625?)

Call for the Robin-Redbreast

Call for the robin-redbreast and the wren,
Since o'er shady groves they hover,
And with leaves and flowers do cover
The friendless bodies of unburied men.
Call unto his funeral Dole
The ant, the field-mouse, and the mole,

To rear him hillocks, that shall keep him warm,
And, when gay tombs are robbed, sustain no harm;
But keep the wolf far thence, that's foe to men,
For with his nails he'll dig them up again.

From *The White Devil*

Hark, now everything is still

Hark, now everything is still—
The screech-owl, and the whistler shrill
Call upon our dame, aloud,
And bid her quickly don her shroud:
Much you had of land and rent,
Your length in clay's now competent.
A long war disturbed your mind,
Here your perfect peace is signed—
Of what is't fools make such vain keeping?
Sin their conception, their birth weeping:
Their life, a general mist of error,
Their death, a hideous storm of terror—
Strew your hair with powders sweet:
Don clean linen, bathe your feet,
And (the foul fiend more to check)
A crucifix let bless your neck,
'Tis now full tide, 'tween night and day,
End your groan, and come away.

From *The Duchess of Malfi*

WILLIAM DRUMMOND (1585—1649)
Madrigal

This life which seems so fair,
Is like a bubble blown up in the air,
By sporting children's breath,
Who chase it everywhere,
And strive who can most motion it bequeath:
And though it sometime seem of its own might
(Like to an eye of gold) to be fixed there,
And firm to hover in that empty height,
That only is *because it is so light*,
But in that Pomp it doth not long appear;
For even when most admired, it in a thought
As swelled from nothing, doth dissolve in nought.

WILLIAM DRUMMOND

89

Like the Idalian queen

Like the Idalian queen,
Her hair about her eyne,
With neck and breast's ripe apples to be seen,
At first glance of the morn
In Cyprus' gardens gathering those fair flowers
Which of her blood were born.
I saw, but fainting saw, my paramours.
The Graces naked danced about the place,
The winds and trees amazed
With silence on her gazed,
The flowers did smile, like those upon her face;
And as their aspen stalks those fingers band,
That she might read my case,
A hyacinth I wished me in her hand.

On the margin wrought

Of this fair volume which we World do name,
If we the sheets and leaves could turn with care,
Of him who it corrects, and did it frame,
We clear might read the art and wisdom rare:
Find out his power which wildest powers doth tame,
His providence extending everywhere,
His justice which proud rebels doth not spare,
In every page, no period of the same.
But silly we, like foolish children, rest
Well pleased with coloured vellum, leaves of gold,
Fair dangling ribbons, leaving what is best,
On the great Writer's sense ne'er taking hold;
    Or if by chance our minds do muse on aught,
    It is some picture on the margin wrought.

Thy sun posts westward

Look how the flower which lingeringly doth fade,
The morning's darling late, the summer's queen,
Spoiled of that juice which kept it fresh and green,
As high as it did raise, bows low the head:
Right so my life, contentments being dead
Or in their contraries but only seen,
With swifter speed declines than erst it spread,
And, blasted, scarce now shows what it hath been.

As doth the pilgrim therefore, whom the night
By darkness would imprison on his way,
Think on thy home, my soul, and think aright
Of what yet rests thee of life's wasting day;
    Thy sun posts westward, passed is thy morn.
    And twice it is not given thee to be born.

JOHN FORD (1586—1639?)

Song

Oh, no more, no more, too late
    Sighs are spent; the burning tapers
Of a life as chaste as fate,
    Pure as are unwritten papers,
    Are burnt out; no heat, no light
    Now remains; 'tis ever night.
Love is dead; let lovers' eyes,
    Locked in endless dreams,
    Th' extremes of all extremes,
Ope no more, for now Love dies.
    Now Love dies, implying
Love's Martyrs must be ever, ever dying.

ROBERT HERRICK (1591—1674)

The Argument of his Book

I sing of *Brooks*, of *Blossoms*, *Birds*, and *Bowers*:
Of *April*, *May*, of *June*, and *July*-Flowers.
I sing of *May-poles*, *Hock-carts*, *Wassails*, *Wakes*,
Of *Bride-grooms*, *Brides*, and of their *Bridal-cakes*.
I write of *Youth*, of *Love*, and have access
By these, to sing of cleanly-*Wantonness*.
I sing of *Dews*, of *Rains*, and piece by piece
Of *Balm*, of *Oil*, of *Spice*, and *Amber-gris*.
I sing of *Times trans-shifting*; and I write
How *Roses* first came *Red*, and *Lilies White*.
I write of *Groves*, of *Twilights*, and I sing
The Court of *Mab*, and of the *Fairy-King*.
I write of *Hell*; I sing (and ever shall)
Of *Heaven*, and hope to have it after all.

Delight in disorder

A sweet disorder in the dress
Kindles in clothes a wantonness:
A lawn about the shoulders thrown
Into a fine distraction:
An erring lace, which here and there
Enthrals the crimson stomacher:
A cuff neglectful, and thereby
Ribbands to flow confusedly:
A winning wave (deserving note)
In the tempestuous petticoat:
A careless shoe-string, in whose tie
I see a wild civility:
Do more bewitch me, than when art
Is too precise in every part.

His Litany, to the Holy Spirit

In the hour of my distress,
When temptations me oppress,
And when I my sins confess,
    Sweet Spirit, comfort me!

When I lie within my bed,
Sick in heart and sick in head,
And with doubts discomforted,
    Sweet Spirit, comfort me!

When the house doth sigh and weep,
And the world is drowned in sleep,
Yet mine eyes the watch do keep,
    Sweet Spirit, comfort me!

When the artless doctor sees
No one hope, but of his fees,
And his skill runs on the lees,
    Sweet Spirit, comfort me!

When his potion and his pill,
Has, or none or little, skill,
Meet for nothing, but to kill,
    Sweet Spirit, comfort me!

When the passing bell doth toll,
And the Furies in a shoal
Come to fright a parting soul,
   Sweet Spirit, comfort me!

When the tapers now burn blue,
And the comforters are few,
And that number more than true,
   Sweet Spirit, comfort me!

When the priest his last hath prayed,
And I nod to what is said,
'Cause my speech is now decayed,
   Sweet Spirit, comfort me!

When, God knows, I'm tossed about,
Either with despair or doubt;
Yet before the glass be out,
   Sweet Spirit, comfort me!

When the tempter me pursueth
With the sins of all my youth,
And half damns me with untruth,
   Sweet Spirit, comfort me!

When the flames and hellish cries
Fright mine ears, and fright mine eyes,
And all terrors me surprise,
   Sweet Spirit, comfort me!

When the judgement is revealed,
And that opened which was sealed,
When to thee I have appealed,
   Sweet Spirit, comfort me!

The Lily in a crystal

You have beheld a smiling rose
  When virgin's hands have drawn
    O'er it a cobweb-lawn:
And here, you see, this Lily shows,
  Tombed in a crystal stone,
More fair in this transparent case,
  Than when it grew alone;
    And had but single grace.

ROBERT HERRICK

You see how cream but naked is;
    Nor dances in the eye
    Without a strawberry:
Or some fine tincture, like to this,
    Which draws the sight thereto,
More by that wantoning with it;
    Than when the paler hue
    No mixture did admit.

You see how amber through the streams
    More gently strokes the sight,
    With some concealed delight
Than when he darts his radiant beams
    Into the boundless air:
Where either too much light his worth
    Doth all at once impair,
    Or set it little forth.

Put purple grapes, or cherries in-
    To glass, and they will send
    More beauty to commend
Them, from that clean and subtle skin,
    Than if they naked stood,
And had no other pride at all,
    But their own flesh and blood,
    And tinctures natural.

Thus lily, rose, grape, cherry, cream
    And strawberry do stir
    More love, when they transfer
A weak, a soft, a broken beam;
    Than if they should discover
At full their proper excellence;
    Without some scene cast over,
    To juggle with the sense.

Thus let this crystalled lily be
    A rule, how far to teach,
    Your nakedness must reach:
And that, no further, than we see
    Those glaring colours laid

By art's wise hand, but to this end
　　They should obey a shade;
　　Lest they too far extend.

So though you're white as swan, or snow,
　　And have the power to move
　　A world of men to love:
Yet, when your lawns and silks shall flow;
　　And that white cloud divide
Into a doubtful twilight; then,
　　Then will your hidden pride
　　Raise greater fires in men.

Upon Sibilla

With paste of almonds, *Syb* her hands doth scoure;
Then gives it to the children to devour.
In cream she bathes her thighs (more soft than silk)
Then to the poor she freely gives the milk.

Upon Julia's voice

So smooth, so sweet, so silvery is thy voice,
As, could they hear, the Damned would make no noise;
But listen to thee (walking in thy chamber)
Melting melodious words to lutes of amber.

HENRY KING (1592—1669)

The exequy

Accept thou shrine of my dead saint,
Instead of dirges this complaint;
And for sweet flowers to crown thy hearse,
Receive a strew of weeping verse
From thy grieved friend, whom thou might'st see
Quite melted into tears for thee.

　　Dear loss! since thy untimely fate
My task hath been to meditate
On thee, on thee: thou art the book,
The library whereon I look

Though almost blind. For thee, loved clay,
I languish out, not live the day,
Using no other exercise
But what I practice with mine eyes:
By which wet glasses I find out
How lazily time creeps about
To one that mourns: this, only this
My exercise and business is:
So I compute the weary hours
With sighs dissolved into showers.

Nor wonder if my time go thus
Backward and most preposterous;
Thou hast benighted me, thy set
This eve of blackness did beget,
Who wast my day, (though overcast
Before thou had'st thy noon-tide past)
And I remember must in tears,
Thou scarce had'st seen so many years
As day tells hours. By thy clear sun
My love and fortune first did run;
But thou wilt never more appear
Folded within my hemisphere,
Since both thy light and motion
Like a fled star is fallen and gone,
And 'twixt me and my soul's dear wish
The earth now interposed is,
Which such a strange eclipse doth make
As ne'er was read in almanac.

I could allow thee for a time
To darken me and my sad clime,
Were it a month, a year, or ten,
I would thy exile live till then;
And all that space my mirth adjourn,
So thou wouldst promise to return;
And putting off thy ashy shroud
At length disperse this sorrow's cloud.

But woe is me! the longest date
Too narrow is to calculate
These empty hopes: never shall I
Be so much blest as to descry
A glimpse of thee, till that day come
Which shall the earth to cinders doom,
And a fierce fever must calcine
The body of this world like thine,
(My little world!); that fit of fire
Once off, our bodies shall aspire
To our souls' bliss: then we shall rise,
And view ourselves with clearer eyes
In that calm region, where no night
Can hide us from each other's sight.

Meantime, thou hast her, earth: much good
May my harm do thee. Since it stood
With Heaven's will I might not call
Her longer mine, I give thee all
My short-lived right and interest
In her, whom living I loved best:
With a most free and bounteous grief,
I give thee what I could not keep.
Be kind to her, and prithee look
Thou write into thy Doomsday Book
Each parcel of this rarity
Which in thy casket shrined doth lie:
See that thou make thy reckoning straight,
And yield her back again by weight
For thou must audit on thy trust
Each grain and atom of this dust,
As thou wilt answer Him that lent,
Not gave thee, my dear monument.

So close the ground, and 'bout her shade
Black curtains draw, my bride is laid.

Sleep on, my love, in thy cold bed
Never to be disquieted!
My last good night! Thou wilt not wake
Till I thy fate shall overtake:

Till age, or grief, or sickness must
Marry my body to that dust
It so much loves; and fill the room
My heart keeps empty in thy tomb.
Stay for me there; I will not fail
To meet thee in that hollow vale.
And think not much of my delay;
I am already on the way,
And follow thee with all the speed
Desire can make, or sorrows breed.
Each minute is a short degree,
And every hour a step towards thee.
At night when I betake to rest,
Next morn I rise nearer my west
Of life, almost by eight hours sail,
Than when sleep breathed his drowsy gale.

Thus from the sun my bottom steers,
And my day's compass downward bears:
Nor labour I to stem the tide
Through which to thee I swiftly glide.

'Tis true, with shame and grief I yield,
Thou like the van first took'st the field,
And gotten hast the victory
In thus adventuring to die
Before me, whose more years might crave
A just precedence in the grave.
But hark! My pulse like a soft drum
Beats my approach, tells thee I come;
And slow howe'er my marches be,
I shall at last sit down by thee.

The thought of this bids me go on,
And wait my dissolution
With hope and comfort. Dear (forgive
The crime) I am content to live
Divided, with but half a heart,
Till we shall meet and never part.

D

Like to the falling of a star

Like to the falling of a star;
Or as the flights of eagles are;
Or like the fresh spring's gaudy hue;
Or silver drops of morning dew;
Or like a wind that chafes the flood;
Or bubbles which on water stood;
Even such is man, whose borrowed light
Is straight called in, and paid to night.

The wind blows out; the bubble dies;
The spring entombed in autumn lies;
The dew dries up; the star is shot;
The flight is past; and man forgot.

FRANCIS QUARLES (1592—1644)

On the infancy of our Saviour

Hail, blessed Virgin, full of heavenly grace,
Blest above all that sprang from human race;
Whose heaven-saluted womb brought forth in one,
A blessed Saviour, and a blessed son:
Oh! what a ravishment 't had been to see
Thy little Saviour perking on thy knee!
To see him nuzzle in thy virgin breast,
His milk-white body all unclad, undressed!
To see thy busy fingers clothe and wrap
His spradling limbs in thy indulgent lap!
To see his desperate eyes, with childish grace,
Smiling upon his smiling mother's face!
And, when his forward strength began to bloom,
To see him diddle up and down the room!
O, who would think so sweet a babe as this,
Should e'er be slain by a false-hearted kiss!
Had I a rag, if sure thy body wore it,
Pardon, sweet Babe, I think I should adore it:
Till then, O grant this boon (a boon far dearer),
The weed not being, I may adore the wearer.

False world, thou liest

Wilt thou set thine eyes upon that which is not? for riches make themselves wings,
they fly away as an eagle.

Proverbs xxiii. 5

False world, thou liest: Thou canst not lend
   The least delight:
Thy favours cannot gain a friend,
   They are so slight:
Thy morning pleasures make an end
   To please at night:
Poor are the wants that thou suppliest:
And yet thou vauntest, and yet thou viest
With heaven; Fond earth, thou boasts; false world, thou liest.

Thy babbling tongue tells golden tales
   Of endless treasure;
Thy bounty offers easy sales
   Of lasting pleasure;
Thou ask'st the Conscience what she ails,
   And swearest to ease her;
There's none can want where thou suppliest:
There's none can give where thou deniest.
Alas, fond world, thou boasts; false world, thou liest.

What well-advised ear regards
   What earth can say?
Thy words are gold, but thy rewards
   Are painted clay;
Thy cunning can but pack the cards;
   Thou canst not play:
Thy game at weakest, still thou viest;
If seen, and then revied[1], deniest;
Thou art not what thou seem'st: false world, thou liest.

Thy tinsel bosom seems a mint
   Of new-coined treasure,
A Paradise, that has no stint,
   No change, no measure;
A painted cask, but nothing in't,
   Nor wealth, nor pleasure:

Vain earth! that falsly thus compliest
With man: Vain man! that thus reliest
On earth: Vain man, thou dot'st: Vain earth, thou liest.

What mean dull souls, in this high measure
    To haberdash
In earth's base wares; whose greatest treasure
    Is dross and trash?
The height of whose enchanting pleasure
    Is but a flash?
Are these the goods that thou suppliest
Us mortals with? Are these the highest?
Can these bring cordial peace? False world, thou liest.

1. *revied*=challenged.

THE DUKE OF NEWCASTLE (1592—1676)

Love's matrimony

There is no happy life
But in a wife;
The comforts are so sweet
When they do meet:
'Tis plenty, peace, a calm
Like dropping balm:
Love's weather is so fair,
Perfumed air,
Each word such pleasure brings
Like soft-touched strings;
Love's passion moves the heart
On either part.
Such harmony together,
So pleased in either,
No discords, concords still,
Sealed with one will.
By love, God man made one,
Yet not alone:
Like stamps of king and queen

It may be seen,
Two figures but one coin;
So they do join,
Only they not embrace,
We face to face.

GEORGE HERBERT (1593—1633)

Discipline

Throw away thy rod,
Throw away thy wrath:
  O my God,
Take the gentle path.

For my heart's desire
Unto thine is bent:
  I aspire
To a full consent.

Not a word or look
I affect to own,
  But by book,
And thy book alone.

Though I fail, I weep:
Though I halt in pace,
  Yet I creep
To the throne of grace.

Then let wrath remove;
Love will do the deed:
  For with love
Stony hearts will bleed.

Love is swift of foot;
Love's a man of war,
  And can shoot,
And can hit from far.

Who can scape his bow?
That which wrought on thee,
   Brought thee low,
Needs must work on me.

Throw away thy rod;
Though man frailties hath,
   Thou art God:
Throw away thy wrath.

The church-floor

Mark you the floor? that square and speckled stone,
  Which looks so firm and strong,
    Is *Patience*:

And th' other black and grave, wherewith each one
  Is checkered all along,
    Humility:

The gentle rising, which on either hand
  Leads to the Quire above,
    Is *Confidence*:

But the sweet cement, which in one sure band
  Ties the whole frame, is *Love*
    And *Charity*.

  Hither sometimes Sin steals, and stains
  The marble's neat and curious veins:
But all is cleansed when the marble weeps.
  Sometimes Death, puffing at the door,
  Blows all the dust about the floor:
But while he thinks to spoil the room, he sweeps.
  Blest be the *Architect*, whose art
  Could build so strong in a weak heart.

The collar

I struck the board, and cried, No more.
    I will abroad.
What? shall I ever sigh and pine?
My lines and life are free; free as the road,
    Loose as the wind, as large as store.
        Shall I be still in suit?
Have I no harvest but a thorn
To let me blood, and not restore
What I have lost with cordial fruit?
        Sure there was wine
    Before my sighs did dry it: there was corn
    Before my tears did drown it.
Is the year only lost to me?
    Have I no bays to crown it?
No flowers, no garlands gay? all blasted?
        All wasted?
    Not so, my heart: but there is fruit,
        And thou hast hands.
    Recover all thy sigh-blown age
On double pleasures: leave thy cold dispute
Of what is fit, and not; forsake thy cage,
        Thy rope of sands,
Which petty thoughts have made, and made to thee
    Good cable, to enforce and draw,
        And be thy law,
    While thou didst wink and wouldst not see.
        Away; take heed:
        I will abroad.
Call in thy death's head there: tie up thy fears.
        He that forbears
    To suit and serve his need,
        Deserves his load.
But as I raved and grew more fierce and wild
        At every word,
    Me thought I heard one calling, *Child:*
        And I replied, *My Lord.*

Love

Love bade me welcome: yet my soul drew back,
    Guilty of dust and sin.
But quick-eyed Love, observing me grow slack
    From my first entrance in,
Drew nearer to me, sweetly questioning,
    If I lacked any thing.

'A guest,' I answered, 'worthy to be here:'
    Love said, 'You shall be he.'
'I the unkind, ungrateful? Ah my dear,
    I cannot look on Thee.'
Love took my hand, and smiling did reply,
    'Who made the eyes but I?'

'Truth Lord, but I have marred them: let my shame
    Go where it doth deserve.'
'And know you not,' says Love, 'Who bore the blame?'
    'My dear, then I will serve.'
'You must sit down,' says Love, 'and taste my meat:'
    So I did sit and eat.

THOMAS CAREW (1595?—1639?)

To my inconstant mistress

When thou, poor excommunicate
    From all the joys of love, shalt see
The full reward, and glorious fate,
    Which my strong faith shall purchase me,
Then curse thine own inconstancy.

A fairer hand than thine, shall cure
    That heart, which thy false oaths did wound;
And to my soul, a soul more pure
    Than thine, shall by Love's hand be bound,
And both with equal glory crowned.

Then shalt thou weep, entreat, complain
    To Love, as I did once to thee;
When all thy tears shall be as vain
    As mine were then, for thou shalt be
Damned for thy false apostasy.

Ask me no more

Ask me no more where Jove bestows,
When June is past, the fading rose:
For in your beauties, orient deep,
These flowers as in their causes sleep.

Ask me no more whither do stray
The golden atoms of the day:
For in pure love heaven did prepare
Those powders to enrich your hair.

Ask me no more whither doth haste
The Nightingale, when May is past:
For in your sweet dividing throat
She winters, and keeps warm her note.

Ask me no more where those stars light,
That downwards fall in dead of night:
For in your eyes they sit, and there
Fixed become, as in their sphere.

Ask me no more if East or West,
The Phoenix builds her spicy nest:
For unto you at last she flies,
And in your fragrant bosom dies.

SIR ROBERT STAPYLTON (1605?—1669)

The bard's song

On the poplars and oaks
When the white raven croaks.
And the crafty young fox withdraws,
With the fair fawn
Through the green lawn
Just into the lion's paws;
Then the scene of blood is acted;
Then the wood-nymphs run distracted;

The mandrake shrieks,
The moon's pale cheeks
Look dark;
But hark,
Brass basons and trumpets are sounding;
See, see, how soon
They thunder the moon
Out of the eclipse she was drowned in
What should we fear?
The sun shines clear;
No mist on the hill,
Not a cloud in the sky;
The lark sings shrill,
And the swallow flies high.

SIR WILLIAM DAVENANT (1606—1668)

Wake all the dead! What ho! What ho!

Wake all the dead! what ho! what ho!
How soundly they sleep whose pillows lie low!
They mind not poor lovers who walk above
On the decks of the world in storms of love.
    No whisper now nor glance can pass
    Through wickets or through panes of glass;
For our windows and doors are shut and barred.
Lie close in the church, and in the churchyard.
    In every grave make room, make room!
    The world's at an end, and we come, we come.

The state is now Love's foe, Love's foe;
Has seized on his arms, his quiver and bow;
Has pinioned his wings, and fettered his feet,
Because he made way for lovers to meet.
    But, O sad chance, his judge was old;
    Hearts cruel grow when blood grows cold.
No man being young his process would draw.
O heavens, that love should be subject to law!
    Lovers go woo the dead, the dead!
    Lie two in a grave, and to bed, to bed!

EDMUND WALLER (1606—1687)

On a girdle

That which her slender waist confined,
Shall now my joyful temples bind;
No Monarch but would give his Crown
His Arms might do what this has 'done.

It is my Heaven's extremest Sphere,
The pale which held the lovely Dear,
My joy, my grief, my hope, my Love,
Do all within this Circle move.

A narrow compass, and yet there
Dwells all that's good, and all that's fair:
Give me but what this Ribbon bound,
Take all the rest the sun goes round.

SIR RICHARD FANSHAWE (1608—1666)

A rose

Blown in the morning, thou shalt fade ere noon:
 What boots a life which in such haste forsakes thee?
 Thou 'rt wond'rous frolic being to die so soon:
 And passing proud a little colour makes thee.

If thee thy brittle beauty so deceives,
 Know then the thing that swells thee is thy bane;
 For the same beauty doth in bloody leaves
 The sentence of thy early death contain.

Some clown's coarse lungs will poison thy sweet flower
 If by the careless plough thou shalt be torn:
 And many *Herods* lie in wait each hour
 To murder thee as soon as thou art born:

Nay, force thy bud to blow; their tyrant breath
Anticipating life, to hasten death.

JOHN MILTON (1608—1674)

On Shakespeare

What needs my Shakespeare for his honoured bones,
The labour of an age in piled stones,
Or that his hallowed reliques should be hid
Under a star-ypointing pyramid?
Dear son of memory, great heir of fame,
What need'st thou such weak witness of thy name?
Thou in our wonder and astonishment
Hast built thyself a live-long monument.
For whilst to the shame of slow-endeavouring art
Thy easy numbers flow, and that each heart
Hath from the leaves of thy unvalued book
Those Delphic lines with deep impression took,
Then thou our fancy of itself bereaving
Dost make us marble with too much conceiving;
And so sepulchered in such pomp dost lie,
That kings for such a tomb would wish to die.

How soon hath time

How soon hath time, the subtle thief of youth,
Stol'n on his wing my three and twentieth year!
My hasting days fly on with full career,
But my late spring no bud or blossom shew'th.
Perhaps my semblance might deceive the truth,
That I to manhood am arrived so near,
And inward ripeness doth much less appear,
That some more timely-happy spirits indu'th.
Yet be it less or more, or soon or slow,
It shall be still in strictest measure even
To that same lot, however mean or high,
Toward which time leads me, and the will of Heaven:
All is, if I have grace to use it so,
As ever in my great Task-master's eye.

O nightingale

O nightingale! that on yon bloomy spray
   Warblest at eve, when all the woods are still,
    Thou with fresh hope the lover's heart dost fill,
While the jolly hours lead on propitious May:

Thy liquid notes that close the eye of day,
   First heard before the shallow cuckoo's bill,
   Portend success in love: oh, if Jove's will
Have linked that amorous power to thy soft lay,
Now timely sing, ere the rude bird of hate
   Foretell my hopeless doom, in some grove nigh;
As thou from year to year hast sung too late
   For my relief, yet hadst no reason why:
Whether the Muse, or Love, call thee his mate,
   Both them I serve, and of their train am I.

L'Allegro

Hence, loathed Melancholy,
   Of Cerberus and blackest Midnight born
In Stygian cave forlorn
   'Mongst horrid shapes, and shrieks, and sights unholy!
Find out some uncouth cell,
   Where brooding Darkness spreads his jealous wings,
And the night-raven sings;
   There, under ebon shades and low-browed rocks
As ragged as thy locks,
   In dark Cimmerian desert ever dwell.
But come, thou Goddess fair and free,
In heaven yclept Euphrosyne,
And by men heart-easing Mirth;
Whom lovely Venus, at a birth,
With two sister Graces more,
To ivy-crowned Bacchus bore:
Or whether (as some sager sing)
The frolic wind that breathes the spring,
Zephyr, with Aurora playing,
As he met her once a-Maying,
There on beds of violet blue,
And fresh-blown roses washed in dew,
Filled her with thee, a daughter fair,
So buxom, blithe, and debonair.
   Haste thee, Nymph, and bring with thee
Jest, and youthful jollity,
Quips and cranks and wanton wiles,
Nods and becks and wreathed smiles,

Such as hang on Hebe's cheek,
And love to live in dimple sleek;
Sport that wrinkled Care derides,
And Laughter holding both his sides:
Come, and trip it, as you go,
On the light fantastic toe;
And in thy right hand lead with thee
The mountain-nymph, sweet Liberty;
And, if I give thee honour due,
Mirth, admit me of thy crew,
To live with her, and live with thee,
In unreproved pleasures free;
To hear the lark begin his flight,
And, singing, startle the dull night,
From his watch-tower in the skies,
Till the dappled dawn doth rise:
Then to come, in spite of sorrow,
And at my window bid good-morrow,
Through the sweet-briar or the vine,
Or the twisted eglantine;
While the cock, with lively din,
Scatters the rear of darkness thin,
And to the stack, or the barn-door,
Stoutly struts his dames before:
Oft listening how the hounds and horn
Cheerly rouse the slumbering morn,
From the side of some hoar hill,
Through the high wood, echoing shrill;
Sometime walking, not unseen,
By hedgerow elms, on hillocks green,
Right against the eastern gate
Where the great Sun begins his state,
Robed in flames and amber light,
The clouds in thousand liveries dight;
While the ploughman, near at hand,
Whistles o'er the furrowed land,
And the milkmaid singeth blithe,
And the mower whets his scythe,
And every shepherd tells his tale
Under the hawthorn in the dale.
    Straight mine eye hath caught new pleasures,

Whilst the landskip round it measures:
Russet lawns, and fallows gray,
Where the nibbling flocks do stray;
Mountains on whose barren breast
The labouring clouds do often rest;
Meadows trim, with daisies pied;
Shallow brooks, and rivers wide;
Towers and battlements it sees
Bosomed high in tufted trees,
Where perhaps some beauty lies,
The cynosure of neighbouring eyes.
Hard by, a cottage chimney smokes
From betwixt two aged oaks,
Where Corydon and Thyrsis met
Are at their savoury dinner set
Of herbs and other country messes,
Which the neat-handed Phyllis dresses;
And then in haste her bower she leaves,
With Thestylis to bind the sheaves;
Or, if the earlier season lead,
To the tanned haycock in the mead.
   Sometimes, with secure delight,
The upland hamlets will invite,
When the merry bells ring round,
And the jocund rebecks sound
To many a youth and many a maid
Dancing in the chequered shade;
And young and old come forth to play
On a sunshine holiday,
Till the livelong daylight fail:
Then to the spicy nut-brown ale,
With stories told of many a feat,
How Faery Mab the junkets eat:
She was pinched and pulled, she said;
And he, by Friar's lantern led,
Tells how the drudging goblin sweat
To earn his cream-bowl duly set,
When in one night, ere glimpse of morn,
His shadowy flail had threshed the corn
That ten day-labourers could not end;
Then lies him down the lubber fiend,

And, stretched out all the chimney's length,
Basks at the fire his hairy strength;
And crop-full out of doors he flings,
Ere the first cock his matin rings.
Thus done the tales, to bed they creep,
By whispering winds soon lulled asleep.
    Towered cities please us then,
And the busy hum of men,
Where throngs of knights and barons bold,
In weeds of peace, high triumphs hold,
With store of ladies, whose bright eyes
Rain influence, and judge the prize
Of wits or arms, while both contend
To win her grace whom all commend.
There let Hymen oft appear
In saffron robe, with taper clear,
And pomp, and feast, and revelry,
With mask and antique pageantry;
Such sights as youthful poets dream
On summer eves by haunted stream.
Then to the well-trod stage anon,
If Jonson's learned sock be on,
Or sweetest Shakespeare, Fancy's child,
Warble his native wood-notes wild.
    And ever, against eating cares,
Lap me in soft Lydian airs,
Married to immortal verse,
Such as the meeting soul may pierce,
In notes with many a winding bout
Of linked sweetness long drawn out
With wanton heed and giddy cunning.
The melting voice through mazes running,
Untwisting all the chains that tie
The hidden soul of harmony;
That Orpheus' self may heave his head
From golden slumber on a bed
Of heaped Elysian flowers, and hear
Such strains as would have won the ear
Of Pluto to have quite set free
His half-regained Eurydice.
    These delights if thou canst give,
Mirth, with thee I mean to live.

Satan

He scarce had ceased when the superior Fiend
Was moving toward the shore; his ponderous shield
Ethereal temper, massy, large and round,
Behind him cast; the broad circumference
Hung on his shoulders like the moon, whose orb
Through optic glass the Tuscan artist views
At evening from the top of Fesole,
Or in Valdarno, to descry new Lands,
Rivers or mountains in her spotty globe.
His spear, to equal which the tallest pine
Hewn on Norwegian hills, to be the mast
Of some great Ammiral, were but a wand,
He walkt with to support uneasy steps
Over the burning marle, not like those steps
On heaven's azure, and the torrid clime
Smote on him sore besides, vaulted with fire;
Nathless he so endured, till on the beach
Of that inflamed sea, he stood and called
His legions, angel forms, who lay entranced
Thick as autumnal leaves that strew the brooks
In Vallombrosa, where the Etrurian shades
High overarch't embower; or scattered sedge
Afloat, when with fierce winds Orion armed
Has vexed the Red-Sea coast, whose waves o'erthrew
Busiris and his Memphian chivalry,
While with perfidious hatred they pursued
The Sojourners of Goshen, who beheld
From the safe shore their floating carcases
And broken chariot wheels, so thick bestrown
Abject and lost lay these, covering the flood,
Under amazement of their hideous change . . .

He ceased; and Satan stayed not to reply,
But glad that now his sea should find a shore,
With fresh alacrity and force renewed
Springs upward like a pyramid of fire
Into the wild expanse, and through the shock
Of fighting elements, on all sides round
Environed wins his way; harder beset

And more endangered, than when Argo passed
Through Bosphorus between the justling rocks:
Or when Ulysses on the larboard shunned
Charybdis, and by the other whirlpool steered.
So he with difficulty and labour hard
Moved on, with difficulty and labour he;
But he once passed, soon after when man fell,
Strange alteration! Sin and Death amain
Following his track, such was the will of Heaven,
Paved after him a broad and beaten way
Over the dark abyss, whose boiling gulf
Tamely endured a bridge of wondrous length
From hell continued reaching th' utmost orb
Of this frail world; by which the spirits perverse
With easy intercourse pass to and fro
To tempt or punish mortals, except whom
God and good angels guard by special grace.
But now at last the sacred influence
Of light appears, and from the walls of Heaven
Shoots far into the bosom of dim night
A glimmering dawn; here Nature first begins
Her farthest verge, and chaos to retire
As from her outmost works a broken foe
With tumult less and with less hostile din,
That Satan with less toil, and now with ease
Wafts on the calmer wave by dubious light
And like a weather-beaten vessel holds
Gladly the port, though shrouds and tackle torn;
Or in the emptier waste, resembling air,
Weighs his spread wings, at leisure to behold
Far off th' empyreal heaven, extended wide
In circuit, undetermined square or round,
With opal towers and battlements adorned
Of living saphire, once his native seat;
And fast by hanging in a golden chain
This pendant world, in bigness as a star
Of smallest magnitude close by the moon.
Thither full fraught with mischievous revenge,
Accursed, and in a cursed hour he hies.

From *Paradise Lost*

Adam and Eve

So passed they naked on, nor shunned the sight
Of God or angel, for they thought no ill:
So hand in hand they passed, the loveliest pair
That ever since in love's embraces met,
Adam the goodliest man of men since born
His sons, the fairest of her daughters Eve.
Under a tuft of shade that on a green
Stood whispering soft, by a fresh fountain side
They sat them down, and after no more toil
Of their sweet gardening labour than sufficed
To recommend cool zephyr, and made ease
More easy, wholesome thirst and appetite
More grateful, to their supper fruits they fell,
Nectarine fruits which the compliant boughs
Yielded them, side-long as they sat recline
On the soft downy bank damasked with flowers:
The savoury pulp they chew, and in the rind
Still as they thirsted scoop the brimming stream;
Nor gentle purpose, nor endearing smiles
Wanted, nor youthful dalliance as beseems
Fair couple, linked in happy nuptial league,
Alone as they. About them frisking played
All beasts of the earth, since wild, and of all chase
In wood of wilderness, forest or den;
Sporting the lion ramped, and in his paw
Dandled the kid; bears, tigers, ounces, pards
Gambolled before them, the unwieldly elephant
To make them mirth used all his might, and wreathed
His lithe proboscis; close the serpent sly
Insinuating, wove with Gordian twine
His braided train, and of his fatal guile
Gave proof unheeded; others on the grass
Couched, and now filled with pasture gazing sat,
Or bedward ruminating; for the sun
Declined was hasting now with prone career
To the ocean isles, and in the ascending scale
Of Heaven the stars that usher evening rose:

From *Paradise Lost*

Their wedded love

Hail wedded love, mysterious law, true source
Of human offspring, sole propriety,
In paradise of all things common else.
By thee adulterous lust was driven from men
Among the bestial herds to range, by thee
Founded in reason, loyal, just, and pure,
Relations dear, and all the charities
Of father, son, and brother first were known.
Far be it, that I should write thee sin or blame,
Of think thee unbefitting holiest place,
Perpetual fountain of domestic sweets,
Whose bed is undefiled and chaste pronounced,
Present, or past, as saints and patriarchs used.
Here love his golden shafts employs, here lights
His constant lamp, and waves his purple wings,
Reigns here and revels; not in the bought smile
Of harlots, loveless, joyless, unendeared,
Casual fruition, nor in court amours
Mixed dance, or wanton mask, or midnight ball,
Or serenade, which the starved lover sings
To his proud fair, best quitted with disdain.
These lulled by Nightingales embracing slept,
And on their naked limbs the flowery roof
Showered roses, which the morn repaired. Sleep on,
Blest pair; and O yet happiest if ye seek
No happier state, and know to know no more.

Their banishment

                    . for now too nigh
The archangel stood, and from the other hill
To their fixed station, all in bright array
The Cherubim descended; on the ground
Gliding meteorous, as evening mist
Risen from a river o'er the marish glides,
And gathers ground fast at the labourer's heel
Homeward returning. High in front advanced,
The brandished sword of God before them blazed
Fierce as a comet; which with torrid heat,
And vapour as the Libyan air adust,

Began to parch that temperate clime; whereat
In either hand the hastening angel caught
Our lingering parents, and to the eastern gate
Led them direct, and down the cliff as fast
To the subjected plain; then disappeared.
They looking back, all the eastern side beheld
Of Paradise, so late their happy seat,
Waved over by that flaming brand, the gate
With dreadful faces thronged and fiery arms:
Some natural tears they dropped, but wiped them soon;
The world was all before them, where to choose
Their place of rest, and providence their guide:
They hand in hand with wandering steps and slow,
Through Eden took their solitary way.

From *Paradise Lost*

Delilah

But who is this, what thing of sea or land?
Female of sex it seems,
That so bedecked, ornate, and gay,
Comes this way sailing
Like a stately ship
Of Tarsus, bound for the isles
Of Javan or Gadier
With all her bravery on, and tackle trim,
Sails filled, and streamers waving,
Courted by all the winds that hold them play,
An Amber scent of odorous perfume
Her harbinger, a damsel train behind;
Some rich Philistian matron she may seem,
And now at nearer view, no other certain
Than Dalila thy wife.

From *Samson Agonistes*

All is best

All is best, though we oft doubt,
What th' unsearchable dispose
Of highest wisdom brings about,
And ever best found in the close.
Oft he seems to hide his face,
But unexpectedly returns

And to his faithful Champion hath in place
Bore witness gloriously; whence Gaza mourns
And all that band them to resist
His uncontrollable intent;
His servants he with new acquist
Of true experience from this great event
With peace and consolation hath dismissed,
And calm of mind all passion spent.

From *Samson Agonistes*

SIR JOHN SUCKLING (1609—1642)

Why so pale and wan

Why so pale and wan fond lover?
　　Prithee why so pale?
Will, when looking well can't move her
　　Looking ill prevail?
　　Prithee, why so pale?

Why so dull and mute, young sinner
　　Prithee why so mute?
Will, when speaking well can't win her,
　　Saying nothing do 't?
　　Prithee, why so mute?

Quit, quit for shame, this will not move,
　　This cannot take her.
If of her self she will not love,
　　Nothing can make her:
　　The devil take her.

A constant lover

Out upon it, I have loved,
Three whole days together;
And am like to love three more,
If it prove fair weather.

Time shall moult away his wings
Ere he shall discover
In the whole wide world again
Such a constant lover.

But the spite on 't is, no praise
Is due at all to me:
Love with me had made no stays,
Had it any been but she.

Had it any been but she
And that very face,
There had been at least ere this
A dozen dozen in her place.

SAMUEL BUTLER (1612—1680)

Hudibras the Sectarian

Beside he was a shrewd *Philosopher*,
And had read every text and gloss over:
What e'er the crabbed'st author hath
He understood b'implicit Faith,
What ever *Sceptick* could inquire for;
For every *why* he had a *wherefore*;
Knew more than forty of them do,
As far as words and terms could go.
All which he understood by rote,
And as occasion served, would quote;
No matter whether right or wrong:
They might be either said or sung.
His notions fitted things so well,
That which was which he could not tell;
But oftentimes mistook th' one
For th' other, as great clerks have done.
He could reduce all things to Acts,
And knew their Natures by Abstracts,
Where Entity and Quiddity
The Ghosts of defunct Bodies fly;
Where Truth in Person does appear,
Like words congealed in Northern Air.
He knew *what's what*, and that's as high
As *Metaphysick* Wit can fly.
In *School Divinity* as able
As he that hight *Irrefragable*;
Profound in all the Nominal

And real ways beyond them all;
And with as delicate a hand,
Could twist as tough a rope of sand,
And weave fine cobwebs, fit for skull
That's empty when the moon is full;
Such as take lodgings in a head
That's to be let unfurnished.
He could raise scruples dark and nice,
And after solve 'em in a trice:
As if Divinity had catched
The itch, of purpose to be scratched;
Or, like a mountebank, did wound
And stab her self with doubts profound,
Only to show with how small pain
The sores of faith are cured again;
Although by woeful proof we find,
They always leave a scar behind.
He knew the seat of Paradise,
Could tell in what degree it lies:
And as he was disposed, could prove it,
Below the moon, or else above it.
What *Adam* dreamt of when his bride
Came from her closet in his side:
Whether the Devil tempted her
By a *High Dutch* interpreter:
If either of them had a navel;
Who first made music malleable:
Whether the Serpent at the fall
Had cloven feet, or none at all.
All this without a gloss or comment,
He would unriddle in a moment:
In proper terms, such as men smatter
When they throw out and miss the matter.
For his *Religion* it was fit
To match his learning and his wit:
'Twas *Presbyterian* true blue,
For he was of that stubborn crew
Of Errant Saints, whom all men grant
To be the true Church *Militant*:
Such as do build their faith upon
The holy text of *Pike* and *Gun*;

Decide all controversies by
Infallible *Artillery*;
And prove their doctrine orthodox
By Apostolic *Blows* and *Knocks*;
Call Fire and Sword and Desolation,
A *godly-thorough-Reformation*,
Which always must be carried on,
And still be doing, never done:
As if Religion were intended
For nothing else but to be mended.
A Sect, whose chief devotion lies
In odd perverse antipathies;
In falling out with that or this,
And finding somewhat still amiss:
More peevish, cross, and splenetic,
Than dog distract, or monkey sick.
That with more care keep Holy-day
The wrong, than others the right way:
Compound for Sins, they are inclined to;
By damning those they have no mind to;
Still so perverse and opposite,
As if they worshipped God for spite,
The self-same thing they will abhor
One way, and long another for.
Free-will they one way disavow,
Another, nothing else allow.
All Piety consists therein
In them, in other men all Sin.

JAMES GRAHAM, MARQUIS OF MONTROSE (1612—1650)

On himself, upon hearing what was his sentence

Let them bestow on ev'ry airth a limb;
Open all my veins, that I may swim
To Thee my Saviour, in that crimson lake;
Then place my purboiled head upon a stake;
Scatter my ashes, throw them in the air:
Lord, since Thou know'st where all these atoms are,
I'm hopeful, once Thou'lt recollect my dust,
And confident Thou'lt raise me with the just.

JOHN CLEVELAND (1613?—1658)

Epitaph on the Earl of Strafford

Here lies wise and valiant dust,
Huddled up 'twixt fit and just:
Strafford, who was hurried hence
'Twixt treason and convenience.
He spent his time here in a mist,
A *Papist*, yet a *Calvinist*;
His Prince's nearest joy and Grief:
He had, yet wanted, all relief:
The Prop and Ruin of the State,
The people's violent love and hate.
One in extremes loved and abhorred.
Riddles lie here, or in a word,
Here lies blood, and let it lie
Speechless still, and never cry.

RICHARD CRASHAW (1613?—1649)

The flaming heart

*Upon the book and picture of the seraphical Saint Teresa
as she is usually expressed with a Seraphim beside her.*

Well-meaning readers! you that come as friends,
And catch the precious name this piece pretends;
Make not too much haste to admire
That fair-cheeked fallacy of fire.
That is a seraphim, they say,
And this the great Teresia.
Readers, be ruled by me; and make
Here a well-placed and wise mistake;
You must transpose the picture quite,
And spell it wrong to read it right;
Read him for her, and her for him,
And call the saint the seraphim.
  Painter, what didst thou understand
To put her dart into his hand?
See, even the years and size of him
Shows this the mother seraphim.
This is the mistress flame; and duteous he
Her happy fire-works, here, comes down to see.

122

O most poor-spirited of men!
Had thy cold pencil kissed her pen,
Thou couldst not so unkindly err
To show us this faint shade for her.
Why, man, this speaks pure mortal frame;
And mocks with female frost Love's manly flame.
One would suspect thou meant'st to paint
Some weak, inferior, woman-saint.
But had thy pale-faced purple took
Fire from the burning cheeks of that bright book,
Thou wouldst on her have heaped up all
That could be formed seraphical;
Whate'er this youth of fire wears fair,
Rosy fingers, radiant hair,
Glowing cheeks, and glistering wings,
All those fair and flagrant things,
But before all, that fiery dart
Had filled the hand of this great heart.
   Do then, as equal right requires;
Since his the blushes be, and hers the fires.
Resume and rectify thy rude design;
Undress thy seraphim into mine;
Redeem this injury of thy art.
Give him the veil, give her the dart.
   Give him the veil, that he may cover
The red cheeks of a rivalled lover;
Ashamed that our world now can show
Nests of new seraphims here below.
   Give her the dart, for it is she,
Fair youth, shoots both thy shaft and thee;
Say, all ye wise and well-pierced hearts
That live and die amidst her darts,
What is't your tasteful spirits do prove
In that rare life of her, and Love?
Say, and bear witness. Sends she not
A seraphim at every shot?
What magazines of immortal arms there shine!
Heaven's great artillery in each love-spun line.
Give then the dart to her who gives the flame;
Give him the veil, who kindly takes the shame.

But if it be the frequent fate
Of worst faults to be fortunate;
If all's prescription; and proud wrong
Harkens not to an humble song;
For all the gallantry of him,
Give me the suffering seraphim.
His be the bravery of all those bright things,
The glowing cheeks, the glistering wings;
The rosy hand, the radiant dart;
Leave her alone the flaming heart.

Leave her that; and thou shalt leave her
Not one loose shaft, but Love's whole quiver;
For in Love's field was never found
A nobler weapon than a wound.
Love's passives are his activ'st part:
The wounded is the wounding heart.
O heart! the equal poise of Love's both parts,
Big alike with wounds and darts,
Live in these conquering leaves; live all the same;
And walk through all tongues one triumphant flame.
Live here, great heart; and love, and die, and kill;
And bleed, and wound; and yield and conquer still.
Let this immortal life where'er it comes
Walk in a crowd of loves and martyrdoms.
Let mystic deaths wait on 't; and wise souls be
The love-slain witnesses of this life of thee.

O sweet incendiary! show here thy art,
Upon this carcass of a hard cold heart:
Let all thy scattered shafts of light that play
Among the leaves of thy large books of day,
Combined against this breast at once break in
And take away from me myself and sin;
This gracious robbery shall thy bounty be,
And my best fortunes such fair spoils of me.
O thou undaunted daughter of desires!
By all thy dower of lights and fires;
By all the eagle in thee, all the dove;
By all thy lives and deaths of love;
By thy large draughts of intellectual day,
And by thy thirsts of love more large than they;
By all thy brim-filled bowls of fierce desire,

By thy last morning's draught of liquid fire;
By the full kingdom of that final kiss
That seized thy parting soul, and sealed thee his;
By all the heavens thou hast in him,
Fair sister of the seraphim!
By all of him we have in thee;
Leave nothing of myself in me.
Let me so read thy life, that I
Unto all life of mine may die.

An epitaph upon a young married couple dead and buried together

To these, whom Death again did wed,
This grave's their second marriage-bed;
For though the hand of Fate could force
'Twixt soul and body a divorce,
It could not sunder man and wife,
'Cause they both lived but one life.
Peace, good Reader, do not weep.
Peace, the lovers are asleep.
They, sweet turtles, folded lie
In the last knot Love could tie.
And though they lie as they were dead,
Their pillow stone, their sheets of lead,
(Pillow hard, and sheets not warm)
Love made the bed; they'll take no harm.
Let them sleep: let them sleep on,
Till this stormy night be gone,
Till the eternal morrow dawn;
Then the curtains will be drawn
And they wake into a light,
Whose day shall never die in night.

SIR JOHN DENHAM (1615—1669)

The Thames from Cooper's Hill

My eye descending from the hill surveys
Where *Thames* amongst the wanton valleys strays.
Thames, the most loved of all the ocean's sons,
By his old sire to his embraces runs,

Hasting to pay his tribute to the sea
Like mortal life to meet eternity.
Though with those streams he no resemblance hold,
Whose foam is amber, and their gravel gold;
His genuine, and less guilty wealth t'explore,
Search not his bottom, but survey his shore;
O'er which he kindly spreads his spacious wing,
And hatches plenty for th' ensuing spring.
Nor then destroys it with too fond a stay,
Like mothers which their infants overlay.
Nor with a sudden and impetuous wave,
Like profuse kings, resumes the wealth he gave.
No unexpected inundations spoil
The mower's hopes, nor mock the plowman's toil:
But God-like his unwearied bounty flows;
First loves to do, then loves the good he does.
Nor are his blessings to his banks confined,
But free, and common, as the sea or wind;
When he to boast, or to disperse his stores
Full of the tributes of his grateful shores,
Visits the world, and in his flying towers
Brings home to us, and makes both *Indies* ours;
Finds wealth where 'tis, bestows it where it wants,
Cities in deserts, woods in cities plants.
So that to us no thing, no place is strange,
While his fair bosom is the world's exchange.
O could I flow like thee, and make thy stream
My great example, as it is my theme!
Though deep, yet clear, though gentle, yet not dull,
Strong without rage, without o'er-flowing full.

ABRAHAM COWLEY (1618—1667)

Anacreontic on drinking

The thirsty earth soaks up the rain,
And drinks and gapes for drink again;
The plants suck in the earth, and are
With constant drinking fresh and fair;

The sea itself (which one would think
Should have but little need of drink)
Drinks twice ten thousand rivers up,
So filled that they o'erflow the cup.
The busy sun (and one would guess
By's drunken fiery face no less)
Drinks up the sea, and when he's done,
The moon and stars drink up the sun:
They drink and dance by their own light,
They drink and revel all the night:
Nothing in Nature's sober found,
But an eternal health goes round.
Fill up the bowl, then, fill it high,
Fill all the glasses there—for why
Should every creature drink but I?
Why, man of mortals, tell me why?

RICHARD LOVELACE (1618—1658)

The grasshopper
To my Noble Friend, Mr. Charles Cotton

Oh thou that swing'st upon the waving ear
   Of some well-filled oaten beard,
Drunk every night with a delicious tear
   Dropped thee from heaven, where now thou'rt reared.

The joys of earth and air are thine entire,
   That with thy feet and wings dost hop and fly:
And when thy poppy works, thou dost retire
   To thy carved acorn-bed to lie.

Up with the day, the sun thou welcom'st then,
   Sport'st in the gilt plaits of his beams,
And all these merry days mak'st merry men,
   Thyself, and melancholy streams.

But ah, the sickle! golden ears are cropped;
   Ceres and Bacchus bid goodnight;
Sharp frosty fingers all your flowers have topped,
   And what scythes spared, winds shave off quite.

Poor verdant fool! and now green ice! thy joys
  Large and as lasting as thy perch of grass,
Bid us lay in 'gainst winter rain, and poise
  Their floods, with an o'erflowing glass.

Thou best of men and friends! we will create
  A genuine summer in each other's breast;
And spite of this cold time and frozen fate
  Thaw us a warm seat to our rest.

Our sacred hearths shall burn eternally
  As vestal flames; the north-wind, he
Shall strike his frost stretched wings, dissolve, and fly
  This Ætna in epitome.

Dropping December shall come weeping in,
  Bewail th'usurping of his reign;
But when in showers of old Greek we begin,
  Shall cry, he hath his crown again!

Night as clear Hesper shall our tapers whip
  From the light casements where we play,
And the dark hag from her black mantle strip,
  And stick there everlasting day.

Thus richer than untempted kings are we,
  That asking nothing, nothing need:
Though Lord of all what seas embrace, yet he
  That wants himself, is poor indeed.

To Lucasta, on going to the wars

Tell me not, Sweet, I am unkind,
  That from the nunnery
Of thy chaste breast, and quiet mind,
  To war and arms I fly.

True; a new mistress now I chase,
  The first foe in the field;
And with a stronger faith embrace
  A sword, a horse, a shield.

Yet this inconstancy is such,
    As you too shall adore;
I could not love thee, Dear, so much,
    Loved I not honour more.

ANDREW MARVELL (1621—1678)

To his coy mistress

Had we but world enough, and time,
This coyness, Lady, were no crime.
We would sit down, and think which way
To walk, and pass our long love's day.
Thou by the Indian Ganges side
Should'st rubies find: I by the tide
Of Humber would complain. I would
Love you ten years before the Flood:
And you should if you please refuse
Till the Conversion of the Jews.
My vegetable Love should grow
Vaster than empires, and more slow.
An hundred years should go to praise
Thine eyes, and on thy forehead gaze.
Two hundred to adore each breast:
But thirty thousand to the rest.
An age at least to every part,
And the last age should show your heart.
For Lady you deserve this state;
Nor would I love at lower rate.
    But at my back I always hear
Time's winged chariot hurrying near:
And yonder all before us lie
Deserts of vast eternity.
Thy beauty shall no more be found;
Nor, in thy marble vault, shall sound
My echoing song: then worms shall try
That long preserved virginity:
And your quaint honour turn to dust;
And into ashes all my lust.

The grave's a fine and private place,
But none, I think, do there embrace.
Now therefore, while the youthful hue
Sits on thy skin like morning dew,
And while thy willing soul transpires
At every pore with instant fires,
Now let us sport us while we may;
And now, like amorous birds of prey,
Rather at once our time devour,
Than languish in his slow-chapt power.
Let us roll all our strength, and all
Our sweetness, up into one ball:
And tear our pleasures with rough strife,
Thorough the iron gates of life.
Thus, though we cannot make our sun
Stand still, yet we will make him run.

The garden

How vainly men themselves amaze
To win the palm, the oak, or bays;
And their uncessant labours see
Crowned from some single herb or tree.
Whose short and narrow verged shade
Does prudently their toils upbraid;
While all flowers and all trees do close
To weave the garlands of repose.

Fair Quiet, have I found thee here,
And Innocence thy sister dear!
Mistaken long, I sought you then
In busy companies of men.
Your sacred plants, if here below,
Only among the plants will grow.
Society is all but rude
To this delicious solitude.

No white nor red was ever seen
So am'rous as this lovely green.
Fond lovers, cruel as their flame,
Cut in these trees their mistress' name.
Little, alas, they know, or heed,

How far these beauties hers exceed!
Fair trees! wheresoe'er your barks I wound,
No name shall but your own be found.

When we have run our passions heat,
Love hither makes his best retreat.
The *Gods*, that a mortal beauty chase,
Still in a tree did end their race.
Apollo hunted *Daphne* so,
Only that she might laurel grow.
And *Pan* did after *Syrinx* speed,
Not as a nymph, but for a reed.

What wond'rous life in this I lead!
Ripe apples drop about my head;
The luscious clusters of the vine
Upon my mouth do crush their wine;
The nectarine, and curious peach,
Into my hands themselves do reach;
Stumbling on melons, as I pass,
Ensnared with flowers, I fall on grass.

Meanwhile the mind, from pleasure less,
Withdraws into its happiness:
The mind, that ocean where each kind
Does straight its own resemblance find;
Yet it creates, transcending these,
Far other worlds, and other seas;
Annihilating all that's made
To a green thought in a green shade.

Here at the fountain's sliding foot,
Or at some fruit-tree's mossy root,
Casting the body's vest aside,
My soul into the boughs does glide:
There like a bird it sits, and sings,
Then whets, and combs its silver wings;
And, till prepared for longer flight,
Waves in its plumes the various light.

Such was that happy garden-state,
While man there walked without a mate:
After a place so pure, and sweet,
What other help could yet be meet!
But 'twas beyond a mortal's share
To wander solitary there:
Two paradises 'twere in one
To live in Paradise alone.

How well the skilful gardener drew
Of flowers and herbs this dial new;
Where from above the milder sun
Does through a fragrant zodiac run;
And, as it works, the industrious bee
Computes its time as well as we.
How could such sweet and wholesome hours
Be reckoned but with herbs and flowers!

The definition of Love

My love is of a birth as rare
    As 'tis for object strange and high:
It was begotten by Despair
    Upon Impossibility.

Magnanimous Despair alone
    Could show me so divine a thing,
Where feeble Hope could ne'er have flown
    But vainly flapped its tinsel wing.

And yet I quickly might arrive
    Where my extended soul is fixed;
But Fate does iron wedges drive,
    And always crowds itself betwixt.

For Fate with jealous eye does see
    Two perfect loves; nor lets them close:
Their union would her ruin be
    And her tyrannic power depose.

And therefore her decrees of steel
 Us as the distant poles have placed,
(Though Love's whole world on us doth wheel)
 Not by themselves to be embraced:

Unless the giddy heaven fall,
 And earth some new convulsion tear,
And, us to join, the world should all
 Be cramped into a planisphere.

As lines, so loves oblique may well
 Themselves in every angle greet:
But ours, so truly parallel,
 Though infinite can never meet.

Therefore the love which us doth bind,
 But Fate so enviously debars,
Is the conjunction of the mind,
 And opposition of the stars.

HENRY VAUGHAN (1622—1695)

They are all gone

They are all gone into the world of light,
 And I alone sit lingering here;
Their very memory is fair and bright,
 And my sad thoughts doth clear.

It glows and glitters in my cloudy breast,
 Like stars upon some gloomy grove,
Or those faint beams in which this hill is dressed
 After the sun's remove.

I see them walking in an air of glory,
 Whose light doth trample on my days:
My days, which are at best but dull and hoary,
 Mere glimmering and decays.

O holy hope, and high humility!
 High as the heavens above!
These are your walks, and you have showed them me,
 To kindle my cold love.

Dear beauteous death! the jewel of the just,
  Shining nowhere but in the dark;
What mysteries do lie beyond thy dust,
  Could man outlook that mark!

He that hath found some fledged bird's nest may know,
  At first sight, if the bird be flown;
But what fair well or grove he sings in now,
  That is to him unknown.

And yet, as angels in some brighter dreams
  Call to the soul when man doth sleep,
So some strange thoughts transcend our wonted themes,
  And into glory peep.

If a star were confined into a tomb,
  Her captive flames must needs burn there;
But when the hand that locked her up gives room,
  She'll shine through all the sphere.

O Father of eternal life, and all
  Created glories under thee!
Resume thy spirit from this world of thrall
  Into true liberty.

Either disperse these mists, which blot and fill
  My perspective still as they pass,
Or else remove me hence unto that hill,
  Where I shall need no glass.

Quickness

False life! a foil and no more, when
    Wilt thou be gone?
Thou foul deception of all men
That would not have the true come on.

Thou art a moon-like toil; a blind
    Self-posing state;
A dark contest of waves and wind;
A mere tempestuous debate.

Life is a fixed, discerning light,
  A knowing joy;
No chance, or fit: but ever bright,
And calm and full, yet doth not cloy.

'Tis such a blissful thing, that still
  Doth vivify,
And shine and smile, and hath the skill
To please without eternity.

Thou art a toilsome mole, or less
  A moving mist,
But life is, what none can express,
A quickness, which my God hath kissed.

The retreat

Happy those early days! when I
Shined in my Angel-infancy.
Before I understood this place
Appointed for my second race,
Or taught my soul to fancy aught
But a white, celestial thought,
When yet I had not walked above
A mile or two from my first love,
And looking back (at that short space),
Could see a glimpse of his bright face;
When on some gilded cloud, or flower
My gazing soul would dwell an hour,
And in those weaker glories spy
Some shadows of eternity;
Before I taught my tongue to wound
My conscience with a sinful sound,
Or had the black art to dispense
A sev'ral sin to every sense,
But felt through all this fleshly dress
Bright shoots of everlastingness.
  O how I long to travel back
And tread again that ancient track!
That I might once more reach that plain,
Where first I left my glorious train,

From whence th'enlightened spirit sees
That shady city of palm trees;
But ah! my soul with too much stay
Is drunk, and staggers in the way.
Some men a forward motion love,
But I by backward steps would move,
And when this dust falls to the urn,
In that state I came, return.

The morning watch

O joys! Infinite sweetness! with what flowers,
And shoots of glory, my soul breaks, and buds!
    All the long hours
    Of night, and rest
    Through the still shrouds
    Of sleep, and clouds,
  This dew fell on my breast;
    O how it bloods,
And spirits all my Earth! Hark! In what rings,
And hymning circulations the quick world
    Awakes, and sings;
    And rising winds,
    And falling springs,
    Birds, beasts, all things
  Adore him in their kinds.
    Thus all is hurled
In sacred hymns, and order, the great chime
And symphony of Nature. Prayer is
    The world in tune,
    A spirit-voice,
    And vocal joys
  Whose echo is Heaven's bliss.
    O let me climb
When I lie down! The pious soul by night
Is like a clouded star, whose beams though said
    To shed their light
    Under some cloud
    Yet are above,
    And shine, and move
  Beyond that misty shroud.
    So in my bed
That curtained grave, though sleep, like ashes, hide
My lamp, and life, both shall in thee abide.

DUCHESS OF NEWCASTLE (1624?—1674)

The soul's garment

Great Nature clothes the soul, which is but thin,
With fleshly garments, which the Fates do spin;
And when these garments are grown old and bare,
With sickness torn, Death takes them off with care,
And folds them up in peace and quiet rest,
And lays them safe within an earthly chest:
Then scours them well and makes them sweet and clean,
Fit for the soul to wear those clothes again.

CHARLES COTTON (1630—1687)

The tempest

Standing upon the margent of the Main,
Whilst the high boiling tide came tumbling in,
I felt my fluctuating thoughts maintain
As great an ocean, and as rude, within;
As full of waves, of depths, and broken grounds,
As that which daily laves her chalky bounds.

Soon could my sad imagination find
A parallel to this half world of flood,
An ocean by my walls of earth confined,
And rivers in the channels of my blood:
Discerning man, unhappy man, to be
Of this great frame Heaven's epitome.

There pregnant Argosies with full sails ride,
To shoot the gulfs of sorrow and despair,
Of which the Love no pilot has to guide,
But to her sea-born mother steers by prayer,
When, oh! the hope her anchor lost, undone,
Rolls at the mercy of the regent moon.

'Tis my adored Diana, then must be
The guid'ress to this beaten bark of mine,
'Tis she must calm and smooth this troubled sea,
And waft my hope over the vaulting brine:
Call home thy venture Dian then at last,
And be as merciful as thou art chaste.

THOMAS TRAHERNE (1637?—1674)

Wonder

How like an angel came I down!
How bright are all things here!
When first among his works I did appear
O, how their glory did me crown!
The world resembled his eternity,
In which my soul did walk;
And every thing that I did see
Did with me talk.

The skies in their magnificence,
The lovely, lively air,
Oh, how divine, how soft, how sweet, how fair!
The stars did entertain my sense,
And all the works of God so bright and pure,
So rich and great, did seem
As if they ever must endure
In my esteem.

A native health and innocence
Within my bones did grow,
And while my God did all his glories show,
I felt a vigour in my sense
That was all spirit; I within did flow
With seas of life like wine;
I nothing in the world did know
But 'twas divine.

Harsh rugged objects were concealed,
Oppressions, tears and cries,
Sins, griefs, complaints, dissensions, weeping eyes
Were hid, and only things revealed
Which heavenly spirits and the angels prize.
The state of innocence
And bliss, not trades and poverties,
Did fill my sense.

The streets seemed paved with golden stones,
The boys and girls all mine;
To me how did their lovely faces shine!
The sons of men all holy ones,

In joy and beauty, then appeared to me;
    And every thing I found,
While like an angel I did see,
    Adorned the ground.

Rich diamonds, and pearl, and gold
    Might every where be seen;
Rare colours, yellow, blue, red, white and green,
    Mine eyes on every side behold:
All that I saw, a wonder did appear,
    Amazement was my bliss:
That and my wealth met everywhere:
    No joy to this!

Cursed, ill-devised proprieties,
    With envy, avarice
And fraud (those fiends that spoil even Paradise),
    Were not the object of mine eyes,
Nor hedges, ditches, limits, narrow bounds:
    I dreamt not aught of those,
But in surveying all men's grounds
    I found repose.

For property its self was mine,
    And hedges, ornaments;
Walls, houses, coffers, and their rich contents,
    To make me rich combine.
Clothes, costly jewels, laces, I esteemed
    My wealth by others worn;
For me they all to wear them seemed
    When I was born.

JOHN DRYDEN (1631—1700)

London

Methinks already from this chymic flame
I see a city of more precious mould,
Rich as the town which gives the Indies name,
With silver paved and all divine with gold.

Already, labouring with a mighty fate,
She shakes the rubbish from her mounting brow
And seems to have renewed her charter's date
Which Heaven will to the death of time allow.

More great than human now and more August,
New deified she from her fires does rise:
Her widening streets on new foundations trust,
And, opening, into larger parts she flies.

Before, she like some shepherdess did show
Who sate to bathe her by a river's side,
Not answering to her fame, but rude and low,
Nor taught the beauteous arts of modern pride.

Now like a maiden queen she will behold
From her high turrets hourly suitors come;
The East with incense and the West with gold
Will stand like suppliants to receive her doom.

The silver Thames, her own domestic flood,
Shall bear her vessels like a sweeping train,
And often wind, as of his mistress proud,
With longing eyes to meet her face again.

The wealthy Tagus and the wealthier Rhine
The glory of their towns no more shall boast,
And Seine, that would with Belgian rivers join,
Shall find her lustre stained and traffic lost.

The venturous merchant who designed more far,
And touches on our hospitable shore,
Charmed with the splendour of this northern star,
Shall here unlade him and depart no more.

Our powerful navy shall no longer meet,
The wealth of France or Holland to invade;
The beauty of this town without a fleet
From all the world shall vindicate her trade.

And while this famed emporium we prepare,
The British ocean shall such triumphs boast,
That those who now disdain our trade to share,
Shall rob like pirates on our wealthy coast.

Already we have conquered half the war,
And the less dangerous part is left behind;
Our trouble now is but to make them dare
And not so great to vanquish as to find.

Thus to the Eastern wealth through storms we go,
But now, the Cape once doubled, fear no more;
A constant trade wind will securely blow,
And gently lay us on the spicy shore.

From *Annus Mirabilis*

Achitophel

Of these the false Achitophel was first,
Of name to all succeeding ages curst:
For close designs and crooked counsels fit,
Sagacious, bold, and turbulent of wit,
Restless, unfixed in principles and place,
In power unpleased, impatient of disgrace;
A fiery soul, which working out its way,
Fretted the pigmy body to decay:
And o'er-informed the tenement of clay.
A daring pilot in extremity,
Pleased with the danger, when the waves went high,
He sought the storms; but, for a calm unfit,
Would steer too nigh the sands to boast his wit.
Great wits are sure to madness near allied
And thin partitions do their bounds divide;
Else, why should he, with wealth and honour blest,
Refuse his age the needful hours of rest?
Punish a body which he could not please,
Bankrupt of life, yet prodigal of ease?
And all to leave what with his toil he won
To that unfeathered two-legged thing, a son.
Got, while his soul did huddled notions try,
And born a shapeless lump, like anarchy.
In friendship false, implacable in hate,
Resolved to ruin or to rule the state;
To compass this the triple bond he broke,
The pillars of the public safety shook,
And fitted Israel for a foreign yoke;
Then, seized with fear, yet still affecting fame,
Usurped a patriot's all-atoning name.

So easy still it proves in factious times
With public zeal to cancel private crimes.
How safe is treason and how sacred ill,
Where none can sin against the people's will,
Where crowds can wink and no offence be known,
Since in another's guilt they find their own!
Yet fame deserved no enemy can grudge;
The statesman we abhor, but praise the judge.
In Israel's courts ne'er sat an Abbethdin
With more discerning eyes or hands more clean,
Unbribed, unsought, the wretched to redress,
Swift of despatch and easy of access.

               From *Absalom and Achitophel*

Zimri

In the first rank of these did Zimri stand,
A man so various that he seemed to be
Not one, but all mankind's epitome:
Stiff in opinions, always in the wrong,
Was everything by starts and nothing long;
But in the course of one revolving moon
Was chymist, fiddler, statesman, and buffoon;
Then all for women, painting, rhyming, drinking,
Besides ten thousand freaks that died in thinking.
Blest madman, who could every hour employ
With something new to wish or to enjoy!
Railing and praising were his usual themes,
And both, to show his judgment, in extremes:
So over violent or over civil
That every man with him was God or Devil.
In squandering wealth was his peculiar art;
Nothing went unrewarded but desert.
Beggared by fools whom still he found too late,
He had his jest, and they had his estate.
He laughed himself from Court; then sought relief
By forming parties, but could ne'er be chief:
For spite of him, the weight of business fell
On Absalom and wise Achitophel;
Thus wicked but in will, of means bereft,
He left not faction, but of that was left.

               From *Absalom and Achitophel*

Can life be a blessing?

Can life be a blessing,
    Or worth the possessing,
Can life be a blessing if love were away?
    Ah, no! though our love all night keep us waking,
And though he torment us with cares all the day,
    Yet he sweetens, he sweetens our pains in the taking;
There's an hour at the last, there's an hour to repay.

In every possessing,
    The ravishing blessing,
In every possessing the fruit of our pain,
    Poor lovers forget long ages of anguish,
Whate'er they have suffered and done to obtain;
    'Tis a pleasure, a pleasure to sigh and to languish,
When we hope, when we hope to be happy again.

Diana's hunting-song

With horns and hounds, I waken the day,
And hie to my woodland-walks away;
I tuck up my robe, and am buskined soon,
And tie to my forehead a waxing moon.
I course the fleet stag, unkennel the fox,
And chase the wild goats o'er summits of rocks;
With shouting and hooting we pierce through the sky
And Echo turns hunter and doubles the cry.
    With shouting and hooting we pierce through the sky
    And Echo turns hunter and doubles the cry.

CHARLES SACKVILLE, EARL OF DORSET (1638—1706)

Dorinda

Dorinda's sparkling wit and eyes,
    Uniting, cast too fierce a light,
Which blazes high, but quickly dies,
    Pains not the heart, but hurts the sight.

Love is a calmer, gentler joy,
    Smooth are his looks and soft his pace;
Her Cupid is a black-guard boy
    That runs his link full in your face.

SIR CHARLES SEDLEY (1639?—1701)

Song to Celia

Not Celia, that I juster am
    Or better than the rest,
For I would change each hour like them,
    Were not my heart at rest.

But I am tied to very thee,
    By every thought I have,
Thy face I only care to see,
    Thy heart I only crave.

All that in woman is adored,
    In thy dear self I find,
For the whole sex can but afford,
    The handsome and the kind.

Why then should I seek farther store,
    And still make love anew;
When change itself can give no more,
    'Tis easy to be true.

JOHN WILMOT, EARL OF ROCHESTER (1648—1680)

A song

Absent from thee I languish still;
    Then ask me not, when I return?
The straying fool 'twill plainly kill,
    To wish all day, all night to mourn.

Dear, from thine arms then let me fly,
    That my fantastic mind may prove,
The torments it deserves to try,
    That tears my fixed heart from my Love.

When wearied with a world of woe,
    To thy safe bosom I retire,
Where love and peace and truth does flow,
    May I contented there expire.

Lest once more wandering from that Heaven,
    I fall on some base heart unblest;
Faithless to thee, false, unforgiven,
    And lose my everlasting rest.

Wretched man

Birds feed on birds, beasts on each other prey;
But savage man alone, does man betray.
Pressed by necessity, *they* kill for food;
Man undoes man, to do himself no good.
With teeth, and claws, by nature armed *they* hunt
Nature's allowance, to supply their want:
But man with smiles, embraces, friendships, praise,
Inhumanly, his fellow's life betrays,
With voluntary pains, works his distress;
Not through necessity, but wantonness.
For hunger, or for love *they* bite or tear,
Whilst wretched man is still in arms for fear;
For fear he arms, and is of arms afraid;
From fear, to fear, successively betrayed.
Base fear, the source whence his best passions came,
His boasted honour, and his dear-bought fame,
The lust of power, to which he's such a slave,
And for the which alone he dares be brave:
To which his various projects are designed,
Which makes him gen'rous, affable, and kind:
For which he takes such pains to be thought wise,
And screws his actions, in a forced disguise:
Leads a most tedious life, in misery,
Under laborious, mean hypocrisy.
Look to the bottom of his vast design,
Wherein man's wisdom, power, and glory join—
The good he acts, the ill he does endure,
'Tis all from fear, to make himself secure.
Merely for safety, after fame they thirst;
For all men would be cowards if they durst:
And honesty's against all common sense—
Men must be knaves; 'tis in their own defence,
Mankind's dishonest; if they think it fair,
Amongst known cheats, to play upon the square,
You'll be undone—
Nor can weak truth, your reputation save;
The knaves will all agree to call you knave.
Wronged shall he live, insulted o'er, opprest,
Who dares be less a villain than the rest.

Thus here you see what human nature craves,
Most men are cowards, all men should be knaves.
The difference lies, as far as I can see,
Not in the thing itself, but the degree;
And all the subject matter of debate,
Is only who's a knave of the first rate.

From *A Satire Against Mankind*

Spoken extempore

*(upon receiving a fall at Whitehall gate
by attempting to kiss the Duchess of
Cleveland as she was stepping out of her
chariot)*

By Heaven's! 'twas bravely done!
    First, to attempt the chariot of the Sun,
    And then to fall like Phaeton.

Song: *The noble name of Spark*

Room, room for a blade of the town,
    That takes delight in roaring,
Who all day long rambles up and down,
    And at night in the street lies snoring.

That for the noble name of Spark
    Does his companions rally;
Commits an outrage in the dark,
    Then slinks into an alley.

To every female that he meets,
    He swears he bears affection,
Defies all laws, arrests, and cheats,
    By the help of a kind protection.

When he intending further wrongs,
    By some resenting cully
Is decently run through the lungs
    And there's an end of Bully.

The King's epitaph

Here lies a great and mighty King,
　　Whose promise none relies on;
He never said a foolish thing,
　　Nor ever did a wise one.

Song

I promised Sylvia to be true;
Nay, out of zeal, I swore it too
And that she might believe me more,
Gave her in writing what I swore:
Not vows, not oaths can lovers bind;
So long as blessed, so long they're kind:
'Twas in a leaf, the wind but blew,
Away both leaf and promise flew.

MATTHEW PRIOR (1664—1721)

On a pretty madwoman

While mad Ophelia we lament,
And her distraction mourn,
Our grief's misplaced, our tears mispent,
Since what for her condition's meant
More justly fits our own.
　　For if 'tis happiness to be,
From all the turns of fate,
From dubious joy, and sorrow free;
Ophelia then is blest, and we
Misunderstand her state.
　　The fates may do whate'er they will,
They can't disturb her mind,
Insensible of good, or ill,
Ophelia is Ophelia still,
Be fortune cross or kind.
　　Then make with reason no more noise,
Since what should give relief,
The quiet of our mind destroys,
Or with a full spring-tide of joys,
Or a dead-ebb of grief.

MATTHEW PRIOR

A letter

My noble, lovely, little Peggy,
Let this my First Epistle beg ye,
At dawn of morn, and close of even,
To lift your heart and hands to Heaven.
In double duty say your prayer:
Our Father first, then *Notre Pere*.
And, dearest child, along the day,
In everything you do and say,
Obey and please my lord and lady,
So God shall love and angels aid ye.

If to these precepts you attend,
No second letter need I send,
And so I rest your constant friend.

Answer to Cloe jealous

Dear Cloe, how blubbered is that pretty face?
    Thy cheek all on fire, and thy hair all uncurled
Pr'ythee quit this caprice; and (as old Falstaff says)
    Let us e'en talk a little like folks of this world.

How can'st thou presume, thou hast leave to destroy
    The beauties, which Venus but lent to thy keeping?
Those looks were designed to inspire love and joy:
    More ord'nary eyes may serve people for weeping.

To be vext at a trifle or two that I writ,
    Your judgment at once, and my passion you wrong:
You take that for fact, which will scarce be found wit:
    Od's life! must one swear to the truth of a song?

What I speak, my fair Cloe, and what I write, shows
    That difference there is betwixt nature and art:
I court others in verse; but I love thee in prose:
    And they have my whimsies; but thou hast my heart.

The god of us verse-men (you know child) the Sun,
    How after his journeys he sets up his rest:
If at morning o'er earth 'tis his fancy to run,
    At night he reclines on his Thetis's breast.

So when I am wearied with wand'ring all day,
    To thee my delight in the evening I come:
No matter what beauties I saw in my way:
    They were but my visits; but thou art my home.

Then finish, dear Cloe, this pastoral war;
    And let us like Horace and Lydia agree:
For thou art a girl as much brighter than her,
    As he was a poet sublimer than me.

ANNE FINCH, COUNTESS OF WINCHILSEA (1666-1720)

A nocturnal reverie

In such a night, when every louder wind
Is to its distant cavern safe confined;
And only gentle Zephyr fans his wings,
And lonely Philomel, still waking, sings;
Or from some tree, famed for the owl's delight,
She, hollowing clear, directs the wanderer right.
In such a night, when passing clouds give place,
Or thinly veil the heaven's mysterious face;
When in some river, overhung with green,
The waving moon and trembling leaves are seen;
When freshened grass now bears itself upright,
And makes cool banks to pleasing rest invite,
Whence spring the woodbind, and the bramble-rose,
And where the sleepy cowslip sheltered grows;
Whilst now a paler hue the foxglove takes,
Yet chequers still with red the dusky brakes:
When scattered glow-worms, but in twilight fine,
Show trivial beauties, watch their hour to shine;
Whilst Salisbury stands the test of every light,
In perfect charms, and perfect virtue bright:
When odours, which declined repelling day,
Through temp'rate air uninterrupted stray;
When darkened groves their softest shadows wear,
And falling waters we distinctly hear;
When through the gloom more venerable shows
Some ancient fabric, awful in repose,
While sunburnt hills their swarthy looks conceal,

And swelling haycocks thicken up the vale:
When the loosed horse now, as his pasture leads,
Comes slowly grazing through th' adjoining meads,
Whose stealing pace, and lengthened shade we fear,
Till torn up forage in his teeth we hear:
When nibbling sheep at large pursue their food,
And unmolested kine rechew the cud;
When curlews cry beneath the village-walls,
And to her straggling brood the partridge calls;
Their shortlived jubilee the creatures keep,
Which but endures, whilst tyrant-man does sleep;
When a sedate content the spirit feels,
And no fierce light disturbs, whilst it reveals;
But silent musings urge the mind to seek
Something too high for syllables to speak;
Till the free soul to a composedness charmed,
Finding the elements of rage disarmed,
O'er all below a solemn quiet grown,
Joys in th' inferior world, and thinks it like her own:
In such a night let me abroad remain,
Till morning breaks, and all's confused again;
Our cares, our toils, our clamours are renewed,
Or pleasures, seldom reached, again pursued.

JONATHAN SWIFT (1667—1745)

A description of a city shower

Careful observers may foretell the hour
By sure prognostics when to dread a shower:
While rain depends, the pensive cat gives o'er
Her frolics, and pursues her tail no more.
Returning home at night, you'll find the sink
Strike your offended sense with double stink.
If you be wise, then go not far to dine,
You'll spend in coach-hire more than save in wine.
A coming shower your shooting corns presage,
Old aches throb, your hollow tooth will rage.
Sauntering in coffee-houses is *Dulman* seen;
He damns the climate, and complains of spleen.

Meanwhile the South rising with dabbled wings,
A sable cloud athwart the welkin flings,
That swilled more liquor than it could contain,
And like a drunkard gives it up again.
Brisk Susan whips her linen from the rope,
While the first drizzling shower is born aslope,
Such is that sprinkling which some careless quean
Flirts on you from her mop, but not so clean.
You fly, invoke the gods; then turning, stop
To rail; she singing, still whirls on her mop.
Not yet, the dust had shunned th' unequal strife,
But aided by the wind, fought still for life;
And wafted with its foe by violent gust,
'Twas doubtful which was rain, and which was dust.
Ah! where must needy poet seek for aid,
When dust and rain at once his coat invade;
His only coat, where dust confused with rain,
Roughen the nap, and leave a mingled stain.

Now in contiguous drops the flood comes down,
Threat'ning with deluge this devoted town.
To shops in crowds the dagged females fly,
Pretend to cheapen goods, but nothing buy.
The Templer spruce, while ev'ry spout's a-broach,
Stays till 'tis fair, yet seems to call a coach.
The tucked-up seamstress walks with hasty strides,
While streams run down her oiled umbrella's sides.
Here various kinds by various fortunes led,
Commence acquaintance underneath a shed.
Triumphant Tories, and desponding Whigs,
Forget their feuds, and join to save their wigs,
Boxed in a chair the beau impatient sits,
While spouts run clatt'ring o'er the roof by fits;
And ever and anon with frightful din
The leather sounds, he trembles from within.
So when Troy chair-men bore the wooden steed,
Pregnant with Greeks, impatient to be freed,
(Those bully Greeks, who, as the moderns do,
Instead of paying chair-men, run them thro')
Laoco'n struck the outside with his spear,
And each imprisoned hero quaked for fear.

Now from all parts the swelling kennels flow,
And bear their trophies with them as they go:
Filth of all hues and odours seem to tell
What street they sailed from, by their sight and smell.
They, as each torrent drives, with rapid force
From Smithfield, or St Pulchre's shape their course,
And in huge confluent join at Snow-Hill Ridge,
Fall from the conduit prone to Holborn-Bridge.
Sweeping from butchers' stalls, dung, guts, and blood,
Drowned puppies, stinking sprats, all drenched in mud,
Dead cats and turnip-tops come tumbling down the flood.

Critics

Hobbes clearly proves that every creature
Lives in a state of war by nature.
The greater for the smallest watch,
But meddle seldom with their match.
A whale of moderate size will draw
A shoal of herrings down his maw.
A fox with geese his belly crams;
A wolf destroys a thousand lambs.
But search among the rhyming race,
The brave are worried by the base.
If on *Parnassus'* top you sit,
You rarely bite, are always bit:
Each poet of inferior size
On you shall rail and criticize;
And strive to tear you limb from limb,
While others do as much for him.
   The vermin only tease and pinch
Their foes superior by an inch.
So, nat'ralists observe, a flea
Hath smaller fleas that on him prey,
And these have smaller fleas to bite 'em,
And so proceed *ad infinitum*:
Thus every poet in his kind
Is bit by him that comes behind;
Who, though too little to be seen,
Can tease, and gall, and give the spleen;
Call dunces, fools and sons of whores,
Lay Grubstreet at each others' doors:

Extol the Greek and Roman masters,
And curse our modern poetasters.
Complain, as many an ancient bard did,
How genius is no more rewarded;
How wrong a taste prevails among us;
How much our ancestors out-sung us:
Can personate an awkward scorn
For those who are not poets born:
And all their brother dunces lash,
Who crowd the press with hourly trash.

Verses on the death of Dr. Swift
Written by himself; Nov. 1731

My female friends, whose tender hearts
Have better learned to act their parts,
Receive the news in doleful dumps:
'The Dean is dead: (Pray what is trumps?)
'Then, Lord have mercy on his soul!
'(Ladies, I'll venture for the vole.)
'Six deans, they say, must bear the pall:
'(I wish I knew what king to call)
'Madam, your husband will attend
'The funeral of so good a friend.
'No, madam, 'tis a shocking sight;
'And he's engaged tomorrow night:
'My lady Club will take it ill,
'If he should fail her at quadrille.
'He loved the Dean (I lead a heart)
'But dearest friends, they say, must part.
'His time was come; he ran his race;
'We hope he's in a better place.' . .

'Perhaps I may allow the Dean
'Had too much satire in his vein;
'And seemed determined not to starve it,
'Because no age could more deserve it.
'Yet malice never was his aim;
'He lashed the vice, but spared the name.
'No individual could resent,
'Where thousands equally were meant;
'His satire points at no defect,
'But what all mortals may correct;

'For he abhorred that senseless tribe
'Who call it humour when they gibe:
'He spared a hump, or crooked nose,
'Whose owners set not up for beaux.
'True genuine dullness moved his pity,
'Unless it offered to be witty.
'Those who their ignorance confest,
'He ne'er offended with a jest;
'But laughed to hear an idiot quote
'A verse from Horace learned by rote.
   'He knew a hundred pleasing stories,
'With all the turns of Whigs and Tories:
'Was cheerful to his dying day;
'And friends would let him have his way.
 'He gave the little wealth he had
'To build a house for fools and mad;
'And showed, by one satiric touch,
'No nation wanted it so much.
'That kingdom he hath left his debtor,
'I wish it soon may have a better.'

ISAAC WATTS (1674—1748)

Against quarrelling and fighting

Let dogs delight to bark and bite,
     For God hath made them so;
Let bears and lions growl and fight,
     For 'tis their nature too.

But, children, you should never let
     Such angry passions rise;
Your little hands were never made
     To tear each other's eyes.

Let love through all your actions run,
     And all your words be mild;
Live like the blessed virgin's son,
     That sweet and lovely child.

His soul was gentle as a lamb;
 And as his stature grew,
He grew in favour both with man,
 And God his father too.

Now, lord of all, he reigns above,
 And from his heavenly throne
He sees what children dwell in love,
 And marks them for his own.

The Day of Judgment

An Ode attempted in English Sapphic

When the fierce Northwind with his airy forces
Rears up the Baltic to a foaming fury;
And the red lightning with a storm of hail comes
    Rushing amain down,

How the poor sailors stand amazed and tremble!
While the hoarse thunder like a bloody trumpet
Roars a loud onset to the gaping waters
    Quick to devour them.

Such shall the noise be, and the wild disorder,
(If things eternal may be like these earthly)
Such the dire terror when the great Archangel
    Shakes the creation;

Tears the strong pillars of the vault of Heaven,
Breaks up old marble the repose of princes;
See the graves open, and the bones arising,
    Flames all around 'em.

Hark the shrill outcries of the guilty wretches!
Lively bright horror and amazing anguish
Stare through their eye-lids, while the living worm lies
    Gnawing within them.

Thoughts like old vultures prey upon their heartstrings,
And the smart twinges, when their eye beholds the
Lofty judge frowning, and a flood of vengeance
    Rolling afore him.

Hopeless immortals! how they scream and shiver
While devils push them to the pit wide yawning
Hideous and gloomy, to receive them headlong
    Down to the centre.

Stop here my fancy: (all away ye horrid
Doleful ideas) come arise to Jesus,
How he sits God-like! and the saints around him
    Throned, yet adoring!

O may I sit there when he comes triumphant
Dooming the nations: then ascend to glory,
While our Hosannahs all along the passage
    Shout the Redeemer.

AMBROSE PHILIPS (1675—1749)

A Winter-piece

To the Earl of Dorset, Copenhagen, March 9, 1709

And yet but lately have I seen, e'en here,
The winter in a lovely dress appear.
E'er yet the clouds let fall the treasured snow,
Or winds begun through hazy skies to blow.
At evening a keen eastern breeze arose;
And the descending rain unsullied froze.
Soon as the silent shades of night withdrew,
The ruddy morn disclosed at once to view
The face of nature in a rich disguise,
And brightened every object to my eyes.
For every shrub, and every blade of grass,
And every pointed thorn, seemed wrought in glass.
In pearls and rubies rich the hawthorns show,
While through the ice the crimson berries glow.
The thick-sprung reeds the watry marshes yield,
Seem polished lances in a hostile field.
The stag in limpid currents with surprize
Sees crystal branches on his forehead rise.

The spreading oak, the beech, and towering pine,
Glazed over, in the freezing aether shine.
The frighted birds the rattling branches shun,
That wave and glitter in the distant sun.
When if a sudden gust of wind arise,
The brittle forest into atoms flies:
The crackling wood beneath the tempest bends,
And in a spangled shower the prospect ends.

THOMAS PARNELL (1679—1718)

A night-piece on death

Those graves, with bending osier bound,
That nameless heave the crumbled ground,
Quick to the glancing thought disclose
Where Toil and Poverty repose.

The flat smooth stones that bear a name,
The chisel's slender help to fame,
(Which e'er our set of friends decay
Their frequent steps may wear away)
A middle race of mortals own,
Men, half ambitious, all unknown.

The marble tombs that rise on high,
Whose dead in vaulted arches lie,
Whose pillars swell with sculptured stones
Arms, angels, epitaphs and bones,
These (all the poor remains of state)
Adorn the rich, or praise the great;
Who while on earth in fame they live,
Are senseless of the fame they give.

Ha! while I gaze, pale Cynthia fades,
The bursting earth unveils the shades!
All slow, and wan, and wrapped with shrouds,
They rise in visionary crowds,
And all with sober accent cry,
Think, mortal, what it is to die.

Now from yon black and funeral yew,
That bathes the charnel house with dew,

Methinks I hear a voice begin;
(Ye ravens, cease your croaking din,
Ye tolling clocks, no time resound
O'er the long lake and midnight ground)
It sends a peal of hollow groans,
Thus speaking from among the bones:
   When men my scythe and darts supply,
How great a king of fears am I!
They view me like the last of things:
They make, and then they dread, my stings.
Fools! if you less provoked your fears,
No more my spectre-form appears.
Death's but a path that must be trod,
If man would ever pass to God:
A port of calms, a state of ease
From the rough rage of swelling seas.
   Why then thy flowing sable stoles,
Deep pendent cypress, mourning poles,
Loose scarfs to fall athwart thy weeds,
Long palls, drawn hearses, covered steeds,
And plumes of black, that as they tread,
Nod o'er the 'scutcheons of the dead?
   Nor can the parted body know,
Nor wants the soul, these forms of woe:
As men who long in prison dwell,
With lamps that glimmer round the cell,
When e'er their suffering years are run,
Spring forth to greet the glittering sun:
Such joy, though far transcending sense,
Have pious souls at parting hence.
On earth, and in the body placed,
A few, and evil years, they waste:
But when their chains are cast aside,
See the glad scene unfolding wide,
Clap the glad wing and tower away,
And mingle with the blaze of day.

EDWARD YOUNG (1683—1765)
Night

Tired nature's sweet restorer, balmy sleep!
He, like the world, his ready visit pays,
Where fortune smiles; the wretched he forsakes:
Swift on his downy pinion flies from woe,
And lights on lids unsullied with a tear.

From short, (as usual) and disturbed repose,
I wake: how happy they who wake no more!
Yet that were vain, if dreams infest the grave.
I wake, emerging from a sea of dreams
Tumultuous; where my wrecked, desponding thought
From wave to wave of fancied misery,
At random drove, her helm of reason lost;
Though now restored, 'tis only change of pain,
A bitter change; severer for severe:
The Day too short for my distress! and Night
Even in the zenith of her dark domain,
Is sunshine, to the colour of my fate.

Night, sable goddess! from her ebon throne,
In rayless majesty, now stretches forth
Her leaden sceptre o'er a slumbering world:
Silence, how dead? and darkness how profound?
Nor eye, nor listening ear an object finds;
Creation sleeps. 'Tis, as the general pulse
Of life stood still, and Nature made a pause;
An aweful pause! prophetic of her end.

.   .   .

The bell strikes one: we take no note of time,
But from its loss. To give it then a tongue,
Is wise in man. As if an angel spoke,
I feel the solemn sound. If heard aright,
It is the knell of my departed hours;
Where are they? with the years beyond the flood:
It is the signal that demands dispatch;
How much is to be done? my hopes and fears
Start up alarmed, and o'er life's narrow verge
Look down—on what? a fathomless abyss;
A dread eternity! how surely mine!
And can Eternity belong to me,
Poor pensioner on the bounties of an hour?

From *Night Thoughts*.

JOHN GAY (1685—1732)

The great frost

O roving muse, recall that wondrous year,
When winter reigned in bleak Britannia's air;
When hoary Thames, with frosted oziers crowned,
Was three long moons in icy fetters bound.
The waterman, forlorn along the shore,
Pensive reclines upon his useless oar,
Sees harnessed steeds desert the stony town,
And wander roads unstable, not their own:
Wheels o'er the hardened waters smoothly glide,
And rase with whitened tracks the slippery tide.
Here the fat cook piles high the blazing fire,
And scarce the spit can turn the steer entire.
Booths sudden hide the Thames, long streets appear,
And numerous games proclaim the crowded fair.
So when a general bids the martial train
Spread their encampment o'er the spacious plain;
Thick-rising tents a canvas city build,
And the loud dice resound through all the field.
'Twas here the matron found a doleful fate:
Let elegaic lay the woe relate,
Soft as the breath of distant flutes, at hours
When silent evening closes up the flowers;
Lulling as falling water's hollow noise;
Indulging grief, like Philomela's voice.
  Doll every day had walked these treacherous roads;
Her neck grew warped beneath autumnal loads
Of various fruit; she now a basket bore,
That head, alas! shall basket bear no more.
Each booth she frequent passed, in quest of gain,
And boys with pleasure heard her shrilling strain.
Ah Doll! all mortals must resign their breath,
And industry itself submit to death!
The crackling crystal yields, she sinks, she dies,
Her head chopped off, from her lost shoulders flies;
Pippins she cried, but death her voice confounds,
And pip-pip-pip along the ice resounds.

So when the Thracian furies Orpheus tore,
And left his bleeding trunk deformed with gore,
His severed head floats down the silver tide,
His yet warm tongue for his lost consort cried;
Eurydice with quivering voice he mourned,
And Heber's banks Eurydice returned.

From *Trivia, or, the art of walking the streets of London*

My Own Epitaph

Life is a jest; and all things show it.
I thought so once; but now I know it.

ALLAN RAMSAY (1685?—1758)

The Caterpillar and the Ant

A pensy Ant, right trig and clean,
Came ae day whiding o'er the green;
Where to advance her pride, she saw
A Caterpillar moving slaw:
Good-e'en t'ye, Mistress Ant, said he,
How's a' at hame? I'm blyth to s'ye.
The sawcy Ant viewed him with scorn,
Nor wad civilities return;
But gecking up her head, quoth she,
Poor animal, I pity thee,
Wha scarce can claim to be a creature,
But some experiment of Nature,
Whase silly shape displeased her eye,
And thus unfinished was flung by.
For me, I'm made with better grace,
With active limbs and lively face;
And cleverly can move with ease
Frae place to place where e'er I please:
Can foot a minuet or jig,

F

And snoov't like ony whirligig;
Which gars my Jo aft grip my hand
Till his heart pitty-pattys, and—
But laigh my qualities I bring,
To stand up clashing with a Thing,
A creeping Thing, the like of thee,
Not worthy of a farewell t'ye.
The airy Ant syne turned awa,
And left him with a proud gaffa.
The Caterpillar was struck dumb,
And never answered her a mum:
The humble reptile fand some pain
Thus to be bantered with disdain.
But tent neist time the Ant came by
The Worm was grown a Butterfly;
Transparent were his wings and fair,
Which bare him flightering throw the air:
Upon a flower he stapt his flight,
And thinking on his former slight,
Thus to the Ant himself addrest,
Pray, Madam, will ye please to rest,
And notice what I now advise,
Inferiors ne'er too much despise;
For fortune may gi'e sic a turn,
To raise aboon ye what ye scorn:
For instance, now I spread my wing
In air, while you're a creeping Thing.

The Rt. Rev. GEORGE BERKELEY, D.D., Bishop of Cloyne (1685—1753)

Verses on the Prospect of Planting Arts and Learning in America

The Muse, disgusted at an age and clime
  Barren of every glorious theme.
In distant lands now waits a better time,
  Producing subjects worthy fame:

In happy climes, where from the genial sun
   And virgin earth such scenes ensue,
The force of art by nature seems outdone,
   And fancied beauties by the true:

In happy climes, the seat of innocence,
   Where nature guides and virtue rules,
Where men shall not impose for truth and sense
   The pedantry of courts and schools:

There shall be sung another golden age,
   The rise of empire and of arts,
The good and great inspiring epic rage,
   The wisest heads, and noblest hearts.

Not such as Europe breeds in her decay;
   Such as she bred when fresh and young,
When heavenly flame did animate her clay,
   By future poets shall be sung.

Westward the course of empire takes its way;
   The four first acts already past,
A fifth shall close the drama with the day;
   Time's noblest offspring is the last.

WILLIAM DIAPER (1685-1717)

Eclogue

Mergus. Lycon begin—begin the mournful tale;
You know what 'tis to love and not prevail:
Describe Pasinthas in his daily moan,
How much he loved, and how he was undone.
   Lycon. Ungrateful Ioessa, vainly coy,
And proud of youthful charms despised the boy;
Has left the calmer sea's pacific arms,

Where constant heat the smiling ocean warms,
To shun the youth: (such is the power of hate)
Some windy bay is now her lone retreat.
In vain Pasinthas sought in every cave,
In every creek, and marked each rising wave;
To every isle he roved with wild despair,
And asked, if Ioessa had been there.
In vain he has the fruitless search pursued,
For she is gone, and will no more be wooed.
Pierced with the killing thought the lover sighs,
And stills the rising storms with louder cries:
While thus he sadly plains, in mournful round,
The air through hollow rocks repeats the distant sounds,
Each winding cavern tells the fruitless care,
And every rock upbraids the absent fair;
By the sad echoes which it still returns,
It seems to pity, when the triton mourns:
But the coy nymph, deaf to the mer-man's cry,
Is still unmoved, and makes no kind reply.
While thus Pasinthas plained, the dolphins came,
And wept to hear his moan; the Nereids swam
In beauteous crowds around, and thus they said;
'Weep not, fond Triton, for a peevish maid,
Tho' she is gone let not the youth despair,
For there are kinder nymphs, and nymphs as fair.'
But, Mergus, love is deaf as well as blind.
The best advice is thought the most unkind.
Restless he goes from the fair pitying throng
To a dark cave, where sea-cows lay their young.
A silent grot sad as his thoughts he found,
Where frightful gloom, and horrors sat around.
There on its slimy bottom careless laid,
He sighed and wept; he sighed, and then he said:
    'Have I then loved to be repaid with scorn?
Ye Gods! 'tis hard, too cruel to be borne.
What?—Have I poisoned too the hated sea,
That Ioessa leaves her home for me?
Had you but told; had you your hatred shown,
I would have loved unpitied, and unknown;
By my own flight I had prevented yours,
And, banished hence, retired to distant shores,

Where rigid lasting cold, and northern blasts
O'er whitened lands a pearly shining cast;
Where icy flakes like floating isles appear,
And fiercely meet; the noise you'll dread to hear,
Nor can your tender limbs the piercing climate bear.
Mussels in shoals on mighty whales attend,
Who feed the worthless fish, and court the puny friend:
Fierce sharks by gentle usage are reclaimed,
But female pride is savage, and untamed.
Go then, ingrate, whom love could never please,
To boist'rous channels, and to foreign seas,
Where rocks like you unmoved with careless pride
Repulse the waves, and check the rising tide.'
    Thus the unhappy youth was heard to moan;
The winds to sigh, the hollow seemed to groan,
And dropping tears fell from the weeping stone.
    Mergus. Thy song's more grateful than a summer's
        breeze,
Whose cooling breath, and gentle fannings please,
And move in wanton rings the listening seas.
Not half so sweet, when first the morning dawns,
Are juicy oysters, or the luscious prawns.
But now the sun is dipt in cooling streams;
The twilight is no more; no doubtful gleams
Of weaker light the flitting shades divide,
But they unmixed prevail, and every object hide.
The sea is heard with deeper sound to roar,
And slumbring waters may be said to snore.
Each nymph is stretching on her oozy bed,
And scarce a fish pops up his sleepy head;
Those who were clung to rocks, the shelly heap
Drop from their hold, and fall into the deep.
Nature herself is still, her labours cease,
And all lies wrapt in silence, and unactive ease.

                    From *Nereides: or, Sea-Eclogues*

HENRY CAREY (1687—1743)

Happy Myrtillo

On a grassy pillow
The youthful Myrtillo
Transported was laid;
In his arms a creature
Whose every feature
For conquest was made.
To his side he clasped her,
And fondly grasped her,
While she cried, Oh dear,
Oh dear Myrtillo,
Had I known your will, Oh,
I'd never come here.

Streams gently flowing,
And zephyrs blowing,
Ambrosial breeze;
A swain admiring,
And all conspiring
The charmer to please:
The dear nymph complying,
No more denying
A silent grove.
Oh blest Myrtillo!
You may if you will, Oh,
Be happy as Jove.

Now the devil's in it
If such a minute
The shepherd would lose;
No, no, no, Myrtillo
Has better skill, Oh
His moments to choose;
The delightful treasure
Of love and pleasure
He boldly seized,
And like Myrtillo,
He had his fill, Oh,
Of what he pleased.

The Huntsman's Rouse

The hounds are all out, and the morning does peep,
Why, how now, you sluggardly sot!
How can you lie snoring asleep while we all
A-horseback have got, my dear boy, my brave boy,
While we all a-horseback have got.

I cannot get up, for the overnight cup
So terribly lies in my head;
Beside, my wife cries, My dear, do not rise,
But cuddle me longer in bed, my dear boy,
But cuddle me longer in bed.

Come, on with your boots, and saddle your mare,
Nor tire us with longer delay;
The cry of the hounds and the sight of the hare
Will chase all our vapours away, my dear boys,
Will chase all our vapours away.

ALEXANDER POPE (1688—1744)

A little learning

A little Learning is a dang'rous thing;
Drink deep, or taste not the Pierian spring:
There shallow draughts intoxicate the brain,
And drinking largely sobers us again.
Fired at first sight with what the Muse imparts,
In fearless youth we tempt the heights of Arts,
While from the bounded level of our mind,
Short views we take, nor see the lengths behind;
But more advanced, behold with strange surprise
New distant scenes of endless science rise!
So pleased at first the towering Alps we try,
Mount o'er the vales, and seem to tread the sky,
Th'eternal snows appear already past,
And the first clouds and mountains seem the last:
But those attained, we tremble to survey
The growing labours of the lengthened way,
Th'increasing prospect tires our wandering eyes,
Hills peep o'er hills, and Alps on Alps arise!

From *An Essay on Criticism*

ALEXANDER POPE

Poetical numbers

But most by numbers judge a Poet's song,
And smooth or rough, with them, is right or wrong:
In the bright Muse though thousand charms conspire,
Her voice is all these tuneful fools admire;
Who haunt Parnassus but to please their ear,
Not mend their minds; as some to Church repair,
Not for the doctrine, but the music there.
These equal syllables alone require,
Though oft the ear the open vowels tire;
While expletives their feeble aid do join;
And ten low words oft creep in one dull line;
While they ring round the same unvaried chimes,
With sure returns of still-expected rhymes.
Where-e'er you find *the cooling western breeze*,
In the next line, *it whispers thro' the trees*;
If crystal streams *with pleasing murmurs creep*,
The reader's threatened (not in vain) with *sleep*.
Then, at the last, and only couplet fraught
With some unmeaning thing they call a thought,
A needless Alexandrine ends the song,
That like a wounded snake, drags its slow length along.
Leave such to tune their own dull rhymes, and know
What's roundly smooth, or languishingly slow;
And praise the easy vigour of a line,
Where Denham's strength, and Waller's sweetness join.
True ease in writing comes from art, not chance,
As those move easiest who have learned to dance.
'Tis not enough no harshness gives offence,
The sound must seem an echo to the sense.
Soft is the strain when Zephyr gently blows,
And the smooth stream in smoother numbers flows;
But when loud surges lash the sounding shore,
The hoarse, rough verse should like the torrent roar.
When Ajax strives, some rock's vast weight to throw,
The line too labours, and the words move slow;
Not so, when swift Camilla scours the plain,
Flies o'er th'unbending corn, and skims along the main.
Hear how Timotheus' various lays surprise
And bid alternate passions fall and rise!
While, at each change, the son of Lybian Jove

Now burns with glory, and then melts with love:
Now his fierce eyes with sparkling fury glow,
Now sighs steal out, and tears begin to flow:
Persians and Greeks like turns of nature found,
And the world's victor stood subdued by sound!
The power of music all our hearts allow;
And what Timotheus was, is Dryden now.

From *An Essay on Criticism*

Field sports

When milder autumn summer's heat succeeds,
And in the new-shorn field the partridge feeds,
Before his lord the ready spaniel bounds,
Panting with hope, he tries the furrowed grounds,
But when the tainted gales the game betray,
Couched close he lies, and meditates the prey;
Secure they trust th'unfaithful field, beset,
Till hovering o'er 'em sweeps the swelling net.
See! from the brake the whirring pheasant springs,
And mounts exulting on triumphant wings.
Short is his joy; he feels the fiery wound,
Flutters in blood, and panting beats the ground.
Ah! what avail his glossy, varying dyes,
His purple crest, and scarlet-circled eyes,
The vivid green his shining plumes unfold,
His painted wings, and breast that flames with gold?
   Nor yet, when moist Arcturus clouds the sky,
The woods and fields their pleasing toils deny.
To plains with well-breathed beagles we repair,
And trace the mazes of the circling hare.
(Beasts, urged by us, their fellow beasts pursue,
And learn of man each other to undo.)
With slaught'ring guns th'unwearied fowler roves,
When frosts have whitened all the naked groves;
Where doves in flocks the leafless trees o'ershade,
And lonely woodcocks haunt the watery glade.
He lifts the tube, and levels with his eye;
Strait a short thunder breaks the frozen sky.

Oft, as in airy rings they skim the heath,
The clam'rous lapwings feel the leaden death:
Oft, as the mounting larks their notes prepare,
They fall, and leave their little lives in air.

From *Windsor Forest*

Atticus

Peace to all such! but were there one whose fires
True genius kindles, and fair fame inspires,
Blest with each talent and each art to please,
And born to write, converse, and live with ease:
Should such a man, too fond to rule alone,
Bear, like the Turk, no brother near the throne,
View him with scornful, yet with jealous eyes,
And hate for arts that caused himself to rise;
Damn with faint praise, assent with civil leer,
And without sneering, teach the rest to sneer;
Willing to wound, and yet afraid to strike,
Just hint a fault, and hesitate dislike;
Alike reserved to blame, or to commend,
A tim'rous foe, and a suspicious friend,
Dreading ev'n fools, by flatterers besieged,
And so obliging that he ne'er obliged;
Like Cato, give his little senate laws,
And sit attentive to his own applause;
While wits and templars every sentence raise,
And wonder with a foolish face of praise.
Who but must laugh, if such a man there be?
Who would not weep, if Atticus were he!

Know then thyself

Know then thyself, presume not God to scan;
The proper study of mankind is man.
Placed on this isthmus of a middle state,
A being darkly wise, and rudely great:
With too much knowledge for the sceptic side,
With too much weakness for the Stoic's pride,
He hangs between; in doubt to act, or rest;
In doubt his mind or body to prefer;
Born but to die, and reas'ning but to err;
Alike in ignorance, his reason such,

Whether he thinks too little, or too much:
Chaos of thought and passion, all confused;
Still by himself abused, or dis-abused;
Created half to rise, and half to fall;
Great lord of all things, yet a prey to all;
Sole judge of truth, in endless error hurled:
The glory, jest, and riddle of the world!

From *An Essay on Man*

Life's poor play

See! some strange comfort every state attend,
And pride bestowed on all, a common friend;
See! some fit passion every age supply,
Hope travels through, nor quits us when we die.
   Behold the child, by Nature's kindly law,
Pleased with a rattle, tickled with a straw:
Some livelier play-thing gives his youth delight,
A little louder, but as empty quite:
Scarfs, garters, gold, amuse his riper stage,
And beads and prayer-books are the toys of age:
Pleased with this bauble still, as that before;
'Till tired he sleeps, and life's poor play is o'er.

From *An Essay on Man*

Eloisa

   What scenes appear where-e'er I turn my view,
The dear ideas, where I fly, pursue,
Rise in the grove, before the altar rise,
Stain all my soul, and wanton in my eyes!
I waste the matin lamp in sighs for thee,
Thy image steals between my God and me,
Thy voice I seem in every hymn to hear,
With every bead I drop too soft a tear.
When from the censer clouds of fragrance roll,
And swelling organs lift the rising soul;
One thought of thee puts all the pomp to flight,
Priests, tapers, temples, swim before my sight:
In seas of flame my plunging soul is drowned,
While altars blaze, and angels tremble round.
   While prostrate here in humble grief I lie,

Kind, virtuous drops just gathering in my eye,
While praying, trembling, in the dust I roll,
And dawning grace is opening on my soul:
Come, if thou darest, all charming as thou art!
Oppose thyself to heaven; dispute my heart;
Come, with one glance of those deluding eyes
Blot out each bright idea of the skies;
Take back that grace, those sorrows, and those tears,
Take back my fruitless penitence and prayers,
Snatch me, just mounting, from the blest abode,
Assist the fiends and tear me from my God!

From Eloisa to Abelard

JOHN BYROM (1692—1763)

On clergymen preaching politics

Indeed, Sir Peter, I could wish, I own,
That parsons would let politics alone!
Plead, if they will, the customary plea
For such like talk, when o'er a dish of tea;
But when they tease us with it from the Pulpit,
I own, Sir Peter, that I cannot gulp it.

If on their rules a Justice should intrench,
And preach, suppose, a sermon from the Bench,
Would you not think your brother magistrate
Was touched a little in his hinder pate?
Now, which is worse, Sir Peter, on the total,—
The lay vagary, or the sacerdotal?

In ancient times, when preachers preached indeed
Their sermons, ere the learned learnt to read,
Another Spirit and another Life
Shut the Church doors against all party strife.
Since then, how often heard from sacred rostrums
The lifeless din of Whig and Tory nostrums!

'Tis wrong, Sir Peter, I insist upon't;
To common sense 'tis plainly an affront.
The parson leaves the Christian in the lurch,
Whene'er he brings his politics to church.
His cant, on either side, if he calls preaching,
The man's wrong-headed, and his brains want bleaching.

Recall the time from conquering William's reign,
And guess the fruits of such a preaching vein:
How oft its nonsense must have veered about,
Just as the politics were in or out;—
The Pulpit governed by no Gospel *data*,
But new Success still mending old *Errata*.

Were I a King (God bless me!) I should hate
My chaplains meddling with affairs of state;
Nor would my subjects, I should think, be fond,
Whenever theirs the Bible went beyond.
How well, methinks, we both should live together,
If these good folks would keep within their tether!

My dog Tray

My Dog I was ever well pleased to see
Come wagging his tail to my fair one and me;
And *Phebe* was pleased too, and to my dog said,
Come hither, poor fellow; and patted his head.
But now, when he's fawning, I with a sour look
Cry, Sirrah; and give him a blow with my crook:
And I'll give him another; for why should not *Tray*
Be as dull as his Master, when *Phebe's* away?

JAMES THOMSON (1700—1748)
Winter

As thus the snows arise, and, foul and fierce,
All Winter drives along the darkened air,
In his own loose-revolving fields, the swain
Disastered stands; sees other hills ascend,
Of unknown joyless brow; and other scenes,
Of horrid prospect, shag the trackless plain;

JAMES THOMSON

Nor finds the river, nor the forest, hid
Beneath the formless wild; but wanders on
From hill to dale, still more and more astray;
Impatient flouncing through the drifted heaps,
Stung with the thoughts of home; the thoughts of home
Rush on his nerves, and call their vigour forth
In many a vain attempt. How sinks his soul!
What black despair, what horror fills his heart!
When for the dusky spot, which fancy feigned
His tufted cottage, rising through the snow,
He meets the roughness of the middle waste,
Far from the track and blessed abode of man;
While round him night resistless closes fast,
And every tempest, howling o'er his head,
Renders the savage wilderness more wild.
Then throng the busy shapes into his mind,
Of covered pits, unfathomably deep,
A dire descent! beyond the power of frost;
Of faithless bogs; of precipices huge,
Smoothed up with snow; and, what is land unknown,
What water, of the still unfrozen spring,
In the loose marsh, or solitary lake,
Where the fresh fountain from the bottom boils.
These check his fearful steps; and down he sinks,
Beneath the shelter of the shapeless drift,
Thinking o'er all the bitterness of death,
Mixed with the tender anguish nature shoots
Through the wrung bosom of the dying man—
His wife, his children, and his friends unseen.
In vain for him the officious wife prepares
The fire fair-blazing, and the vestment warm;
In vain his little children, peeping out
Into the mingling storm, demand their sire,
With tears of artless innocence. Alas!
Nor wife, nor children, more shall he behold,
Nor friends, nor sacred home. On every nerve
The deadly winter seizes; shuts up sense;
And, o'er his inmost vitals creeping cold,
Lays him along the snows, a stiffened corpse,
Stretched out, and bleaching in the northern blast.
    Ah! little think the gay licentious proud,

Whom pleasure, power, and affluence surround;
They, who their thoughtless hours in giddy mirth,
And wanton, often cruel, riot waste;
Ah! little think they, while they dance along,
How many feel, this very moment, death
And all the sad variety of pain.
How many sink in the devouring flood,
Or more devouring flame. How many bleed,
By shameful variance betwixt man and man.
How many pine in want, and dungeon-glooms;
Shut from the common air and common use
Of their own limbs. How many drink the cup
Of baleful grief, or eat the bitter bread
Of misery. Sore pierced by wintry winds,
How many shrink into the sordid hut
Of cheerless poverty. How many shake
With all the fiercer tortures of the mind,
Unbounded passion, madness, guilt, remorse;
Whence tumbled headlong from the height of life,
They furnish matter for the tragic muse.
E'en in the vale, where wisdom loves to dwell,
With friendship, peace, and contemplation joined,
How many, racked with honest passions, droop
In deep retired distress. How many stand
Around the death-bed of their dearest friends,
And point the parting anguish. Thought, fond man,
Of these, and all the thousand nameless ills,
That one incessant struggle render life,
One scene of toil, of suffering, and of fate,
Vice in his high career would stand appalled,
And heedless rambling impulse learn to think;
The conscious heart of charity would warm,
And her wide wish benevolence dilate;
The social tear would rise, the social sigh;
And into clear perfection, gradual bliss,
Refining still, the social passions work.

From *The Seasons*

Happy Britannia

Heavens! what a goodly prospect spreads around,
Of hills, and dales, and woods, and lawns, and spires,
And glittering towns, and gilded streams, till all
The stretching landskip into smoke decays!
Happy Britannia! Where the Queen of Arts,
Inspiring vigour, Liberty abroad
Walks, unconfined, even to thy farthest cots,
And scatters plenty with unsparing hand.

   Rich is thy soil, and merciful thy clime;
Thy streams unfailing in the Summer's drought;
Unmatched thy guardian-oaks; thy valleys float
With golden waves; and on thy mountains flocks
Bleat numberless; while, roving round their sides,
Bellow the blackening herds in lusty droves.
Beneath, thy meadows glow, and rise unquelled
Against the mower's scythe. On every hand,
Thy villas shine. Thy country teems with wealth;
And property assures it to the swain,
Pleased, and unwearied, in his guarded toil.

   Full are thy cities with the sons of art;
And trade and joy, in every busy street,
Mingling are heard: even drudgery himself,
As at the car he sweats, or, dusty, hews
The palace-stone, looks gay. Thy crowded ports,
Where rising masts an endless prospect yield,
With labour burn, and echo to the shouts
Of hurried sailor, as he hearty waves
His last adieu, and loosening every sheet,
Resigns the spreading vessel to the wind.

   Bold, firm, and graceful, are thy generous youth,
By hardship sinewed, and by danger fired,
Scattering the nations where they go; and first
Or in the listed plain, or stormy seas.
Mild are thy glories too, as o'er the plans
Of thriving peace thy thoughtful sires preside;
In genius, and substantial learning, high;
For every virtue, every worth, renowned;
Sincere, plain-hearted, hospitable, kind;
Yet like the mustering thunder when provoked,
The dread of tyrants, and the sole resource
Of those that under grim oppression groan.

From The Seasons

The Land of Indolence

In lowly dale, fast by a river's side,
With woody hill o'er hill encompassed round,
A most enchanting wizard did abide,
Than whom a fiend more fell is nowhere found.
It was, I ween, a lovely spot of ground;
And there a season atween June and May,
Half prankt with spring, with summer half imbrowned,
A listless climate made, where, sooth to say,
No living wight could work, ne cared even for play.

Was nought around but images of rest:
Sleep-soothing groves, and quiet lawns between;
And flowery beds that slumbrous influence kest,
From poppies breathed; and beds of pleasant green,
Where never yet was creeping creature seen.
Meantime unnumbered glittering streamlets played,
And hurled every-where their waters sheen;
That, as they bickered through the sunny glade,
Though restless still themselves, a lulling murmur made.

Joined to the prattle of the purling rills,
Were heard the lowing herds along the vale,
And flocks loud-bleating from the distant hills,
And vacant shepherds piping in the dale;
And now and then sweet Philomel would wail,
Or stock-doves plain amid the forest deep,
That drowsy rustled to the sighing gale;
And still a coil the grasshopper did keep:
Yet all these sounds yblent inclined all to sleep.

Full in the passage of the vale, above,
A sable, silent, solemn forest stood;
Where nought but shadowy forms were seen to move,
As Idless fancied in her dreaming mood.
And up the hills, on either side, a wood
Of blackening pines, ay waving to and fro,
Sent forth a sleepy horror through the blood;
And where this valley winded out, below,
The murmuring main was heard, and scarcely heard, to flow.

A pleasing land of drowsy-hed it was:
Of dreams that wave before the half-shut eye;
And of gay castles in the clouds that pass,
For ever flushing round a summer-sky:
There eke the soft delights, that witchingly
Instil a wanton sweetness through the breast,
And the calm pleasures always hovered nigh;
But whate'er smacked of noyance, or unrest,
Was far far off expelled from this delicious nest.

From *The Castle of Indolence*

JOHN DYER (1700—1758)

Grongar Hill

Ever charming, ever new
When will the landskip tire the view!
The fountain's fall, the river's flow,
The woody vallies, warm and low;
The windy summit, wild and high,
Roughly rushing on the sky!
The pleasant seat, the ruined tower,
The naked rock, the shady bower;
The town and village, dome and farm,
Each give each a double charm,
As pearls upon an Æthiop's arm.
See on the mountain's southern side,
Where the prospect ópens wide,
Where the evening gilds the tide;
How close and small the hedges lie!
What streaks of meadows cross the eye!
A step methinks may pass the stream,
So little distant dangers seem;
So we mistake the future's face,
Eyed through hope's deluding glass;
As yon summits soft and fair,
Clad in colours of the air,
Which, to those who journey near,
Barren, and brown, and rough appear.
Still we tread tired the same coarse way
The present's still a cloudy day.

The wool trade

Thus all is here in motion, all is life:
The creaking wain brings copious store of corn:
The grazier's sleeky kine obstruct the roads;
The neat-dressed housewives, for the festal board
Crowned with full baskets, in the field-way paths
Come tripping on; the' echoing hills repeat
The stroke of axe and hammer; scaffolds rise,
And growing edifices; heaps of stone,
Beneath the chisel, beauteous shapes assume
Of frieze and column. Some, with even line,
New streets are marking in the neighbouring fields,
And sacred domes of worship. Industry,
Which dignifies the artist, lifts the swain,
And the straw cottage to a palace turns,
Over the work presides. Such was the scene
Of hurrying Carthage, when the Trojan chief
First viewed her growing turrets. So appear
The increasing walls of busy Manchester,
Sheffield, and Birmingham, whose reddening fields
Rise and enlarge their suburbs. Lo, in throngs
For every realm, the careful factors meet,
Whispering each other. In long ranks the bales,
Like war's bright files, beyond the sight extend.
          .   .   .   Pursue,
Ye sons of Albion, with unyielding heart,
Your hardy labours: let the sounding loom
Mix with the melody of every vale.

CHARLES WESLEY (1707—1788)

Hymn

O Thou who camest from above,
　　The pure, celestial fire t' impart,
Kindle a flame of sacred love
　　On the mean altar of my heart,
There let it for thy glory burn
　　With inextinguishable blaze,
And trembling to it's Source return,
　　In humble prayer, and fervent praise.

Jesus, confirm my heart's desire
   To work, and speak, and think for thee,
Still let me guard the holy fire,
   And still stir up thy gift in me,
Ready for all thy perfect will
   My acts of faith and love repeat,
'Till death thy endless mercies seal,
   And make thy sacrifice complete.

Wrestling Jacob

Come, O thou traveller unknown,
   Whom still I hold, but cannot see,
My company before is gone,
   And I am left alone with thee,
With thee all night I mean to stay,
And wrestle till the break of day.

I need not tell thee who I am,
   My misery, or sin declare,
Thyself hast called me by my name,
   Look on thy hands, and read it there,
But who, I ask thee, who art thou,
Tell me thy name, and tell me now?

In vain thou strugglest to get free,
   I never will unloose my hold:
Art thou the man that died for me?
   The secret of thy love unfold;
Wrestling I will not let thee go,
Till I thy name, thy nature know.

Wilt thou not yet to me reveal
   Thy new, unutterable name?
Tell me, I still beseech thee, tell,
   To know it now resolved I am;
Wrestling I will not let thee go,
Till I thy name, thy nature know.

'Tis all in vain to hold thy tongue,
   Or touch the hollow of my thigh:
Though every sinew be unstrung,

Out of my arms thou shalt not fly;
Wrestling I will not let thee go,
Till I thy name, thy nature know.

What though my shrinking flesh complain,
   And murmur to contend so long,
I rise superior to my pain,
   When I am weak then I am strong,
And when my all of strength shall fail,
I shall with the God-man prevail.

My strength is gone, my nature dies,
   I sink beneath thy weighty hand,
Faint to revive, and fall to rise;
   I fall, and yet by faith I stand,
I stand, and will not let thee go,
Till I thy name, thy nature know.

Yield to me now—for I am weak;
   But confident in self-despair:
Speak to my heart, in blessings speak,
   Be conquered by my instant prayer,
Speak, or thou never hence shalt move,
And tell me, if thy name is love.

'Tis love, 'tis love! Thou diedst for me,
   I hear thy whisper in my heart.
The morning breaks, the shadows flee:
   Pure Universal Love thou art,
To me, to all thy Bowels move,
Thy nature, and thy name is love.

My prayer hath power with God; the grace
   Unspeakable I now receive,
Through faith I see thee face to face,
   I see thee face to face, and live:
In vain I have not wept, and strove,
Thy nature, and thy name is love.

I know thee, saviour, who thou art,
   Jesus the feeble sinner's friend;
Nor wilt thou with the night depart,
   But stay, and love me to the end;
Thy mercies never shall remove,
Thy nature, and thy name is love.

The sun of righteousness on me
   Hath rose with healing in his wings,
Withered my nature's strength; from thee
   My soul its life and succour brings,
My help is all laid up above;
Thy nature, and thy name is love.

Contented now upon my thigh
   I halt, till life's short journey end;
All helplessness, all weakness I,
   On thee alone for strength depend,
Nor have I power, from thee, to move;
Thy nature, and thy name is love.

Lame as I am, I take the prey,
   Hell, earth, and sin with ease o'ercome;
I leap for joy, pursue my way,
   And as a bounding hart fly home,
Through all eternity to prove
Thy nature, and thy name is love.

SAMUEL JOHNSON (1709—1784)
The scholar's life

When first the college rolls receive his name,
The young enthusiast quits his ease for fame;
Through all his veins the fever of renown
Burns from the strong contagion of the gown;
O'er Bodley's dome his future labours spread,
And Bacon's mansion trembles o'er his head;
Are these thy views? proceed, illustrious youth,
And Virtue guard thee to the throne of Truth.
Yet should thy soul indulge the gen'rous heat

Till captive Science yields her last retreat;
Should Reason guide thee with her brightest ray,
And pour on misty doubt resistless day;
Should no false kindness lure to loose delight,
Nor praise relax, nor difficulty fright;
Should tempting novelty thy cell refrain,
And sloth effuse her opiate fumes in vain;
Should beauty blunt on fops her fatal dart,
Nor claim the triumph of a lettered heart;
Should no disease thy torpid veins invade,
Nor melancholy's phantoms haunt thy shade;
Yet hope not life from grief or danger free,
Nor think the doom of man reversed for thee.
Deign on the passing world to turn thine eyes
And pause awhile from letters to be wise;
There mark what ills the scholar's life assail,
Toil, envy, want, the patron, and the jail.
See nations slowly wise, and meanly just,
To buried merit raise the tardy bust.
If dreams yet flatter, once again attend,
Hear Lydiat's life, and Galileo's end.

From *The Vanity of Human Wishes*

Life's last scene

But grant, the virtues of a temp'rate prime
Bless with an age exempt from scorn or crime;
An age that melts with unperceived decay,
And glides in modest Innocence away;
Whose peaceful day Benevolence endears,
Whose night congratulating conscience cheers;
The gen'ral fav'rite as the gen'ral friend:
Such age there is, and who shall wish its end?
Yet ev'n on this her load Misfortune flings,
To press the weary minutes' flagging wings;
New Sorrow rises as the day returns,
A sister sickens, or a daughter mourns.
Now kindred Merit fills the sable bier,
Now lacerated Friendship claims a tear.
Year chases year, decay pursues decay,
Still drops some joy from with'ring life away;
New forms arise, and diff'rent views engage,

Superfluous lags the vet'ran on the stage,
Till pitying Nature signs the last release,
And bids afflicted worth retire to peace.
   But few there are whom hours like these await,
Who set unclouded in the gulphs of fate.
From Lydia's monarch should the search descend,
By Solon cautioned to regard his end,
In life's last scene what prodigies surprise,
Fears of the brave, and follies of the wise!
From Marlb'rough's eyes the streams of dotage flow,
And Swift expires a driv'ler and a show.

           From *The Vanity of Human Wishes*

WILLIAM SHENSTONE (1714—1763)

O sweet Anne Page

Beneath a churchyard yew
   Decayed and worn with age,
At dusk of eve, methought I spied
Poor Slender's ghost, that whimpering cried,
   O sweet, O sweet Anne Page!

Ye gentle bards, give ear!
   Who talk of amorous rage,
Who spoil the lily, rob the rose;
Come learn of me to weep your woes;
   O sweet! O sweet Anne Page!

Why should such laboured strains
   Your formal Muse engage?
I never dreamt of flame or dart,
That fired my breast, or pierced my heart,
   But sighed, O sweet Anne Page! . . .

Hence every fond conceit
   Of shepherd, or of sage!
'Tis Slender's voice, 'tis Slender's way,
Expresses all you have to say—
   O sweet! O sweet Anne Page!

WILLIAM SHENSTONE 185 / 5

The Landscape

How pleased within my native bowers
    Erewhile I passed the day!
Was ever scene so decked with flowers?
    Were ever flowers so gay?

How sweetly smiled the hill, the vale,
    And all the landscape round!
The river gliding down the dale!
    The hill with beeches crowned!

But now, when urged by tender woes
    I speed to meet my dear,
That hill and stream my zeal oppose,
    And check my fond career.

No more, since Daphne was my theme,
    Their wonted charms I see:
That verdant hill, and silver stream,
    Divide my love and me.

THOMAS GRAY (1716—1771)

The Bard

A Pindaric Ode

On a rock, whose haughty brow
Frowns o'er old Conway's foaming flood,
Robed in the sable garb of woe,
With haggard eyes the Poet stood;
(Loose his beard, and hoary hair
Streamed, like a meteor, to the troubled air)
And with a Master's hand, and Prophet's fire,
Struck the deep sorrows of his lyre.
Hark, how each giant-oak, and desert cave,
Sighs to the torrent's aweful voice beneath!
O'er thee, oh King! their hundred arms they wave,
Revenge on thee in hoarser murmurs breath;
Vocal no more, since Cambria's fatal day,
To high-born Hoel's harp, or soft Llewellyn's lay.

Cold is Cadwallo's tongue,
That hushed the stormy main:
Brave Urien sleeps upon his craggy bed:
Mountains, ye mourn in vain
Modred, whose magic song
Made huge Plinlimmon bow his cloud-top'd head.
On dreary Arvon's shore they lie,
Smeared with gore, and ghastly pale:
Far, far aloof th' affrighted ravens sail;
The famished Eagle screams, and passes by.
Dear lost companions of my tuneful art,
Dear, as the light that visits these sad eyes,
Dear, as the ruddy drops that warm my heart,
Ye died amidst your dying country's cries—
No more I weep. They do not sleep.
On yonder cliffs, a griesly band,
I see them sit; they linger yet,
Avengers of their native land:
With me in dreadful harmony they join,
And weave with bloody hands the tissue of thy line.

Weave the warp, and weave the woof,
The winding-sheet of Edward's race.
Give ample room, and verge enough
The characters of hell to trace.
Mark the year, and mark the night,
When Severn shall re-echo with affright
The shrieks of death, through Berkley's roof that ring,
Shrieks of an agonizing King!
She-Wolf of France, with unrelenting fangs,
That tear'st the bowels of thy mangled Mate,
From thee be born, who o'er thy country hangs
The scourge of Heaven. What Terrors round him wait!
Amazement in his van, with Flight combined,
And Sorrow's faded form, and Solitude behind . . .

The verse adorn again
Fierce War, and faithful Love,
And Truth severe, by fairy Fiction drest.
In buskin'd measures move
Pale Grief, and pleasing Pain,
With Horror, Tyrant of the throbbing breast.

A Voice, as of the Cherub-Choir,
Gales from blooming Eden bear;
And distant warblings lessen on my ear,
That lost in long futurity expire.
Fond impious Man, think'st thou, yon sanguine cloud,
Raised by thy breath, has quenched the Orb of day?
To-morrow he repairs the golden flood,
And warms the nations with redoubled ray.
Enough for me: with joy I see
The different doom our Fates assign.
Be thine Despair, and sceptered Care,
To triumph, and to die, are mine.'
He spoke, and headlong from the mountain's height
Deep in the roaring tide he plunged to endless night.

Sonnet on the death of Richard West

In vain to me the smiling mornings shine,
    And reddening Phoebus lifts his golden fire:
The birds in vain their amorous descant join;
    Or cheerful fields resume their green attire:
These ears, alas! for other notes repine,
    A different object do these eyes require.
My lonely anguish melts no heart, but mine;
    And in my breast the imperfect joys expire.
Yet morning smiles the busy race to cheer,
    And new-born pleasure brings to happier men:
The fields to all their wonted tribute bear:
    To warm their little loves the birds complain:
I fruitless mourn to him, that cannot hear,
    And weep the more because I weep in vain.

Impromptu

suggested by a view, in 1766, of the seat and ruins of a
nobleman, at Kingsgate, Kent

Old, and abandoned by each venal friend,
Here Holland formed the pious resolution
To smuggle a few years, and strive to mend
A broken character and constitution.

On this congenial spot he fixed his choice;
Earl Goodwin trembled for his neighbouring sand;
Here sea-gulls scream, and cormorants rejoice,
And mariners, though shipwrecked, dread to land.

Here reigns the blustering North, and blighting East,
No tree is heard to whisper, bird to sing;
Yet Nature could not furnish out the feast,
Art he invokes new horrors still to bring.

Here mouldering fanes and battlements arise,
Turrets and arches nodding to their fall,
Unpeopled monasteries delude our eyes,
And mimic desolation covers all.

'Ah!' said the sighing peer, 'had Bute been true,
Nor Shelburne's, Rigby's, Calcraft's friendship vain,
Far better scenes than these had blest our view,
And realised the beauties which we feign:

'Purged by the sword, and purified by fire,
Then had we seen proud London's hated walls;
Owls would have hooted in St. Peter's choir,
And foxes stunk and littered in St. Paul's.

MARK AKENSIDE (1721—1770)

For a grotto

To me, whom in their lays the shepherds call
Actaea, daughter of the neighbouring stream,
This cave belongs. The figtree and the vine,
Which o'er the rocky entrance downward shoot,
Were placed by Glycon. He with cowslips pale,
Primrose, and purple lychnis, decked the green
Before my threshold, and my shelving walls
With honeysuckle covered. Here at noon,
Lulled by the murmur of my rising fount,
I slumber: here my clustering fruits I tend;
Or from the humid flowers, at break of day,
Fresh garlands weave, and chase from all my bounds

Each thing impure or noxious. Enter-in,
O stranger, undismayed. Nor bat, nor toad
Here lurks: and if thy breast of blameless thoughts
Approve thee, not unwelcome shalt thou tread
My quiet mansion: chiefly, if thy name
Wise Pallas and the immortal Muses own.

For a statue of Chaucer at Woodstock

Such was old Chaucer. Such the placid mien
Of him who first with harmony informed
The language of our fathers. Here he dwelt
For many a cheerful day. These ancient walls
Have often heard him, while his legends blithe
He sang; of love, or knighthood, or the wiles
Of homely life: through each estate and age,
The fashions and the follies of the world
With cunning hand portraying. Though perchance
From Blenheim's towers, O stranger, thou art come,
Glowing with Churchill's trophies; yet in vain
Dost thou applaud them, if thy breast be cold
To him, this other hero; who, in times
Dark and untaught, began with charming verse
To tame the rudeness of his native land.

That delightful time

Would I again were with you!—O ye dales
Of Tyne, and ye most ancient woodlands; where
Oft as the giant flood obliquely strides,
And his banks open, and his lawns extend,
Stops short the pleased traveller to view
Presiding o'er the scene some rustic tower
Founded by Norman or by Saxon hands:
O ye Northumbrian shades, which overlook
The rocky pavement and the mossy falls
Of solitary Wensbeck's limpid stream;
How gladly I recall your well-known seats
Beloved of old, and that delightful time
When all alone, for many a summer's day,
I wandered through your calm recesses, led
In silence by some powerful hand unseen.

Nor will I e'er forget you. Nor shall e'er
The graver tasks of manhood, or the advice
Of vulgar wisdom, move me to disclaim
Those studies which possessed me in the dawn
Of life, and fixed the colour of my mind
For every future year.

From *The Pleasures of the Imagination*

WILLIAM COLLINS (1721—1759)

Ode to Evening

If aught of oaten stop, or pastoral song,
May hope, chaste Eve, to sooth thy modest ear,
   Like thy own solemn springs,
   Thy springs, and dying gales,
O Nymph reserved, while now the bright-haired sun
Sits in yon western tent, whose cloudy skirts,
   With brede ethereal wove,
   O'erhang his wavy bed:
Now air is hushed, save where the weak-eyed bat,
With short shrill shriek flits by on leathern wing,
   Or where the beetle winds
   His small but sullen horn,
As oft he rises 'midst the twilight path,
Against the pilgrim borne in heedless hum:
   Now teach me, Maid composed,
   To breath some softened strain,
Whose numbers stealing through thy dark'ning vale,
May not unseemly with its stillness suit,
   As musing slow, I hail
   Thy genial loved return!
For when thy folding star arising shows
His paly circlet, at his warning lamp
   The fragrant hours, and elves
   Who slept in flowers the day,
And many a nymph who wreaths her brows with sedge,
And sheds the fresh'ning dew, and lovelier still,
   The Pensive Pleasures sweet
   Prepare thy shadowy car.

Then lead, calm Vot'ress, where some sheety lake
Cheers the lone heath, or some time-hallowed pile,
   Or upland fallows grey
   Reflect its last cool gleam.
But when chill blustering winds, or driving rain,
Forbid my willing feet, be mine the hut,
   That from the mountain's side,
   Views wilds, and swelling floods,
And hamlets brown, and dim-discovered spires,
And hears their simple bell, and marks o'er all
   Thy dewy fingers draw
   The gradual dusky veil.
While Spring shall pour his showers, as oft he wont,
And bathe thy breathing tresses, meekest Eve!
   While Summer loves to sport
   Beneath thy lingering light;
While sallow Autumn fills thy lap with leaves;
Or Winter yelling through the troublous air,
   Affrights thy shrinking train,
   And rudely rends thy robes;
So long, sure-found beneath thy sylvan shed,
Shall Fancy, Friendship, Science, rose-lipped Health,
   Thy gentlest influence own,
   And hymn thy fav'rite name!

Ode on the death of Thomson

In yonder grave a druid lies
   Where slowly winds the stealing wave!
The year's best sweets shall duteous rise
   To deck it's poet's sylvan grave!

In yon deep bed of whispering reeds
   His airy harp shall now be laid,
That he, whose heart in sorrow bleeds,
   May love through life the soothing shade.

Then maids and youths shall linger here,
   And while its sounds at distance swell,
Shall sadly seem in pity's ear
   To hear the woodland pilgrim's knell.

Remembrance oft shall haunt the shore
    When Thames in summer-wreaths is dressed,
And oft suspend the dashing oar
    To bid his gentle spirit rest!

And oft as Ease and Health retire
    To breezy lawn, or forest deep,
The friend shall view yon whit'ning spire,
    And 'mid the varied landscape weep.

But thou, who own'st that earthly bed,
    Ah! what will every dirge avail?
Or tears, which Love and Pity shed,
    That mourn beneath the gliding sail!

Yet lives there one, whose heedless eye
    Shall scorn thy pale shrine glimm'ring near?
With him, sweet bard, may Fancy die,
    And Joy desert the blooming year.

But thou, lorn Stream, whose sullen tide
    No sedge-crowned sisters now attend,
Now waft me from the green hill's side
    Whose cold turf hides the buried friend!

And see, the fairy valleys fade,
    Dun Night has veiled the solemn view!
—Yet once again, dear parted Shade,
    Meek Nature's Child, again adieu!

The genial meads assigned to bless
    Thy life, shall mourn thy early doom;
Their hinds, and shepherd-girls shall dress
    With simple hands thy rural tomb.

Long, long, thy stone and pointed clay
    Shall melt the musing Briton's eyes
O! Vales, and Wild Woods, shall he say
    In yonder grave your druid lies!

Dirge in Cymbeline

Sung by Guiderius and Arviragus over Fidele, supposed to be dead.

To fair Fidele's grassy tomb
    Soft maids and village hinds shall bring
Each opening sweet of earliest bloom,
    And rifle all the breathing spring.

No wailing ghost shall dare appear
    To vex with shrieks this quiet grove:
But shepherd lads assemble here,
    And melting virgins own their love.

No withered witch shall here be seen,
    No goblins lead their nightly crew;
The female fays shall haunt the green,
    And dress thy grave with pearly dew!

The red-breast oft at evening hours
    Shall kindly lend his little aid:
With hoary moss, and gathered flowers,
    To deck the ground where thou art laid.

When howling winds, and beating rain,
    In tempests shake the sylvan cell,
Or 'midst the chase on every plain,
    The tender thought on thee shall dwell.

Each lonely scene shall thee restore,
    For thee the tear be duly shed:
Beloved till life could charm no more,
    And mourned, till pity's self be dead.

CHRISTOPHER SMART (1722—1771)

My Cat Jeoffrey

For I will consider my Cat Jeoffrey.
For he is the servant of the Living God, duly and daily serving him.
For at the First glance of the glory of God in the East he worships
in his way.

For is this done by wreathing his body seven times round with elegant quickness.

For then he leaps up to catch the musk, which is the blessing of God upon his prayer.

For he rolls upon prank to work it in.

For having done duty and received blessing he begins to consider himself.

For this he performs in ten degrees.

For first he looks upon his fore-paws to see if they are clean.

For secondly he kicks up behind to clear away there.

For thirdly he works it upon stretch with the fore-paws extended.

For fourthly he sharpens his paws by wood.

For fifthly he washes himself.

For sixthly he rolls upon wash.

For seventhly he fleas himself, that he may not be interrupted upon the beat.

For eighthly he rubs himself against a post.

For ninthly he looks up for his instructions.

For tenthly he goes in quest of food.

For having considered God and himself he will consider his neighbour.

For if he meets another cat he will kiss her in kindness.

For when he takes his prey he plays with it to give it a chance.

For one mouse in seven escapes by his dallying.

For when his day's work is done his business more properly begins.

For he keeps the Lord's watch in the night against the adversary.

For he counteracts the powers of darkness by his electrical skin and glaring eyes.

For he counteracts the Devil, who is death, by brisking about the life.

For in his morning orisons he loves the sun and the sun loves him.

For he is of the tribe of Tiger.

For the Cherub Cat is a term of the Angel Tiger.

For he has the subtlety and hissing of a serpent, which in goodness he suppresses.

For he will not do destruction, if he is well fed, neither will he spit without provocation.

For he purrs in thankfulness, when God tells him he's a good Cat.

For he is an instrument for the children to learn benevolence upon.

For every house is incomplete without him and a blessing is lacking in the spirit.

For the Lord commanded Moses concerning the cats at the departure of the Children of Israel from Egypt.

For every family had one cat at least in the bag.

For the English Cats are the best in Europe.

For he is the cleanest in the use of his fore-paws of any quadrupede.

For the dexterity of his defence is an instance of the love of God to him exceedingly.

For he is the quickest to his mark of any creature.

For he is tenacious of his point.

For he is a mixture of gravity and waggery.

For he knows that God is his Saviour.

For there is nothing sweeter than his peace when at rest.

For there is nothing brisker than his life when in motion.

For he is of the Lord's poor and so indeed is he called by benevolence perpetually—Poor Jeoffry! poor Jeoffry! the rat has bit thy throat.

For I bless the name of the Lord Jesus that Jeoffry is better.

For the divine spirit comes about his body to sustain it in complete cat.

For his tongue is exceedingly pure so that it has in purity what it wants in music.

For he is docile and can learn certain things.

For he can set up with gravity which is patience upon approbation.

For he can fetch and carry, which is patience in employment.

For he can jump over a stick which is patience upon proof positive.

For he can spraggle upon waggle at the word of command.

For he can jump from an eminence into his master's bosom.

For he can catch the cork and toss it again.

For he is hated by the hypocrite and miser.

For the former is afraid of detection.

For the latter refuses the charge.

For he camels his back to bear the first notion of business.

For he is good to think on, if a man would express himself neatly.

For he made a great figure in Egypt for his signal services.

For he killed the Ichneumon-rat very pernicious by land.

For his ears are so acute that they sting again.

For from this proceeds the passing quickness of his attention.

For by stroking of him I have found out electricity.

For I perceived God's light about him both wax and fire.

For the Electrical fire is the spiritual substance, which God sends
    from heaven to sustain the bodies both of man and beast.
For God has blessed him in the variety of his movements.
For, though he cannot fly, he is an excellent clamberer.
For his motions upon the face of the earth are more than any other
    quadrupede.
For he can tread to all the measures upon the music.
For he can swim for life.
For he can creep.

From Jubilate Agno

JOSEPH WARTON (1722—1800)

The charms of nature

    What are the lays of artful Addison,
Coldly correct, to Shakespeare's warblings wild?
Whom on the winding Avon's willowed banks
Fair fancy found, and bore the smiling babe
To a close cavern: (still the shepherds show
The sacred place, whence with religious awe
They hear, returning from the field at eve,
Strange whispering of sweet music through the air)
Here, as with honey gathered from the rock,
She fed the little prattler, and with songs
Oft' soothed his wondering ears, with deep delight
On her soft lap he sat, and caught the sounds.

OLIVER GOLDSMITH (1728—1774)

Song

When lovely woman stoops to folly,
    And finds too late that men betray,
What charm can sooth her melancholy,
    What art can wash her guilt away?

The only art her guilt to cover,
    To hide her shame from every eye,
To give repentance to her lover,
    And wring his bosom—is to die.

From The Vicar of Wakefield

Sir Joshua Reynolds

Here Reynolds is laid, and to tell you my mind,
He has not left a better or wiser behind;
His pencil was striking, resistless and grand,
His manners were gentle, complying and bland;
Still born to improve us in every part,
His pencil our faces, his manners our heart:
To coxcombs averse, yet most civilly steering,
When they judged without skill he was still hard of hearing:
When they talked of their Raphaels, Corregios and stuff,
He shifted his trumpet, and only took snuff.

Auburn

Sweet Auburn, loveliest village of the plain,
Where health and plenty cheered the labouring swain,
Where smiling spring its earliest visit paid,
And parting summer's lingering blooms delayed,
Dear lovely bowers of innocence and ease,
Seats of my youth, when every sport could please,
How often have I loitered o'er thy green,
Where humble happiness endeared each scene.
How often have I paused on every charm,
The sheltered cot, the cultivated farm,
The never failing brook, the busy mill,
The decent church that topt the neighbouring hill,
The hawthorn bush, with seats beneath the shade,
For talking age and whispering lovers made!
How often have I blest the coming day,
When toil remitting lent its turn to play,
And all the village train from labour free
Led up their sports beneath the spreading tree,
While many a pastime circled in the shade,
The young contending as the old surveyed;
And many a gambol frolicked o'er the ground,
And slights of art and feats of strength went round;
And still as each repeated pleasure tired,
Succeeding sports the mirthful band inspired;
The dancing pair that simply sought renown
By holding out to tire each other down;
The swain mistrustless of his smutted face,
While secret laughter tittered round the place;

The bashful virgin's side-long looks of love,
The matron's glance that would those looks reprove!
These were thy charms, sweet village; sports like these,
With sweet succession taught even toil to please;
These round thy bowers their cheerful influence shed,
These were thy charms—But all these charms are fled.
Sweet smiling village, loveliest of the lawn,
Thy sports are fled, and all thy charms withdrawn;
Amidst thy bowers the tyrant's hand is seen,
And desolation saddens all the green:
One only master grasps the whole domain,
And half a tillage stints thy smiling plain;
No more thy glassy brook reflects the day,
But choaked with sedges, works its weedy way;
Along thy glades, a solitary guest,
The hollow sounding bittern guards its nest;
Amidst thy desert walks the lapwing flies,
And tires their echoes with unvaried cries.
Sunk are thy bowers, in shapeless ruin all,
And the long grass o'ertops the mouldering wall;
And trembling, shrinking from the spoiler's hand,
Far, far away thy children leave the land.
    Ill fares the land, to hastening ills a prey,
Where wealth accumulates, and men decay:
Princes and lords may flourish, or may fade;
A breath can make them, as a breath has made;
But a bold peasantry, their country's pride,
When once destroyed, can never be supplied.

                           From *The Deserted Village*

THOMAS WARTON (1728—1790)

Sonnet

Written in a blank leaf of Dugdale's Monasticon

Deem not, devoid of elegance, the sage,
    By Fancy's genuine feelings unbeguiled,
    Of painful Pedantry the poring child,
    Who turns, of these proud domes, th' historic page,
Now sunk by Time, and Henry's fiercer rage.
    Think'st thou the warbling Muses never smiled

On his lone hours? Ingenuous views engage
His thought, on themes, unclassic falsely stiled,
Intent. While cloistered Piety displays
Her mouldering roll, the piercing eye explores
New manners, and the pomp of elder days,
Whence culls the pensive bard his pictured stores.
Nor rough, nor barren, are the winding ways
Of hoar Antiquity, but strown with flowers.

The Solemn Noon of Night

Beneath yon ruined Abbey's moss-grown piles
Oft let me sit, at twilight hour of Eve,
Where through some western window the pale moon
Pours her long-levelled rule of streaming light;
While sullen sacred silence reigns around,
Save the lone Screech-owl's note, who builds his bow'r
Amid the mouldering caverns dark and damp,
Or the calm breeze, that rustles in the leaves
Of flaunting Ivy, that with mantle green
Invests some wasted tower. Or let me tread
It's neighb'ring walk of pines, where mused of old
The cloistered brothers: through the gloomy void
That far extends beneath their ample arch
As on I pace, religious horror wraps
My soul in dread repose. But when the world
Is clad in Midnight's raven-coloured robe,
'Mid hollow charnel let me watch the flame
Of taper dim, shedding a livid glare
O'er the wan heaps; while airy voices talk
Along the glimm'ring walls, or ghostly shape
At distance seen, invites with beck'ning hand
My lonesome steps, through the far-winding vaults.
Nor undelightful is the solemn noon
Of night, when haply wakeful from my couch
I start: lo, all is motionless around!
Roars not the rushing wind; the sons of men
And every beast in mute oblivion lie;
All Nature's hushed in silence and in sleep.
O then how fearful is it to reflect,
That through the still globe's awful solitude
No being wakes but me! 'till stealing sleep

My drooping temples bathes in opiate dews.
Nor then let dreams, of wanton Folly born,
My senses lead through flowery paths of joy;
But let the sacred Genius of the night
Such mystic visions send, as SPENSER saw,
When through bewildering Fancy's magic maze,
To the fell house of Busyrane, he led
Th' unshaken Britomart; or MILTON knew,
When in abstracted thought he first conceived
All heaven in tumult, and the Seraphim
Come towering, armed in adamant and gold.

WILLIAM COWPER (1731—1800)

Light shining out of darkness

God moves in a mysterious way,
   His wonders to perform;
He plants His footsteps in the sea,
   And rides upon the storm.

Deep in unfathomable mines
   Of never failing skill;
He treasures up His bright designs,
   And works His sovereign will.

Ye fearful saints fresh courage take,
   The clouds ye so much dread
Are big with mercy, and shall break
   In blessings on your head.

Judge not the Lord by feeble sense,
   But trust Him for His grace;
Behind a frowning providence,
   He hides a smiling face.

His purposes will ripen fast,
   Unfolding every hour;
The bud may have a bitter taste,
   But sweet will be the flower.

Blind unbelief is sure to err,
    And scan His work in vain;
God is his own interpreter,
    And he will make it plain.

The winter evening

Hark! 'tis the twanging horn o'er yonder bridge,
That with its wearisome but needful length
Bestrides the wintry flood, in which the moon
Sees her unwrinkled face reflected bright:—
He comes, the herald of a noisy world,
With spattered boots, strapped waist, and frozen locks;
News from all nations lumb'ring at his back.
True to his charge, the close-packed load behind,
Yet careless what he brings, his one concern
Is to conduct it to the destined inn:
And, having dropped th' expected bag, pass on.
He whistles as he goes, light-hearted wretch,
Cold and yet cheerful: messenger of grief
Perhaps to thousands, and of joy to some;
To him indiff'rent whether grief or joy.
Houses in ashes, and the fall of stocks,
Births, deaths, and marriages, epistles wet
With tears, that trickled down the writer's cheeks
Fast as the periods from his fluent quill,
Or charged with am'rous sighs of absent swains,
Or nymphs responsive, equally affect
His horse and him, unconscious of them all.
But oh th' important budget! ushered in
With such heart-shaking music, who can say
What are its tidings? have our troops awaked?
Or do they still, as if with opium drugged,
Snore to the murmurs of th' Atlantic wave?
Is India free? and does she wear her plumed
And jewelled turban with a smile of peace,
Or do we grind her still? The grand debate,
The popular harangue, the tart reply,
The logic, and the wisdom, and the wit,
And the loud laugh—I long to know them all;

I burn to set th' imprisoned wranglers free,
And give them voice and utt'rance once again.
  Now stir the fire, and close the shutters fast,
Let fall the curtains, wheel the sofa round,
And, while the bubbling and loud-hissing urn
Throws up a steamy column, and the cups,
That cheer but not inebriate, wait on each,
So let us welcome peaceful ev'ning in.

To the Immortal Memory of the Halibut on which I dined this day, Monday, April 26, 1784.

Where hast thou floated? in what seas pursued
Thy pastime? When wast thou an egg new spawned,
Lost in the immensity of ocean's waste?
Roar as they might, the overbearing winds
That rocked the deep, thy cradle, thou wast safe—
And in thy minnikin and embryo state,
Attached to the firm leaf of some salt weed,
Didst outlive tempests, such as wrung and racked
The joints of many a stout and gallant bark,
And whelmed them in the unexplored abyss.
Indebted to no magnet and no chart,
Nor under guidance of the polar fire,
Thou wast a voyager on many coasts,
Grazing at large in meadows submarine,
Where flat Batavia, just emerging, peeps
Above the brine—where Caledonia's rocks
Beat back the surge—and where Hibernia shoots
Her wondrous causeway far into the main.
Wherever thou hast fed, thou little thought'st,
And I not more, that I should feed on thee.
Peace, therefore, and good health, and much good fish,
To him who sent thee! and success, as oft
As it descends into the billowy gulf,
To the same drag that caught thee!—Fare thee well!
Thy lot thy brethren of the slimy fin
Would envy, could they know that thou wast doomed
To feed a bard, and to be praised in verse.

ERASMUS DARWIN (1731—1802)

Vegetable Loves

From giant Oaks, that wave their branches dark,
To the dwarf Moss that clings upon their bark,
What Beaux and Beauties crowd the gaudy groves,
And woo and win their vegetable Loves.
How Snowdrops cold, and blue-eyed Harebels blend
Their tender tears, as o'er the stream they bend;
The love-sick Violet, and the Primrose pale,
Bow their sweet heads, and whisper to the gale;
With secret sighs the Virgin Lily droops,
And jealous Cowslips hang their tawny cups.
How the young Rose in beauty's damask pride
Drinks the warm blushes of his bashful bride;
With honey'd lips enamoured Woodbines meet,
Clasp with fond arms, and mix their kisses sweet.
    Stay thy soft murmuring waters, gentle Rill;
Hush, whispering Winds; ye rustling Leaves, be still;
Rest, silver Butterflies, your quivering wings;
Alight, ye Beetles, from your airy rings;
Ye painted Moths, your gold-eyed plumage furl,
Bow your wide horns, your spiral trunks uncurl;
Glitter, ye Glow-worms, on your mossy beds;
Descend, ye Spiders, on your lengthened threads;
Slide here, ye horned Snails, with varnished shells;
Ye Bee-nymphs, listen in your waxen cells!
    Botanic Muse, who in this latter age
Led by your airy hand the Swedish sage,
Bade his keen eye your secret haunts explore
On dewy dell, high wood, and winding shore;
Say on each leaf how tiny Graces dwell;
How laugh the Pleasures in a blossom's bell;
How insect Loves arise on cobweb wings,
Aim their light shafts, and point their little stings.

From *The loves of the plants*

CHARLES CHURCHILL (1731—1764)

What is't to us?

The Cit, a Common-Council-Man by place
Ten thousand mighty nothings in his face,
By situation as by nature great,
With nice precision parcels out the state;
Proves and disproves, affirms, and then denies,
Objects himself, and to himself replies;
Wielding aloft the Politician rod,
Makes Pitt by turns a devil and a god;
Maintains, e'en to the very teeth of pow'r,
The same thing right and wrong in half an hour.
Now all is well, now he suspects a plot,
And plainly proves, WHATEVER IS, IS NOT.
Fearfully wise, he shakes his empty head,
And deals out empires as he deals out thread.
His useless scales are in a corner flung,
And Europe's balance hangs upon his tongue.

Peace to such triflers, be our happier plan
To pass through life as easy as we can,
Who's in or out, who moves this grand machine,
Nor stirs my curiosity, nor spleen.
Secrets of state no more I wish to know
Than secret movements of a Puppet-Show;
Let but the puppets move, I've my desire,
Unseen the hand which *guides* the Master-Wire.

What is't to us, if taxes rise or fall,
Thanks to our fortune *we* pay none at all.
Let muckworms, who in dirty acres deal,
Lament those hardships which *we* cannot feel.
His Grace, who smarts, may bellow if he please,
But must I bellow too, who sit at ease?
By custom safe, the poet's numbers flow,
Free as the light and air some years ago.
No stateman e'er will find it worth his pains
To tax our labours, and excise our brains.
Burthens like these vile earthly buildings bear,
No tribute's laid on *Castles* in the *Air*.

From *Night*

204

JAMES BEATTIE (1735—1803)

Nature and the poets

But who the melodies of morn can tell?
The wild brook babbling down the mountain side;
The lowing herd; the sheepfold's simple bell;
The pipe of early shepherd dim descried
In the lone valley; echoing far and wide
The clamorous horn along the cliffs above;
The hollow murmur of the ocean-tide;
The hum of bees, the linnet's lay of love,
And the full choir that wakes the universal grove.

The cottage-curs at early pilgrim bark;
Crowned with her pail the tripping milkmaid sings;
The whistling plowman stalks afield; and, hark!
Down the rough slope the ponderous waggon rings;
Through rustling corn the hare astonished springs;
Slow tolls the village-clock the drowsy hour;
The partridge bursts away on whirring wings;
Deep mourns the turtle in sequestered bower,
And shrill lark carols clear from her aereal tour.

O Nature, how in every charm supreme!
Whose votaries feast on raptures ever new!
O for the voice and fire of seraphim,
To sing thy glories with devotion due!
Blest be the day I 'scaped the wrangling crew,
From Pyrrho's maze, and Epicurus' sty;
And held high converse with the godlike few,
Who to th' enraptured heart, and ear, and eye,
Teach beauty, virtue, truth, and love, and melody.

From *The Minstrel*.

JOHN PHILPOT CURRAN (1750—1817)

The deserter's lamentation

If sadly thinking,
And spirits sinking,
Could more than drinking
Our griefs compose—

A cure for sorrow
From care I'd borrow;
And hope tomorrow
  Might end my woes.

But since in wailing
There's naught availing,
For Death, unfailing,
  Will strike the blow;
Then, for that reason,
And for the season,
Let us be merry
  Before we go!

A wayworn ranger,
To joy a stranger,
Through every danger
  My course I've run.
Now, death befriending,
His last aid lending,
My griefs are ending,
  My woes are done.

No more a rover,
Or hapless lover,
Those cares are over—
  'My cup runs low;'
Then, for that reason,
And for the season,
Let us be merry
Before we go!

ROBERT FERGUSSON (1750—1774)

My winsome dear

In July month, ae bonny morn,
  Whan Nature's rokelay green
Was spread o'er ilka rigg o' corn
  To charm our roving een;

Glouring about I saw a quean,
   The fairest 'neath the lift;
Her EEN ware o' the siller sheen,
   Her SKIN like snawy drift,
                Sae white that day.

Quod she, "I ferly unco sair,
   That ye sud musand gae,
Ye wha hae sung o' HALLOW-FAIR,
   Her winter's pranks and play:
Whan on LEITH-SANDS the racers rare,
   Wi' Jocky louns are met,
Their orro pennies there to ware,
   And drown themsel's in debt
              Fu' deep that day."

An' wha are ye, my winsome dear,
   That takes the gate sae early?
Whare do ye win, gin ane may speir,
   For I right meikle ferly,
That sic braw buskit laughing lass
   Thir bonny blinks shou'd gi'e,
An' loup like HEBE o'er the grass,
   As wanton and as free
              Frae dule this day.

"I dwall amang the caller springs
   That weet the LAND O' CAKES.
And aften tune my canty strings
   At BRIDALS and LATE-WAKES :
They ca' me MIRTH; I ne'er was kend
   To grumble or look sour,
But blyth wad be a lift to lend,
   Gif ye wad sey my pow'r
              An' pith this day."

A bargain be't, and by my feggs
   Gif ye will be my mate,
Wi' you I'll screw the cheery pegs,
   Ye shanna find me blate;
We'll reel an' ramble thro' the sands,
   And jeer wi' a' we meet;

Nor hip the daft and gleesome bands
That fill EDINA's street
                    Sae thrang this day.

                                        From *Leith Races*

THOMAS CHATTERTON (1752—1770)

*An Excelente Balade of Charitie
As Wroten Bie The Gode Prieste
Thomas Rowley*, 1464

In Virgyne the sweltrie sun gan sheene,
And hotte upon the mees did caste his raie;
The apple rodded from its palie greene,
And the mole peare did bende the leafy spraie;
The peede chelandri sunge the livelong daie;
'Twas nowe the pride, the manhode of the yeare,
And eke the grounde was dighte in its mose defte aumere.

The sun was glemeing in the middle of daie,
Deadde still the aire, and eke the welken blue,
When from the sea arist in drear arraie
A hepe of cloudes of sable sullen hue,
The which full fast unto the woodlande drewe,
Hiltring attenes the sunnis fetive face,
And the blacke tempeste swolne and gatherd up apace.

Beneathe an holme, faste by a pathwaie side,
Which dide unto Seyncte Godwine's covent lede,
A hapless pilgrim moneynge did abide,
Pore in his viewe, ungentle in his weede,
Long bretful of the miseries of neede,
Where from the hail-stone coulde the almer flie?
He had no housen theere, ne anie covent nie.

Look in his glommed face, his sprighte there scanne;
Howe woe-be-gone, how withered, forwynd, deade!
Haste to thie church-glebe-house, asshrewed manne!
Haste to thie kiste, thie onlie dortoure bedde.

Cale, as the claie whiche will gre on thie hedde,
Is Charitie and Love aminge highe elves;
Knightis and Barons live for pleasure and themselves.

The gatherd storme is rype; the bigge drops falle;
The forswat meadowes smethe, and drenche the raine;
The comyng ghastness do the cattle pall,
And the full flockes are drivynge ore the plaine;
Dashde from the cloudes the waters flott againe;
The welkin opes; the yellow levynne flies;
And the hot fierie smothe in the wide lowings dies.

Liste! now the thunder's rattling clymmynge sound
Cheves slowlie on, and then embollen clangs,
Shakes the hie spyre, and losst, dispended, drowned,
Still on the gallard eare of terroure hanges;
The windes are up; the lofty elmen swanges;
Again the levynne and the thunder poures,
And the full cloudes are braste attenes in stonen showers.

Spurreynge his palfrie oere the watrie plaine,
The Abbote of Seyncte Godwynes convente came;
His chapournette was drented with the reine,
And his pencte gyrdle met with mickle shame;
He aynewarde tolde his bedroll at the same;
The storme encreasen, and he drew aside,
With the mist almes craver neere to the holme to bide.

His cope was all of Lyncolne clothe so fyne,
With a gold button fasten'd neere his chynne;
His autremete was edged with golden twynne,
And his shoone pyke a loverds mighte have binne;
Full well it shewn he thoughten coste no sinne:
The trammels of the palfrye pleasde his sighte,
For the horse-millanare his head with roses dighte.

An almes, sir prieste! the droppynge pilgrim saide,
O! let me waite within your covente dore,
Till the sunne sheneth hie above our heade,

And the loude tempeste of the aire is oer;
Helpless and ould am I alas! and poor;
No house, ne friend, ne moneie in my pouche;
All yatte I call my owne is this my silver crouche.

Varlet, replyd the Abbatte, cease your dinne;
This is no season almes and prayers to give;
Mie porter never lets a faitour in;
None touch mie rynge who not in honour live.
And now the sonne with the blacke cloudes did stryve,
And shettynge on the grounde his glairie raie,
The Abbatte spurrde his steede, and eftsoones roadde awaie.

Once moe the skie was blacke, the thounder rolde;
Faste reyneynge oer the plaine a prieste was seen;
Ne dighte full proude, ne buttoned up in golde;
His cope and jape were graie, and eke were clene;
A Limitoure he was of order seene;
And from the pathwaie side then turned hee,
Where the pore almer laie binethe the holmen tree.

An almes, sir priest! the droppynge pilgrim sayde,
For sweet Seyncte Marie and your order sake.
The Limitoure then loosen'd his pouche threade,
And did thereoute a groate of silver take;
The mister pilgrim dyd for halline shake.
Here take this silver, it maie eathe thie care;
We are Goddes stewards all, nete of oure owne we bare.

But ah! unhailie pilgrim, lerne of me,
Scathe anie give a rentrolle to their Lorde.
Here take my semecope, thou arte bare I see;
Tis thyne; the Seynctes will give me mie rewarde.
He left the pilgrim, and his waie aborde.
Virgynne and hallie Seyncte, who sitte yn gloure,
Or give the mittee will, or give the gode man power.

GEORGE CRABBE (1754—1832)

Truth in poetry

I grant indeed that Fields and Flocks have charms,
For him that gazes or for him that farms;
But when amid such pleasing scenes I trace
The poor laborious natives of the place
And see the mid-day sun, with fervid ray,
On their bare heads and dewy temples play;
While some, with feebler heads and fainter hearts,
Deplore their fortune, yet sustain their parts,
Then shall I dare these real ills to hide,
In tinsel trappings of poetic pride?
No; cast by Fortune on a frowning coast,
Which neither groves nor happy valleys boast;
Where other cares than those the Muse relates,
And other Shepherds dwell with other mates;
By such examples taught, I paint the Cot,
As truth will paint it and as bards will not.
Nor you, ye Poor, of lettered scorn complain,
To you, the smoothest song is smooth in vain;
O'ercome by labour and bowed down by time,
Feel you the barren flattery of a rhyme?
Can Poets sooth you, when you pine for bread,
By winding myrtles round your ruined shed?
Can their light tales your weighty griefs o'erpower,
Or glad with airy mirth the toilsome hour?
Lo! where the heath, with withering brake grown o'er,
Lends the light turf that warms the neighbouring poor;
From thence a length of burning sand appears,
Where the thin harvest waves its withered ears;
Rank weeds, that every art and care defy,
Reign o'er the land and rob the blighted rye:
There Thistles stretch their prickly arms afar,
And to the ragged infant threaten war;
There Poppies nodding, mock the hope of toil,
There the blue Bugloss paints the sterile soil;
Hardy and high, above the slender sheaf,
The slimy Mallow waves her silky leaf;
O'er the young shoot the Charlock throws a shade,
And clasping Tares cling round the sickly blade;

211

With mingled tints the rocky coasts abound,
And a sad splendour vainly shines around.
  So looks the Nymph whom wretched arts adorn,
Betrayed by Man, then left for Man to scorn;
Whose cheek in vain assumes the mimic rose,
While her sad eyes the troubled breast disclose;
Whose outward splendour is but folly's dress,
Exposing most, when most it gilds distress.

From The Village

Peter Grimes

  Thus by himself compelled to live each day,
To wait for certain hours the tide's delay;
At the same times the same dull views to see,
The bounding marsh-bank and the blighted tree;
The water only, when the tides were high,
When low, the mud half-covered and half-dry;
The sun-burnt tar that blisters on the planks,
And bank-side stakes in their uneven ranks;
Heaps of entangled weeds that slowly float,
As the tide rolls by the impeded boat.
  When tides were neap, and, in the sultry day,
Through the tall bounding mud-banks made their way,
Which on each side rose swelling, and below
The dark warm flood ran silently and slow;
There anchoring, Peter chose from man to hide,
There hang his head, and view the lazy tide
In its hot slimy channel slowly glide;
Where the small eels that left the deeper way
For the warm shore, within the shallows play;
Where gaping mussels, left upon the mud,
Slope their slow passage to the fallen flood;—
Here dull and hopeless he'd lie down and trace
How sidelong crabs had scrawled their crooked race;
Or sadly listen to the tuneless cry
Of fishing gull or clanging golden-eye;
What time the sea-birds to the marsh would come,
And the loud bittern, from the bulrush home,
Gave from the salt-ditch side the bellowing boom:
He nursed the feelings these dull scenes produce,
And loved to stop beside the opening sluice;

Where the small stream, confined in narrow bound,
Ran with with a dull, unvaried, saddening sound;
Where all, presented to the eye or ear,
Oppressed the soul with misery, grief, and fear.

From *The Borough*

The Caroline

Third in our Borough's list appears the sign
Of a fair queen—the gracious Caroline;
But in decay—each feature in the face
Has stain of Time, and token of disgrace.
The storm of winter, and the summer-sun,
Have on that form their equal mischief done;
The features now are all disfigured seen,
And not one charm adorn's th' insulted queen:
To this poor face was never paint applied,
Th' unseemly work of cruel Time to hide;
Here we may rightly such neglect upbraid,
Paint on such faces is by prudence laid.
Large the domain, but all within combine
To correspond with the dishonoured sign;
And all around dilapidates; you call—
But none replies—they're inattentive all:
At length a ruined stable holds your steed,
While you through large and dirty rooms proceed,
Spacious and cold; a proof they once had been
In honour—now magnificently mean;
Till in some small half-furnished room you rest,
Whose dying fire denotes it had a guest.
In those you passed where former splendour reigned,
You saw the carpets torn, the paper stained;
Squares of discordant glass in windows fixed,
And paper oiled in many a space betwixt;
A soiled and broken sconce, a mirror cracked,
With table underpropped, and chairs new-backed;
A marble side-slab with ten thousand stains,
And all an ancient tavern's poor remains.
With much entreaty, they your food prepare,
And acid wine afford, with meagre fare;
Heartless you sup; and when a dozen times
You've read the fractured window's senseless rhymes;

Have been assured that Phoebe Green was fair,
And Peter Jackson took his supper there;
You reach a chilling chamber, where you dread
Damps, hot or cold, from a tremendous bed;
Late comes your sleep, and you are wakened soon
By rustling tatters of the old festoon.

From *The Borough*

WILLIAM BLAKE (1757—1827)

How sweet I roamed from field to field

How sweet I roamed from field to field
And tasted all the summer's pride,
Till I the Prince of Love beheld
Who in the sunny beams did glide!

He showed me lilies for my hair,
And blushing roses for my brow;
He led me through his gardens fair
Where all his golden pleasures grow.

With sweet May dews my wings were wet,
And Phoebus fired my vocal rage;
He caught me in his silken net,
And shut me in his golden cage.

He loves to sit and hear me sing,
Then, laughing, sports and plays with me;
Then stretches out my golden wing,
And mocks my loss of liberty.

The Tyger

Tyger! Tyger! burning bright
In the forests of the night,
What immortal hand or eye
Could frame thy fearful symmetry?

In what distant deeps or skies
Burnt the fire of thine eyes?
On what wings dare he aspire?
What the hand dare seize the fire?

And what shoulder, and what art,
Could twist the sinews of thy heart?
And when thy heart began to beat,
What dread hand? and what dread feet?

What the hammer? what the chain?
In what furnace was thy brain?
What the anvil? what dread grasp
Dare its deadly terrors clasp?

When the stars threw down their spears,
And watered heaven with their tears,
Did he smile his work to see?
Did he who made the Lamb make thee?

Tyger! Tyger! burning bright
In the forests of the night,
What immortal hand or eye,
Dare frame thy fearful symmetry?

London

I wander through each chartered street,
Near where the chartered Thames does flow,
And mark in every face I meet
Marks of weakness, marks of woe,

In every cry of every Man,
In every Infant's cry of fear,
In every voice, in every ban,
The mind-forged manacles I hear.

How the Chimney-sweeper's cry
Every blackening Church appalls;
And the hapless Soldier's sigh
Runs in blood down Palace walls.

But most through midnight streets I hear
How the youthful Harlot's curse
Blasts the new born Infant's tear,
And blights with plagues the Marriage hearse.

WILLIAM BLAKE

In deadly fear

And Los beheld the mild Emanation, Jerusalem, eastward bending
Her revolutions toward the Starry Wheels in maternal anguish,
Like a pale cloud, arising from the arms of Beulah's Daughters
In Entuthon Benython's deep Vales beneath Golgonooza.

And Hand and Hyle rooted into Jerusalem by a fibre
Of strong revenge, and Skofeld Vegetated by Reuben's Gate
In every Nation of the Earth, till the Twelve Sons of Albion
Enrooted into every nation, a mighty Polypus growing
From Albion over the whole Earth: such is my awful Vision.

I see the Four-fold Man, The Humanity in deadly sleep
And its fallen Emanation, The Spectre and its cruel Shadow.
I see the Past, Present and Future existing all at once
Before me. O Divine Spirit, sustain me on thy wings,
That I may awake Albion from his long and cold repose;
For Bacon and Newton, sheathed in dismal steel, their terrors hang
Like iron scourges over Albion: Reasonings like vast Serpents
Infold around my limbs, bruising my minute articulations.

I turn my eyes to the Schools and Universities of Europe
And there behold the Loom of Locke, whose Woof rages dire,
Washed by the Water-wheels of Newton: black the cloth
In heavy wreathes folds over every Nation: cruel Works
Of many Wheels I view, wheel without wheel, with cogs tyrannic
Moving by compulsion each other, not as those in Eden, which,
Wheel within Wheel, in freedom revolve in harmony and peace.

I see in deadly fear in London Los raging round his Anvil
Of death, forming an Axe of gold; the Four Sons of Los
Stand round him cutting the Fibres from Albion's hills
That Albion's Sons may roll apart over the Nations,
While Reuben enroots his brethren in the narrow Canaanite
From the Limit Noah to the Limit Abram, in whose Loins
Reuben in his Twelve-fold majesty and beauty shall take refuge
As Abraham flees from Chaldea shaking his goary locks.
But first Albion must sleep, divided from the Nations.

I see Albion sitting upon his Rock in the first Winter,
And thence I see the Chaos of Satan and the World of Adam
When The Divine Hand went forth on Albion in the mid Winter
And at the place of Death, when Albion sat in Eternal Death
Among the Furnaces of Los in the Valley of the Son of Hinnom.

From *Jerusalem*

It is not so with me

Ah, happy blindness! Enion sees not the terrors of the uncertain,
And thus she wails from the dark deep; the golden heavens tremble:

"I am made to sow the thistle for wheat, the nettle for a nourishing
   dainty.
"I have planted a false oath in the earth; it has brought forth a
   poison tree.
"I have chosen the serpent for a councillor, and the dog
"For a schoolmaster to my children.
"I have blotted out from light and living the dove and nightingale,
"And I have caused the earth worm to beg from door to door.

"I have taught the thief a secret path into the house of the just.
"I have taught pale artifice to spread his nets upon the morning.
"My heavens are brass, my earth is iron, my moon a clod of clay,
"My sun a pestilence burning at noon and a vapour of death in night.

"What is the price of Experience? do men buy it for a song?
"Or wisdom for a dance in the street? No, it is bought with the price
"Of all that a man hath, his house, his wife, his children.
"Wisdom is sold in the desolate market where none come to buy,
"And in the withered field where the farmer plows for bread in vain.

"It is an easy thing to triumph in the summer's sun
"And in the vintage and to sing on the waggon loaded with corn.
"It is an easy thing to talk of patience to the afflicted,
"To speak the laws of prudence to the houseless wanderer,
"To listen to the hungry raven's cry in wintry season
"When the red blood is filled with wine and with the marrows of
   lambs.

"It is an easy thing to laugh at wrathful elements,
"To hear the dog howl at the wintry door, the ox in the slaughter house moan;
"To see a god on every wind and a blessing on every blast;

"To hear sounds of love in the thunder storm that destroys our enemies' house;
"To rejoice in the blight that covers his field, and the sickness that cuts off his children,
"While our olive and vine sing and laugh round our door, and our children bring fruit and flowers.

"Then the groan and the dolor are quite forgotten, and the slave grinding at the mill,
"And the captive in chains, and the poor in the prison, and the soldier in the field
"When the shattered bone hath laid him groaning among the happier dead.

"It is an easy thing to rejoice in the tents of prosperity:
"Thus could I sing and thus rejoice: but it is not so with me."

From *Vala, or The Four Zoas*

ROBERT BURNS (1759—1796)

Green grow the rashes O

Green grow the rashes O,
Green grow the rashes O,
The sweetest hours that e'er I spend,
Are spent amang the lasses O!

There's nought but care on ev'ry han',
In ev'ry hour that passes O;
What signifies the life o' man,
An' 'twere na for the lasses O.

The warly race may riches chase,
An' riches still may fly them O;
An' tho at last they catch them fast,
Their hearts can ne'er enjoy them O.

But gie me a canny hour at e'en,
My arms about my dearie O;
An' warly cares, an' warly men,
May a' gae tapsalteerie O!

For you sae douce, ye sneer at this,
Ye're nought but senseless asses O:
The wisest man the warl' saw,
He dearly loved the lasses O.

Auld nature swears, the lovely dears
Her noblest work she classes O;
Her prentice han' she tried on man,
An' then she made the lasses O.

Tam O' Shanter

When chapman billies leave the street,
And drouthy neibors neibors meet,
As market-days are wearing late,
An' folk begin to tak the gate;
While we sit bousing at the nappy,
An' getting fou and unco happy,
We think na on the lang Scots miles,
The mosses, waters, slaps, and stiles,
That lie between us and our hame,
Whare sits our sulky sullen dame,
Gathering her brows like gathering storm,
Nursing her wrath to keep it warm.
  This truth fand honest Tam o' Shanter,
As he frae Ayr ae night did canter—
(Auld Ayr, wham ne'er a town surpasses
For honest men and bonnie lasses).
  O Tam! hadst thou but been sae wise
As ta'en thy ain wife Kate's advice!
She tauld thee weel thou was a skellum,
A bletherin', blusterin', drunken blellum;
That frae November till October,
Ae market-day thou was na sober;
That ilka melder wi' the miller
Thou sat as lang as thou had siller;
That every naig was ca'd a shoe on,

The smith and thee gat roarin' fou on;
That at the Lord's house, even on Sunday,
Thou drank wi' Kirkton Jean till Monday.
She prophesied that, late or soon,
Thou would be found deep drowned in Doon;
Or catched wi' warlocks in the mirk
By Alloway's auld haunted kirk.

    Ah, gentle dames! it gars me greet
To think how mony counsels sweet,
How mony lengthened sage advices,
The husband frae the wife despises!

    But to our tale: Ae market night,
Tam had got planted unco right,
Fast by an ingle, bleezing finely,
Wi' reaming swats, that drank divinely;
And at his elbow, Souter Johnny,
His ancient, trusty, drouthy crony;
Tam lo'ed him like a very brither;
They had been fou for weeks thegither.
The night drave on wi' songs and clatter,
And aye the ale was growing better:
The landlady and Tam grew gracious,
Wi' favours secret, sweet, and precious;
The souter tauld his queerest stories;
The landlord's laugh was ready chorus:
The storm without might rair and rustle,
Tam did na mind the storm a whistle.

    Care, mad to see a man sae happy,
E'en drowned himsel amang the nappy.
As bees flee hame wi' lades o' treasure,
The minutes winged their way wi' pleasure;
Kings may be blest, but Tam was glorious,
O'er a' the ills o' life victorious!

    But pleasures are like poppies spread—
You seize the flow'r, its bloom is shed;
Or like the snow falls in the river—
A moment white, then melts for ever;
Or like the borealis race,
That flit ere you can point their place;
Or like the rainbow's lovely form
Evanishing amid the storm.

Nae man can tether time nor tide;
The hour approaches Tam maun ride;
That hour, o' night's black arch the key-stane,
That dreary hour, he mounts his beast in;
And sic a night he taks the road in,
As ne'er poor sinner was abroad in.

 The wind blew as 'twad blawn its last;
The rattling show'rs rose on the blast;
The speedy gleams the darkness swallowed;
Loud, deep, and lang, the thunder bellowed:
That night, a child might understand,
The Deil had business on his hand.

 Weel mounted on his gray mare, Meg,
A better never lifted leg,
Tam skelpit on thro' dub and mire,
Despising wind, and rain, and fire;
Whiles holding fast his gude blue bonnet;
Whiles crooning o'er some auld Scots sonnet;
Whiles glow'ring round wi' prudent cares,
Lest bogles catch him unawares.
Kirk-Alloway was drawing nigh,
Whare ghaists and houlets nightly cry.

 By this time he was cross the ford,
Whare in the snaw the chapman smoored;
And past the birks and meikle stane,
Whare drunken Charlie brak's neck-bane;
And thro' the whins, and by the cairn
Whare hunters fand the murder'd bairn;
And near the thorn, aboon the well,
Whare Mungo's mither hanged hersel.
Before him Doon pours all his floods;
The doubling storm roars thro' the woods;
The lightnings flash from pole to pole;
Near and more near the thunders roll:
When, glimmering thro' the groaning trees,
Kirk-Alloway seem'd in a bleeze;
Thro' ilka bore the beams were glancing;
An' loud resounded mirth and dancing.

 Inspiring bold John Barleycorn!
What dangers thou canst mak us scorn!
Wi' tippenny, we fear nae evil;

Wi' usquebae, we'll face the devil!
The swats sae reamed in Tammie's noddle,
Fair play, he cared na deils a boddle!
But Maggie stood right sair astonished,
Till, by the heel and hand admonished,
She ventured forward on the light;
And, vow! Tam saw an unco sight!
Warlocks and witches in a dance!
Nae cotillion brent new frae France,
But hornpipes, jigs, strathspeys, and reels,
Put life and mettle in their heels.
A winnock-bunker in the east,
There sat auld Nick, in shape o' beast—
A touzie tyke, black, grim, and large!
To gie them music was his charge:
He screwed the pipes and gart them skirl.
Till roof and rafters a' did dirl.
Coffins stood round like open presses,
That shawed the dead in their last dresses;
And by some devilish cantraip sleight
Each in its cauld hand held a light,
By which heroic Tam was able
To note upon the haly table
A murderer's banes in gibbet-airns;
Twa span-lang, wee, unchristened bairns;
A thief new-cutted frae the rape—
Wi' his last gasp his gab did gape;
Five tomahawks, wi' blude red-rusted;
Five scymitars, wi' murder crusted;
A garter, which a babe had strangled;
A knife, a father's throat had mangled,
Whom his ain son o' life bereft—
The grey hairs yet stack to the heft;
Wi' mair o' horrible and awefu',
Which even to name wad be unlawfu'.

As Tammie glowred, amazed, and curious,
The mirth and fun grew fast and furious:
The piper loud and louder blew;
The dancers quick and quicker flew;
They reeled, they set, they crossed, they cleekit,
Till ilka carlin swat and reekit,

And coost her duddies to the wark,
And linket at it in her sark!
   Now Tam, O Tam! had thae been queans,
A' plump and strapping in their teens;
Their sarks, instead o' creeshie flannen,
Been snaw-white seventeen hunder linen!
Thir breeks o' mine, my only pair,
That ance were plush, o' gude blue hair,
I wad hae gi'en them off my hurdies,
For ae blink o' the bonnie burdies!
   But wither'd beldams, auld and droll,
Rigwoodie hags wad spean a foal,
Louping and flinging on a crummock,
I wonder didna turn thy stomach.
   But Tam kend what was what fu' brawlie
There was ae winsome wench and walie
That night enlisted in the core,
Lang after kend on Carrick shore!
(For mony a beast to dead she shot,
And perished mony a bonnie boat,
And shook baith meikle corn and bear,
And kept the country-side in fear.)
Her cutty sark, o' Paisley harn,
That while a lassie she had worn,
In longitude tho' sorely scanty,
It was her best, and she was vauntie.
Ah! little kend thy reverend grannie
That sark she coft for her wee Nannie
Wi' twa pund Scots ('twas a' her riches)
Wad ever graced a dance of witches!
   But here my muse her wing maun cour;
Sic flights are far beyond her pow'r—
To sing how Nannie lap and flang,
(A souple jade she was, and strang);
And how Tam stood, like ane bewitched,
And thought his very een enriched;
Even Satan glowred, and fidged fu' fain,
And hotched and blew wi' might and main:
Till first ae caper, syne anither,
Tam tint his reason a' thegither,

And roars out 'Weel done, Cutty-sark!'
And in an instant all was dark!
And scarcely had he Maggie rallied,
When out the hellish legion sallied.

   As bees bizz out wi' angry fyke
When plundering herds assail their byke,
As open pussie's mortal foes
When pop! she starts before their nose,
As eager runs the market-crowd,
When 'Catch the thief!' resounds aloud.
So Maggie runs; the witches follow,
Wi' mony an eldritch skriech and hollow.

   Ah, Tam! ah, Tam! thou'll get thy fairin'!
In hell they'll roast thee like a herrin'!
In vain thy Kate awaits thy comin'!
Kate soon will be a woefu' woman!
Now do thy speedy utmost, Meg,
And win the key-stane o' the brig:
There at them thou thy tail may toss,
A running stream they dare na cross.
But ere the key-stane she could make,
The fient a tail she had to shake!
For Nannie, far before the rest,
Hard upon noble Maggie prest,
And flew at Tam wi' furious ettle;
But little wist she Maggie's mettle!
Ae spring brought off her master hale,
But left behind her ain gray tail:
The carlin claught her by the rump,
And left poor Maggie scarce a stump.

   Now, wha this tale o' truth shall read,
Ilk man and mother's son, take heed:
Whene'er to drink you are inclined,
Or cutty-sarks rin in your mind,
Think! ye may buy the joys o'er dear;
Remember Tam o' Shanter's mare.

WILLIAM WORDSWORTH (1770—1850)

The fountain

A Conversation

We talked with open heart, and tongue
Affectionate and true,
A pair of friends, though I was young,
And Matthew seventy-two.

We lay beneath a spreading oak,
Beside a mossy seat;
And from the turf a fountain broke,
And gurgled at our feet.

'Now, Matthew!' said I, 'let us match
This water's pleasant tune
With some old border-song, or catch
That suits a summer's noon;

'Or of the church-clock and the chimes
Sing here beneath the shade,
That half-mad thing of witty rhymes
Which you last April made!

In silence Matthew lay, and eyed
The spring beneath the tree;
And thus the dear old man replied,
The grey-haired man of glee:

'No check, no stay, this streamlet fears;
How merrily it goes!
'Twill murmur on a thousand years,
And flow as now it flows.

'And here, on this delightful day,
I cannot choose but think
How oft, a vigorous man, I lay
Beside this fountain's brink.

'My eyes are dim with childish tears,
My heart is idly stirred,
For the same sound is in my ears
Which in those days I heard.

'Thus fares it still in our decay:
And yet the wiser mind
Mourns less for what age takes away
Than what it leaves behind.

'The blackbird amid leafy trees,
The lark above the hill,
Let loose their carols when they please,
Are quiet when they will.

'With Nature never do *they* wage
A foolish strife; they see
A happy youth, and their old age
Is beautiful and free:

'But we are pressed by heavy laws;
And often, glad no more,
We wear a face of joy, because
We have been glad of yore.

'If there be one who need bemoan
His kindred laid in earth,
The household hearts that were his own;
It is the man of mirth.

'My days, my Friend, are almost gone,
My life has been approved,
And many love me! but by none
Am I enough beloved.'

'Now both himself and me he wrongs,
The man who thus complains!
I live and sing my idle songs
Upon these happy plains;

'And, Matthew, for thy children dead
I'll be a son to thee!'
At this he grasped my hand, and said,
'Alas! that cannot be.'

We rose up from the fountain-side;
And down the smooth descent
Of the green sheep-track did we glide;
And through the wood we went;

And, ere we came to Leonard's rock,
He sang those witty rhymes
About the crazy old church-clock,
And the bewildered chimes.

*Lines composed a few miles above Tintern Abbey on revisiting the
banks of the Wye during a tour. July 13, 1798*

Five years have past; five summers, with the length
Of five long winters! and again I hear
These waters, rolling from their mountain-springs
With a soft inland murmur.—Once again
Do I behold these steep and lofty cliffs,
That on a wild secluded scene impress
Thoughts of more deep seclusion; and connect
The landscape with the quiet of the sky.
The day is come when I again repose
Here, under this dark sycamore, and view
These plots of cottage-ground, these orchard-tufts,
Which at this season, with their unripe fruits,
Are clad in one green hue, and lose themselves
'Mid groves and copses. Once again I see
These hedge-rows, hardly hedge-rows, little lines
Of sportive wood run wild: these pastoral farms,
Green to the very door; and wreaths of smoke
Sent up, in silence, from among the trees!
With some uncertain notice, as might seem
Of vagrant dwellers in the houseless woods,
Or of some Hermit's cave, where by his fire
The Hermit sits alone.

              These beauteous forms,
Through a long absence, have not been to me
As is a landscape to a blind man's eye:
But oft, in lonely rooms, and 'mid the din
Of towns and cities, I have owed to them,
In hours of weariness, sensations sweet,
Felt in the blood, and felt along the heart;
And passing even into my purer mind,
With tranquil restoration:—feelings too
Of unremembered pleasure: such, perhaps,
As have no slight or trivial influence
On that best portion of a good man's life,
His little, nameless, unremembered, acts
Of kindness and of love. Nor less, I trust,
To them I may have owed another gift,
Of aspect more sublime; that blessed mood,
In which the burthen of the mystery,
In which the heavy and the weary weight
Of all this unintelligible world,
Is lightened:—that serene and blessed mood,
In which the affections gently lead us on,—
Until, the breath of this corporeal frame
And even the motion of our human blood
Almost suspended, we are laid asleep
In body, and become a living soul:
While with an eye made quiet by the power
Of harmony, and the deep power of joy,
We see into the life of things.

              If this
Be but a vain belief, yet, oh! how oft—
In darkness and amid the many shapes
Of joyless daylight; when the fretful stir
Unprofitable, and the fever of the world,
Have hung upon the beatings of my heart—
How oft, in spirit, have I turned to thee,
O sylvan Wye! thou wanderer thro' the woods,
How often has my spirit turned to thee!

And now, with gleams of half-extinguished thought,
With many recognitions dim and faint,
And somewhat of a sad perplexity,
The picture of the mind revives again:

While here I stand, not only with the sense
Of present pleasure, but with pleasing thoughts
That in this moment there is life and food
For future years. And so I dare to hope,
Though changed, no doubt, from what I was when first
I came among these hills; when like a roe
I bounded o'er the mountains, by the sides
Of the deep rivers, and the lonely streams,
Wherever nature led: more like a man
Flying from something that he dreads than one
Who sought the thing he loved. For nature then
(The coarser pleasures of my boyish days,
And their glad animal movements all gone by)
To me was all in all.—I cannot paint
What then I was. The sounding cataract
Haunted me like a passion: the tall rock,
The mountain, and the deep and gloomy wood,
Their colours and their forms, were then to me
An appetite; a feeling and a love,
That had no need of a remoter charm,
By thought supplied, nor any interest
Unborrowed from the eye.—That time is past,
And all its aching joys are now no more,
And all its dizzy raptures. Not for this
Faint I, nor mourn nor murmur; other gifts
Have followed; for such loss, I would believe,
Abundant recompense. For I have learned
To look on nature, not as in the hour
Of thoughtless youth; but hearing oftentimes
The still, sad music of humanity,
Nor harsh nor grating, though of ample power
To chasten and subdue. And I have felt
A presence that disturbs me with the joy
Of elevated thoughts; a sense sublime
Of something far more deeply interfused,
Whose dwelling is the light of setting suns,
And the round ocean and the living air,
And the blue sky, and in the mind of man:
A motion and a spirit, that impels
All thinking things, all objects of all thought,
And rolls through all things. Therefore am I still
A lover of the meadows and the woods,

And mountains; and of all that we behold
From this green earth; of all the mighty world
Of eye, and ear,—both what they half create,
And what perceive; well pleased to recognise
In nature and the language of the sense
The anchor of my purest thoughts, the nurse,
The guide, the guardian of my heart, and soul
Of all my moral being.
                         Nor perchance,
If I were not thus taught, should I the more
Suffer my genial spirits to decay:
For thou art with me here upon the banks
Of this fair river; thou my dearest Friend,
My dear, dear Friend; and in thy voice I catch
The language of my former heart, and read
My former pleasures in the shooting lights
Of thy wild eyes. Oh! yet a little while
May I behold in thee what I was once,
My dear, dear Sister! and this prayer I make,
Knowing that Nature never did betray
The heart that loved her; 'tis her privilege,
Through all the years of this our life, to lead
From joy to joy: for she can so inform
The mind that is within us, so impress
With quietness and beauty, and so feed
With lofty thoughts, that neither evil tongues,
Rash judgments, nor the sneers of selfish men,
Nor greetings where no kindness is, nor all
The dreary intercourse of daily life,
Shall e'er prevail against us, or disturb
Our cheerful faith, that all which we behold
Is full of blessings. Therefore let the moon
Shine on thee in thy solitary walk;
And let the misty mountain-winds be free
To blow against thee: and, in after years,
When these wild ecstasies shall be matured
Into a sober pleasure; when thy mind
Shall be a mansion for all lovely forms,
Thy memory be as a dwelling-place
For all sweet sounds and harmonies; oh! then,
If solitude, or fear, or pain, or grief,

Should be thy portion, with what healing thoughts
Of tender joy wilt thou remember me,
And these my exhortations! Nor, perchance—
If I should be where I no more can hear
Thy voice, nor catch from thy wild eyes these gleams
Of past existence—wilt thou then forget
That on the banks of this delightful stream
We stood together; and that I, so long
A worshipper of Nature, hither came
Unwearied in that service: rather say
With warmer love—oh! with far deeper zeal
Of holier love. Nor wilt thou then forget
That after many wanderings, many years
Of absence, these steep woods and lofty cliffs,
And this green pastoral landscape, were to me
More dear, both for themselves and for thy sake!

It is a beauteous evening

It is a beauteous evening, calm and free,
The holy time is quiet as a Nun
Breathless with adoration; the broad sun
Is sinking down in its tranquility;
The gentleness of heaven broods o'er the Sea:
Listen! the mighty Being is awake,
And doth with his eternal motion make
A sound like thunder—everlastingly.
Dear Child! dear Girl! that walkest with me here,
If thou appear untouched by solemn thought,
Thy nature is not therefore less divine:
Thou liest in Abraham's bosom all the year;
And worshipp'st at the Temple's inner shrine,
God being with thee when we know it not.

From *Miscellaneous Sonnets*

Afterthought

I thought of Thee, my partner and my guide,
As being past away.—Vain sympathies!
For, backward, Duddon! as I cast my eyes,
I see what was, and is, and will abide;
Still glides the Stream, and shall for ever glide;

The Form remains, the Function never dies;
While we, the brave, the mighty, and the wise,
We Men, who in our morn of youth defied
The elements, must vanish;—be it so!
Enough, if something from our hands have power
To live, and act, and serve the future hour;
And if, as toward the silent tomb we go,
Through love, through hope, and faith's transcendent dower,
We feel that we are greater than we know.

The Trosachs

There's not a nook within this solemn Pass
But were an apt confessional for One
Taught by his summer spent, his autumn gone,
That Life is but a tale of morning grass
Withered at eve. From scenes of art which chase
That thought away, turn, and with watchful eyes
Feed it 'mid Nature's old felicities,
Rocks, rivers, and smooth lakes more clear than glass
Untouched, unbreathed upon. Thrice happy quest,
If from a golden perch of aspen spray
(October's workmanship to rival May)
The pensive warbler of the ruddy breast
That moral sweeten by a heaven-taught lay,
Lulling the year, with all its cares, to rest!

A dedicated spirit

As one who hangs down-bending from the side
Of a slow-moving boat, upon the breast
Of a still water, solacing himself
With such discoveries as his eye can make
Beneath him in the bottom of the deep,
Sees many beauteous sights—weeds, fishes, flowers,
Grots, pebbles, roots of trees, and fancies more,
Yet often is perplexed and cannot part
The shadow from the substance, rocks and sky,
Mountains and clouds, reflected in the depth
Of the clear flood, from things which there abide
In their true dwelling; now is crossed by gleam
Of his own image, by a sunbeam now,

And wavering motions sent he knows not whence,
Impediments that make his task more sweet;
Such pleasant office have we long pursued
Incumbent o'er the surface of past time
With like success, nor often have appeared
Shapes fairer or less doubtfully discerned
Than these to which the Tale, indulgent Friend!
Would now direct thy notice. Yet in spite
Of pleasure won, and knowledge not withheld,
There was an inner falling off—I loved,
Loved deeply all that had been loved before,
More deeply even than ever: but a swarm
Of heady schemes jostling each other, gawds,
And feast and dance, and public revelry,
And sports and games (too grateful in themselves,
Yet in themselves less grateful, I believe,
Than as they were a badge glossy and fresh
Of manliness and freedom) all conspired
To lure my mind from firm habitual quest
Of feeding pleasures, to depress the zeal
And damp those yearnings which had once been mine—
A wild, unworldly-minded youth, given up
To his own eager thoughts. It would demand
Some skill, and longer time than may be spared,
To paint these vanities, and how they wrought
In haunts where they, till now, had been unknown.
It seemed the very garments that I wore
Preyed on my strength, and stopped the quiet stream
Of self-forgetfulness.
                    Yes, that heartless chase
Of trivial pleasures was a poor exchange
For books and nature at that early age.
'Tis true, some casual knowledge might be gained
Of character or life; but at that time,
Of manners put to school I took small note,
And all my deeper passions lay elsewhere.
Far better had it been to exalt the mind
By solitary study, to uphold
Intense desire through meditative peace;
And yet, for chastisement of these regrets,
The memory of one particular hour

Doth here rise up against me. 'Mid a throng
Of maids and youths, old men, and matrons staid,
A medley of all tempers, I had passed
The night in dancing, gaiety, and mirth,
With din of instruments and shuffling feet,
And glancing forms, and tapers glittering,
And unaimed prattle flying up and down;
Spirits upon the stretch, and here and there
Slight shocks of young love-liking interspersed,
Whose transient pleasure mounted to the head,
And tingled through the veins. Ere we retired,
The cock had crowed, and now the eastern sky
Was kindling, not unseen, from humble copse
And open field, through which the pathway wound,
And homeward led my steps. Magnificent
The morning rose, in memorable pomp,
Glorious as e'er I had beheld—in front,
The sea lay laughing at a distance; near,
The solid mountains shone, bright as the clouds,
Grain-tinctured, drenched in empyrean light;
And in the meadows and the lower grounds
Was all the sweetness of a common dawn—
Dews, vapours, and the melody of birds,
And labourers going forth to till the fields.
Ah! need I say, dear Friend! that to the brim
My heart was full; I made no vows, but vows
Were then made for me; bond unknown to me
Was given, that I should be, else sinning greatly,
A dedicated Spirit. On I walked
In thankful blessedness, which yet survives.

From *The Prelude*

SIR WALTER SCOTT (1771—1832)

Melrose Abbey

If thou would'st view fair Melrose aright,
Go visit it by the pale moonlight;
For the gay beams of lightsome day
Gild, but to flout, the ruins gray.

When the broken arches are black in night,
And each shafted oriel glimmers white;
When the cold light's uncertain shower
Streams on the ruined central tower;
When buttress and buttress, alternately,
Seem framed of ebon and ivory;
When silver edges the imagery,
And the scrolls that teach thee to live and die;
When distant Tweed is heard to rave,
And the owlet hoot o'er the dead man's grave,
Then go—but go alone the while—
Then view St. David's ruined pile;
And, home returning, soothly swear,
Was never scene so sad and fair!

From *The Lay of the Last Minstrel*

Proud Maisie

Proud Maisie is in the wood,
    Walking so early;
Sweet Robin sits on the bush,
    Singing so rarely.

'Tell me, thou bonny bird,
    When shall I marry me?'
'When six braw gentlemen
    Kirkward shall carry ye.'

'Who makes the bridal bed,
    Birdie, say truly?'
'The grey-headed sexton
    That delves the grave duly.

'The glow-worm o'er grave and stone
    Shall light thee steady.
The owl from the steeple sing,
    "Welcome, proud lady",'

SAMUEL TAYLOR COLERIDGE (1772—1834)

Christabel

'Tis the middle of night by the castle clock,
And the owls have wakened the crowing cock;
Tu-whit!—Tu-whoo!
And hark, again! the crowing cock,
How drowsily it crew.

Sir Leoline, the Baron rich,
Hath a toothless mastiff bitch;
From her kennel beneath the rock
She maketh answer to the clock,
Four for the quarters, and twelve for the hour;
Ever and aye, by shine and shower,
Sixteen short howls, not over loud;
Some say, she sees my lady's shroud.

Is the night chilly and dark?
The night is chilly, but not dark.
The thin grey cloud is spread on high,
It covers but not hides the sky.
The moon is behind, and at the full;
And yet she looks both small and dull.
The night is chill, the cloud is gray;
'Tis a month before the month of May,
And the spring comes slowly up this way.

The lovely lady, Christabel,
Whom her father loves so well,
What makes her in the wood so late,
A furlong from the castle gate?
She had dreams all yesternight
Of her own betrothed knight;
And she in the midnight wood will pray
For the weal of her lover that's far away.

She stole along, she nothing spoke,
The sighs she heaved were soft and low,
And naught was green upon the oak,
But moss and rarest mistletoe:
She kneels beneath the huge oak tree,
And in silence prayeth she.

The lady sprang up suddenly,
The lovely lady, Christabel!
It moaned as near, as near can be,
But what it is she cannot tell.—
On the other side it seems to be,
Of the huge, broad-breasted, old oak tree.

The night is chill; the forest bare;
Is it the wind that moaneth bleak?
There is not wind enough in the air
To move away the ringlet curl
From the lovely lady's cheek—
There is not wind enough to twirl
The one red leaf, the last of its clan,
That dances as often as dance it can,
Hanging so light, and hanging so high,
On the topmost twig that looks up at the sky.
Hush beating heart of Christabel!
Jesu, Maria, shield her well!
She folded her arms beneath her cloak,
And stole to the other side of the oak.
　　What sees she there?

There she sees a damsel bright,
Drest in a silken robe of white,
That shadowy in the moonlight shone:
The neck that made that white robe wan,
Her stately neck, and arms were bare;
Her blue-veined feet unsandalled were
And wildly glittered here and there
The gems entangled in her hair.
I guess, 'twas frightful there to see
A lady so richly clad as she—
Beautiful exceedingly!

'Mary mother, save me now!'
(Said Christabel) 'And who art thou?'

Dejection

Well! If the Bard was weather-wise, who made
　The grand old ballad of Sir Patrick Spence,

This night, so tranquil now, will not go hence
Unroused by winds, that ply a busier trade
Than those which mould yon cloud in lazy flakes,
Or the dull sobbing draft, that moans and rakes
    Upon the strings of this Aeolian lute,
    Which better far were mute.
    For lo! the new moon winter-bright!
    And overspread with phantom light,
    (With swimming phantom light o'erspread
    But rimmed and circled by a silver thread)
I see the old moon in her lap, foretelling
    The coming-on of rain and squally blast.
And oh! that even now the gust were swelling,
    And the slant night-shower driving loud and fast!
Those sounds which oft have raised me, whilst they awed,
    And sent my soul abroad,
Might now perhaps their wonted impulse give,
Might startle this dull pain, and make it move and live!

The pains of sleep

    Ere on my bed my limbs I lay,
    It hath not been my use to pray
    With moving lips or bended knees;
    But silently, by slow degrees,
    My spirit I to Love compose,
    In humble trust mine eyelids close,
    With reverential resignation,
    No wish conceived, no thought exprest!
    Only a sense of supplication;
    A sense o'er all my soul imprest
    That I am weak, yet not unblest,
    Since in me, round me, everywhere
    Eternal Strength and Wisdom are.

    But yesternight I prayed aloud
    In anguish and in agony,
    Up-starting from the fiendish crowd
    Of shapes and thoughts that tortured me:
    A lurid light, a trampling throng,
    Sense of intolerable wrong,
    And whom I scorned, those only strong!

Thirst of revenge, the powerless will
Still baffled, and yet burning still!
Desire with loathing strangely mixed
On wild or hateful objects fixed.
Fantastic passions! maddening brawl!
And shame and terror over all!
Deeds to be hid which were not hid,
Which all confused I could not know
Whether I suffered, or I did:
For all seemed guilt, remorse or woe,
My own or others still the same
Life-stifling fear, soul-stifling shame.

So two nights passed: the night's dismay
Saddened and stunned the coming day.
Sleep, the wide blessing, seemed to me
Distemper's worst calamity.
The third night, when my own loud scream
Had waked me from the fiendish dream,
O'ercome with sufferings strange and wild,
I wept as I had been a child;
And having thus by tears subdued
My anguish to a milder mood,
Such punishments, I said, were due
To natures deepliest stained with sin:
For aye entempesting anew
The unfathomable hell within
The horror of their deeds to view,
To know and loathe, yet wish and do !
Such griefs with such men well agree,
But wherefore, wherefore fall on me?
To be beloved is all I need,
And when I love, I love indeed.

Self-knowledge

E coelo descendit γνῶθι σεαυτόν. *Juvenal*

Γνῶθι σεαυτόν—and is this the prime
And heaven-sprung adage of the olden time!
Say, canst thou make thyself? Learn first that trade;

Haply thou mayst know that thou thyself had made.
What hast thou, Man, that thou darest call thine own?
What is there in thee, Man, that can be known?
Dark fluxion, all unfixable by thought,
A phantom dim of past and future wrought,
Vain sister of the worm—life, death, soul, clod—
Ignore thyself, and strive to know thy God!

ROBERT SOUTHEY (1774—1843)

Thalaba and the banquet

Still a bare, silent, solitary glen,
A tearful silence, and a solitude
    That made itself be felt;
    And steeper now the ascent,
    A rugged path, that tired
The straining muscles, toiling slowly up,
    At length again a rock
    Stretched o'er the narrow vale;
There also had a portal-way been hewn,
But gates of massy iron barred the pass,
    Huge, solid, heavy-hinged.

Was it to earthly Eden, lost so long,
The fated Youth had found his wondrous way?
    But earthly Eden boasts
    No terraced palaces,
No rich pavilions bright with woven gold,
    Like these that in the vale
    Rise amid odorous groves.
    The astonished Thalaba,
Doubting as though an unsubstantial dream
    Beguiled him, closed his eyes,
    And opened them again;
    And yet uncertified,
He prest them close, and as he looked around
    Questioned the strange reality again.
    He did not dream;
    They still were there,

The glittering tents,
The odorous groves,
The gorgeous palaces.

Full of the bliss, yet still awake
To wonder, on went Thalaba;
On every side the song of mirth,
The music of festivity,
Invite the passing youth.
Wearied at length with hunger and with heat,
He enters in a banquet room,
Where round a fountain brink,
On silken carpets sate the festive train.
Instant through all his frame
Delightful coolness spread;
The playing fount refreshed
The agitated air;
The very light came cooled through silvered panes
Of pearly shell, like the pale moon-beam tinged;
Or where the wine-vase filled the aperture,
Rosy as rising morn, or softer gleam
Of saffron, like the sunny evening mist:
Through every hue, and streaked by all,
The flowing fountain played.
Around the water-edge
Vessels of wine, alternate placed,
Ruby and amber, tinged its little waves.
From golden goblets there
The guests sate quaffing the delicious juice
Of Shiraz' golden grape.

But Thalaba took not the draught;
For rightly he knew had the Prophet forbidden
That beverage, the mother of sins.
Nor did the urgent guests
Proffer a second time the liquid fire,
When in the youth's strong eye they saw
No moveable resolve.
Yet not uncourteous, Thalaba
Drank the cool draught of innocence,
That fragrant from its dewy vase

Came purer than it left its native bed;
 And he partook the odorous fruits,
  For all rich fruits were there;
   Water-melons rough of rind,
    Whose pulp the thirsty lip
    Dissolved into a draught;
Pistachios from the heavy-clustered trees
  Of Malavert, or Haleb's fertile soil;
And Casbin's luscious grapes of amber hue,
  That many a week endure
   The summer sun intense,
   Till by its powerful heat
All watery particles exhaled, alone
The strong essential sweetness ripens there.
  Here cased in ice the apricot,
   A topaz, crystal-set:
   Here, on a plate of snow,
   The sunny orange rests;
And still the aloes and the sandal-wood,
From golden censers, o'er the banquet room
  Diffuse their dying sweets.

Anon a troop of females formed the dance,
Their ankles bound with bracelet-bells,
 That made the modulating harmony.
Transparent garments to the greedy eye
  Exposed their harlot limbs,
Which moved, in every wanton gesture skilled.

 With earnest eyes the banqueters
  Fed on the sight impure;
   And Thalaba, he gazed,
 But in his heart he bore a talisman,
  Whose blessed alchemy
  To virtuous thoughts refined
The loose suggestions of the scene impure.
Oneiza's image swam before his sight,
  His own Arabian Maid.
He rose, and from the banquet room he rushed,
  Tears coursed his burning cheek;
And nature for a moment woke the thought,

And murmured, that, from all domestic joys
Estranged, he wandered o'er the world
   A lonely being, far from all he loved.
Son of Hodeirah, not among thy crimes
    That momentary murmur shall be written!

      From tents of revelry,
From festal bowers, to solitude he ran;
   And now he came where all the rills
Of that well-watered garden in one tide
    Rolled their collected waves.
   A straight and stately bridge
Stretched its long arches o'er the ample stream.
Strong in the evening and distinct its shade
Lay on the watery mirror, and his eye
   Saw it united with its parent pile,
One huge fantastic fabric. Drawing near,
   Loud from the chambers of the bridge below,
    Sounds of carousal came and song,
And unveiled women bade the advancing youth
    Come merry-make with them!
     Unhearing, or unheeding, he
    Passed o'er with hurried pace,
And sought the shade and silence of the grove.

      Deserts of Araby!
    His soul returned to you.
He cast himself upon the earth,
    And closed his eyes and called
    The voluntary vision up.
    A cry, as of distress,
Aroused him; loud it came and near!
He started up, he strung his bow,
    He plucked an arrow forth.
Again a shriek . . a woman's shriek!
And lo! she rushes through the trees,
    Her veil is rent, her garments torn!
    The ravisher follows close.
'Prophet, save me! save me, God!
Help! Help me, man!' to Thalaba she cried;
    Thalaba drew the bow.

The unerring arrow did its work of death.
Then turning to the woman, he beheld
His own Oneiza, his Arabian Maid.

Thalaba and the magic thread

He found a Woman in the cave,
A solitary Woman,
Who by the fire was spinning,
And singing as she spun.
The pine boughs were cheerfully blazing,
And her face was bright with the flame;
Her face was as the damsel's face,
And yet her hair was grey.
She bade him welcome with a smile,
And still continued spinning,
And singing as she spun . . . .

The thread she spun it gleamed like gold
In the light of the odorous fire,
Yet was it so wondrously thin,
That, save when it shone in the light,
You might look for it closely in vain.
The youth sate watching it,
And she observed his wonder,
And then again she spake,
And still her speech was song;
'Now twine it round thy hands I say,
Now twine it round thy hands I pray;
My thread is small, my thread is fine,
But he must be
A stronger man than thee,
Who can break this thread of mine!'

And up she raised her bright blue eyes,
And sweetly she smiled on him,
And he conceived no ill;
And round and round his right hand,
And round and round his left,
He wound the thread so fine.
And then again the Woman spake,
And still her speech was song,
'Now thy strength, O Stranger, strain!
Now then break the slender chain.'

Thalaba strove, but the thread
    By magic hands was spun,
And in his cheek the flush of shame
    Arose, commixed with fear.
She beheld and laughed at him,
    And then again she sung,
'My thread is small, my thread is fine,
      But he must be
    A stronger man than thee,
Who can break this thread of mine!'

And up she raised her bright blue eyes,
    And fiercely she smiled on him:
'I thank thee, I thank thee, Hodeirah's son!
I thank thee for doing what can't be undone!'
For binding thyself in the chain I have spun!'
    Then from his head she wrenched
      A lock of his raven hair,
      And cast it in the fire,
    And cried aloud as it burnt,
    Sister! Sister! hear my voice!
    Sister! Sister! come and rejoice!
      The thread is spun,
      The prize is won,
      The work is done,
For I have made captive Hodeirah's Son.'

From Thalaba the Destroyer

WALTER SAVAGE LANDOR (1775—1864)

Faesulan idyl

Here, when precipitate Spring with one light bound
Into hot Summer's lusty arms expires;
And where go forth at morn, at eve, at night,
Soft airs, that want the lute to play with them,
And softer sighs, that know not what they want;
Under a wall, beneath an orange-tree,
Whose tallest flowers could tell the lowlier ones
Of sights in Fiesole right up above,

While I was gazing a few paces off
At what they seemed to show me with their nods,
Their frequent whispers and their pointing shoots,
A gentle maid came down the garden steps
And gathered the pure treasure in her lap.
I heard the branches rustle, and stept forth
To drive the ox away, or mule, or goat,
(Such I believed it must be); for sweet scents
Are the swift vehicles of still sweeter thoughts,
And nurse and pillow the dull memory
That would let drop without them her best stores.
They bring me tales of youth and tones of love,
And 'tis and ever was my wish and way
To let all flowers live freely, and all die,
Whene'er their Genius bids their souls depart,
Among their kindred in their native place.
I never pluck the rose; the violet's head
Hath spaken with my breath upon its bank
And not reproacht me; the ever-sacred cup
Of the pure lily hath between my hands
Felt safe, unsoiled, nor lost one grain of gold.
I saw the light that made the glossy leaves
More glossy; the fair arm, the fairer cheek
Warmed by the eye intent on its pursuit;
I saw the foot, that although half-erect
From its grey slipper could not lift her up
To what she wanted; I held down a branch,
And gathered her some blossoms, since their hour
Was come, and bees had wounded them, and flies
Of harder wing were working their way through
And scattering them in fragments under foot.
So crisp were some, they rattled unevolved,
Others, ere broken off, fell into shells,
For such appear the petals when detacht,
Unbending, brittle, lucid, white like snow,
And like snow not seen through, by eye or sun;
Yet every one her gown received from me
Was fairer than the first; . . . I thought not so,
But so she praised them to reward my care.
I said: *You find the largest.*

This indeed,
Cried she, *is large and sweet.*
                    She held one forth,
Whether for me to look at or to take
She knew not, nor did I; but taking it
Would best have solved (and this she felt) her doubt.
I dared not touch it; for it seemed a part
Of her own self; fresh, full, the most mature
Of blossoms, yet a blossom; with a touch
To fall, and yet unfallen.
                    She drew back.
The boon she tendered, and then, finding not
The ribbon at her waist to fix it in,
Dropt it, as loth to drop it, on the rest.

The end

I strove with none, for none was worth my strife;
    Nature I loved, and, next to Nature, Art;
I warmed both hands before the fire of life;
    It sinks, and I am ready to depart.

Florence

I leave with unreverted eye the towers
    Of Pisa pining o'er her desert stream.
Pleasure (they say) yet lingers in thy bowers,
    Florence, thou patriot's sigh, thou poet's dream!

O could I find thee as thou once wert known,
    Thoughtful and lofty, liberal and free!
But the pure Spirit from thy wreck has flown,
    And only Pleasure's phantom dwells with thee.

The last fruit off an old tree

There falls with every wedding chime
A feather from the wing of Time.
You pick it up, and say 'How fair
To look upon its colours are!'
Another drops day after day
Unheeded; not one word you say.
When bright and dusky are blown past,
Upon the hearse there nods the last.

THOMAS MOORE (1779—1852)

The journey onwards

As slow our ship her foamy track
    Against the wind was cleaving,
Her trembling pennant still looked back
    To that dear isle 'twas leaving.
So loath we part from all we love,
    From all the links that bind us;
So turn our hearts, as on we rove,
    To those we've left behind us!

When, round the bowl, of vanished years
    We talk with joyous seeming—
With smiles that might as well be tears,
    So faint, so sad their beaming;
While memory brings us back again
    Each early tie that twined us,
O, sweet's the cup that circles then
    To those we've left behind us!

And when in other climes we meet
    Some isle or vale enchanting,
Where all looks flowery, wild, and sweet,
    And nought but love is wanting;
We think how great had been our bliss
    If heaven had but assigned us
To live and die in scenes like this,
    With some we've left behind us!

As travellers oft look back at eve
    When eastward darkly going,
To gaze upon that light they leave
    Still faint behind them glowing,—
So, when the close of pleasure's day
    To gloom hath near consigned us,
We turn to catch one fading ray
    Of joy that's left behind us.

LEIGH HUNT (1784—1859)

The Fish, the Man, and the Spirit

TO A FISH

You strange, astonished-looking, angle-faced,
  Dreary-mouthed, gaping wretches of the sea,
  Gulping salt-water everlastingly,
Cold-blooded, though with red your blood be graced,
And mute, though dwellers in the roaring waste;
  And you, all shapes beside, that fishy be,—
  Some round, some flat, some long, all devilry,
Legless, unloving, infamously chaste:—

O scaly, slippery, wet, swift, staring wights,
  What is't ye do? What life lead? eh, dull goggles?
How do ye vary your vile days and nights?
  How pass your Sundays? Are ye still but joggles
In ceaseless wash? Still nought but gapes, and bites,
  And drinks, and stares, diversified with boggles?

A FISH ANSWERS

Amazing monster! that, for aught I know,
  With the first sight of thee didst make our race
  For ever stare! O flat and shocking face,
Grimly divided from the breast below!
Thou that on dry land horribly dost go
  With a split body and most ridiculous pace,
  Prong after prong, disgracer of all grace,
Long-useless-finned, haired, upright, unwet, slow!

O breather of unbreathable, sword-sharp air,
  How canst exist? How bear thyself, thou dry
And dreary sloth? What particle canst share
  Of the only blessed life, the watery?
I sometimes see of ye an actual *pair*
  Go by! linked fin by fin! most odiously.

THE FISH TURNS INTO A MAN, AND THEN INTO A SPIRIT, AND AGAIN SPEAKS

Indulge thy smiling scorn, if smiling still,
  O man! and loathe, but with a sort of love;
    For difference must its use by difference prove,
And, in sweet clang, the spheres with music fill.
One of the spirits am I, that at his will
  Live in whate'er has life—fish, eagle, dove—
    No hate, no pride, beneath nought, nor above,
A visitor of the rounds of God's sweet skill.

Man's life is warm, glad, sad, 'twixt loves and graves,
  Boundless in hope, honoured with pangs austere,
Heaven-gazing; and his angel-wings he craves:—
  The fish is swift, small-needing, vague yet clear,
A cold, sweet, silver life, wrapped in round waves,
  Quickened with touches of transporting fear.

GEORGE GORDON, LORD BYRON (1788—1824)

The poet and the world

I have not loved the world, nor the world me;
I have not flattered its rank breath, nor bowed
To its idolatries a patient knee,—
Nor coined my cheek to smiles,—nor cried aloud
In worship of an echo; in the crowd
They could not deem me one of such; I stood
Among them, but not of them; in a shroud
Of thoughts which were not their thoughts, and still could,
Had I not filed my mind, which thus itself subdued.

I have not loved the world, nor the world me,—
But let us part fair foes; I do believe,
Though I have found them not, that there may be
Words which are things,—hopes which will not deceive,
And virtues which are merciful, nor weave
Snares for the failing: I would also deem
O'er others' griefs that some sincerely grieve;
That two, or one, are almost what they seem,—
That goodness is no name, and happiness no dream.

From *Childe Harold's Pilgrimage*

Haidee

One of the two according to your choice,
Woman or wine, you'll have to undergo,
Both maladies are taxes on our joys:
But which to choose I really hardly know;
And if I had to give a casting voice,
For both sides I could many reasons show,
And then decide, without great wrong to either,
It were much better to have both than neither.

Juan and Haidee gazed upon each other
With swimming looks of speechless tenderness,
Which mixed all feelings, friend, child, lover, brother,
All that the best can mingle and express,
When two pure hearts are poured in one another,
And love too much, and yet can not love less;
But almost sanctify the sweet excess,
By the immortal wish and power to bless.

Mixed in each other's arms, and heart in heart,
Why did they not then die?—they had lived too long.
Should an hour come to bid them breathe apart;
Years could not bring them cruel things or wrong;
The world was not for them, nor the world's art
For beings passionate as Sappho's song:
Love was born *with* them, *in* them, so intense,
It was their very spirit—not a sense.

They should have lived together deep in woods,
Unseen as sings the nightingale; they were
Unfit to mix in these thick solitudes
Called social, haunts of Hate, and Vice, and Care:
How lonely every freeborn creature broods!
The sweetest song-birds nestle in a pair:
The eagle soars alone; the gull and crow
Flock o'er their carrion, just like men below.

Now pillowed cheek to cheek, in loving sleep,
Haidee and Juan their siesta took,
A gentle slumber, but it was not deep,

For ever and anon a something shook
Juan, and shuddering o'er his frame would creep;
And Haidee's sweet lips murmured like a brook,
A wordless music, and her face so fair
Stirred with her dreams, as rose-leaves with the air.

Or as the stirring of a deep clear stream
Within an Alpine hollow, when the wind
Walks o'er it, was she shaken by the dream,
The mysterious usurper of the mind—
O'erpowering use to be whate'er may seem
Good to the soul which we no more can bind;
Strange state of being! (for 'tis still to be)
Senseless to feel, and with sealed eyes to see.

She dreamed of being alone on the sea shore,
Chained to a rock; she knew not how, but stir
She could not from the spot, and the loud roar
Grew, and each wave rose roughly, threatening her;
And o'er her upper lip they seemed to pour
Until she sobbed for breath, and soon they were
Foaming o'er her lone head, so fierce and high—
Each broke to drown her, yet she could not die.

Anon—she was released, and then she strayed
O'er the sharp shingles with her bleeding feet,
And stumbled almost every step she made:
And something rolled before her in a sheet
Which she must still pursue, howe'er afraid;
'Twas white and indistinct, nor stopped to meet
Her glance or grasp, for still she gazed, and grasped,
And ran, but it escaped her as she clasped.

The dream changed;—in a cave she stood, its walls
Were hung with marble icicles; the work
Of ages on its water-fretted halls,
Where waves might wash, and seals might breed and lurk;
Her hair was dripping and the very balls
Of her black eyes seemed turned to tears, and murk
The sharp rocks looked below each drop they caught,
Which froze to marble as it fell,—she thought.

And wet, and cold, and lifeless, at her feet,
Pale as the foam that frothed on his dead brow,
Which she essayed in vain to clear, (how sweet
Were once her cares, how idle seemed they now!)
Lay Juan, nor could aught renew the beat
Of his quenched heart; and the sea-dirges low
Rang in her sad ears like a mermaid's song,
And that brief dream appeared a life too long.

And gazing on the dead, she thought his face
Faded, or altered into something new—
Like to her father's features, till each trace
More like and like to Lambro's aspect grew—
With all his keen worn look and Grecian grace;
And starting, she awoke, and what to view?
O powers of heaven (what dark eye meets she there)
'Tis—'tis her father's—fixed upon the pair!

Then shrieking, she arose, and shrieking fell,
With joy and sorrow, hope and fear, to see
Him whom she deemed a habitant where dwell
The ocean-buried, risen from death, to be
Perchance the death of one she loved too well:
Dear as a father had been to Haidee,
It was a moment of that awful kind—
I have seen much—but must not call to mind.

Up Juan sprung to Haidee's bitter shriek,
And caught her falling, and from off the wall
Snatched down his sabre, in hot haste to wreak
Vengeance on him who was the cause of all:
Then Lambro, who till now forbore to speak,
Smiled scornfully, and said, 'Within my call,
A thousand scimitars await the word;
Put up, young man, put up your silly sword.'

And Haidee clung around him; 'Juan, 'tis—
'Tis Lambro—'tis my father! Kneel with me—
He will forgive us—yes—it must be—yes.
O dearest father, in this agony
Of pleasure and of pain—even while I kiss

Thy garment's hem with transport, can it be
That doubt should mingle with my filial joy?
Deal with me as thou wilt, but spare this boy.'

High and inscrutable the old man stood,
Calm in his voice, and calm within his eye—
Not always signs with him of calmest mood:
He looked upon her, but gave no reply;
Then turned to Juan, in whose cheek the blood
Oft came and went, as there resolved to die,
In arms, at least, he stood in act to spring
On the first foe whom Lambro's call might bring.

From *Don Juan*

Poet's credo

If ever I should condescend to prose,
    I'll write poetical commandments, which
Shall supersede beyond all doubt all those
    That went before; in these I shall enrich
My text with many things that no one knows,
    And carry precept to the highest pitch:
I'll call the work 'Longinus o'er Bottle;
Or, Every Poet his *own* Aristotle.'

Thou shalt believe in Milton, Dryden, Pope;
    Thou shalt not set up Wordsworth, Coleridge, Southey;
Because the first is crazed beyond all hope,
    The second drunk, the third so quaint and mouthy:
With Crabbe it may be different to cope,
    And Campbell's Hippocrene is somewhat drouthy:
Thou shalt not steal from Samuel Rogers, nor
Commit—flirtation with the muse of Moore.

Thou shalt not covet Mr. Sotheby's muse,
    His Pegasus, nor anything that's his;
Thou shalt not bear false witness like 'the Blues'—
    (There's one, at least, is very fond of this);
Thou shalt not write, in short, but what I choose;
    This is true criticism, and you may kiss—
Exactly as you please, or not—the rod;
But if you don't, I'll lay it on, by G-d!

From *Don Juan*

Italy

With all its sinful doings, I must say,
That Italy's a pleasant place to me,
Who love to see the Sun shine every day,
And vines (not nailed to walls) from tree to tree
Festooned, much like the back scene of a play,
Or melodrame, which people flock to see,
When the first act is ended by a dance
In vineyards copied from the south of France.

I like on Autumn evenings to ride out,
Without being forced to bid my groom be sure
My cloak is round his middle strapped about,
Because the skies are not the most secure;
I know too that, if stopped upon my route,
Where the green alleys windingly allure,
Reeling with grapes red waggons choke the way,—
In England 'twould be dung, dust, or a dray.

I also like to dine on becaficas,
To see the Sun set, sure he'll rise to-morrow,
Not through a misty morning, twinkling weak as
A drunken man's dead eye in maudlin sorrow,
But with all Heaven t'himself; that day will break as
Beauteous as cloudless, not be forced to borrow
That sort of farthing candlelight which glimmers
Where reeking London's smoky caldron simmers.

I love the language, that soft bastard Latin,
Which melts like kisses from a female mouth,
And sounds as if it should be writ on satin,
With syllables which breathe of the sweet South,
And gentle liquids gliding all so pat in,
That not a single accent seems uncouth,
Like our harsh northern whistling, grunting guttural,
Which we're obliged to hiss, and spit, and sputter all.

I like the women too (forgive my folly),
From the rich peasant cheek of ruddy bronze,
And large black eyes that flash on you a volley
Of rays that say a thousand things at once,

To the high dame's brow, more melancholy,
But clear, and with a wild and liquid glance,
Heart on her lips, and soul within her eyes,
Soft as her clime, and sunny as her skies.

From *Beppo*

PERCY BYSSHE SHELLEY (1792—1822)

Ever as we sailed

. . . like gossamer
On the swift breath of morn, the vessel flew
O'er the bright whirlpools of that fountain fair,
Whose shores receded fast, whilst we seemed lingering there;

Till down that mighty stream, dark, calm, and fleet,
Between a chasm of cedarn mountains riven,
Chased by the thronging winds whose viewless feet
As swift as twinkling beams, had, under Heaven,
From woods and waves wild sounds and odours driven,
The boat fled visibly—three nights and days,
Borne like a cloud through morn, and noon, and even,
We sailed along the winding watery ways
Of the vast stream, a long and labyrinthine maze.

A scene of joy and wonder to behold
That river's shapes and shadows changing ever,
When the broad sunrise filled with deepening gold
Its whirlpools, where all hues did spread and quiver;
And where melodious falls did burst and shiver
Among rocks clad with flowers, the foam and spray
Sparkled like stars upon the sunny river,
Or when the moon light poured a holier day,
One vast and glittering lake around green islands lay.

Morn, noon, and even, that boat of pearl outran
The streams which bore it, like the arrowy cloud
Of tempest, or the speedier thought of man,
Which flieth forth and cannot make abode;
Sometimes through forests, deep like night, we glode,

Between the walls of mighty mountains crowned
With Cyclopean piles, whose turrets proud,
The homes of the departed, dimly frowned
O'er the bright waves which girt their dark foundations round.

Sometimes between the wide and flowering meadows,
Mile after mile we sailed, and 'twas delight
To see far off the sunbeams chase the shadows
Over the grass; sometimes beneath the night
Of wide and vaulted caves, whose roofs were bright
With starry gems, we fled, whilst from their deep
And dark-green chasms, shades beautiful and white,
Amid sweet sounds across our path would sweep,
Like swift and lovely dreams that walk the waves of sleep.

And ever as we sailed, our minds were full
Of love and wisdom, which would overflow
In converse wild, and sweet, and wonderful,
And in quick smiles whose light would come and go
Like music o'er wide waves, and in the flow
Of sudden tears, and in the mute caress—
For a deep shade was cleft, and we did know,
That virtue, though obscured on Earth, not less
Survives all mortal change in lasting loveliness.

Three days and nights we sailed, as thought and feeling
Number delightful hours—for through the sky
The sphered lamps of day and night, revealing
New changes and new glories, rolled on high,
Sun, moon, and moonlike lamps, the progeny
Of a diviner Heaven, serene and fair;
Of the fourth day, wild as a windwrought sea
The stream became, and fast and faster bare
The spirit-winged boat, steadily speeding there.

Steady and swift, where the waves rolled like mountains
Within the ravine, whose rifts did pour
Tumultuous floods from their ten thousand fountains,
The thunder of whose earth-uplifting roar
Made the air sweep in whirlwinds from the shore,
Calm as a shade, the boat of that fair child

I

Securely fled, that rapid stress before,
Amid the topmost spray, and sunbows wild,
Wreathed in the silver mist; in joy and pride we smiled.

The torrent of that wide and raging river
Is passed, and our aereal speed suspended.
We look behind; a golden mist did quiver
Where its wild surges with the lake were blended,—
Our bark hung there, as on a line suspended
Between two heavens,—that windless waveless lake
Which four great cataracts from four vales, attended
By mists, aye feed; from rocks and clouds they break,
And of that azure sea a silent refuge make.

Motionless resting on the lake awhile,
I saw its marge of snow-bright mountains rear
Their peaks aloft, I saw each radiant isle,
And in the midst, afar, even like a sphere
Hung in one hollow sky did there appear
The temple of the Spirit; on the sound
Which issued thence, drawn nearer and more near,
Like the swift moon this glorious earth around,
The charmed boat approached, and there its haven found.

From *The Revolt of Islam*

Who reigns?

Who reigns? There was the Heaven and Earth at first,
And Light and Love; then Saturn, from whose throne
Time fell, an envious shadow: such the state
Of the earth's primal spirits beneath his sway,
As the calm joy of flowers and living leaves
Before the wind or sun has withered them
And semivital worms; but he refused
The birthright of their being, knowledge, power,
Which pierces this dim universe like light,
Self-empire, and the majesty of love;
For thirst of which they fainted. Then Prometheus
Gave wisdom, which is strength, to Jupiter,
And with this law alone, 'Let man be free',
Clothed him with the dominion of wide Heaven.

To know nor faith, nor love, nor law; to be
Omnipotent but friendless is to reign;
And Jove now reigned; for on the race of man
First famine, and then toil, and then disease,
Strife, wounds, and ghastly death unseen before,
Fell; and the unseasonable seasons drove
With alternating shafts of frost and fire,
Their shelterless, pale tribes to mountain caves:
And in their desert hearts fierce wants he sent,
And mad disquietudes, and shadows idle
Of unreal good, which levied mutual war,
So ruining the lair wherein they raged.
Prometheus saw, and waked the legioned hopes
Which sleep within folded Elysian flowers,
Nepenthe, Moly, Amaranth, fadeless blooms,
That they might hide with thin and rainbow wings
The shape of Death; and love he sent to bind
The disunited tendrils of that vine
Which bears the wine of life, the human heart;
And he tamed fire which, like some beast of prey,
Most terrible, but lovely, played beneath
The frown of man; and tortured to his will
Iron and gold, the slaves and signs of power,
And gems and poisons, and all subtlest forms
Hidden beneath the mountains and the waves.
He gave man speech, and speech created thought,
Which is the measure of the universe;
And Science struck the thrones of earth and heaven,
Which shook, but fell not; and the harmonious mind
Poured itself forth in all-prophetic song;
And music lifted up the listening spirit
Until it walked, exempt from mortal care,
Godlike, o'er the clear billows of sweet sound;
And human hands first mimicked and then mocked,
With moulded limbs more lovely than its own,
The human form, till marble grew divine;
And mothers, gazing, drank the love men see
Reflected in their race, behold, and perish.
He told the hidden power of herbs and springs,
And Disease drank and slept. Death grew like sleep.
He taught the implicated orbits woven

Of the wide-wandering stars; and how the sun
Changes his lair, and by what secret spell
The pale moon is transformed, when her broad eye
Gazes not on the interlunar sea:
He taught to rule, as life directs the limbs,
The tempest-winged chariots of the Ocean,
And the Celt knew the Indian. Cities then
Were built, and through their snow-like columns flowed
The warm winds, and the azure aether shone,
And the blue sea and shadowy hills were seen.
Such, the alleviations of his state,
Prometheus gave to man, for which he hangs
Withering in destined pain: but who rains down
Evil, the immedicable plague, which, while
Man looks on his creation like a God
And sees that it is glorious, drives him on,
The wreck of his own will, the scorn of earth,
The outcast, the abandoned, the alone?
Not Jove: while yet his frown shook Heaven, ay, when
His adversary from adamantine chains
Cursed him, he trembled like a slave. Declare
Who is his master? Is he too a slave?

From *Prometheus Unbound*

Sonnet: England in 1819

An old, mad, blind, despised, and dying king,—
Princes, the dregs of their dull race, who flow
Through public scorn,—mud from a muddy spring,—
Rulers who neither see, nor feel, nor know,
But leech-like to their fainting country cling,
Till they drop, blind in blood, without a blow,—
A people starved and stabbed in the untilled field,—
An army, which liberticide and prey
Makes as a two-edged sword to all who wield,—
Golden and sanguine laws which tempt and slay;
Religion Christless, Godless—a book sealed;
A Senate,—Time's worse statute unrepealed,—
Are graves, from which a glorious Phantom may
Burst, to illumine our tempestuous day.

To ———

Music, when soft voices die,
Vibrates in the memory—
Odours, when sweet violets sicken,
Live within the sense they quicken.

Rose leaves, when the rose is dead,
Are heaped for the beloved's bed;
And so thy thoughts, when thou art gone,
Love itself shall slumber on.

The Final Chorus

The world's great age begins anew,
The golden years return,
The earth doth like a snake renew
Her winter weeds outworn:
Heaven smiles, and faiths and empires gleam
Like wrecks of a dissolving dream.

A brighter Hellas rears its mountains
From waves serener far;
A new Peneus rolls his fountains
Against the morning star;
Where fairer Tempes bloom, there sleep
Young Cyclads on a sunnier deep.

A loftier Argo cleaves the main,
Fraught with a later prize;
Another Orpheus sings again,
And loves, and weeps, and dies;
A new Ulysses leaves once more
Calypso for his native shore.

Oh! write no more the Tale of Troy,
If earth Death's scroll must be!
Nor mix with Laian rage the joy
Which dawns upon the free,
Although a subtler sphinx renew
Riddles of death Thebes never knew.

Another Athens shall arise,
And to remoter time
Bequeath, like sunset to the skies,
The splendour of its prime;
And leave, if nought so bright may live,
All earth can take or heaven can give.

Saturn and Love their long repose
Shall burst, more bright and good
Than all who fell, than one who rose,
Than many unsubdued:
Not gold, not blood, their altar dowers,
But votive tears and symbol flowers.

Oh cease! must hate and death return?
Cease! must men kill and die?
Cease! drain not to its dregs the urn
Of bitter prophecy.
The world is weary of the past,
Oh might it die or rest at last!

From Hellas

JOHN CLARE (1793—1864)

Noon

All how silent and how still,
Nothing heard but yonder mill;
While the dazzled eye surveys
All around a liquid blaze;
And amid the scorching gleams,
If we earnest look, it seems
As if crooked bits of glass
Seemed repeatedly to pass.
Oh, for a puffing breeze to blow
But breezes are all strangers now
Not a twig is seen to shake
Nor the smallest bent to quake
From the river's muddy side
Not a curve is seen to glide;

And no longer on the stream
Watching lies the silver bream,
Forcing, from repeated springs,
'Verges in successive rings.'
Bees are faint, and cease to hum;
Birds are overpowered and dumb.
Rural voices all are mute,
Tuneless lie the pipe and flute;
Shepherds, with their panting sheep,
In the swaliest corner creep;
And from the tormenting heat
All are wishing to retreat.
Huddled in grass and flowers,
Mowers wait for cooler hours;
And the cow-boy seeks the sedge,
Ramping in the woodland hedge,
While his cattle o'er the vales
Scamper, with uplifted tails;
Others not so wild and mad,
That can better bear the gad,
Underneath the hedgerow lunge,
Or, if nigh, in waters plunge.
Oh! to see how flowers are took,
How it grieves me when I look:
Ragged-robins, once so pink,
Now are turned as black as ink,
And the leaves, being scorched so much,
Even crumble at the touch;
Drowking lies the meadow-sweet,
Flopping down beneath one's feet;
While to all the flowers that blow,
If in open air they grow,
Th'injurious deed alike is done
By the hot relentless sun.
E'en the dew is parched up
From the teasel's jointed cup:
O poor birds! where must ye fly,
Now your water-pots are dry?
If ye stay upon the heath,
Ye'll be choked and clammed to death:
Therefore leave the shadeless goss,

Seek the spring-head lined with moss;
There your little feet may stand,
Safely printing on the sand;
While, in full possession, where
Purling eddies ripple clear,
You with ease and plenty blest,
Sip the coolest and the best.
Then away! and wet your throats;
Cheer me with your warbling notes;
'Twill hot noon the more revive;
While I wander to contrive
For myself a place as good,
In the middle of a wood:
There aside some mossy bank,
Where the grass in bunches rank
Lifts its down on spindles high,
Shall be where I'll choose to lie;
Fearless of the things that creep,
There I'll think, and there I'll sleep,
Caring not to stir at all,
Till the dew begins to fall.

I feel I am

I feel I am, I only know I am,
   And plod upon the earth as dull and void;
Earth's prison chilled my body with its dram
   Of dullness, and my soaring thoughts destroyed.
I fled to solitudes from passion's dream,
   But strife pursued—I only know I am.
I was a being created in the race
   Of men, disdaining bounds of place and time;
A spirit that could travel o'er the space
   Of earth and heaven, like a thought sublime;
Tracing creation, like my Maker free,—
   A soul unshackled like eternity:
Spurning earth's vain and soul-debasing thrall—
But now I only know I am,—that's all.

                   Written in Northampton Asylum

JOHN KEATS (1795—1821)

Sleep and poetry

Stop and consider! life is but a day;
A fragile dew-drop on its perilous way
From a tree's summit; a poor Indian's sleep
While his boat hastens to the monstrous steep
Of Montmorenci. Why so sad a moan?
Life is the rose's hope while yet unblown;
The reading of an ever-changing tale;
The light uplifting of a maiden's veil;
A pigeon tumbling in clear summer air;
A laughing school-boy, without grief or care,
Riding the springy branches of an elm.

O for ten years, that I may overwhelm
Myself in poesy; so I may do the deed
That my soul has to itself decreed.
Then will I pass the countries that I see
In long perspective, and continually
Taste their pure fountains. First the realm I'll pass
Of Flora, and old Pan: sleep in the grass,
Feed upon apples red, and strawberries,
And choose each pleasure that my fancy sees;
Catch the white-handed nymphs in shady places,
To woo sweet kisses from averted faces,—
Play with their fingers, touch their shoulders white
Into a pretty shrinking with a bite
As hard as lips can make it: till agreed,
A lovely tale of human life we'll read.
And one will teach a tame dove how it best
May fan the cool air gently o'er my rest;
Another, bending o'er her nimble tread,
Will set a green robe floating round her head,
And still will dance with ever varied ease,
Smiling upon the flowers and the trees:
Another will entice me on, and on
Through almond blossoms and rich cinnamon;
Till in the bosom of a leafy world
We rest in silence, like two gems upcurled
In the recesses of a pearly shell.

And can I ever bid these joys farewell?
Yes, I must pass them for a nobler life,
Where I may find the agonies, the strife
Of human hearts: for lo! I see afar,
O'ersailing the blue cragginess, a car
And steeds with streamy manes—the charioteer
Looks out upon the winds with glorious fear:
And now the numerous tramplings quiver lightly
Along a huge cloud's ridge; and now with sprightly
Wheel downward come they into fresher skies,
Tipt round with silver from the sun's bright eyes.
Still downward with capacious whirl they glide;
And now I see them on the green-hill's side
In breezy rest among the nodding stalks.
The charioteer with wond'rous gesture talks
To the trees and mountains; and there soon appear
Shapes of delight, of mystery, and fear,
Passing along before a dusky space
Made by some mighty oaks: as they would chase
Some ever-fleeting music on they sweep.
Lo! how they murmur, laugh, and smile, and weep:
Some with upholden hand and mouth severe;
Some with their faces muffled to the ear
Between their arms; some, clear in youthful bloom,
Go glad and smilingly athwart the gloom;
Some looking back, and some with upward gaze;
Yes, thousands in a thousand different ways
Flit onward—now a lovely wreath of girls
Dancing their sleek hair into tangled curls;
And now broad wings. Most awfully intent
The driver of those steeds is forward bent,
And seems to listen: O that I might know
All that he writes with such a hurrying glow.

The visions all are fled—the car is fled
Into the light of heaven, and in their stead
A sense of real things comes doubly strong,
And, like a muddy stream, would bear along
My soul to nothingness: but I will strive
Against all doubtings, and will keep alive
The thought of that same chariot, and the strange
Journey it went.

Life again

O magic sleep! O comfortable bird,
That broodest o'er the troubled sea of the mind
Till it is hushed and smooth! O unconfined
Restraint! imprisoned liberty! great key
To golden palaces, strange minstrelsy,
Fountains grotesque, new trees, bespangled caves,
Echoing grottos, full of tumbling waves
And moonlight; aye, to all the mazy world
Of silvery enchantment!—who, upfurled
Beneath thy drowsy wing a triple hour,
But renovates and lives?—Thus, in the bower,
Endymion was calmed to life again.
Opening his eyelids with a healthier brain,
He said: 'I feel this thine endearing love
All through my bosom: thou art as a dove
Trembling its closed eyes and sleeked wings
About me; and the pearliest dew not brings
Such morning incense from the fields of May,
As do those brighter drops that twinkling stray
From those kind eyes,—the very home and haunt
Of sisterly affection. Can I want
Aught else, aught nearer heaven, than such tears?
Yet dry them up, in bidding hence all fears
That, any longer, I will pass my days
Alone and sad. No, I will once more raise
My voice upon the mountain-heights; once more
Make my horn parley from their foreheads hoar:
Again my trooping hounds their tongues shall loll
Around the breathed boar: again I'll poll
The fair-grown yew tree, for a chosen bow:
And, when the pleasant sun is getting low,
Again I'll linger in a sloping mead
To hear the speckled thrushes, and see feed
Our idle sheep. So be thou cheered sweet,
And, if thy lute is here, softly intreat
My soul to keep in its resolved course.'

From *Endymion*

JOHN KEATS

A sleeping youth

After a thousand mazes overgone,
At last, with sudden step, he came upon
A chamber, myrtle walled, embowered high,
Full of light, incense, tender minstrelsy,
And more of beautiful and strange beside:
For on a silken couch of rosy pride,
In midst of all, there lay a sleeping youth
Of fondest beauty; fonder, in fair sooth,
Than sighs could fathom, or contentment reach:
And coverlids gold-tinted like the peach,
Or ripe October's faded marigolds,
Fell sleek about him in a thousand folds—
Not hiding up an Apollonian curve
Of neck and shoulder, nor the tenting swerve
Of knee from knee, nor ankles pointing light;
But rather, giving them to the filled sight
Officiously. Sideway his face reposed
On one white arm, and tenderly unclosed,
By tenderest pressure, a faint damask mouth
To slumbery pout; just as the morning south
Disparts a dew-lipped rose. Above his head,
Four lily stalks did their white honours wed
To make a coronal; and round him grew
All tendrils green, of every bloom and hue,
Together intertwined and trammelled fresh:
The vine of glossy sprout; the ivy mesh,
Shading its Ethiop berries; and woodbine,
Of velvet leaves and bugle-blooms divine;
Convolvulus in streaked vases flush;
The creeper, mellowing for an autumn blush;
And virgin's bower, trailing airily;
With others of the sisterhood. Hard by,
Stood serene Cupids watching silently.
One, kneeling to a lyre, touched the strings,
Muffling to death the pathos with his wings;
And, ever and anon, uprose to look
At the youth's slumber; while another took
A willow-bough, distilling odorous dew,
And shook it on his hair; another flew

In through the woven roof, and fluttering-wise
Rained violets upon his sleeping eyes.

                              From *Endymion*

*

Hyperion and Saturn

All eyes were on Enceladus's face,
And they beheld, while still Hyperion's name
Flew from his lips up to the vaulted rocks,
A pallid gleam across his features stern:
Not savage, for he saw full many a God
Wroth as himself. He looked upon them all,
And in each face he saw a gleam of light,
But splendider in Saturn's, whose hoar locks
Shone like the bubbling foam about a keel
When the prow sweeps into a midnight cove.
In pale and silver silence they remained,
Till suddenly a splendour, like the morn,
Pervaded all the beetling gloomy steeps,
All the sad spaces of oblivion,
And every gulf, and every chasm old,
And every height, and every sullen depth,
Voiceless, or hoarse with loud tormented streams:
And all the everlasting cataracts
And all the headlong torrents far and near,
Mantled before in darkness and huge shade,
Now saw the light and made it terrible.
It was Hyperion:—a granite peak
His bright feet touched, and there he stayed to view
The misery his brilliance had betrayed
To the most hateful seeing of itself.
Golden his hair of short Numidian curl,
Regal his shape majestic, a vast shade
In midst of his own brightness, like the bulk
Of Memnon's image at the set of sun
To one who travels from the dusking East:
Sighs, too, as mournful as that Memnon's harp
He uttered, while his hands contemplative
He pressed together, and in silence stood.
Despondence seized again the fallen Gods

At sight of the dejected King of Day,
And many hid their faces from the light:
But fierce Enceladus sent forth his eyes
Among the brotherhood; and, at their glare,
Uprose Iapetus, and Creus too,
And Phorcus, sea-born, and together strode
To where he towered on his eminence.
There those four shouted forth old Saturn's name;
Hyperion from the peak loud answered, 'Saturn!'
Saturn sat near the Mother of the Gods,
In whose face was no joy, though all the Gods
Gave from their hollow throats the name of 'Saturn!'

From *Hyperion*

The banquet

Of wealthy lustre was the banquet-room,
Filled with pervading brilliance and perfume:
Before each lucid pannel fuming stood
A censer fed with myrrh and spiced wood,
Each by a sacred tripod held aloft,
Whose slender feet wide-swerved upon the soft
Wool-woofed carpets: fifty wreaths of smoke
From fifty censers their light voyage took
To the high roof, still mimicked as they rose
Along the mirrored walls by twin-clouds odorous.
Twelve sphered tables, by silk seats insphered,
High as the level of a man's breast reared
On libbard's paws, upheld the heavy gold
Of cups and goblets, and the store thrice told
Of Ceres' horn, and, in huge vessels, wine
Come from the gloomy tun with merry shine.
Thus loaded with a feast the tables stood,
Each shrining in the midst the image of a God.

When in an antichamber every guest
Had felt the cold full sponge to pleasure pressed,
By minist'ring slaves, upon his hands and feet,
And fragrant oils with ceremony meet
Poured on his hair, they all moved to the feast

In white robes, and themselves in order placed
Around the silken couches, wondering
Whence all this mighty cost and blaze of wealth could spring.

Soft went the music the soft air along,
While fluent Greek a vowelled undersong
Kept up among the guests, discoursing low
At first, for scarcely was the wine at flow;
But when the happy vintage touched their brains,
Louder they talk, and louder come the strains
Of powerful instruments:—the gorgeous dyes,
The space, the splendour of the draperies,
The roof of awful richness, nectarous cheer,
Beautiful slaves, and Lamia's self, appear,
Now, when the wine has done its rosy deed,
And every soul from human trammels freed,
No more so strange; for merry wine, sweet wine,
Will make Elysian shades not too fair, too divine.
Soon was God Bacchus at meridian height;
Flushed were their cheeks, and bright eyes double bright:
Garlands of every green, and every scent
From vales deflowered, or forest-trees branch-rent,
In baskets of bright osiered gold were brought
High as the handles heaped, to suit the thought
Of every guest; that each, as he did please,
Might fancy-fit his brows, silk-pillowed at his ease.

                                        From *Lamia*

Sonnet on the sea

It keeps eternal whispering around
Desolate shores, and with its mighty swell
Gluts twice ten thousand caverns, till the spell
Of Hecate leaves them their old shadowy sound.
Often 'tis in such gentle temper found,
That scarcely will the very smallest shell
Be moved for days from where it sometime fell,
When last the winds of Heaven were unbound.
Oh ye! who have your eye-balls vexed and tired,
Feast them upon the wideness of the sea;

JOHN KEATS

Oh ye! whose ears are dinned with uproar rude,
Or fed too much with cloying melody—
Sit ye near some old cavern's mouth, and brood
Until ye start, as if the sea-nymphs quired!

THOMAS HOOD (1799—1845)

The Haunted House

O, very gloomy is the House of Woe,
Where tears are falling while the bell is knelling,
With all the dark solemnities which show
That Death is in the dwelling!

O very, very dreary is the room
Where love, domestic Love, no longer nestles,
But smitten by the common stroke of doom,
The Corpse lies on the trestles!

But House of Woe, and hearse, and sable pall,
The narrow home of the departed mortal,
Ne'er looked so gloomy as that Ghostly Hall,
With its deserted portal!

The centipede along the threshold crept,
The cobweb hung across in mazy tangle,
And in its winding-sheet the maggot slept,
At every nook and angle.

The keyhold lodged the earwig and her brood,
The emmets of the steps had old possession,
And marched in search of their diurnal food
In undisturbed procession.

As undisturbed as the prehensile cell
Of moth or maggot, or the spider's tissue,
For never foot upon that threshold fell,
To enter or to issue.

O'er all there hung the shadow of a fear,
A sense of mystery the spirit daunted,
And said, as plain as whisper in the ear,
The place is Haunted . . .

Some tale that might, perchance, have solved the doubt,
Wherefore amongst those flags so dull and livid,
The banner of the Bloody Hand shone out
So ominously vivid . . .

If but a rat had lingered in the house,
To lure the thought into a social channel!
But not a rat remained, or tiny mouse,
To squeak behind the panel.

Huge drops rolled down the walls, as if they wept;
And where the cricket used to chirp so shrilly,
The toad was squatting, and the lizard crept
On that damp hearth and chilly.

For years no cheerful blaze had sparkled there,
Or glanced on coat of buff or knightly metal;
The slug was crawling on the vacant chair,—
The snail upon the settle.

The floor was redolent of mould and must,
The fungus in the rotten seams had quickened;
While on the oaken table coats of dust
Perennially had thickened.

No mark of leathern jack or metal can,
No cup—no horn—no hospitable token—
All social ties between that board and Man
Had long ago been broken.

There was so foul a rumour in the air,
The shadow of a Presence so atrocious;
No human creature could have feasted there,
Even the most ferocious.

For over all there hung a cloud of fear,
A sense of mystery the spirit daunted,
And said, as plain as whisper in the ear,
The place is Haunted!

WINTHROP MACKWORTH PRAED (1802—1839)

Fairy song

He has conned the lesson now;
    He has read the book of pain:
There are furrows on his brow;
    I must make it smooth again.

Lo! I knock the spurs away;
    Lo! I loosen belt and brand;
Hark! I hear the courser neigh
    For his stall in Fairy-land.

Bring the cap, and bring the vest;
    Buckle on his sandal shoon;
Fetch his memory from the chest
    In the treasury of the moon.

I have taught him to be wise
    For a little maiden's sake;—
Lo! he opens his glad eyes,
    Softly, slowly: Minstrel, wake!

JAMES CLARENCE MANGAN (1803—1849)

Gone in the wind

An adaptation from Rückert

Solomon! where is thy throne? It is gone in the wind.
Babylon! where is thy might? It is gone in the wind.
Like the swift shadows of noon, like the dreams of the blind,
Vanish the glories and pomps of the earth in the wind.

Man! canst thou build upon aught in the pride of thy mind?
Wisdom will teach thee that nothing can tarry behind;
Though there be thousand bright actions embalmed and enshrined,
Myriads and millions of brighter are snow in the wind.

Solomon! where is thy throne? It is gone in the wind.
Babylon! where is thy might? It is gone in the wind.
All that the genius of Man hath achieved or designed
Waits but its hour to be dealt with as dust by the wind.

Say, what is Pleasure? A phantom, a mask undefined;
Science? An almond, whereof we can pierce but the rind;
Honour and Affluence? Firmans that Fortune hath signed
Only to glitter and pass on the wings of the wind.

Solomon! where is thy throne? It is gone in the wind.
Babylon! where is thy might? It is gone in the wind.
Who is the Fortunate? He who in anguish hath pined!
He shall rejoice when his relics are dust in the wind!

Mortal! be careful with what thy best hopes are entwined;
Woe to the miners for Truth—where the Lampless have mined!
Woe to the seekers on earth for—what none ever find!
They and their trust shall be scattered like leaves on the wind.

Solomon! where is thy throne? It is gone in the wind.
Babylon! where is thy might? It is gone in the wind.
Happy in death are they only whose hearts have consigned
All earth's affections and longings and cares to the wind.

Pity, thou, reader! the madness of poor Humankind,
Raving of Knowledge,—and Satan so busy to blind!
Raving of Glory—like me,—for the garlands I bind
(Garlands of song) are but gathered, and—strewn in the wind!

Solomon! where is thy throne? It is gone in the wind.
Babylon! where is thy might? It is gone in the wind.
I, Abul-Namez, must rest; for my fire hath declined,
And I hear voices from Hades like bells on the wind.

O'Hussey's ode to the Maguire

Where is my Chief, my Master, this bleak night, *mavrone*!
O, cold, cold, miserably cold is this bleak night for Hugh,
It's showery, arrowy, speary sleet pierceth one through and through,
Pierceth one to the very bone!

Rolls real thunder? Or was that red, livid light
Only a meteor? I scarce know; but through the midnight dim
The pitiless ice-wind streams. Except the hate that persecutes *him*
Nothing hath crueller venomy might.

An awful, a tremendous night is this, meseems!
The flood-gates of the rivers of heaven, I think, have been burst wide-
Down from the overcharged clouds, like unto headlong ocean's tide,
Descends grey rain in roaring streams.

Though he were even a wolf ranging the round green woods,
Though he were even a pleasant salmon in the unchainable sea,
Though he were a wild mountain eagle, he could scarce bear, he,
This sharp, sore sleet, these howling floods.

O, mournful is my soul this night for Hugh Maguire!
Darkly, as in a dream, he strays! Before him and behind
Triumphs the tyrannous anger of the wounding wind,
The wounding wind, that burns as fire!

It is my bitter grief—it cuts me to the heart—
That in the country of Clan Darry this should be his fate!
O, woe is me, where is he? Wandering, houseless, desolate,
Alone, without or guide or chart!

Medreams I see just now his face, the strawberry bright,
Uplifted to the blackened heavens, while the tempestuous winds
Blow fiercely over and round him, and the smiting sleet-shower blinds
The hero of Galang to-night!

Large, large affliction unto me and mine it is,
That one of his majestic bearing, his fair, stately form,
Should thus be tortured and o'erborne—that this unsparing storm
Should wreak its wrath on head like his!

That his great hand, so oft the avenger of the oppressed,
Should this chill, churlish night, perchance, be paralysed by frost—
While through some icicle-hung thicket—as one lorn and lost—
He walks and wanders without rest.

The tempest-driven torrent deluges the mead,
It overflows the low banks of the rivulets and ponds—
The lawns and pasture-grounds lie locked in icy bonds
So that the cattle cannot feed.

The pale bright margins of the streams are seen by none.
Rushes and sweeps along the untamable flood on every side—
It penetrates and fills the cottagers' dwellings far and wide—
Water and land are blent in one.

Through some dark woods, 'mid bones of monsters, Hugh now strays,
As he confronts the storm with anguished heart, but manly brow—
O! what a sword-wound to that tender heart of his were now
A backward glance at peaceful days.

But other thoughts are his—thoughts that can still inspire
With joy and an onward-bounding hope the bosom of MacNee—
Thoughts of his warriors charging like bright billows of the sea,
Borne on the wind's wings, flashing fire!

And though frost glaze to-night the clear dew of his eyes,
And white ice-gauntlets glove his noble fine fair fingers o'er,
A warm dress is to him that lightning-garb he ever wore,
The lightning of the soul, not skies.

Avran

Hugh marched forth to the fight—I grieved to see him so depart;
And lo! to-night he wanders frozen, rain-drenched, sad, betrayed—
But the memory of the lime-white mansions his right hand hath laid
In ashes warms the hero's heart!

From the Irish

EDWARD FITZGERALD (1809—1883)

Quatrains

A book of Verses underneath the Bough,
A Jug of Wine, a Loaf of Bread—and Thou
   Beside me singing in the Wilderness—
O, Wilderness were Paradise enow!

Some for the Glories of This World; and some
Sigh for the Prophet's Paradise to come;
   Ah, take the Cash, and let the Credit go,
Nor heed the rumble of a distant Drum!

Think, in this battered Caravanserai
Whose Portals are alternate Night and Day,
   How Sultan after Sultan with his Pomp
Abode his destined Hour, and went his way.

They say the Lion and the Lizard keep
The Courts were Jamshyd gloried and drank deep:
   And Bahram, that great Hunter—the wild Ass
Stamps o'er his Head, but cannot break his Sleep.

I sometimes think that never blows so red
The Rose as where some buried Cæsar bled;
   That every Hyacinth the Garden wears
Dropt in her lap from some once lovely Head.

From *Rubaiyat of Omar Khayyam*

ALFRED, LORD TENNYSON (1809—1892)

The deep dark night

The mighty waste of moaning waters lay
So goldenly in moonlight, whose clear lamp
With its long line of vibratory lustre
Trembled on the dun surface, that my Spirit
Was buoyant with rejoicings. Each hoar wave
With crisped undulation arching rose,
Thence falling in white ridge with sinuous slope
Dashed headlong to the shore and spread along
The sands its tender fringe of creamy spray.

Thereat my shallop lightly I unbound,
Spread my white sail and rode exulting on
The placid murmurings of each feathery wave
That hurried into sparkles round the cleaving
Of my dark Prow; but scarcely had I past
The third white line of breakers when a squall
Fell on me from the North, an inky Congress
Of the Republican clouds unto the zenith
Rushed from the horizon upwards with the speed
Of their own thunder-bolts.
The seas divided and dim Phantasies
Came thronging thickly round me, with hot eyes
Unutterable things flitting by me;
Semblance of palpability was in them,
Albeit the wavering lightnings glittered through
Their shadowed immaterialities.
Black shapes clung to my boat; a sullen owl
Perched on the Prow, and overhead the hum
As of infernal Spirits in mid Heaven
Holding aerial council caught mine ear.
Then came a band of melancholy sprites,
White as their shrouds and motionlessly pale
Like some young Ashwood when the argent Moon
Looks in upon its many silver stems.
And thrice my name was syllabled in the air
And thrice upon the wave, like that loud voice
Which through the deep dark night in the olden time
Came sounding o'er the lone Ionian.

From *The Devil and the Lady* (written at the age of fourteen)

Fatima

O Love, Love, Love! O withering might!
O sun, that from thy noonday height
Shudderest when I strain my sight,
Throbbing through all thy heat and light,
   Lo, falling from my constant mind,
    Lo, parched and withered, deaf and blind,
    I whirl like leaves in roaring wind.

Last night I wasted hateful hours
Below the city's eastern towers:
I thirsted for the brooks, the showers:
I rolled among the tender flowers:
   I crushed them on my breast, my mouth:
   I looked athwart the burning drouth
   Of that long desert to the south.

Last night, when some one spoke his name,
From my swift blood that went and came
A thousand little shafts of flame
Were shivered in my narrow frame.
   O Love, O fire! once he drew
   With one long kiss my whole soul through
   My lips, as sunlight drinketh dew.

Before he mounts the hill, I know
He cometh quickly: from below
Sweet gales, as from deep gardens, blow
Before him, striking on my brow.
   In my dry brain my spirit soon,
   Down-deepening from swoon to swoon,
   Faints like a dazzled morning moon.

The wind sounds like silver wire,
And from beyond the noon a fire
Is poured upon the hills, and nigher
The skies stoop down in their desire;
   And, isled in sudden seas of light,
   My heart, pierced through with fierce delight,
   Bursts into blossom in his sight.

My whole soul waiting silently,
All naked in a sultry sky,
Droops blinded with his shining eye:
I *will* possess him or will die.
   I will grow round him in his place,
   Grow, live, die looking on his face,
   Die, dying clasped in his embrace.

Ulysses

It little profits that an idle king,
By this still hearth, among these barren crags,
Matched with an aged wife, I mete and dole
Unequal laws unto a savage race,
That hoard, and sleep, and feed, and know not me.
I cannot rest from travel: I will drink
Life to the lees: all times I have enjoyed
Greatly, have suffered greatly, both with those
That loved me, and alone; on shore, and when
Through scudding drifts the rainy Hyades
Vext the dim sea: I am become a name;
For always roaming with a hungry heart
Much have I seen and known; cities of men
And manners, climates, councils, governments,
Myself not least, but honoured of them all;
And drunk delight of battle with my peers,
Far on the ringing plains of windy Troy.
I am a part of all that I have met;
Yet all experience is an arch wherethrough
Gleams that untravelled world, whose margin fades
For ever and for ever when I move.
How dull it is to pause, to make an end,
To rust unburnished, not to shine in use!
As though to breathe were life. Life piled on life
Were all too little, and of one to me
Little remains: but every hour is saved
From that eternal silence, something more,
A bringer of new things; and vile it were
For some three suns to store and hoard myself,
And this gray spirit yearning in desire
To follow knowledge like a sinking star,
Beyond the utmost bound of human thought.

　　This is my son, mine own Telemachus,
To whom I leave the sceptre and the isle—
Well-loved of me, discerning to fulfil
This labour, by slow prudence to make mild
A rugged people, and through soft degrees
Subdue them to the useful and the good.
Most blameless is he, centred in the sphere
Of common duties, decent not to fail

In offices of tenderness, and pay
Meet adoration to my household gods,
When I am gone. He works his work, I mine.
    There lies the port; the vessel puffs her sail:
There gloom the dark broad seas. My mariners,
Souls that have toiled, and wrought, and thought with me—
That ever with a frolic welcome took
The thunder and the sunshine, and opposed
Free hearts, free foreheads—you and I are old;
Old age hath yet his honour and his toil;
Death closes all: but something ere the end,
Some work of noble note, may yet be done,
Not unbecoming men that strove with Gods.
The lights begin to twinkle from the rocks:
The long day wanes: the slow moon climbs: the deep
Moans round with many voices. Come, my friends,
'Tis not too late to seek a newer world.
Push off, and sitting well in order smite
The sounding furrows; for my purpose holds
To sail beyond the sunset, and the baths
Of all the western stars, until I die.
It may be that the gulfs will wash us down:
It may be we shall touch the Happy Isles,
And see the great Achilles, whom we knew.
Though much is taken, much abides; and though
We are not now that strength which in old days
Moved earth and heaven; that which we are, we are:
One equal temper of heroic hearts,
Made weak by time and fate, but strong in will
To strive, to seek, to find, and not to yield.

Summer night

    Now sleeps the crimson petal, now the white;
Nor waves the cypress in the palace walk;
Nor winks the gold fin in the porphyry font:
The firefly wakens: waken thou with me.

    Now droops the milk white peacock like a ghost,
And like a ghost she glimmers on to me.

Now lies the Earth all Danae to the stars,
And all thy heart lies open unto me.

Now slides the silent meteor on, and leaves
A shining furrow, as thy thoughts in me.

Now folds the lily all her sweetness up,
And slips into the bosom of the lake:
So fold thyself, my dearest, thou, and slip
Into my bosom and be lost in me.

From The Princess

In Memoriam

(*xxxiv*)

My own dim life should teach me this,
   That life shall live for evermore,
   Else earth is darkness at the core,
And dust and ashes all that is;

This round of green, this orb of flame,
   Fantastic beauty; such as lurks
   In some wild poet, when he works
Without a conscience or an aim.

What then were God to such as I?
   'Twere hardly worth my while to choose
   Of things all mortal, or to use
A little patience ere I die;

'Twere best at once to sink to peace,
   Like birds the charming serpent draws,
   To drop head-foremost in the jaws
Of vacant darkness and to cease.

(*lxvii*)

When on my bed the moonlight falls,
   I know that in thy place of rest
   By that broad water of the west,
There comes a glory on the walls:

Thy marble bright in dark appears,
  As slowly steals a silver flame
  Along the letters of thy name,
And o'er the number of thy years.

The mystic glory swims away;
  From off my bed the moonlight dies;
  And closing eaves of wearied eyes
I sleep till dusk is dipt in gray:

And then I know the mist is drawn
  A lucid veil from coast to coast,
  And in the dark church like a ghost
Thy tablet glimmers to the dawn.

(cxx)

I trust I have not wasted breath:
  I think we are not wholly brain,
  Magnetic mockeries; not in vain,
Like Paul with beasts, I fought with Death;

Not only cunning casts in clay:
  Let Science prove we are, and then
  What matters Science unto men,
At least to me? I would not stay.

Let him, the wiser man who springs
  Hereafter, up from childhood shape
  His action like the greater ape,
But I was *born* to other things.

(cxxiii)

There rolls the deep where grew the tree.
  O earth, what changes hast thou seen!
  There where the long street roars, hath been
The stillness of the central sea.

The hills are shadows, and they flow
  From form to form, and nothing stands;
  They melt like mist, the solid lands,
Like clouds they shape themselves and go.

But in my spirit will I dwell,
  And dream my dream, and hold it true;
  For though my lips may breathe adieu,
I cannot think the thing farewell.

The Eagle

He clasps the crag with crooked hands;
Close to the sun in lonely lands,
Ringed with the azure world, he stands.

The wrinkled sea beneath him crawls;
He watches from his mountain walls,
And like a thunderbolt he falls.

To E.L., on his travels in Greece

Illyrian woodlands, echoing falls
  Of water, sheets of summer glass,
  The long divine Peneian pass,
The vast Akrokeraunian walls,

Tomohrit, Athos, all things fair,
  With such a pencil, such a pen,
  You shadow forth to distant men,
I read and felt that I was there:

And trust me while I turned the page,
  And tracked you still on classic ground,
  I grew in gladness till I found
My spirits in the golden age.

For me the torrent ever poured
  And glistened—here and there alone
  The broad-limbed Gods at random thrown
By fountain-urns;—and Naiads oared

A glimmering shoulder under gloom
  Of cavern pillars; on the swell
  The silver lily heaved and fell;
And many a slope was rich in bloom

From him that on the mountain lea
  By dancing rivulets fed his flocks
  To him who sat upon the rocks,
And fluted to the morning sea.

SIR SAMUEL FERGUSON (1810-1886)

Ceann Dubh Deelish

Put your head, darling, darling, darling,
  Your darling black head my heart above;
Oh, mouth of honey, with the thyme for fragrance,
  Who, with heart in breast, could deny you love?
Oh, many and many a young girl for me is pining
  Letting her locks of gold to the cold wind free,
For me, the foremost of our gay young fellows;
  But I'd leave a hundred, pure love, for thee!
Then put your head, darling, darling, darling,
  Your darling black head my heart above;
Oh, mouth of honey, with the thyme for fragrance,
  Who, with heart in breast, could deny you love?

From the Irish

Deidre's lament for the Sons of Usnach

The lions of the hill are gone,
And I am left alone—alone—
Dig the grave both wide and deep,
For I am sick, and fain would sleep!

The falcons of the wood are flown.
And I am left alone—alone
Dig the grave both deep and wide,
And let us slumber side by side.

The dragons of the rock are sleeping,
Sleep that wakes not for our weeping:
Dig the grave and make it ready;
Lay me on my true Love's body.

Lay their spears and bucklers bright
By the warriors' sides aright;
Many a day the three before me
On their linked bucklers bore me.

Lay upon the low grave floor,
'Neath each head, the blue claymore;
Many a time the noble three
Reddened those blue blades for me.

Lay the collars, as is meet,
Of their greyhounds at their feet;
Many a time for me have they
Brought the tall red deer to bay.

Oh! to hear my true love singing,
Sweet as sound of trumpets ringing:
Like the sway of ocean swelling
Rolled his deep voice round our dwelling.

Oh! to hear the echoes pealing
Round our green and fairy sheeling,
When the three, with soaring chorus,
Passed the silent skylark o'er us.

Echo now, sleep, morn and even—
Lark alone enchant the heaven!—
Ardan's lips are scant of breath,—
Neesa's tongue is cold in death.

Stag, exult on glen and mountain—
Salmon, leap from loch to fountain—
Heron, in the free air warm ye—
Usnach's Sons no more will harm ye!

Erin's stay no more you are,
Rulers of the ridge of war;
Never more 'twill be your fate
To keep the beam of battle straight.

Woe is me! by fraud and wrong—
Traitors false and tyrants strong—
Fell Clan Usnach, bought and sold,
For Barach's feast and Conor's gold!

Woe to Eman, roof and wall!—
Woe to Red Branch, hearth and hall!—
Tenfold woe and black dishonour
To the false and foul Clan Conor!

Dig the grave both wide and deep,
Sick I am, and fain would sleep!
Dig the grave and make it ready,
Lay me on my true Love's body.

                                    From the Irish

ROBERT BROWNING (1812—1889)

Meeting at night

The grey sea and the long black land;
And the yellow half-moon large and low;
And the startled little waves that leap
In fiery ringlets from their sleep,
As I gain the cove with pushing prow,
And quench its speed i' the slushy sand.

Then a mile of warm sea-scented beach;
Three fields to cross till a farm appears;
A tap at the pane, the quick sharp scratch
And blue spurt of a lighted match,
And a voice less loud, through its joys and fears,
Than the two hearts beating each to each!

The Englishman in Italy

Time for rain! for your long hot dry Autumn
    Had net-worked with brown
The white skin of each grape on the bunches,
    Marked like a quail's crown,
Those creatures you make such account of,
    Whose heads,—speckled white
Over brown like a great spider's back,
    As I told you last night,—
Your mother bites off for her supper.
    Red-ripe as could be,
Pomegranates were chapping and splitting
    In halves on the tree:
And betwixt the loose walls of great flint-stone,
    Or in the thick dust
On the path, or straight out of the rock-side,
    Wherever could thrust
Some burnt sprig of bold hardy rock-flower
    Its yellow face up,
For the prize were great butterflies fighting,
    Some five for one cup.
So, I guessed, ere I got up this morning,
    What change was in store,
By the quick rustle-down of the quail-nets
    Which woke me before
I could open my shutter, made fast
    With a bough and a stone,
And look through the twisted dead vine-twigs,
    Sole lattice that's known.
Quick and sharp rang the rings down the net-poles,
    While, busy beneath,
Your priest and his brother tugged at them,
    The rain in their teeth.
And out upon all the flat house-roofs
    Where split figs lay drying,
The girls took the frails under cover:
    Nor use seemed in trying
To get out the boats and go fishing,
    For, under the cliff,
Fierce the black water frothed o'er the blind-rock.

J

No seeing our skiff
Arrive about noon from Amalfi,
　—Our fisher arrive,
And pitch down his basket before us,
　All trembling alive
With pink and grey jellies, your sea-fruit;
　You touch the strange lumps,
And mouths gape there, eyes open, all manner
　Of horns and of humps,
Which only the fisher looks grave at,
　While round him like imps
Cling screaming the children as naked
　And brown as his shrimps;
Himself too as bare to the middle
　—You see round his neck
The string and its brass coin suspended,
　That saves him from wreck.
But to-day not a boat reached Salerno,
　So back, to a man,
Came our friends, with whose help in the vineyards
　Grape-harvest began.
In the vat, halfway up in our house-side,
　Like blood the juice spins,
While your brother all bare-legged is dancing
　Till breathless he grins
Dead-beaten in effort on effort
　To keep the grapes under,
Since still when he seems all but master,
　In pours the fresh plunder
From girls who keep coming and going
　With basket on shoulder,
And eyes shut against the rain's driving;
　Your girls that are older,—
For under the hedges of aloe,
　And where, on its bed
Of the orchard's black mould, the love-apple
　Lies pulpy and red,
All the young ones are kneeling and filling
　Their laps with the snails
Tempted out by this first rainy weather,—
　Your best of regales,

As to-night will be proved to my sorrow,
    When, supping in state,
We shall feast our grape-gleaners (two dozen,
    Three over one plate)
With lasagne so tempting to swallow
    In slippery ropes,
And gourds fried in great purple slices,
    That colour of popes.
Meantime, see the grape bunch they've brought you:
    The rain-water slips
O'er the heavy blue bloom on each globe
    Which the wasp to your lips
Still follows with fretful persistence:
    Nay, taste, while awake,
This half of a curd-white smooth cheese-ball
    That peels, flake by flake,
Like an onion, each smoother and whiter;
    Next, sip this weak wine
From the thin green glass flask, with its stopper,
    A leaf of the vine;
And end with the prickly-pear's red flesh
    That leaves through its juice
The stony black seeds on your pearl-teeth.
    Scirocco is loose!
Hark, the quick, whistling pelt of the olives
    Which, thick in one's track,
Tempt the stranger to pick up and bite them,
    Though not yet half black!
How the old twisted olive trunks shudder,
    The medlars let fall
Their hard fruit, and the brittle great fig-trees
    Snap off, figs and all. . . . .

Two in the Campagna

I wonder do you feel today
    As I have felt since, hand in hand,
We sat down on the grass, to stray
    In spirit better through the land,
This morn of Rome and May?

For me, I touched a thought, I know,
   Has tantalized me many times,
(Like turns of thread the spiders throw
   Mocking across our path) for rhymes
To catch at and let go.

Help me to hold it! First it left
   The yellowing fennel, run to seed
There, branching from the brickwork's cleft,
   Some old tomb's ruin: yonder weed
Took up the floating weft,

Where one small orange cup amassed
   Five beetles,—blind and green they grope
Among the honey-meal: and last,
   Everywhere on the grassy slope
I traced it. Hold it fast!

The champaign with its endless fleece
   Of feathery grasses everywhere!
Silence and passion, joy and peace,
   An everlasting wash of air—
Rome's ghost since her decease.

Such life here, through such lengths of hours,
   Such miracles performed in play,
Such primal naked forms of flowers,
   Such letting nature have her way
While heaven looks from its towers!

How say you? Let us, O my dove,
   Let us be unashamed of soul,
As earth lies bare to heaven above!
   How is it under our control
To love or not to love?

I would that you were all to me,
   You that are just so much, no more.
Nor yours nor mine, nor slave nor free!
   Where does the fault lie? What the core
O' the wound, since wound must be?

I would I could adopt your will,
　See with your eyes, and set my heart
Beating by yours, and drink my fill
　At your soul's springs,—your part my part
In life, for good and ill.

No. I yearn upward, touch you close,
　Then stand away. I kiss your cheek,
Catch your soul's warmth,—I pluck the rose
　And love it more than tongue can speak—
Then the good minute goes.

Already how am I so far
　Out of that minute? Must I go
Still like the thistle-ball, no bar,
　Onward, whenever light winds blow,
Fixed by no friendly star?

Just when I seemed about to learn!
　Where is the thread now? Off again!
The old trick! Only I discern—
　Infinite passion, and the pain
Of finite hearts that yearn.

Memorabilia

Ah, did you once see Shelley plain,
　And did he stop and speak to you
And did you speak to him again?
　How strange it seems and new!

But you were living before that,
　And also you are living after;
And the memory I started at—
　My starting moves your laughter.

I crossed a moor, with a name of its own
　And a certain use in the world no doubt,
Yet a hand's-breadth of it shines alone
　'Mid the blank miles round about:

For there I picked up on the heather
And there I put inside my breast
A moulted feather, an eagle-feather!
Well, I forget the rest.

EMILY JANE BRONTE (1818—1848)

I'm happiest when most away

I'm happiest when most away
I can bear my soul from its home of clay
On a windy night when the moon is bright
And the eye can wander through worlds of light—

When I am not and none beside—
No earth nor sea nor cloudless sky—
But only spirit wandering wide
Through infinite immensity.

There let thy bleeding branch atone

There let thy bleeding branch atone
For every torturing tear:
Shall my young sins, my sins alone,
Be everlasting here?

Who bade thee keep that cursed name
A pledge for memory?
As if oblivion ever came
To breathe its bliss on me;

As if, through all the 'wildering maze
Of mad hours left behind,
I once forgot the early days
That thou wouldst call to mind.

ARTHUR HUGH CLOUGH (1819—1861)

So pleasant it is to have money

As I sat at the cafe, I said to myself,
They may talk as they please about what they call pelf,
They may sneer as they like about eating and drinking,
But help it I cannot, I cannot help thinking
   How pleasant it is to have money, heigh ho!
   How pleasant it is to have money.

I sit at my table, *en grand seigneur*,
And when I have done, throw a crust to the poor;
Not only the pleasure, one's self, of good living,
But also the pleasure of now and then giving.
   So pleasant it is to have money, heigh ho!
   So pleasant it is to have money.

It was but last winter I came up to Town,
But already I'm getting a little renown;
I make new acquaintance where'er I appear;
I am not too shy, and have nothing to fear.
   So pleasant it is to have money, heigh ho!
   So pleasant it is to have money.

I drive through the streets, and I care not a damn;
The people they stare, and they ask who I am;
And if I should chance to run over a cad,
I can pay for the damage if ever so bad.
   So pleasant it is to have money, heigh ho!
   So pleasant it is to have money.

We stroll to our box and look down on the pit,
And if it weren't low should be tempted to spit;
We loll and we talk until people look up,
And when it's half over we go out and sup.
   So pleasant it is to have money, heigh ho!
   So pleasant it is to have money.

The best of the tables and the best of the fare—
And as for the others, the devil may care;
It isn't our fault if they dare not afford
To sup like a prince and be drunk as a lord.
   So pleasant it is to have money, heigh ho!
   So pleasant it is to have money.

We sit at our tables and tipple champagne;
Ere one bottle goes, comes another again;
The waiters they skip and they scuttle about,
And the landlord attends us so civilly out.
   So pleasant it is to have money, heigh ho!
   So pleasant it is to have money.

It was but last winter I came up to town,
But already I'm getting a little renown;
I get to good houses without much ado,
Am beginning to see the nobility too.
   So pleasant it is to have money, heigh ho!
   So pleasant it is to have money.

O dear! what a pity they ever should lose it!
For they are the gentry that know how to use it;
So grand and so graceful, such manners, such dinners,
But yet, after all, it is we are the winners.
   So pleasant it is to have money, heigh ho!
   So pleasant it is to have money.

From *Dipsychus*

MATTHEW ARNOLD (1822—1888)

A Summer night

In the deserted, moon-blanched street,
How lonely rings the echo of my feet!
Those windows, which I gaze at, frown,
Silent and white, unopening down,
Repellent as the world;—but see,
A break between the housetops shows
The moon! and, lost behind her, fading dim

Into the dewy dark obscurity
Down at the far horizon's rim,
Doth a whole tract of heaven disclose!

And to my mind the thought
Is on a sudden brought
Of a past night, and a far different scene.
Headlands stood out into the moonlit deep
As clearly as at noon;
The spring-tide's brimming flow
Heaved dazzlingly between;
Houses, with long white sweep,
Girdled the glistening bay;
Behind, through the soft air,
The blue haze-cradled mountains spread away,
That night was far more fair—
But the same restless pacings to and fro,
And the same vainly throbbing heart was there,
And the same bright, calm moon.
And the calm moonlight seems to say:
Hast thou then still the old unquiet breast,
Which neither deadens into rest,
Nor ever feels the fiery glow
That whirls the spirit from itself away,
But fluctuates to and fro,
Never by passion quite possessed
And never quite benumbed by the world's sway?—
And I, I know not if to pray
Still to be what I am, or yield and be
Like all the other men I see.

For most men in a brazen prison live,
Where, in the sun's hot eye,
With heads bent o'er their toil, they languidly
Their lives to some unmeaning taskwork give,
Dreaming of nought beyond their prison-wall.
And as, year after year,
Fresh products of their barren labour fall
From their tired hands, and rest
Never yet comes more near,
Gloom settles slowly down over their breast;

And while they try to stem
The waves of mournful thought by which they are prest,
Death in their prison reaches them,
Unfreed, having seen nothing, still unblest.

And the rest, a few,
Escape their prison and depart
On the wide ocean of life anew.
There the freed prisoner, where'er his heart
Listeth, will sail;
Nor doth he know how there prevail,
Despotic on that sea,
Trade-winds which cross it from eternity.
Awhile he holds some false way, undebarred
By thwarting signs, and braves
The freshening wind and blackening waves.
And then the tempest strikes him; and between
The lightning bursts is seen
Only a driving wreck,
And the pale master on his spar-strewn deck
With anguished face and flying hair
Grasping the rudder hard,
Still bent to make some port he knows not where,
Still standing for some false, impossible shore.
And sterner comes the roar
Of sea and wind, and through the deepening gloom
Fainter and fainter wreck and helmsman loom,
And he too disappears, and comes no more.

Is there no life, but these alone?
Madman or slave, must man be one?

Plainness and clearness without shadow of stain!
Clearness divine!
Ye heavens, whose pure dark regions have no sign
Of languor, though so calm, and, though so great,
Are yet untroubled and unpassionate;
Who, though so noble, share in the world's toil,
And, though so tasked, keep free from dust and soil!
I will not say that your mild deeps retain
A tinge, it may be, of their silent pain

Who have longed deeply once, and longed in vain—
But I will rather say that you remain
A world above man's head, to let him see
How boundless might his soul's horizons be,
How vast, yet of what clear transparency!
How it were good to abide there, and breathe free;
How fair a lot to fill
Is left to each man still!

A dream

Was it a dream? We sailed, I thought we sailed,
Martin and I, down a green Alpine stream,
Under o'erhanging pines; the morning sun,
On the wet umbrage of their glossy tops,
On the red pinings of their forest floor,
Drew a warm scent abroad; behind the pines
The mountain skirts, with all their sylvan change
Of bright-leafed chestnuts, and mossed walnut-trees,
And the frail scarlet-berried ash, began.
Swiss chalets glittered on the dewy slopes,
And from some swarded shelf high up, there came
Notes of wild pastoral music: over all
Ranged, diamond-bright, the eternal wall of snow.
Upon the mossy rocks at the stream's edge,
Backed by the pines, a plank-built cottage stood,
Bright in the sun; the climbing gourd-plant's leaves
Muffled its walls, and on the stone-strewn roof
Lay the warm golden gourds; golden, within,
Under the eaves, peered rows of Indian corn.
We shot beneath the cottage with the stream.
On the brown rude-carved balcony two forms
Came forth—Olivia's, Marguerite! and thine.
Clad were they both in white, flowers in their breast;
Straw hats bedecked their heads, with ribbons blue
Which waved, and on their shoulders, fluttering, played.
They saw us, they conferred; their bosoms heaved,
And more than mortal impulse filled their eyes.
Their lips moved; their white arms, waved eagerly,
Flashed once, like falling streams; we rose, we gazed:
One moment, on the rapid's top, our boat
Hung poised—and then the darting river of Life,

Loud thundering, bore us by: swift, swift it foamed;
Black under cliffs it raced, round headlands shone.
Soon the planked cottage 'mid the sun-warmed pines
Faded, the moss, the rocks; us burning plains
Bristled with cities, as the sea received.

Dover beach

The sea is calm to-night,
The tide is full, the moon lies fair
Upon the Straits;—on the French coast, the light
Gleams, and is gone; the cliffs of England stand,
Glimmering and vast, out in the tranquil bay.
Come to the window, sweet is the night air!
Only, from the long line of spray
Where the sea meets the moon-blanched land,
Listen! you hear the grating roar
Of pebbles which the waves draw back, and fling,
At their return, up the high strand,
Begin, and cease, and then again begin,
With tremulous cadence slow, and bring
The eternal note of sadness in.

Sophocles long ago
Heard it on the Aegean, and it brought
Into his mind the turbid ebb and flow
Of human misery; we
Find also in the sound a thought,
Hearing it by this distant northern sea.

The Sea of Faith
Was once, too, at the full, and round earth's shore
Lay like the folds of a bright girdle furled;
But now I only hear
Its melancholy, long, withdrawing roar,
Retreating, to the breath
Of the night-wind, down the vast edges drear
And naked shingles of the world.

Ah, love, let us be true
To one another! for the world, which seems
To lie before us like a land of dreams,
So various, so beautiful, so new;
Hath really neither joy, nor love, nor light,
Nor certitude, nor peace, nor help for pain;
And we are here as on a darkling plain
Swept with confused alarms of struggle and flight,
Where ignorant armies clash by night.

WILLIAM (JOHNSON) CORY (1823—1892)

Heraclitus

They told me, Heraclitus, they told me you were dead,
They brought me bitter news to hear and bitter tears to shed.
I wept as I remembered how often you and I
Had tired the sun with talking and sent him down the sky.

And now that thou art lying, my dear old Carian guest,
A handful of grey ashes, long long ago at rest,
Still are thy pleasant voices, thy nightingales, awake;
For Death, he taketh all away, but them he cannot take.

COVENTRY PATMORE (1823—1896)

Departure

It was not like your great and gracious ways!
Do you, that have nought other to lament,
Never, my Love, repent
Of how, that July afternoon,
You went,
With sudden, unintelligible phrase,
And frightened eye,
Upon your journey of so many days
Without a single kiss, or a good-bye?
I knew, indeed, that you were parting soon;
And so we sate, within the low sun's rays,
You whispering to me, for your voice was weak,

Your harrowing praise.
Well, it was well
To hear you such things speak,
And I could tell
What made your eyes a growing gloom of love,
As a warm South-wind sombres a March grove.
And it was like your great and gracious ways
To turn your talk on daily things, my Dear,
Lifting the luminous, pathetic lash
To let the laughter flash,
Whilst I drew near,
Because you spoke so low that I could scarcely hear.
But all at once to leave me at the last,
More at the wonder than the loss aghast,
With huddled, unintelligible phrase,
And frightened eye,
And go your journey of all days
With not one kiss, or a good-bye,
And the only loveless look the look with which you passed:
'Twas all unlike your great and gracious ways.

Arbor vitæ

With honeysuckle, over-sweet, festooned;
With bitter ivy bound;
Terraced with funguses unsound;
Deformed with many a boss
And closed scar, o'ercushioned deep with moss;
Bunched all about with pagan mistletoe;
And thick with nests of the hoarse bird
That talks, but understands not his own word;
Stands, and so stood a thousand years ago,
A single tree.
Thunder has done its worst among its twigs,
Where the great crest yet blackens, never pruned,
But in its heart, alway
Ready to push new verdurous boughs, whene'er
The rotting saplings near it fall and leave it air,
Is all antiquity and no decay.
Rich, though rejected by the forest-pigs,
Its fruit, beneath whose rough, concealing rind
They that will break it find

Heart-succouring savour of each several meat,
And kernelled drink of brain-renewing power,
With bitter condiment and sour,
And sweet economy of sweet,
And odours that remind
Of haunts of childhood and a different day.
Beside this tree,
Praising no Gods nor blaming, sans a wish,
Sits, Tartar-like, the Time's civility,
And eats its dead-dog off a golden dish.

WILLIAM ALLINGHAM (1824—1889)

The girl's lamentation

With grief and mourning I sit and spin;
My Love passed by, and he didn't come in;
He passes by me, both day and night,
And carries off my poor heart's delight.

There is a tavern in yonder town,
My Love goes there and he spends a crown;
He takes a strange girl upon his knee,
And never more gives a thought to me.

Says he, 'We'll wed without loss of time,
And sure our love's but a little crime';—
My apron-string now it's wearing short,
And my Love he seeks other girls to court.

O with him I'd go if I had my will,
I'd follow him barefoot o'er rock and hill;
I'd never once speak of all my grief
If he'd give me a smile for my heart's relief.

In our wee garden the rose unfolds,
With bachelor's-buttons and marigolds;
I'll tie no posies for dance or fair,
A willow-twig is for me to wear.

For a maid again I can never be,
Till the red rose blooms on the willow tree.
Of such a trouble I've heard them tell,
And now I know what it means full well.

As through the long lonesome night I lie,
I'd give the world if I might but cry;
But I mus'n't moan there or raise my voice,
And the tears run down without any noise.

And what, O what will my mother say?
She'll wish her daughter was in the clay.
My father will curse me to my face;
The neighbours will know of my black disgrace.

My sister's buried three years, come Lent;
But sure we made far too much lament.
Beside her grave they still say a prayer—
I wish to God 'twas myself was there!

The Candlemas crosses hang near my bed,
To look at them puts me much in dread,
They mark the good time that's gone and past:
It's like this year's one will prove the last.

The oldest cross it's a dusty brown,
But the winter winds didn't shake it down;
The newest cross keeps the colour bright;
When the straw was reaping my heart was light.

Now summer or winter to me it's one;
But oh! for a day like the time that's gone.
I'd little care was it storm or shine,
If I had but peace in this heart of mine.

Oh, light and false is a young man's kiss,
And a foolish girl gives her soul for this.
Oh! light and short is the young man's blame,
And a helpless girl has the grief and shame.

To the river-bank once I thought to go,
And cast myself in the stream below;
I thought 'twould carry us far out to sea,
Where they'd never find my poor babe and me.

Sweet Lord, forgive me that wicked mind!
You know I used to be well-inclined.
Oh, take compassion upon my state,
Because my trouble is so very great.

My head turns round with the spinning-wheel,
And a heavy cloud on my eyes I feel.
But the worst of all is at my heart's core;
For my innocent days will come back no more.

A mill

Two leaps the water from its race
    Made to the brook below,
The first leap it was curving glass,
    The second bounding snow.

DANTE GABRIEL ROSSETTI (1828—1882)

The bride's prelude

Although the lattice had dropped loose,
    There was no wind; the heat
Being so at rest that Amelotte
Heard far beneath the plunge and float
Of a hound swimming in the moat.

Some minutes since, two rooks had toiled
    Home to the nests that crowned
Ancestral ash-trees. Through the glare
Beating again, they seemed to tear
With that thick caw the woof o' the air.

But else, 'twas at the dead of noon
    Absolute silence; all,
From the raised bridge and guarded sconce
To green-clad places of pleasaunce
Where the long lake was white with swans.

Amelotte spoke not any word
    Nor moved she once; but felt
Between her hands in narrow space
Her own hot breath upon her face,
And kept in silence the same place.

Lost on both sides

As when two men have loved a woman well,
    Each hating each, through Love's and Death's deceit;
    Since not for either this stark marriage-sheet
And the long pauses of this wedding-bell;
    Yet o'er her grave the night and day dispel
    At last their feud forlorn, with cold and heat;
    Nor other than dear friends to death may fleet
The two lives left that most of her can tell:—

So separate hopes, which in a soul had wooed
    The one same Peace, strove with each other long,
        And Peace before their faces perished since:
So through that soul, in restless brotherhood,
    They roam together now, and wind among
        Its bye-streets, knocking at the dusty inns.

A superscription

Look in my face; my name is Might-have-been;
    I am also called No-more, Too-late, Farewell;
    Unto thine ear I hold the dead-sea shell
Cast up thy Life's foam-fretted feet between;
Unto thine eyes the glass where that is seen
    Which had Life's form and Love's, but by my spell
    Is now a shaken shadow intolerable,
Of ultimate things unuttered the frail screen.

Mark me, how still I am! But should there dart
  One moment through thy soul the soft surprise
  Of that winged Peace which lulls the breath of sighs,—
Then shalt thou see me smile, and turn apart
Thy visage to mine ambush at thy heart
  Sleepless with cold commemorative eyes.

GEORGE MEREDITH (1828—1909)

Love dies

In our old shipwrecked days there was an hour,
When in the firelight steadily aglow,
Joined slackly, we beheld the red chasm grow
Among the clicking coals. Our library-bower
That eve was left to us; and hushed we sat
As lovers to whom Time is whispering.
From sudden-opened doors we heard them sing:
The nodding elders mixed good wine with chat.
Well knew we that Life's greatest treasure lay
With us, and of it was our talk. 'Ah, yes!
Love dies!' I said: I never thought it less.
She yearned to me that sentence to unsay.
Then when the fire domed blackening, I found
Her cheek was salt against my kiss, and swift
Up the sharp scale of sobs her breast did lift:—
Now am I haunted by that taste! that sound!

From *Modern Love*

A dusty answer

Thus piteously Love closed what he begat:
The union of this ever-diverse pair!
These two were rapid falcons in a snare,
Condemned to do the flitting of the bat.
Lovers beneath the singing sky of May,
They wandered once; clear as the dew on flowers.
But they fed not on the advancing hours:
Their hearts held cravings for the buried day.
Then each applied to each that fatal knife,
Deep questioning, which probes to endless dole.

Ah, what a dusty answer gets the soul
When hot for certainties in this our life!—
In tragic hints here see what evermore
Moves dark as yonder midnight ocean's force,
Thundering like rampant hosts of warrior horse,
To throw that faint thin line upon the shore!

From *Modern Love*

Juggling Jerry

Pitch here the tent, while the old horse grazes:
By the old hedge-side we'll halt a stage.
It's nigh my last above the daisies:
My next leaf'll be man's blank page.
Yes, my old girl! and it's no use crying:
Juggler, constable, king, must bow.
One that outjuggles all's been spying
Long to have me, and he has me now.

We've travelled times to this old common:
Often we've hung our pots in the gorse.
We've had a stirring life, old woman!
You, and I, and the old grey horse.
Races, and fairs, and royal occasions,
Round us coming to their call:
Now they'll miss us at our stations:
There's a Juggler outjuggles all!

Up goes the lark, as if all were jolly!
Over the duck-pond the willow shakes.
Easy to think that grieving's folly,
When the hand's firm as driven stakes!
Ay, when we're strong, and braced, and manful,
Life's a sweet fiddle: but we're a batch
Born to become the Great Juggler's han'ful:
Balls he shies up, and is safe to catch.

Here's where the lads of the village cricket:
I was a lad not wide from here:
Couldn't I whip off the bail from the wicket?
Like an old world those days appear!

Donkey, sheep, geese, and thatched ale-house—
I know them!
They are old friends of my halts, and seem,
Somehow, as if kind thanks I owe them:
Juggling don't hinder the heart's esteem.

Juggling's no sin, for we must have victual:
Nature allows us to bait for the fool.
Holding one's own makes us juggle no little;
But, to increase it, hard juggling's the rule.
You that are sneering at my profession,
Haven't you juggled a vast amount?
There's the Prime Minister, in one Session
Juggles more games than my sins 'll count.

I've murdered insects with mock thunder:
Conscience, for that, in men don't quail.
I've made bread from the bump of wonder:
That's my business, and there's my tale.
Fashion and rank all praised the professor:
Ay! and I've had my smile from the Queen:
Bravo, Jerry! she meant: God bless her!
Ain't this a sermon on that scene?

I've studied man from my topsy-turvy
Close, and, I reckon, rather true.
Some are fine fellows: some, right scurvy:
Most, a dash between the two.
But it's a woman, old girl, that makes me
Think more kindly of the race:
And it's a woman, old girl, that shakes me
When the Great Juggler I must face.

We two were married, due and legal:
Honest we've lived since we've been one.
Lord! I could then jump like an eagle:
You danced bright as a bit o' the sun.
Birds in May-bush we were! right merry!
All night we kissed, we juggled all day.
Joy was the heart of Juggling Jerry!
Now from his old girl he's juggled away.

It's past parsons to console us:
No, nor no doctor fetch for me:
I can die without my bolus;
Two of a trade, lass, never agree!
Parson and Doctor!—don't they love rarely,
Fighting the devil in other men's fields!
Stand up yourself and match him fairly:
Then see how the rascal yields!

I, lass, have lived no gipsy, flaunting
Finery while his poor helpmate grubs:
Coin I've stored, and you won't be wanting:
You shan't beg from the troughs and tubs.
Nobly you've stuck to me, though in his kitchen
Many a Marquis would hail you Cook!
Palaces you could have ruled and grown rich in,
But your old Jerry you never forsook.

Hand up the chirper! ripe ale winks in it;
Let's have comfort and be at peace.
Once a stout draught made me light as a linnet.
Cheer up! the Lord must have his lease.
May be—for none see in that black hollow—
It's just a place where we're held in pawn,
And, when the Great Juggler makes as to swallow,
It's just the sword-trick—I ain't quite gone!

Yonder came smells of the gorse, so nutty,
Gold-like and warm: it's the prime of May.
Better than mortar, brick and putty,
Is God's house on a blowing day.
Lean me more up the mound; now I feel it:
All the old heath-smells! Ain't it strange?
There's the world laughing, as if to conceal it,
But He's by us, juggling the change.

I mind it well, by the sea-beach lying,
Once—it's long gone—when two gulls we beheld,
Which, as the moon got up, were flying
Down a big wave that sparked and swelled.
Crack, went a gun: one fell: the second
Wheeled round him twice, and was off for new luck:
There in the dark her white wing beckoned:—
Drop me a kiss—I'm the bird dead-struck!

CHRISTINA GEORGINA ROSSETTI (1830—1894)

Weary in well-doing

I would have gone; God bade me stay:
I would have worked; God bade me rest.
He broke my will from day to day;
He read my yearnings unexpressed,
And said them nay.

Now I would stay; God bids me go:
Now I would rest; God bids me work.
He breaks my heart tossed to and fro;
My soul is wrung with doubts that lurk
And vex it so.

I go, Lord, where Thou sendest me;
Day after day I plod and moil:
But, Christ my God, when will it be
That I may let alone my toil
And rest with thee?

Luscious and sorrowful

Beautiful, tender, wasting away for sorrow;
Thus to-day; and how shall it be with thee to-morrow?
Beautiful, tender—what else?
  A hope tells.

Beautiful, tender, keeping the jubilee
In the land of home together, past death and sea;
No more change or death, no more
  Salt sea-shore.

WILLIAM MORRIS (1834—1896)

An ancient castle

Midways of a walled garden,
  In the happy poplar land,
  Did an ancient castle stand,
With an old knight for a warden.

Many scarlet bricks there were
  In its walls, and old grey stone;
  Over which red apples shone
At the right time of the year. .

On the bricks the green moss grew,
  Yellow lichen on the stone,
  Over which red apples shone;
Little war that castle knew.

Deep green water filled the moat,
  Each side had a red-brick lip,
  Green and mossy with the drip
Of dew and rain; there was a boat

Of carven wood, with hangings green
  About the stern; it was great bliss
  For lovers to sit there and kiss
In the hot summer noons, not seen.

Across the moat the fresh west wind
  In very little ripples went;
  The way the heavy aspens bent
Towards it, was a thing to mind.

The painted drawbridge over it
  Went up and down with gilded chains,
  'Twas pleasant in the summer rains
Within the bridge-house there to sit.

There were five swans that ne'er did eat
  The water-weeds, for ladies came
  Each day, and young knights did the same,
And gave them cakes and bread for meat.

They had a house of painted wood,
  A red roof gold-spiked over it,
  Wherein upon their eggs to sit
Week after week; no drop of blood,

Drawn from men's bodies by sword-blows,
   Came ever there, or any tear;
   Most certainly from year to year
'Twas pleasant as a Provence rose.

The banners seemed quite full of ease,
   That over the turret-roofs hung down;
   The battlements could get no frown
From the flower-moulded cornices.

Who walked in that garden there?
   Miles and Giles and Isabeau,
   Tall Jehane de Castel beau,
Alice of the golden hair,

Big Sir Gervaise, the good knight,
   Fair Ellayne le Violet,
   Mary, Constance fille de fay,
Many dames with footfall light. . . . .

From *Golden wings*

The brooding of Sigurd

But the morn to the noon hath fallen, and the afternoon to the eve,
And the beams of the westering sun the Niblung wall-stones leave,
And yet sitteth Sigurd alone; then the sun sinketh down into night,
And the moon ariseth in heaven, and the earth is pale with her light:
And there sitteth Sigurd the Volsung in the gold and the harness of war
That was won from the heart-wise Fafnir and the guarded Treasure of yore,
But pale is the Helm of Aweing, and wan are the ruddy rings:
So whiles in a city forsaken ye see the shapes of kings,
And the lips that the carvers wrought, while their words were remembered and known,
And the brows men trembled to look on in the long-enduring stone,
And their hands once unforgotten, and their breasts, the walls of war;
But now are they hidden marvels to the wise and the master of lore,
And he nameth them not, nor knoweth, and their fear is faded away.

E'en so sat Sigurd the Volsung till the night waxed moonless and grey,
Till the chill dawn spread o'er the lowland, and the purple fells grew
    clear
In the cloudless summer dawn-dusk, and the sun was drawing anear:
Then reddened the Burg of the Niblungs, and the walls of the ancient
    folk,
And a wind came down from the mountains and the living things
    awoke
And cried out for need and rejoicing; till, lo, the rim of the sun
Showed over the eastern ridges, and the new day was begun;
And the beams rose higher and higher, and white grew the Niblung
    wall,
And the spears on the ramparts glistered and the windows blazed
    withal,
And the sunlight flooded the courts, and throughout the chambers
    streamed:
Then bright as the flames of the heaven the Helm of Aweing gleamed,
Then clashed the red rings of the Treasure, as Sigurd stood on his feet,
And went through the echoing chambers, as the winds in the wall-
    nook beat;
And there in the earliest morning while the lords of the Niblungs lie
'Twixt light sleep and awakening they hear the clash go by,
And their dreams are of happy battle, and the songs that follow fame,
And the hope of the Gods accomplished, and the tales of the ancient
    name,
Ere Sigurd came to the Niblungs and faced their gathered foes.

From *The Story of Sigurd the Volsung*

ALGERNON CHARLES SWINBURNE (1837—1909)

The garden of Proserpine

Here, where the world is quiet,
   Here, where all trouble seems
Dead winds' and spent waves' riot
   In doubtful dreams of dreams;
I watch the green field growing
For reaping folk and sowing,
For harvest-time and mowing,
   A sleepy world of streams.

I am tired of tears and laughter,
  And men that laugh and weep
Of what may come hereafter
  For men that sow to reap:
I am weary of days and hours,
Blown buds of barren flowers,
Desires and dreams and powers
  And everything but sleep.

Here life has death for neighbour
  And far from eye or ear
Wan waves and wet winds labour,
  Weak ships and spirits steer;
They drive adrift, and whither
They wot not who make thither;
But no such winds blow hither,
  And no such things grow here.

No growth of moor or coppice,
  No heather-flower or vine,
But bloomless buds of poppies,
  Green grapes of Proserpine,
Pale beds of blowing rushes
Where no leaf blooms or blushes
Save this whereout she crushes
  For dead men deadly wine.

Pale, without name or number,
  In fruitless fields of corn,
They bow themselves and slumber
  All night till light is born;
And like a soul belated,
In hell and heaven unmated,
By cloud and mist abated
  Comes out of darkness morn.

Though one were strong as seven,
  He too with death shall dwell,
Nor wake with wings in heaven,
  Nor weep for pains in hell;
Though one were fair as roses,
His beauty clouds and closes;
And well though love reposes,
  In the end it is not well.

Pale, beyond porch and portal,
  Crowned with calm leaves, she stands
Who gathers all things mortal
  With cold immortal hands;
Her languid lips are sweeter
Than love's who fears to greet her,
To men that mix and meet her
  From many times and lands.

She waits for each and other,
  She waits for all men born;
Forgets the earth her mother,
  The life of fruits and corn;
And spring and seed and swallow
Take wing for her and follow
Where summer song rings hollow
  And flowers are put to scorn.

There go the loves that wither,
  The old loves with wearier wings;
And all dead years draw thither,
  And all disastrous things;
Dead dreams of days forsaken,
Blind buds that snows have shaken,
Wild leaves that winds have taken,
  Red strays of ruined springs.

We are not sure of sorrow,
  And joy was never sure;
To-day will die to-morrow;
  Time stoops to no man's lure;
And love, grown faint and fretful,
With lips but half regretful
Sighs, and with eyes forgetful
  Weeps that no loves endure.

From too much love of living,
  From hope and fear set free,
We thank with brief thanksgiving
  Whatever gods may be
That no life lives for ever;
That dead men rise up never;
That even the weariest river
  Winds somewhere safe to sea.

Then star nor sun shall waken,
  Nor any change of light:
Nor sounds of waters shaken,
  Nor any sound or sight:
Nor wintry leaves nor vernal.
Nor days nor things diurnal;
Only the sleep eternal
  In an eternal night.

THOMAS HARDY (1840—1928)

When I set out for Lyonnesse

When I set out for Lyonnesse,
  A hundred miles away,
  The rime was on the spray,
And starlight lit my lonesomeness
When I set out for Lyonnesse
  A hundred miles away.

What would bechance at Lyonnesse
  While I should sojourn there
  No prophet durst declare,
Nor did the wisest wizard guess
What would bechance at Lyonnesse
  While I should sojourn there.

When I came back from Lyonnesse
  With magic in my eyes,
  All marked with mute surmise
My radiance rare and fathomless,
When I came back from Lyonnesse
  With magic in my eyes.

Weathers

This is the weather the cuckoo likes,
And so do I;
When showers betumble the chestnut spikes,
And nestlings fly:
And the little brown nightingale bills his best,
And they sit outside at 'The Traveller's Rest',
And maids come forth sprig-muslin drest,
And citizens dream of the south and west,
And so do I.

This is the weather the shepherd shuns,
And so do I;
When beeches drip in browns and duns,
And thresh, and ply;
And hill-hid tides throb, throe on throe,
And meadow rivulets overflow,
And drops on gate-bars hang in a row,
And rooks in families homeward go,
And so do I.

In Tenebris

I

Percussus sum sicut foenum, et aruit cor neum. Psalms CI.

Wintertime nighs;
But my bereavement-pain
It cannot bring again:
   Twice no one dies.

Flower-petals flee;
But, since it once hath been,
No more that severing scene
   Can harrow me.

Birds faint in dread:
I shall not lose old strength
In the lone frost's black length:
   Strength long since fled!

Leaves freeze to dun;
But friends can not turn cold
This season as of old
   For him with none.

Tempests may scath;
But love can not make smart
Again this year his heart
   Who no heart hath.

Black is night's cope;
But death will not appal
One who, past doubtings all,
   Waits in unhope.

II

Considerabam ad dexteram, et videbam; et non erat qui cognosceret me . . . Non est qui requirat animam meam. Psalms CXLI.

When the clouds' swoln bosoms echo back the shouts of the many and strong
That things are all as they best may be, save a few to be right ere long,
And my eyes have not the vision in them to discern what to these is so clear,
The blot seems straightway in me alone; one better he were not here.

The stout upstanders say, All's well with us: ruers have nought to rue!
And what the potent say so oft, can it fail to be somewhat true?
Breezily go they, breezily come; their dust smokes around their career,
Till I think I am one born out of due time, who has no calling here.

Their dawns bring lusty joys, it seems; their eves exultance sweet;
Our times are blessed times, they cry: Life shapes it as is most meet,
And nothing is much the matter; there are many smiles to a tear;
Then what is the matter is I, I say. Why should such an one be here..?

Let him to whose ears the low-voiced Best seems stilled by the clash of the First,
Who holds that if way to the Better there be, it exacts a full look at the Worst,
Who feels that delight is a delicate growth cramped by crookedness, custom, and fear,
Get him up and be gone as one shaped awry; he disturbs the order here.

III

Heu mihi, quia incolatus meus prolongatus est! Habitavi cum habitantibus Cedar; multum incola fuit anima mea. Psalms CXIX.

There have been times when I well might have passed and the ending have come—
Points in my path when the dark might have stolen on me, artless, unrueing—
Ere I had learnt that the world was a welter of futile doing:
Such had been times when I might well have passed, and the ending have come!

Say, on the noon when the half-sunny hours told that April was nigh,
And I upgathered and cast forth the snow from the crocus-border,
Fashioned and furbished the soil into a summer-seeming order,
Glowing in gladsome faith that I quickened the year thereby.

Or on that loneliest of eves when afar and benighted we stood,
She who upheld me and I, in the midmost of Egdon together,
Confident I in her watching and ward through the blackening
heather,
Deeming her matchless in might and with measureless scope endued.

Or on that winter-wild night when, reclined by the chimney-nook
quoin,
Slowly a drowse overgat me, the smallest and feeblest of folk there,
Weak from my baptism of pain; when at times and anon I awoke
there—
Heard of a world wheeling on, with no listing or longing to join.

Even then! while unweeting that vision could vex or that knowledge
could numb,
That sweets to the mouth in the belly are bitter, and tart, and
untoward,
Then, on some dim-coloured scene should my briefly raised curtain
have lowered,
Then might the Voice that is law have said 'Cease!' and the ending
have come.

GERARD MANLEY HOPKINS (1844—1889)

The starlight night

Look at the stars ! look, look up at the skies !
  O look at all the fire-folk sitting in the air!
  The bright boroughs, the circle-citadels there!
Down in dim woods the diamond delves! the elves'-eyes!
The grey lawns cold where gold, where quickgold lies!
  Wind-beat whitebeam! airy abeles set on a flare!
  Flake-doves sent floating forth at a farmyard scare!—
Ah well! it is all a purchase, all is a prize.

Buy then! bid then!—What ?—Prayer, patience, alms, vows.
Look, look: a May-mess, like on orchard boughs!
  Look! March-bloom, like on mealed-with-yellow sallows!

These are indeed the barn; withindoors house
The shocks. This piece-bright paling shuts the spouse
   Christ home, Christ and his mother and all his hallows.

The wreck of the Deutschland

On Saturday sailed from Bremen,
American-outward-bound,
Take settler and seamen, tell men with women,
Two hundred souls in the round—
O Father, not under thy feathers nor ever as guessing
The goal was a shoal, of a fourth the doom to be drowned;
Yet did the dark side of the bay of thy blessing
Not vault them, the millions of rounds of thy mercy not reeve
   even them in?

Into the snows she sweeps,
Hurling the haven behind,
The Deutschland, on Sunday; and so the sky keeps,
For the infinite air is unkind,
And the sea flint-flake, black-backed in the regular blow,
Sitting Eastnortheast, in cursed quarter, the wind;
Wiry and white-fiery and whirlwind-swivelled snow
Spins to the widow-making unchilding unfathering deeps.

She drove in the dark to leeward,
She struck—not a reef or a rock
But the combs of a smother of sand; night drew her
Dead to the Kentish Knock;
And she beat the bank down with her bows and the ride of her keel:
The breakers rolled on her beam with ruinous shock;
And canvas and compass, the whorl and the wheel
Idle for ever to waft her or wind her with, these sh ndured...

Hope had grown grey hairs,
Hope had mourning on,
Trenched with tears, carved with cares,
Hope was twelve hours gone;
And frightful a nightfall folded rueful a day
Nor rescue, only rocket and lightship, shone,
And lives at last were washing away:
To the shrouds they took,—they shook in the hurling and horrible
   airs.

K

One stirred from the rigging to save
The wild woman-kind below,
With a rope's end round the man, handy and brave—
He was pitched to his death at a blow,
For all his dreadnought breast and braids of thew:
They could tell him for hours, dandled the to and fro
Through the cobbled foam-fleece, what could he do
With the burl of the fountains of air, buck and the flood of the wave?

They fought with God's cold—
And they could not and fell to the deck
(Crushed them) or water (and drowned them) or rolled
With the sea-romp over the wreck.
Night roared, with the heart-break hearing a heart-broke rabble,
The woman's wailing, the crying of child without check—
Till a lioness arose breasting the babble,
A prophetess towered in the tumult, a virginal tongue told.

Ah, touched in your bower of bone
Are you! turned for an exquisite smart,
Have you! make words break from me here all alone,
Do you!—mother of being in me, heart.
O unteachably after evil, but uttering truth,
Why, tears! is it? tears; such a melting, a madrigal start!
Never-eldering revel and river of youth,
What can it be, this glee? the good you have there of your own?

Sister, a sister calling
A master, her master and mine!—
And the inboard seas run swirling and hawling;
The rash smart sloggering brine
Blinds her; but she that weather sees one thing, one;
Has one fetch in her: she rears herself to divine
Ears, and the call of the tall nun
To the men in the tops and the tackle rode over the storm's brawling.

She was first of a five and came
Of a coifed sisterhood.
(O Deutschland, double a desperate name!
O world wide of its good!

But Gertrude, lily, and Luther, are two of a town,
Christ's lily and beast of the waste wood:
From life's dawn it is drawn down,
Abel is Cain's brother and breasts they have sucked the same.)

Loathed for a love of men knew in them,
Banned by the land of their birth,
Rhine refused them. Thames would ruin them;
Surf, snow, river and earth
Gnashed: but thou art above, thou Orion of light;
Thy unchancelling poising palms were weighing the worth,
Thou martyr-master: in thy sight
Storm flakes were scroll-leaved flowers, lily showers—sweet heaven
    was astrew in them.

Five! the finding and sake
And cipher of suffering Christ.
Mark, the mark is of man's make
And the word of it Sacrificed.
But he scores it in scarlet himself on his own bespoken,
Before-time-taken, dearest prized and priced—
Stigma, signal, cinquefoil token
For lettering of the lamb's fleece, ruddying of the rose-flake.

Joy fall to thee, father Francis,
Drawn to the Life that died;
With the gnarls of the nails in thee, niche of the lance, his
Lovescape crucified
And seal of his seraph-arrival! and these thy daughters
And five-lived and leaved favour and pride,
Are sisterly sealed in wild waters,
To bathe in his fall-gold mercies, to breathe in his all-fire glances.

Away in the loveable west,
On a pastoral forehead of Wales,
I was under a roof here, I was at rest,
And they the prey of the gales;
She to the black-about air, to the breaker, the thickly
Falling flakes, to the throng that catches and quails
Was calling 'O Christ, Christ, come quickly':
The cross to her she calls Christ to her, christens her wild-worst Best.

The majesty! what did she mean?
Breathe, arch and original Breath.
Is it love in her of the being as her lover had been?
Breathe, body of lovely Death.
They were else-minded then, altogether, the men
Woke thee with a *we are perishing* in the weather of Gennesareth.
Or is it that she cried for the crown then,
The keener to come at the comfort for feeling the combating keen?

For how to the heart's cheering
The down-dugged ground-hugged grey
Hovers off, the jay-blue heavens appearing
Of pied and peeled May!
Blue-beating and hoary-glow height; or night, still higher,
With belled fire and the moth-soft Milky Way,
What by your measure is the heaven of desire,
The treasure never eyesight got, nor was ever guessed what for the
    hearing?

No, but it was not these.
The jading and jar of the cart,
Time's tasking, it is fathers that asking for ease
Of the sodden-with-its-sorrowing heart,
Not danger, electrical horror; then further it finds
The appealing of the Passion is tenderer in prayer apart:
Other, I gather, in measure her mind's
Burden, in wind's burly and beat of endragoned seas.

But how shall I . . . make me room there:
Reach me a . . . Fancy, come faster—
Strike you the sight of it? look at it loom there,
Thing that she . . . there then! the Master,
Ipse, the only one, Christ, King, Head:
He was to cure the extremity where he had cast her;
Do, deal, lord it with living and dead;
Let him ride, her pride, in his triumph, despatch and have done
    with his doom there.

Ah! there was a heart right
There was single eye!
Read the unshapeable shock night
And knew the who and the why;

Wording it how but by him that present and past,
Heaven and earth are word of, worded by?—
The Simon Peter of a soul! to the blast
Tarpeian-fast, but a blown beacon of light.

Jesu, heart's light,
Jesu, maid's son,
What was the feast followed the night
Thou hadst glory of this nun?—
Feast of the one woman without stain.
For so conceived, so to conceive thee is done;
But here was heart-throe, birth of a brain,
Word, that heard and kept thee and uttered thee outright.

Well, she has thee for the pain, for the
Patience; but pity of the rest of them!
Heart, go and bleed at a bitterer vein for the
Comfortless unconfessed of them—
No not uncomforted: lovely-felicitous Providence
Finger of a tender of, O of a feather delicacy, the breast of the
Maiden could obey so, be a bell to, ring of it, and
Startle the poor sheep back! is the shipwreck then a harvest, does
   tempest carry the grain for thee?

I admire thee, master of the tides,
Of the Yore-flood, of the year's fall;
The recurb and the recovery of the gulf's sides,
The girth of it and the wharf of it and the wall;
Stanching, quenching ocean of a motionable mind;
Ground of being, and granite of it: past all
Grasp God, throned behind
Death with a sovereignty that heeds but hides, bodes but abides;

With a mercy that outrides
The all of water, an ark
For the listener; for the lingerer with a love glides
Lower than death and the dark;
A vein for the visiting of the past-prayer, pent in prison,
The-last-breath penitent spirits—the uttermost mark
Our passion-plunged giant risen,
The Christ of the Father compassionate, fetched in the storm of his
   strides.

Now burn, new born to the world,
Doubled-natured name,
The heaven-flung, heart-fleshed, maiden-furled
Miracle-in-Mary-of-flame,
Mid-numbered He in three of the thunder-throne!
Not a dooms-day dazzle in his coming nor dark as he came;
Kind, but royally reclaiming his own;
A released shower, let flash to the shire, not a lightning of fire
    hard-hurled.

Dame, at our door
Drowned, and among our shoals,
Remember us in the roads, the heaven-haven of the Reward:
Our King back, oh, upon English souls!
Let him easter in us, be a dayspring to the dimness of us, be a
    crimson-cresseted east,
More brightening her, rare-dear Britain, as his reign rolls,
Pride, rose, prince, hero of us, high-priest,
Our hearts' charity's hearth's fire, our thoughts' chivalry's throng's
    Lord.

Life death does end

No worst, there is none. Pitched past pitch of grief,
More pangs will, schooled at forepangs, wilder wring.
Comforter, where, where is your comforting?
Mary, mother of us, where is your relief?

My cries heave, herds-long; huddle in a main, a chief
Woe, world-sorrow; on an age-old anvil wince and sing—
Then lull, then leave off. Fury had shrieked 'No ling—
ering! Let me be fell: force I must be brief.'

O the mind, mind has mountains; cliffs of fall
Frightful, sheer, no-man-fathomed. Hold them cheap
May who ne'er hung there. Nor does long our small
Durance deal with that steep or deep. Here! creep,
Wretch, under a comfort serves in a whirlwind: all
Life death does end and each day dies with sleep.

From *Six Epigrams*

No, they are come; their horn is lifted up;
They stand, they shine in the sun; Fame has foregone
All quests save the recital of their greatness;
Their clarions from all corners of the field
With potent lips call down cemented towers;
Their harness beams like scythes in morning grass;
Like flame they gather on our cliffs at evening,
At morn they come upon our lands like rains;
They plough our vales; you see the unsteady flare
Flush through their heaving columns; when they halt
They seem to fold the hills with golden capes;
They draw all coverts, cut the fields, and suck
The treasure from all cities . . . .

Moonrise

I awoke in the Midsummer not to call night, in the white and the
    walk of the morning:
The moon, dwindled and thinned to the fringe of a fingernail held
    to the candle,
Or paring of paradisaïcal fruit, lovely in waning but lustreless,
Stepped from the stool, drew back from the barrow, of dark Maenefa
    the mountain;
A cusp still clasped him, a fluke yet fanged him, entangled him,
    not quit utterly.
This was the prized, the desirable sight, unsought, presented so
    easily,
Parted me leaf and leaf, divided me, eyelid and eyelid of slumber.

ROBERT BRIDGES (1844-1930)

Triolet

All women born are so perverse
No man need boast their love possessing.
If nought seem better, nothing's worse:
All women born are so perverse.
From Adam's wife, that proved a curse
Though God had made her for a blessing,
All women born are so perverse
No man need boast their love possessing.

Cheddar pinks

Mid the squandered colour
  idling as I lay
Reading the Odyssey
  in my rock-garden
I espied the clustered
  tufts of Cheddar pinks
Burgeoning with promise
  of their scented bloom
All the modish motley
  of their bloom to-be
Thrust up in narrow buds
  on the slender stalks
Thronging springing urgent
  hasting (so I thought)
As if they feared to be
  too late for summer—
Like schoolgirls overslept
  wakened by the bell
Leaping from bed to don
  their muslin dresses
    On a May morning:

Then felt I like to one
  indulging in sin
(Whereto Nature is oft
  a blind accomplice)
Because my aged bones
  so enjoyed the sun
There as I lay along
  idling with my thoughts
Reading an old poet
  while the busy world
Toiled moiled fussed and scurried
  worried bought and sold
Plotted stole and quarrelled
  fought and God knows what.
I had forgotten Homer
  dallying with my thoughts
Till I fell to making
  these little verses

Communing with the flowers
in my rock-garden
On a May morning.

London snow

When men were all asleep the snow came flying,
In large white flakes falling on the city brown,
Stealthily and perpetually settling and loosely lying,
 Hushing the latest traffic of the drowsy town;
Deadening, muffling, stifling its murmurs failing;
Lazily and incessantly floating down and down:
 Silently sifting and veiling road, roof and railing;
Hiding difference, making unevenness even,
Into angles and crevices softly drifting and sailing.
 All night it fell, and when full inches seven
It lay in the depth of its uncompacted lightness,
The clouds blew off from a high and frosty heaven;
 And all woke earlier for the unaccustomed brightness
Of the winter dawning, the strange unheavenly glare:
The eye marvelled—marvelled at the dazzling whiteness;
 The ear hearkened to the stillness of the solemn air;
No sound of wheel rumbling nor of foot falling,
And the busy morning cries came thin and spare.
 Then boys I heard, as they went to school, calling,
They gathered up the crystal manna to freeze
Their tongues with tasting, their hands with snowballing;
 Or rioted in a drift, plunging up to the knees;
Or peering up from under the white-mossed wonder,
'O look at the trees!' they cried, 'O look at the trees!'
 With lessened load a few carts creak and blunder,
Following along the white deserted way,
A country company long dispersed asunder:
 When now already the sun, in pale display
Standing by Paul's high dome, spread forth below
His sparkling beams, and awoke the stir of the day.
 For now doors open, and war is waged with the snow;
And trains of sombre men, past tale of number,
Tread long brown paths, as toward their toil they go:
 But even for them awhile no cares encumber
Their minds diverted; the daily word is unspoken,
The daily thoughts of labour and sorrow slumber
At the sight of the beauty that greets them, for the charm
 they have broken.

ALICE MEYNELL (1847—1922)

The threshing machine

No 'fan is in his hand' for these
Young villagers beneath the trees,
Watching the wheels. And I recall
The rhythm of rods that rise and fall,
Purging the harvest, over-seas.

No fan, no flail, no threshing floor!
And all their symbols evermore
Forgone in England now—the sign,
The visible pledge, the threat divine,
The chaff dispersed, the wheat in store.

The unbreathing engine makes no tune,
Steady at sunrise, steady at noon,
Inhuman, perfect, saving time,
And saving measure, and saving rhyme—
And did our Ruskin speak too soon?

'No noble strength on earth' he sees
'Save Hercules' arm'; his grave decrees
Curse wheel and stream. As the wheels run
I saw the other strength of man,
I knew the brain of Hercules!

The wind is blind

'*Eyeless, in Gaza, at the mill, with slaves.*'
—MILTON's *Samson*

The wind is blind.
The earth sees sun and moon; the height
Is watch-tower to the dawn; the plain
Shines to the summer; visible light
Is scattered in the drops of rain.

The wind is blind.
The flashing billows are aware;
With open eyes the cities see;
Light leaves the ether, everywhere
Known to the homing bird and bee.

330

The wind is blind.
Is blind alone. How has he hurled
His ignorant lash, his aimless dart,
His eyeless rush upon the world,
Unseeing, to break his unknown heart!

The wind is blind.
And the sail traps him, and the mill
Captures him; and he cannot save
His swiftness and his desperate will
From those blind uses of the slave.

WILLIAM ERNEST HENLEY (1849—1903)

Villon's straight tip to all cross coves
Tout aux tavernes et aux filles

Suppose you screeve? or go cheap-jack?
Or fake the broads? or fig a nag?
Or thimble rig? or knap a yack?
Or pitch a snide? or smash a rag?
Suppose you duff? or nose and lag?
Or get the straight, and land your pot?
How do you melt the multy swag?
Booze and the blowens cop the lot.

Fiddle, or fence, or mace, or mack;
Or moskeneer, or flash the drag;
Dead-lurk a crib, or do a crack;
Pad with a slang, or chuck a fag;
Bonnet, or tout, or mump and gag;
Rattle the tats, or mark the spot;
You cannot bank a single stag;
Booze and the blowens cop the lot.

Suppose you try a different tack,
And on the square you flash your flag?
At penny-a-lining make your whack,
Or with the mummers mug and gag?
For nix, for nix the dibbs you bag!
At any graft, no matter what,
Your merry goblins soon stravag:
Booze and the blowens cop the lot.

It's up the spout and Charley Wag
With wipes and tickers and what not
Until the squeezer nips your scrag,
Booze and the blowens cop the lot.

ROBERT LOUIS STEVENSON (1850—1894)

A portrait

I am a kind of farthing dip,
    Unfriendly to the nose and eyes;
A blue-behinded ape, I skip
    Upon the trees of Paradise.

At mankind's feast, I take my place
    In solemn, sanctimonious state,
And have the air of saying grace
    While I defile the dinner plate.

I am 'the smiler with the knife',
    The battener upon garbage, I—
Dear Heaven, with such a rancid life,
    Were it not better far to die?

Yet still, about the human pale,
    I love to scamper, love to race,
To swing by my irreverent tail
    All over the most holy place;

And when at length, some golden day,
    The unfailing sportsman, aiming at,
Shall bag, me—all the world shall say:
    Thank God, and there's an end of that.

A mile an' a bittock

A mile an' a bittock, a mile or twa,
Abune the burn, ayont the law,
Davie an' Donal' an' Cherlie an' a',
An' the mune was shinin' clearly!

Ane went hame wi' the ither, an' then
The ither went hame wi' the ither twa men,
An' baith wad return him the service again,
An' the mune was shinin' clearly!

The clocks were chappin' in house an' ha',
Eleeven, twal an' ane an' twa;
An' the guidman's face was turnt to the wa',
An' the mune was shinin' clearly!

A wind got up frae affa the sea,
It blew the stars as clear's could be,
It blew in the een of a' o' the three,
An' the mune was shinin' clearly!

Noo, Davie was first to get sleep in his head,
'The best o' frien's maun twine,' he said;
I'm weariet, an' here I'm awa' to my bed.'
An' the mune was shinin' clearly!

Twa o' them walkin' an' crackin' their lane,
The mornin' licht cam gray an' plain,
An' the birds they yammert on stick an' stane,
An' the mune was shinin' clearly!

O years ayont, O years awa',
My lads, ye'll mind whate'er befa'—
My lads, ye'll mind on the bield o' the law,
When the mune was shinin' clearly.

WILLIAM WILKINS (1852—1915)

The Magazine Fort, Phoenix Park, Dublin

Inside its zig-zag lines the little camp is asleep,
  Embalmed in the infinite breath of the greensward, the river,
    the stars.
Round the staff, the yellow leopards of England, weary of wars,
Curl and uncurl, to the murmurous voice of the greenwood deep.
On the lonely terrace their watch the shadowy sentinels keep,
  Each bayonet a spire of silver—high over the silvery jars
  Of the streamtide, swooning in starlight adown its foam-fretted bars
To the city, that lies in a shroud as of ashes under the steep.
  To the south are the hills everlasting; eastward the sea-capes and
    isles;
  Inland, the levels of emerald stretch for a hundred miles.

OSCAR WILDE (1856—1900)

Le Jardin

The lily's withered chalice falls
  Around its rod of dusty gold,
  And from the beech-trees on the wold
The last wood-pigeon coos and calls.

The gaudy leonine sunflower
  Hangs black and barren on its stalk,
  And down the windy garden walk
The dead leaves scatter,—hour by hour.

Pale privet-petals white as milk
  Are blown into a snowy mass
  The roses lie upon the grass
Like little shreds of crimson silk.

ALFRED EDWARD HOUSMAN (1859—1936)

Yon far country

Into my heart an air that kills
  From yon far country blows:
What are those blue remembered hills,
  What spires, what farms are those?

That is the land of lost content,
  I see it shining plain,
The happy highways where I went
  And cannot come again.

Wenlock

'Tis time, I think, by Wenlock town
  The golden broom should blow;
The hawthorn sprinkled up and down
  Should charge the land with snow.

Spring will not wait the loiterer's time
  Who keeps so long away;
So others wear the broom and climb
  The hedgerows heaped with may.

Oh tarnish late on Wenlock Edge,
  Gold that I never see;
Lie long, high snowdrifts in the hedge
  That will not shower on me.

Friends

When I came last to Ludlow
  Amidst the moonlight pale,
Two friends kept step beside me,
  Two honest lads and hale.

Now Dick lies long in the churchyard,
  And Ned lies long in jail,
And I come home to Ludlow
  Amidst the moonlight pale.

FRANCIS THOMPSON (1859—1907)

To a snowflake

What heart could have thought you?—
Past our devisal
(O filigree petal!)
Fashioned so purely,
Fragilely, surely,
From what Paradisal
Imagineless metal,
Too costly for cost?
Who hammered you, wrought you,
From argentine vapour?—
'God was my shaper.
Passing surmisal,
He hammered, He wrought me,
From curled silver vapour,
To lust of His mind:—
Thou couldst not have thought me!
So purely, so palely,
Tinily, surely,
Mightily, fraily,
Insculped and embossed,
With His hammer of wind,
And His graver of frost.'

The Hound of Heaven

I fled Him, down the nights and down the days;
    I fled Him, down the arches of the years;
I fled Him, down the labyrinthine ways
    Of my own mind; and in the mist of tears
I hid from Him, and under running laughter.
        Up vistaed hopes I sped;
        And shot, precipitated,
Adown Titanic glooms of chasmèd fears,
From those strong Feet that followed, followed after.
        But with unhurrying chase,
        And unperturbèd pace,
    Deliberate speed, majestic instancy,
        They beat—and a Voice beat
        More instant than the Feet—
'All things betray thee, who betrayest Me.'

        I pleaded, outlaw-wise,
By many a hearted casement, curtained red,
Trellised with intertwining charities;
(For though I knew His love Who followed,
        Yet was I sore adread
Lest, having Him, I must have naught beside);
But, if one little casement parted wide,
The gust of His approach would clash it to.
Fear wist not to evade, as Love wist to pursue.
Across the margent of the world I fled,
    And troubled the gold gateways of the stars,
    Smiting for shelter on their clangèd bars;
        Fretted to dulcet jars
And silvern chatter the pale ports o' the moon.
I said to Dawn: Be sudden—To Eve: Be soon;
    With thy young skiey blossoms heap me over
        From this tremendous Lover—
Float thy vague veil about me, lest He see!
I tempted all His servitors, but to find
My own betrayal in their constancy,
In faith to Him their fickleness to me,
Their traitorous trueness, and their loyal deceit.
To all swift things for swiftness did I sue;

Clung to the whistling mane of every wind.
    But whether they swept, smoothly fleet,
The long savannahs of the blue;
      Or whether, Thunder-driven,
    They clanged his chariot 'thwart a heaven,
Plashy with flying lightnings round the spurn o' their feet:—
Fear wist not to evade as Love wist to pursue.
      Still with unhurrying chase,
      And unperturbed pace,
    Deliberate speed, majestic instancy,
      Came on the following Feet,
      And a voice above their beat—
    'Naught shelters thee, who wilt not shelter Me.'

I sought no more that after which I strayed
      In face of man or maid;
But still within the little children's eyes
    Seems something, something that replies,
They at least are for me, surely for me!
I turned me to them very wistfully;
But, just as their young eyes grew sudden fair
    With dawning answers there,
Their angel plucked them from me by the hair.
'Come then, ye other children, Nature's—share
With me' (said I) 'Your delicate fellowship;
      Let me greet you lip to lip,
      Let me twine with you caresses,
        Wantoning
      With our Lady-Mother's vagrant tresses,
        Banqueting
      With her in her wind-walled palace,
      Underneath her azured dais,
      Quaffing as your taintless way is,
        From a chalice
Lucent-weeping out of the dayspring.'

      So it was done:
I in their delicate fellowship was one—
Drew the bolt of Nature's secrecies.
      I knew all the swift importings
      On the wilful face of skies;

I knew how the clouds arise
Spumed of the wild sea-snortings;
    All that's born or dies
Rose and drooped with; made them shapers
Of mine own moods, or wailful or divine;
    With them joyed and was bereaven.
    I was heavy with the even,
When she lit her glimmering tapers
Round the day's dead sanctities.
I laughed in the morning's eyes.
I triumphed and I saddened with all weather,
    Heaven and I wept together,
And its sweet tears were salt with mortal mine;
Against the red throb of its sunset-heart
    I laid my own to beat,
    And share commingling heat;
But not by that, by that, was eased my human smart.
In vain my tears were wet on Heaven's grey cheek.
For ah! we know not what each other says
    These things and I; in sound I speak—
Their sound is but their stir, they speak by silences.
Nature, poor stepdame, cannot slake my drouth;
    Let her, if she would owe me,
Drop yon blue bosom-veil of sky, and show me
    The breasts o' her tenderness:
Never did any milk of hers once bless
    My thirsting mouth.
    Nigh and nigh draws the chase
    With unperturbed pace,
Deliberate speed, majestic instancy;
    And past those noised Feet
    A voice comes yet more fleet—
'Lo! naught contents thee, who content'st not Me.'

Naked I wait Thy love's uplifted stroke!
My harness piece by piece Thou hast hewn from me,
    And smitten me to my knee;
    I am defenceless utterly.
    I slept, methinks, and woke,
And, slowly gazing, find me stripped in sleep.

In the rash lustihead of my young powers,
      I shook the pillaring hours
And pulled my life upon me; grimed with smears,
I stand amid the dust o' the mounded years—
My mangled youth lies dead beneath the heap.
My days have crackled and gone up in smoke,
Have puffed and burst as sun-starts on a stream.
      Yea, faileth now even dream
The dreamer, and the lute the lutanist;
Even the linked fantasies, in whose blossomy twist
I swung the earth a trinket at my wrist,
Are yielding; cords of all too weak account
For earth with heavy griefs so overplussed.
      Ah! is Thy love indeed
A weed, albeit an amaranthine weed,
Suffering no flowers except its own to mount?
      Ah! must—
      Designer infinite!—
Ah! must Thou char the wood ere Thou canst limn with it?
My freshness spent its wavering shower i' the dust;
And now my heart is as a broken fount,
Wherein tear-drippings stagnate, spilt down ever
      From the dank thoughts that shiver
Upon the sighful branches of my mind.
      Such is; what is to be?
The pulp so bitter, how shall taste the rind?
I dimly guess what Time in mists confounds;
Yet ever and anon a trumpet sounds
From the hid battlements of Eternity;
Those shaken mists a space unsettle, then
Round the half glimpsed turrets slowly wash again.
      But not ere him who summoneth
      I first have seen, enwound
With glooming robes purpureal cypress-crowned;
His name I know, and what his trumpet saith.
Whether man's heart or life it be which yields
      Thee harvest, must Thy harvest-fields
      Be dunged with rotten death?

      Now of that long pursuit
      Comes on at hand the bruit;

That Voice is round me like a bursting sea:
'And is thy earth so marred,
Shattered in shard on shard?
Lo, all things fly thee, for thou fliest Me!
Strange, piteous, futile thing,
Wherefore should any set thee love apart?
Seeing none but I makes much of naught' (He said),
'And human love needs human meriting:
How hast thou merited—
Of all man's clotted clay the dingiest clot?
Alack, thou knowest not
How little worthy of any love thou art!
Whom wilt thou find to love ignoble thee,
Save Me, save only Me?
All which I took from thee I did but take
Not for thy harms,
But just that thou might'st seek it in My arms.
All which thy child's mistake
Fancies as lost, I have stored for thee at home:
Rise, clasp My hand, and come!'

Halts by me that footfall:
Is my gloom, after all,
Shade of His hand, outstretched caressingly?
'Ah, fondest, blindest, weakest,
I am He Whom thou seekest!
Thou dravest love from thee, who dravest Me.'

DOUGLAS HYDE (1862—1949)

The Red man's wife

'Tis what they say,
    Thy little heel fits in a shoe.
'Tis what they say,
    Thy little mouth kisses well, too.
'Tis what they say,
    Thousand loves that you leave me to rue;
That the tailor went the way
    That the wife of the Red man knew.

Nine months did I spend
   In a prison closed tightly and bound;
Bolts on my smalls
   And a thousand locks frowning around;
But o'er the tide
   I would leap with the leap of a swan,
Could I once set my side
   By the bride of the Red-haired man.

I thought, O my life,
   That one house between us love would be;
And I thought I would find
   You once coaxing my child on your knee:
But now the curse of the High One
   On him let it be,
And on all of the band of the liars
   Who put silence between you and me.

There grows a tree in the garden
   With blossoms that tremble and shake,
I lay my hand on its bark
   And I feel that my heart must break.
On one wish alone
   My soul through the long months ran,
One little kiss
   From the wife of the Red-haired man.

But the Day of Doom shall come,
   And hills and harbours be rent;
A mist shall fall on the sun
   From the dark clouds heavily sent;
The sea shall be dry,
   And earth under mourning and ban;
Then loud shall he cry
   For the wife of the Red-haired man.

I am Raftery

I am Raftery the Poet
   Full of hope and love,
With eyes that have no light,
   With gentleness that has no misery.

Going west upon my pilgrimage
   By the light of my heart,
Feeble and tired
   To the end of my road.

Behold me now,
   And my face to the wall,
A-playing music
   Unto empty pockets.

              From the Irish of Raftery

RUDYARD KIPLING (1865—1936)

Danny Deever

'What are the bugles blowin' for?' said Files-on-Parade.
'To turn you out, to turn you out,' the Colour-Sergeant said.
'What makes you look so white, so white?' said Files-on-Parade.
'I'm dreadin' what I've got to watch,' the Colour-Sergeant said.
  For they're hangin' Danny Deever, you can hear the Dead March
    play,
  The regiment's in 'ollow square—they're hangin' him to-day;
  They've taken of his buttons off an' cut his stripes away,
  An' they're hangin' Danny Deever in the mornin'.

'What makes the rear-rank breathe so 'ard?' said Files-on-Parade.
'It's bitter cold, it's bitter cold,' the Colour-Sergeant said.
'What makes that front-rank man fall down?' said Files-on-Parade.
'A touch o' sun, a touch o' sun,' the Colour-Sergeant said.
  They are hangin' Danny Deever, they are marchin' of 'im round,
  They 'ave 'alted Danny Deever by 'is coffin on the ground;
  An' 'e'll swing in 'arf a minite for a sneakin' shootin' hound—
  O they're hangin' Danny Deever in the mornin'.

' 'Is cot was right-'and cot to mine,' said Files-on-Parade.
' 'E's sleepin' out an' far to-night,' the Colour-Sergeant said.
'I've drunk 'is beer a score o' times' said Files-on-Parade.
' 'E's drinkin' bitter beer alone,' the Colour-Sergeant said.
  They are hangin' Danny Deever, you must mark 'im to 'is place,
  For 'e shot a comrade sleepin'—you must look 'im in the face;
  Nine 'undred of 'is county an' the Regiment's disgrace,
  While they're hangin' Danny Deever in the mornin'.

'What's that so black agin the sun?' said Files-on-Parade.
'It's Danny fightin' 'ard for life,' the Colour-Sergeant said.
'What's that that whimpers over'ead?' said Files-on-Parade.
'It's Danny's soul that's passin' now,' the Colour-Sergeant said.
  For they're done with Danny Deever, you can 'ear the quickstep
    play,
  The regiment's in column, an' they're marchin' us away;
  Ho! the young recruits are shakin', and' they'll want their beer
    to-day,
  After hangin' Danny Deever in the mornin'!

Harp song of the Dane women

What is a woman that you forsake her,
And the hearth-fire and the home-acre,
To go with the old grey Widow-maker?

She has no house to lay a guest in—
But one chill bed for all to rest in,
That the pale suns and the stray bergs nest in.

She has no strong white arms to fold you,
But the ten-times-fingering weed to hold you—
Out on the rocks where the tide has rolled you.

Yet, when the signs of summer thicken,
And the ice breaks, and the birch-buds quicken,
Yearly you turn from our side, and sicken—

Sicken again for the shouts and the slaughters.
You steal away to the lapping waters,
And look at your ship in her winter-quarters.

You forget our mirth, and talk at the tables,
The kine in the shed and the horse in the stables—
To pitch her sides and go over her cables.

Then you drive out where the storm-clouds swallow,
And the sound of your oar-blades, falling hollow,
Is all we have left through the months to follow.

Ah, what is Woman that you forsake her,
And the hearth-fire and the home-acre,
To go with the old grey Widow-maker?

WILLIAM BUTLER YEATS (1865—1939)

The wanderings of Oisin

We galloped over the glossy sea:
I know not if days passed or hours,
And Niamh sang continually
Danaan songs, and their dewy showers
Of pensive laughter, unhuman sound,
Lulled weariness, and softly round
My human sorrow her white arms wound.
We galloped; now a hornless deer
Passed by us, chased by a phantom hound
All pearly white, save one red ear;
And now a lady rode like the wind
With an apple of gold in her tossing hand;
And a beautiful young man followed behind
With quenchless gaze and fluttering hair.

The horse towards the music raced,
Neighing along the lifeless waste;
Like sooty fingers, many a tree
Rose ever out of the warm sea;
And they were trembling ceaselessly,
As though they all were beating time,
Upon the centre of the sun,
To that low laughing woodland rhyme.
And, now our wandering hours were done,
We cantered to the shore, and knew
The reason of the trembling trees:
Round every branch the song-birds flew,
Or clung thereon like swarming bees;
While round the shore a million stood
Like drops of frozen rainbow light,
And pondered in a soft vain mood
Upon their shadows in the tide,
And told the purple deeps their pride,
And murmured snatches of delight;
And on the shores were many boats
With bending sterns and bending bows,
And carven figures on their prows
Of bitterns, and fish-eating stoats,
And swans with their exultant throats:

And where the wood and waters meet
We tied the horse in a leafy clump,
And Niamh blew three merry notes
Out of a little silver trump;
And then an answering whispering flew
Over the bare and woody land,
A whisper of impetuous feet,
And ever nearer, nearer grew;
And from the woods rushed out a band
Of men and ladies, hand in hand,
And singing, singing all together;
Their brows were white as fragrant milk,
Their cloaks made out of yellow silk,
And trimmed with many a crimson feather;
And when they saw the cloak I wore
Was dim with mire of a mortal shore,
They fingered it and gazed on me
And laughed like murmurs of the sea;

No second Troy

Why should I blame her that she filled my days
With misery, or that she would of late
Have taught to ignorant men most violent ways,
Or hurled the little streets upon the great,
Had they but courage equal to desire?
What could have made her peaceful with a mind
That nobleness made simple as a fire,
With beauty like a tightened bow, a kind
That is not natural in an age like this,
Being high and solitary and most stern?
Why, what could she have done, being what she is?
Was there another Troy for her to burn?

The Second Coming

Turning and turning in the widening gyre
The falcon cannot hear the falconer;
Things fall apart; the centre cannot hold;
Mere anarchy is loosed upon the world,
The blood-dimmed tide is loosed, and everywhere
The ceremony of innocence is drowned;
The best lack all conviction, while the worst
Are full of passionate intensity.

Surely some revelation is at hand;
Surely the Second Coming is at hand.
The Second Coming! Hardly are those words out
When a vast image out of *Spiritus Mundi*
Troubles my sight: somewhere in sands of the desert
A shape with lion body and the head of a man,
A gaze blank and pitiless as the sun,
Is moving its slow thighs, while all about it
Reel shadows of the indignant desert birds.
The darkness drops again; but now I know
That twenty centuries of stony sleep
Were vexed to nightmare by a rocking cradle,
And what rough beast, its hour come round at last,
Slouches towards Bethlehem to be born?

Sailing to Byzantium

That is no country for old men. The young
In one another's arms, birds in the trees,
—Those dying generations—at their song,
The salmon-falls, the mackerel-crowded seas,
Fish, flesh, or fowl, commend all summer long
Whatever is begotten, born, and dies.
Caught in that sensual music all neglect
Monuments of unageing intellect.

An aged man is but a paltry thing,
A tattered coat upon a stick, unless
Soul clap its hands and sing, and louder sing
For every tatter in its mortal dress,
Nor is there singing school but studying
Monuments of its own magnificence;
And therefore I have sailed the seas and come
To the holy city of Byzantium.

O sages standing in God's holy fire
As in the gold mosaic of a wall,
Come from the holy fire, perne in a gyre,
And be the singing-masters of my soul.
Consume my heart away; sick with desire
And fastened to a dying animal
It knows not what it is; and gather me
Into the artifice of eternity.

Once out of nature I shall never take
My bodily form from any natural thing,
But such a form as Grecian goldsmiths make
Of hammered gold and gold enamelling
To keep a drowsy Emperor awake;
Or set upon a golden bough to sing
To lords and ladies of Byzantium
Of what is past, or passing, or to come.

Byzantium

The unpurged images of day recede;
The Emperor's drunken soldiery are abed;
Night resonance recedes, night-walkers' song
After great cathedral gong;
A starlit or a moonlit dome disdains
All that man is,
All mere complexities,
The fury and the mire of human veins.

Before me floats an image, man or shade,
Shade more than man, more image than a shade;
For Hades' bobbin bound in mummy-cloth
May unwind the winding path;
A mouth that has no moisture and no breath
Breathless mouths may summon;
I hail the superhuman;
I call it death-in-life and life-in-death.

Miracle, bird or golden handiwork,
More miracle than bird or handiwork,
Planted on the star-lit golden bough,
Can like the cocks of Hades crow,
Or, by the moon embittered, scorn aloud
In glory of changeless metal
Common bird or petal
And all complexities of mire or blood.

At midnight on the Emperor's pavement flit
Flames that no faggot feeds, nor steel has lit.
Nor storm disturbs, flames begotten of flame,
Where blood-begotten spirits come

And all complexities of fury leave,
Dying into a dance,
An agony of trance,
An agony of flame that cannot singe a sleeve.

Astraddle on the dolphin's mire and blood,
Spirit after spirit! The smithies break the flood,
The golden smithies of the Emperor!
Marbles of the dancing floor
Break bitter furies of complexity,
Those images that yet
Fresh images beget,
That dolphin-torn, that gong-tormented sea.

The curse of Cromwell

You ask what I have found, and far and wide I go:
Nothing but Cromwell's house and Cromwell's murderous crew,
The lovers and the dancers are beaten into the clay,
And the tall men and the swordsmen and the horsemen, where are
    they?
And there is an old beggar wandering in his pride—
His fathers served their fathers before Christ was crucified.
                        O what of that, O what of that,
                        What is there left to say?

All neighbourly content and easy talk are gone,
But there's no good complaining, for money's rant is on.
He that's mounting up must on his neighbour mount.
And we and all the Muses are things of no account.
They have schooling of their own, but I pass their schooling by,
What can they know that we know that know the time to die?
                        O what of that, O what of that,
                        What is there left to say?

But there's another knowledge that my heart destroys,
As the fox in the old fable destroyed the Spartan boy's,
Because it proves that things both can and cannot be;
That the swordsmen and the ladies can still keep company,
Can pay the poet for a verse and hear the fiddle sound,
That I am still their servant though all are underground.
                        O what of that, O what of that,
                        What is there left to say?

I came on a great house in the middle of the night,
Its open lighted doorway and its windows all alight,
And all my friends were there and made me welcome too;
But I woke in an old ruin that the winds howled through;
And when I pay attention I must out and walk
Among the dogs and horses that understand my talk.
                    O what of that, O what of that,
                    What is there left to say?

ERNEST CHRISTOPHER DOWSON (1867—1900)

Dreg.

The fire is out, and spent the warmth thereof,
(This is the end of every song man sings!)
The golden wine is drunk, the dregs remain,
Bitter as wormwood and as salt as pain;
And health and hope have gone the way of love
Into the drear oblivion of lost things,
Ghosts go along with us until the end;
This was a mistress, this, perhaps, a friend.
With pale, indifferent eyes, we sit and wait
For the dropt curtain and the closing gate:
This is the end of all the songs man sings.

LIONEL JOHNSON (1867—1902)

Mystic and cavalier

Go from me: I am one of those who fall.
What! hath no cold wind swept your heart at all,
In my sad company? Before the end,
    Go from me, dear my friend!

Yours are the victories of light: your feet
Rest from good toil, where rest is brave and sweet.
But after warfare in a mourning gloom,
    I rest in clouds of doom.

Have you not read so, looking in these eyes?
Is it the common light of the pure skies,
Lights up their shadowy depths? The end is set:
    Though the end be not yet.

When gracious music stirs, and all is bright,
And beauty triumphs through a courtly night;
When I too joy, a man like other men:
    Yet, am I like them, then?

And in the battle, when the horsemen sweep
Against a thousand deaths, and fall on sleep:
Who ever sought that sudden calm, if I
    Sought not? Yet, could not die.

Seek with thine eyes to pierce this crystal sphere:
Canst read a fate there, prosperous and clear?
Only the mists, only the weeping clouds:
    Dimness, and airy shrouds.

Beneath, what angels are at work? What powers
Prepare the secret of the fatal hours?
See! the mists tremble, and the clouds are stirred:
    When comes the calling word?

The clouds are breaking from the crystal ball,
Breaking and clearing: and I look to fall.
When the cold winds and airs of portent sweep,
    My spirit may have sleep.

O rich and sounding voices of the air!
Interpreters and prophets of despair:
Priests of a fearful sacrament! I come,
    To make with you my home.

Æ (GEORGE RUSSELL) (1867—1935)

Ancient

The sky is cold as pearl
Over a milk-white land.
The snow seems older than Time,
Though it fell through a dreaming, and
Will vanish itself as a dream
At the dimmest touch of a hand.

Out of a timeless world
Shadows fall upon Time,
From a beauty older than earth
A ladder the soul may climb.
I climb by the phanton stair
To a whiteness older than Time.

Dark rapture

Ah, did he climb, that man, nigher to heaven than I,
Babbling inarticulately along the road
His drunken chaotic rapture, lifting to the sky,
His wild darkness, his hands, his voice, his heart that glowed;
Gazing with intoxicated imagination on
The dance the tireless fiery-footed watchers make
Through unending ages on the blue, luminous lawn?
Oh, could that maddened will, those riotous senses break
Into the astral ecstacy, for a moment feel
The profundities? Did he offer his sin to the Most High?
Or was he like those spoilers who break through and steal,
Not by the strait gate, into the city of the sky?
I heard him cry GOD in amazement as if his eyes
Saw through those reeling lights the one eternal Light.
Was that madness of his accepted as sacrifice?
Did fire fall on him from some archangelic height?
I, who was stricken to dumbness of awe, could not endure
The intolerable vastness still to the uttermost star.
Was it not enough the heart humble, contrite and pure?
Must hell with heaven be knit ere the ancient gates unbar,
The Pleroma open? I hurried, unaccepted, forlorn,
From the deep slumbering earth, the heavens that were not mine,
Hearing murmurs still from the dark rapture born
Where the Holy Breath was mixed with the unholy wine.

THOMAS STURGE MOORE (1870—1944)

The dying swan

O silver-throated swan
Struck, struck! a golden dart
Clean through thy breast has gone
Home to thy heart.
Thrill, thrill, O silver throat!

O silver trumpet, pour
Love for defiance back
On him who smote!
And brim, brim o'er
With love; and ruby-dye thy track
Down thy last living reach
Of river, sail the golden light . .
Enter the sun's heart . . even teach,
O wondrous-gifted Pain, teach thou
The god to love, let him learn how.

Shells

Nature nothing shows more rare
Than shells, not even flowers; no,
Unfading petals tinted glow
Where ocean's obscure weight is air;
Where winds are currents, streams or tides,
Life to perfect their beauty hides.

Each hinged valve curves out and rims
Pink, yellow, purple, green or blue,
A colour-whisper's graded tune;
While dinted lobe, spine or rib limns
Crisp helmet, cusped shard to wing,
Full panoply for fairy wing.

In easy air and warm light nursed
Bloom yet and love with glamour fraught,
And brave but flower-like youth:
Like brittle shells, long years immersed,
Secreted by toil, conscience, thought,
Are formed art, virtue, truth.

WILLIAM HENRY DAVIES (1871—1940)

Leisure

What is this life if, full of care,
We have no time to stand and stare.

No time to stand beneath the boughs
And stare as long as sheep or cows.

No time to see, when woods we pass,
Where squirrels hide their nuts in grass.

No time to see, in broad daylight,
Streams full of stars like skies at night.

No time to turn at Beauty's glance,
And watch her feet, how they can dance.

No time to wait till her mouth can
Enrich that smile her eyes began.

A poor life this if, full of care,
We have no time to stand and stare.

The wind

Sometimes he roars among the leafy trees
Such sounds as in a narrow cove, when Seas
Rush in between high rocks; or grandly rolled,
Like music heard in churches that are old.
Sometimes he makes the children's happy sound,
When they play hide and seek, and one is found.
Sometimes he whineth like a dog in sleep,
Bit by the merciless, small fleas; then deep
And hollow sounds come from him, as starved men
Oft hear rise from their empty parts; and then
He'll hum a hollow groan, like one sick lain,
Who fears a move will but increase his pain.

And now he makes an awful wail, as when
From dark coal-pits are brought up crushed, dead men
To frantic wives. When he's on mischief bent,
He breeds more ill than that strange Parliament
Held by the witches, in the Hebrides;
He's here, he's there, to do what'er he please.
For well he knows the spirits' tricks at night,
Of slamming doors, and blowing out our light,
And tapping at our windows, rattling pails,
And making sighs and moans, and shouts and wails.
'Twas he no doubt made that young man's hair white,
Who slept alone in a strange house one night,
And was an old man in the morn and crazed,
And all who saw and heard him were amazed.

L

WALTER DE LA MARE (1873—1956)

Breughel's Winter

Jagg'd mountain peaks and skies ice-green
Wall in the wild cold scene below.
Churches, farms, bare copse, the sea
In freezing quiet of winter show;
Where ink-black shapes on fields in flood
Curling, skating, and sliding go.
To left, a gabled tavern; a blaze;
Peasants; a watching child; and lo,
Muffled, mute—beneath naked trees
In sharp perspective set a-row—
Trudge huntsmen, sinister spears aslant,
Dogs snuffling behind them in the snow;
And arrowlike, lean, athwart the air
    Swoops into space a crow.

But flame, nor ice, nor piercing rock,
Nor silence, as of a frozen sea,
Nor that slant inward infinite line
Of signboard, bird, and hill, and tree,
Give more than subtle hint of him
Who squandered here life's mystery.

Slim cunning hands

Slim cunning hands at rest, and cozening eyes—
Under this stone one loved too wildly lies;
How false she was, no granite could declare;
    Nor all earth's flowers, how fair.

The last coachload
To Colin

Crashed through the woods that lumbering Coach. The dust
Of flinted roads bepowdering felloe and hood.
Its gay paint cracked, its axles red with rust,
It lunged, lurched, toppled through a solitude

Of whispering boughs, and feathery, nid-nod grass.
Plodded the fetlocked horses. Glum and mum,
Its ancient Coachman recked not where he was,
Nor into what strange haunt his wheels were come.

354

Crumbling the leather of his dangling reins;
Worn to a cow's tuft his stumped, idle whip;
Sharp eyes of beast and bird in the trees' green lanes
Gleamed out like stars above a derelict ship.

'Old Father Time—Time—Time!' jeered twittering throat.
A squirrel capered on the leader's rump,
Slithered a weasel, peered a thief-like stoat,
In sandy warren beat on the coney's thump.

Mute as a mammet in his saddle sate
The hunched Postilion, clad in magpie trim;
The bright flies buzzed around his hairless pate;
Yaffle and jay squawked mockery at him.

Yet marvellous peace and amity breathed there.
Tranquil the labyrinths of this sundown wood.
Musking its chaces, bloomed the brier-rose fair;
Spellbound as if in trance the pine-trees stood.

Through moss and pebbled rut the wheels rasped on;
That Ancient drowsing on his box. And still
The bracken track with glazing sunbeams shone;
Laboured the horses, straining at the hill . . .

But now—a verdurous height with eve-shade sweet;
Far, far to West the Delectable Mountains glowed.
Above, Night's canopy; at the horses' feet
A sea-like honied waste of flowers flowed.

There fell a pause of utter quiet. And—
Out from one murky window glanced an eye,
Stole from the other a lean, groping hand,
The padded door swung open with a sigh.

And—*Exeunt Omnes*! None to ask the fare—
A myriad human Odds in a last release
Leap out incontinent, snuff the incensed air;
A myriad parched-up voices whisper, 'Peace.'

On, on, and on—a stream, a flood, they flow.
O wondrous vale of jocund buds and bells!
Like vanishing smoke the rainbow legions glow,
Yet still the enravished concourse sweeps and swells.

All journeying done. Rest now from lash and spur—
Laughing and weeping, shoulder and elbow—'twould seem
That Coach capacious all Infinity were,
And these the fabulous figments of a dream.

Mad for escape; frenzied each breathless mote,
Lest rouse the Old Enemy from his death-still swoon,
Lest crack that whip again—they fly, they float,
Scamper, breathe—'Paradise!' abscond, are gone . . .

GILBERT KEITH CHESTERTON (1874—1936)

Antichrist, or the reunion of Christendom: An ode

*"A Bill which has shocked the conscience of every
Christian community in Europe."—Mr. F. E. Smith,
on the Welsh Disestablishment Bill.*

Are they clinging to their crosses,
  F. E. Smith,
Where the Breton boat-fleet tosses,
  Are they, Smith?
Do they, fasting, trembling, bleeding,
 Wait the news from this our city?
Groaning 'That's the Second Reading!'
 Hissing 'There is still Committee!'
If the voice of Cecil falters,
 If McKenna's point has pith,
Do they tremble for their altars?
  Do they, Smith?

Russian peasants round their pope
  Huddled, Smith,
Hear about it all, I hope,
  Don't they, Smith?
In the mountain hamlets clothing
 Peaks beyond Caucasian pales,

Where Establishment means nothing
    And they never heard of Wales,
Do they read it all in Hansard
    With a crib to read it with—
'Welsh Tithes: Dr. Clifford Answered.'
                Really, Smith?

In the lands where Christians were,
                F. E. Smith,
In the little lands laid bare,
                Smith, O Smith!
Where the Turkish bands are busy,
    And the Tory name is blessed
Since they hailed the Cross of Dizzy
    On the banners from the West!
Men don't think it half so hard if
    Islam burns their kin and kith,
Since a curate lives in Cardiff
                Saved by Smith.

It would greatly, I must own,
                Soothe me, Smith!
If you left this theme alone,
                Holy Smith!
For your legal cause or civil
    You fight well and get your fee;
For your God or dream or devil
    You will answer, not to me.
Talk about the pews and steeples
    And the Cash that goes therewith!
But the souls of Christian peoples . . .
                Chuck it, Smith!

EDWARD THOMAS (1878—1917)

Haymaking

After night's thunder far away had rolled
The fiery day had a kernel sweet of cold
And in the perfect blue the clouds uncurled,
Like the first gods before they made the world
And misery, swimming the stormless sea
In beauty and in divine gaiety.

The smooth white empty road was lightly strewn
With leaves—the holly's Autumn falls in June—
And fir cones standing up stiff in the heat.
The mill-foot water tumbled white and lit
With tossing crystals, happier than any crowd
Of children pouring out of school aloud.
And in the little thickets where a sleeper
For ever might lie lost, the nettle creeper
And garden-warbler sang unceasingly;
While over them shrill shrieked in his fierce glee
The swift with wings and tail as sharp and narrow
As if the bow had flown off with the arrow.
Only the scent of woodbine and hay new mown
Travelled the road. In the field sloping down,
Park-like, to where its willow showed the brook,
Haymakers rested. The tosser lay forsook
Out in the sun; and the long waggon stood
Without its team: it seemed it never would
Move from the shadow of that single yew.
The team, as still, until their task was due,
Beside the labourers enjoyed the shade
That three squat oaks mid-field together made
Upon a circle of grass and weed uncut,
And on the hollow, once a chalk pit, but
Now brimmed with nut and elder-flower so clean.
The men leaned on their rakes, about to begin,
But still. And all were silent. All was old,
This morning time, with a great age untold,
Older than Clare and Cobbett, Morland and Crome,
Than at the field's far edge, the farmer's home,
A white house crouched at the foot of a great tree.
Under the heavens that know not what years be
The men, the beasts, the trees, the implements
Uttered even what they will in times far hence—
All of us gone out of the reach of change—
Immortal in a picture of an old grange.

Health

Four miles at a leap, over the dark hollow land,
To the frosted steep of the down and its juniper black,
Travels my eye with equal ease and delight:
And scarce could my body leap four yards.

This is the best and the worst of it—
Never to know,
Yet to imagine gloriously, pure health.

To-day, had I suddenly health,
I could not satisfy the desire of my heart
Unless health abated it,
So beautiful is the air in its softness and clearness, while Spring
Promises all and fails in nothing as yet;
And what blue and what white is I never knew
Before I saw this sky blessing the land.

For had I health I could not ride or run or fly
So far or so rapidly over the land
As I desire: I should reach Wiltshire tired;
I should have changed my mind before I could be in Wales.
I could not love; I could not command love.
Beauty would still be far off
However many hills I climbed over;
Peace would still be farther.
Maybe I should not count it anything
To leap these four miles with the eye;
And either I should not be filled almost to bursting with desire,
Or with my power desire would still keep pace.

Yet I am not satisfied
Even with knowing I never could be satisfied.
With health and all the power that lies
In maiden beauty, poet and warrior,
In Caesar, Shakespeare, Alcibiades,
Mazeppa, Leonardo, Michelangelo,
In any maiden whose smile is lovelier
Than sunlight upon dew,
I could not be as the wagtail running up and down
The warm tiles of the roof slope, twittering
Happily and sweetly as if the sun itself
Extracted the song
As the hand makes sparks from the fur of a cat:
I could not be as the sun.
Nor should I be content to be
As little as the bird or as mighty as the sun.

For the bird knows not of the sun,
And the sun regards not the bird.
But I am almost proud to love both bird and sun,
Though scarce this Spring could my body leap four yards.

JOHN MASEFIELD (b. 1878)

Sonnet

Flesh, I have knocked at many a dusty door,
Gone down full many a windy midnight lane,
Probed in old walls and felt along the floor,
Pressed in blind hope the lighted window-pane.
But useless all, though sometimes, when the moon
Was full in heaven and the sea was full,
Along my body's alleys came a tune
Played in the tavern by the Beautiful.

Then for an instant I have felt at point
To find and seize her, whosoe'er she be,
Whether some saint whose glory doth anoint
Those whom she loves, or but a part of me,
Or something that the things not understood
Make for their uses out of flesh and blood.

HAROLD MONRO (1879—1932)

Living

Slow bleak awakening from the morning dream
Brings me in contact with the sudden day.
I am alive—this I.
I let my fingers move along my body.
Realisation warns them, and my nerves
Prepare their rapid messages and signals.
While Memory begins recording, coding,
Repeating; all the time Imagination
Mutters: You'll only die.

Here's a new day. O pendulum move slowly!
My usual clothes are waiting on their peg.
I am alive—this I.

And in a moment Habit, like a crane,
Will bow its neck and dip its pulleyed cable,
Gathering me, my body, and our garment,
And swing me forth, oblivious of my question,
Into the daylight—why?

I think of all the others who awaken,
And wonder if they go to meet the morning
More valiantly than I;
Nor asking of this Day they will be living:
What have I done that I should be alive?
O, can I not forget that I am living?
How shall I reconcile the two conditions:
Living, and yet—to die?

Between the curtains the autumnal sunlight
With lean and yellow finger points me out;
The clock moans: Why? Why? Why?
But suddenly, as if without a reason,
Heart, Brain and Body, and Imagination
All gather in tumultuous joy together,
Running like children down the path of morning
To fields where they can play without a quarrel:
A country I'd forgotten, but remember,
And welcome with a cry.

O cool glad pasture; living tree, tall corn,
Great cliff, or languid sloping sand, cold sea,
Waves; rivers curving: you, eternal flowers,
Give me content, while I can think of you:
Give me your living breath!
Back to your rampart, Death.

Week-end

The ninth sonnet

Be staid; be careful; and be not too free.
Temptation to enjoy your liberty
may rise against you, break into a crime,
and smash the habit of employing time.

It serves no purpose that the careful clock
mark the appointment, the officious train
hurry to keep it, if the minutes mock
loud in your ear: 'Late, late. Late. Late again.'
Week-end is very well on Saturday:
A little episode, a trivial story
In some oblivious spot somehow, somewhere.
On Sunday nights we hardly laugh or speak:
Week-end begins to merge itself in Week.

ROBIN FLOWER (1881—1946)

Troy

I read last night with many pauses
—For the flesh is weak though the spirit be willing—
A book I bought for a pound and a shilling:
'The Trojan War's Economic Causes',
Till slumber at last through my eyelids crept,
And I let the book fall from my hands and slept.
Then, as the hours of the night grew deep,
A dream came through the passes of sleep
Of the silly stories of Homer's telling:
The press of the ships, the gathering hum,
Iphigeneia dying dumb,
The Greek tents white on the Trojan shore,
Achilles' anger and Nestor's lore,
The dabbled hair of the heroes lying
Mid the peace of the dead and the groans of the dying,
Hector dragged through the battle's lust,
The locks of Priam down in the dust,
Andromache's agony, Ilion's fall,
And, over all,
The lovely vision of naked Helen.

JAMES STEPHENS (1882—1950)

A glass of beer

The lanky hank of a she in the inn over there
Nearly killed me for asking the loan of a glass of beer;
May the devil grip the whey-faced slut by the hair,
And beat bad manners out of her skin for a year.

That parboiled ape, with the toughest jaw you will see
On virtue's path, and a voice that would rasp the dead,
Came roaring and raging the minute she looked at me,
And threw me out of the house on the back of my head!

If I asked her master he'd give me a cask a day;
But she, with the beer at hand, not a gill would arrange!
May she marry a ghost and bear him a kitten, and may
The High King of Glory permit her to get the mange.

Egan O Rahilly

Here in a distant place I hold my tongue;
I am O Rahilly!

When I was young,
Who now am young no more,
I did not eat things picked up from the shore:
The periwinkle, and the tough dog-fish
At even-tide have got into my dish!

The great, where are they now! the great had said—
This is not seemly! Bring to him instead
That which serves his and serves our dignity—
And that was done.

I am O Rahilly!
Here in a distant place he holds his tongue,
Who once said all his say, when he was young!

THOMAS ERNEST HULME (1883—1917)

Autumn

A touch of cold in the Autumn night
I walked abroad,
And saw the ruddy moon lean over a hedge,
Like a red-faced farmer.
I did not stop to speak, but nodded;
And round about were the wistful stars
With white faces like town children,

Fantasia of a fallen gentleman on a cold bitter night on the Embankment

Once, in finesse of fiddles found I ecstasy,
In a flash of gold heels on the hard pavement.
Now see I
That warmth's the very stuff of poesy.
Oh, God, make small
The old star-eaten blanket of the sky
That I may fold it round me and in comfort lie.

JAMES ELROY FLECKER (1884—1915)

Saadabad

Let us deal kindly with a heart of old by sorrow torn:
Come with Nedim to Saadabad, my love, this silver morn:
I hear the boatmen singing from our caïque on the Horn,
Waving cypress, waving cypress, let us go to Saadabad.

We shall watch the Sultan's fountains ripple, rumble, splash and rise
Over terraces of marble, under the blue balconies,
Leaping through the plaster dragon's hollow mouth and empty eyes:
Waving cypress, waving cypress, let us go to Saadabad.

Lie a little to your mother: tell her you must out to pray,
And we'll slink along the alleys, thieves of all a summer day,
Down the worn old watersteps, and then, my love, away:
Waving cypress, waving cypress, let us go to Saadabad.

You and I, and with us only some poor lover in a dream:
I and you—perhaps one minstrel who will sing beside the stream.
Ah Nedim will be the minstrel, and the lover be Nedim,
Waving cypress, waving cypress, when we go to Saadabad!

Down Horn Constantinople fades and flashes in the blue,
Rose of cities dropping with the heavy summer's burning dew,
Fading now as falls the Orient evening round the sky and you,
Fading into red and silver as we row to Saadabad.

Banish, then, O Grecian eyes, the passion of the waiting West!
Shall God's holy monks not enter on a day God knoweth best
To crown the Roman king again, and hang a cross upon his breast?
Daughter of the Golden Islands, come away to Saadabad.

And a thousand swinging steeples shall begin as they began
When Heraclius rode home from the wrack of Ispahan,
Naked captives pulled behind him, double eagles in the van—
But is this a tale for lovers on the way to Saadabad?

Rather now shall you remember how of old two such as we,
You like her the laughing mistress of a poet, him or me,
Came to find the flowery lawns that give the soul tranquillity:
Let the boatmen row no longer—for we land at Saadabad.

See you not that moon-dim caïque with the lovers at the prow,
Straining eyes and aching lips, and touching hands as we do now,
See you not the turbaned shadows passing, whence? and moving,
  how?
Are the ghosts of all the Moslems floating down to Saadabad?

Broken fountains, phantom waters, nevermore to glide and gleam
From the dragon-mouth in plaster sung of old by old Nedim,
Beautiful and broken fountains, keep you still your Sultan's dream,
Or remember how his poet took a girl to Saadabad?

DAVID HERBERT LAWRENCE (1885—1930)

Humming-bird

I can imagine, in some other world
Primeval-dumb, far back
In that most awful stillness, that only gasped and hummed,
Humming-birds raced down the avenues.

Before anything had a soul,
While life was a heave of Matter, half inanimate,
This little bit chipped off in brilliance
And went whizzing through the slow, vast, succulent stems.

I believe there were no flowers then,
In the world where the humming-bird flashed ahead of creation.
I believe he pierced the slow vegetable veins with his long beak.
Probably he was big
As mosses, and little lizards, they say, were once big.
Probably he was a jabbing, terrifying monster.

We look at him through the wrong end of the long telescope of Time.
Luckily for us.

Giorno dei Morti

Along the avenue of cypresses,
All in their scarlet cloaks, and surplices
Of linen, go the chanting choristers,
The priests in gold and black, the villagers . . .

And all along the path to the cemetery
The round dark heads of men crowd silently,
And black-scarved faces of women-folk, wistfully
Watch at the banner of death, and the mystery.

And at the foot of a grave a father stands
With sunken head, and forgotten, folded hands;
And at the foot of a grave a mother kneels
With pale shut face, and neither hears nor feels

The coming of the chanting choristers
Between the avenue of cypresses,
The silence of the many villagers,
The candle-flames beside the surplices.

ANDREW YOUNG (b. 1885)

In December

I watch the dung-cart stumble by
   Leading the harvest to the fields,
That from cow-byre and stall and sty
   The farmstead in the winter yields.

Like shocks in a reaped field of rye
   The small black heaps of lively dung
Sprinkled in the grass-meadow lie
   Licking the air with smoky tongue.

This is Earth's food that man piles up
   And with his fork will thrust on her,
And Earth will lie and slowly sup
   With her moist mouth through half the year.

The round barrow

A lark as small as a flint arrow
Rises and falls over this ancient barrow
And seems to mock with its light tones
The silent man of bones;

Some prince that earth drew back again
From his long strife with wind and mist and rain,
Baring for him this broad round breast
In token of her rest.

But as I think how Death sat once
And with sly fingers picked those princely bones,
I feel my bones are verily
The stark and final I.

I climbed the hill housed in warm flesh,
But now as one escaped from its false mesh
Through the wan mist I journey on,
A clanking skeleton.

RUPERT BROOKE (1887—1915)

Menelaus and Helen

Hot through Troy's ruin Menelaus broke
    To Priam's palace, sword in hand, to sate
    On that adulterous whore a ten years' hate
And a king's honour. Through red death, and smoke
And cries, and then by quieter ways he strode,
    Till the still innermost chamber fronted him.
    He swung his sword, and crashed into the dim
Luxurious bower, flaming like a god.

High sat white Helen, lonely and serene.
    He had not remembered that she was so fair
And that her neck curved down in such a way;
And he felt tired. He flung the sword away,
    And kissed her feet, and knelt before her there,
The perfect Knight before the perfect Queen.

So far the poet. How should he behold
   That journey home, the long connubial years?
   He does not tell you how white Helen bears
Child on legitimate child, becomes a scold,
Haggard with virtue. Menelaus bold
   Waxed garrulous, and sacked a hundred Troys
   'Twixt noon and supper. And her golden voice
Got shrill as he grew deafer. And both were old.

Often he wonders why on earth he went
   Troyward, or why poor Paris ever came.
Oft she weeps, gummy-eyed and impotent;
   Her dry shanks twitch at Paris' mumbled name.
So Menelaus nagged; and Helen cried;
And Paris slept on by Scamander side.

EDWIN MUIR (1887—1959)

Childhood

Long time he lay upon the sunny hill,
   To his father's house below securely bound.
Far off the silent, changing sound was still,
   With the black islands lying thick around.

He saw each separate height, each vaguer hue,
   Where the massed islands rolled in mist away,
And though all ran together in his view
   He knew that unseen straits between them lay.

Often he wondered what new shores were there.
   In thought he saw the still light on the sand,
The shallow water clear in tranquil air,
   And walked through it in joy from strand to strand.

Over the sound a ship so slow would pass
   That in the black hill's gloom it seemed to lie.
The evening sound was smooth like sunken glass,
   And time seemed finished ere the ship passed by.

Grey tiny rocks slept round him where he lay,
   Moveless as they, more still as evening came,
The grasses threw straight shadows far away,
   And from the house his mother called his name.

Horses

Those lumbering horses in the steady plough,
On the bare field—I wonder why, just now,
They seemed so terrible, so wild and strange,
Like magic power on the stony grange,

Perhaps some childish hour has come again,
When I watched fearful, through the blackening rain,
Their hooves like pistons in an ancient mill
Move up and down, yet seem as standing still.

Their conquering hooves which trod the stubble down
Were ritual that turned the field to brown,
And their great hulks were seraphim of gold,
Or mute ecstatic monsters on the mould.

And oh the rapture, when, one furrow done,
They marched broad-breasted to the sinking sun!
The light flowed off their bossy sides in flakes;
The furrows rolled behind like struggling snakes.

But when at dusk with steaming nostrils home
They came, they seemed gigantic in the gloam,
And warm and glowing with mysterious fire,
Which lit their smouldering bodies in the mire.

Their eyes as brilliant and as wide as night
Gleamed with a cruel apocalyptic light.
Their manes the leaping ire of the wind
Lifted with rage invisible and blind.

Ah now it fades! it fades! and I must pine
Again for that dread country crystalline,
Where the blank field and the still-standing tree
Were bright and fearful presences to me.

The interrogation

We could have crossed the road but hesitated.
And then came the patrol;
The leader conscientious and intent,
The men surly, indifferent.
While we stood by and waited
The interrogation began. He says the whole
Must come out now, who, what we are,
Where we have come from, with what purpose, whose
Country or camp we plot for or betray.
Question on question.
We have stood and answered through the standing day
And watched across the road beyond the hedge
The careless lovers in pairs go by,
Hand linked in hand, wandering another star,
So near we could shout to them. We cannot choose
Answer or action here,
Though still the careless lovers saunter by
And the thoughtless field is near.
We are on the very edge,
Endurance almost done,
And still the interrogation is going on.

DAME EDITH SITWELL (b. 1887)

Hornpipe

Sailors come
To the drum
Out of Babylon;
   Hobby-horses
Foam, the dumb
Sky rhinoceros-glum

Watched the courses of the breakers' rocking-horses and with Glaucis
Lady Venus on the settee of the horsehair sea!
Where Lord Tennyson in laurels wrote a gloria free,
In a borealic iceberg came Victoria; she
Knew Prince Albert's tall memorial took the colours of the floreal
And the borealic iceberg; floating on they see
New-arisen Madam Venus for whose sake from far

Came the fat and zebra'd emperor from Zanzibar
Where like golden bouquets lay far Asia, Africa, Cathay,
All laid before that shady lady by the fibroid Shah.
Captain Fracasse stout as any water-butt came, stood
With Sir Bacchus both a-drinking the black tarr'd grapes' blood
Plucked among the tartan leafage
By the furry wind whose grief age
Could not wither—like a squirrel with a gold star-nut.
Queen Victoria sitting shocked upon the rocking horse
Of a wave said to the Laureate, 'This minx of course
Is as sharp as any lynx and blacker-deeper than the drinks and quite as
Hot as any hottentot, without remorse!
                    For the minx,'
                              Said she,
                    'And the drinks,
                              You can see
Are hot as any hottentot and not the goods for me!'

Still falls the Rain
The Raids, 1940. Night and Dawn

Still falls the Rain—
Dark as the world of man, black as our loss—
Blind as the nineteen hundred and forty nails
Upon the Cross.

Still falls the Rain
With a sound like the pulse of the heart that is changed to the
   hammer-beat
In the Potter's Field, and the sound of the impious feet

On the Tomb:
                    Still falls the Rain
In the Field of Blood where the small hopes breed and the human
   brain
Nurtures its greed, that worm with the brow of Cain.

Still falls the Rain
At the feet of the Starved Man hung upon the Cross.
Christ that each day, each night, nails there, have mercy on us—
On Dives and on Lazarus:
Under the rain the sore and the gold are as one.

Still falls the Rain—
Still falls the Blood from the Starved Man's wounded Side:
He bears in His Heart all wounds,—those of the light that died,
The last faint spark
In the self-murdered heart, the wounds of the sad uncomprehending
   dark,
The wounds of the baited bear,—
The blind and weeping bear whom the keepers beat
On his helpless flesh ... the tears of the hunted hare.

Still falls the Rain—
Then—O Ile leape up to my God: who pulles me doune—
See, see where Christ's blood streames in the firmament:
It flows from the Brow we nailed upon the tree
Deep to the dying, to the thirsting heart
That holds the fires of the world,—dark-smirched with pain
As Caesar's laurel crown.

Then sounds the voice of One who like the heart of man
Was once a child who among beasts has lain—
'Still do I love, still shed my innocent light, my Blood, for thee.'

Dirge for the New Sunrise

*Fifteen minutes past eight o'clock, on the morning of
Monday the 6th August 1945*

Bound to my heart as Ixion to the wheel,
Nailed to my heart as the Thief upon the Cross,
I hang between our Christ and the gap where the world was lost

And watch the phantom Sun in Famine Street
—The ghost of the heart of Man ... red Cain
And the more murderous brain
Of Man, still redder Nero that conceived the death
Of his mother Earth, and tore
Her womb, to know the place where he was conceived.

But no eyes grieved—
For none were left for tears:
They were blinded as the years
Since Christ was born. Mother or Murderer, you have given or
   taken life—
Now all is one!

There was a morning when the holy Light
Was young. The beautiful First Creature came
To our water-springs, and thought us without blame.

Our hearts seemed safe in our breasts and sang to the Light—
The marrow in the bone
We dreamed was safe . . . the blood in the veins, the sap
　in the tree
Were springs of Deity.

But I saw the little Ant-men as they ran
Carrying the world's weight of the world's filth
And the filth in the heart of Man—
Compressed till those lusts and greeds had a greater heat
　than that of the Sun.

And the ray from that heat came soundless, shook the sky
As if in search of food, and squeezed the stems
Of all that grows on the earth till they were dry
—And drank the marrow of the bone:
The eyes that saw, the lips that kissed, are gone
Or black as thunder lie and grin at the murdered Sun.

The living blind and seeing Dead together lie
As if in love . . . There was no more hating then,
And no more love: Gone is the heart of Man.

From *Three poems of the Atomic Bomb*

THOMAS STEARNS ELIOT (b. 1888)

Preludes

I

The winter evening settles down
With smell of steaks in passageways.
Six o'clock.
The burnt-out ends of smoky days.
And now a gusty shower wraps
The grimy scraps
Of withered leaves about your feet
And newspapers from vacant lots;

The showers beat
On broken blinds and chimney-pots,
And at the corner of the street
A lonely cab-horse steams and stamps.
And then the lighting of the lamps.

II

The morning comes to consciousness
Of faint stale smells of beer
From the sawdust-trampled street
With all its muddy feet that press
To early coffee-stands.
With the other masquerades
That time resumes,
One thinks of all the hands
That are raising dingy shades
In a thousand furnished rooms.

III

You tossed a blanket from the bed,
You lay upon your back, and waited;
You dozed, and watched the night revealing
The thousand sordid images
Of which your soul was constituted;
They flickered against the ceiling.
And when all the world came back
And the light crept up between the shutters,
And you heard the sparrows in the gutters,
You had such a vision of the street
As the street hardly understands;
Sitting along the bed's edge, where
You curled the papers from your hair,
Or clasped the yellow soles of feet
In the palms of both soiled hands.

IV

His soul stretched tight across the skies
That fade behind a city block,
Or trampled by insistent feet
At four and five and six o'clock;

And short square fingers stuffing pipes,
And evening newspapers, and eyes
Assured of certain certainties,
The conscience of a blackened street
Impatient to assume the world.

I am moved by fancies that are curled
Around these images, and cling:
The notion of some infinitely gentle
Infinitely suffering thing.

Wipe your hand across your mouth, and laugh;
The worlds revolve like ancient women
Gathering fuel in vacant lots.

Gerontion

*Thou hast nor youth nor age
But as it were an after dinner sleep
Dreaming of both.*

Here I am, an old man in a dry month,
Being read to by a boy, waiting for rain.
I was neither at the hot gates
Nor fought in the warm rain
Nor knee deep in the salt marsh, heaving a cutlass,
Bitten by flies, fought.
My house is a decayed house,
And the jew squats on the window-sill, the owner,
Spawned in some estaminet of Antwerp,
Blistered in Brussels, patched and peeled in London.
The goat coughs at night in the field overhead;
Rocks, moss, stonecrop, iron, merds.
The woman keeps the kitchen, makes tea,
Sneezes at evening, poking the peevish gutter.
                         I an old man,
A dull head among windy spaces.

Signs are taken for wonders. "We would see a sign!"
The word within a word, unable to speak a word,
Swaddled with darkness. In the juvescence of the year
Came Christ the tiger

In depraved May, dogwood and chestnut, flowering judas.
To be eaten, to be divided, to be drunk
Among whispers; by Mr. Silvero
With caressing hands, at Limoges
Who walked all night in the next room;
By Hakagawa, bowing among the Titians;
By Madame de Tornquist, in the dark room
Shifting the candles; Fraülein von Kulp
Who turned in the hall, one hand on the door. Vacant shuttles
Weave the wind. I have no ghosts,
An old man in a draughty house
Under a windy knob.

After such knowledge, what forgiveness? Think now
History has many cunning passages, contrived corridors
And issues, deceives with whispering ambitions,
Guides us by vanities. Think now
She gives when our attention is distracted
And what she gives, gives with such supple confusions
That the giving famishes the craving. Gives too late
What's not believed in, or if still believed,
In memory only, reconsidered passion. Gives too soon
Into weak hands, what's thought can be dispensed with
Till the refusal propagates a fear. Think
Neither fear nor courage saves us. Unnatural vices
Are fathered by our heroism. Virtues
Are forced upon us by our impudent crimes.
These tears are shaken from the wrath-bearing tree.

The tiger springs in the new year. Us he devours. Think at last
We have not reached conclusion, when I
Stiffen in a rented house. Think at last
I have not made this show purposelessly
And it is not by any concitation
Of the backward devils.
I would meet you upon this honestly.
I that was near your heart was removed therefrom
To lose beauty in terror, terror in inquisition.
I have lost my passion: why should I need to keep it
Since what is kept must be adulterated?
I have lost my touch, smell, hearing, taste and touch:
How should I use them for your closer contact?

These with a thousand small deliberations
Protract the profit of their chilled delirium,
Excite the membrane, when the sense has cooled,
With pungent sauces, multiply variety
In a wilderness of mirrors. What will the spider do,
Suspend its operations, will the weevil
Delay? De Bailhache, Fresca, Mrs. Cammel, whirled
Beyond the circuit of the shuddering Bear
In fractured atoms. Gull against the wind, in the windy straits
Of Belle Isle, or running on the Horn,
White feathers in the snow, the Gulf claims,
And an old man driven by the Trades
To a sleepy corner.
                                        Tenants of the house,
Thoughts of a dry brain in a dry season.

The Dry Salvages

The Dry Salvages—presumably *les trois sauvages*—is a small group of rocks,
with a beacon, off the north-east coast of Cape Ann, Massachusetts. *Salvages* is
pronounced to rhyme with *assuages*. *Groaner:* a whistling buoy.

I

I do not know much about gods; but I think that the river
Is a strong brown god—sullen, untamed and intractable,
Patient to some degree, at first recognised as a frontier;
Useful, untrustworthy, as a conveyor of commerce;
Then only a problem confronting the builder of bridges.
The problem once solved, the brown god is almost forgotten
By the dwellers in cities—ever, however, implacable,
Keeping his seasons and rages, destroyer, reminder
Of what men choose to forget. Unhonoured, unpropitiated
By worshippers of the machine, but waiting, watching and
    waiting.
His rhythm was present in the nursery bedroom,
In the rank ailanthus of the April dooryard,
In the smell of grapes on the autumn table,
And the evening circle in the winter gaslight.

The river is within us, the sea is all about us;
The sea is the land's edge also, the granite
Into which it reaches, the beaches where it tosses

Its hints of earlier and other creation:
The starfish, the horseshoe crab, the whale's backbone;
The pools where it offers to our curiosity
The more delicate algae and the sea anemone.
It tosses up our losses, the torn seine,
The shattered lobsterpot, the broken oar
And the gear of foreign dead men. The sea has many voices,
Many gods and many voices.
                              The salt is on the briar rose,
The fog is in the fir trees.
                    The sea howl
And the sea yelp, are different voices
Often together heard: the whine in the rigging,
The menace and caress of wave that breaks on water,
The distant rote in the granite teeth,
And the wailing warning from the approaching headland
Are all sea voices, and the heaving groaner
Rounded homewards, and the seagull:
And under the oppression of the silent fog
The tolling bell
Measures time not our time, rung by the unhurried
Ground swell, a time
Older than the time of chronometers, older
Than time counted by anxious worried women
Lying awake, calculating the future,
Trying to unweave, unwind, unravel
And piece together the past and the future,
Between midnight and dawn, when the past is all deception,
The future futureless, before the morning watch
When time stops and time is never ending;
And the ground swell, that is and was from the beginning,
Clangs
The bell.

II

Where is there an end of it, the soundless wailing,
The silent withering of autumn flowers
Dropping their petals and remaining motionless;
Where is there an end to the drifting wreckage,
The prayer of the bone on the beach, the unprayable
Prayer at the calamitous annunciation?

There is no end, but addition: the trailing
Consequence of further days and hours,
While emotion takes to itself the emotionless
Years of living among the breakage
Of what was believed in as the most reliable—
And therefore the fittest for renunciation.

There is the final addition, the failing
Pride or resentment at failing powers,
The unattached devotion which might pass for devotionless,
In a drifting boat with a slow leakage,
The silent listening to the undeniable
Clamour of the bell of the last annunciation.

Where is the end of them, the fishermen sailing
Into the wind's tail, where the fog cowers?
We cannot think of a time that is oceanless
Or of an ocean not littered with wastage
Or of a future that is not liable
Like the past, to have no destination.

We have to think of them as forever bailing,
Setting and hauling, while the North East lowers
Over shallow banks unchanging and erosionless
Or drawing their money, drying sails at dockage;
Not as making a trip that will be unpayable
For a haul that will not bear examination.

There is no end of it, the voiceless wailing,
No end to the withering of withered flowers,
To the movement of pain that is painless and motionless,
To the drift of the sea and the drifting wreckage,
The bone's prayer to Death its God. Only the hardly, barely
    prayable
Prayer of the one Annunciation.

It seems, as one becomes older,
That the past has another pattern, and ceases to be a mere
    sequence—
Or even development: the latter a partial fallacy
Encouraged by superficial notions of evolution
Which becomes, in the popular mind, a means of disowning
    the past.

The moments of happiness—not the sense of well-being,
Fruition, fulfilment, security or affection,
Or even a very good dinner, but the sudden illumination—
We had the experience but missed the meaning,
And approach to the meaning restores the experience
In a different form, beyond any meaning
We can assign to happiness. I have said before
That the past experience revived in the meaning
Is not the experience of one life only
But of many generations—not forgetting
Something that is probably quite ineffable:
The backward look behind the assurance
Of recorded history, the backward half-look
Over the shoulder, towards the primitive terror.
Now, we come to discover that the moments of agony
(Whether, or not, due to misunderstanding,
Having hoped for the wrong things or dreaded the wrong things,
Is not in question) are likewise permanent
With such permanence as time has. We appreciate this better
In the agony of others, nearly experienced,
Involving ourselves, than in our own.
For our own past is covered by the currents of action,
But the torment of others remains an experience
Unqualified, unworn by subsequent attrition.
People change, and smile: but the agony abides.
Time the destroyer is time the preserver,
Like the river with its cargo of dead negroes, cows and chicken
    coops,
The bitter apple and bite in the apple.
And the ragged rock in the restless waters,
Waves wash over it, fogs conceal it;
On a halcyon day it is merely a monument,
In navigable weather it is always a seamark
To lay a course by: but in the sombre season
Or the sudden fury, is what it always was.

III

I sometimes wonder if that is what Krishna meant—
Among other things—or one way of putting the same thing:
That the future is a faded song, a Royal Rose or a lavender spray
Of wistful regret for those who are not yet here to regret,

Pressed between yellow leaves of a book that has never been
  opened.
And the way up is the way down, the way forward is the way
  back.
You cannot face it steadily, but this thing is sure,
That time is no healer: the patient is no longer here.
When the train starts, and the passengers are settled
To fruit, periodicals and business letters
(And those who saw them off have left the platform)
Their faces relax from grief into relief,
To the sleepy rhythm of a hundred hours.
Fare forward, travellers! not escaping from the past
Into different lives, or into any future;
You are not the same people who left that station
Or who will arrive at any terminus,
While the narrowing rails slide together behind you;
And on the deck of the drumming liner
Watching the furrow that widens behind you,
You shall not think 'the past is finished'
Or 'the future is before us'.
At nightfall, in the rigging and the aerial,
Is a voice descanting (though not to the ear,
The murmuring shell of time, and not in any language)
'Fare forward, you who think that you are voyaging;
You are not those who saw the harbour
Receding, or those who will disembark.
Here between the hither and the farther shore
While time is withdrawn, consider the future
And the past with an equal mind.
At the moment which is not of action or inaction
You can receive this: "on whatever sphere of being
The mind of a man may be intent
At the time of death"—that is the one action
(And the time of death is every moment)
Which shall fructify in the lives of others:
And do not think of the fruit of action.
Fare forward.
                    O voyagers, O seamen,
You who come to port, and you whose bodies
Will suffer the trial and judgement of the sea,
Or whatever event, this is your real destination.'

So Krishna, as when he admonished Arjuna
On the field of battle.
                        Not fare well,
But fare forward, voyagers.

IV

Lady, whose shrine stands on the promontory,
Pray for all those who are in ships, those
Whose business has to do with fish, and
Those concerned with every lawful traffic
And those who conduct them.

Repeat a prayer also on behalf of
Women who have seen their sons or husbands
Setting forth, and not returning:
Figlia del tuo figlio,
Queen of Heaven.
Also pray for those who were in ships, and
Ended their voyage on the sand, in the sea's lips
Or in the dark throat which will not reject them
Or wherever cannot reach them the sound of the sea bell's
Perpetual angelus.

V

To communicate with Mars, converse with spirits,
To report the behaviour of the sea monster,
Describe the horoscope, haruspicate or scry,
Observe disease in signatures, evoke
Biography from the wrinkles of the palm
And tragedy from fingers; release omens
By sortilege, or tea leaves, riddle the inevitable
With playing cards, fiddle with pentagrams
Or barbituric acids, or dissect
The recurrent image into pre-conscious terrors—
To explore the womb, or tomb, or dreams; all these are usual
Pastimes and drugs, and features of the press:
And always will be, some of them especially
When there is distress of nations and perplexity
Whether on the shores of Asia, or in the Edgware Road.
Men's curiosity searches past and future
And clings to that dimension. But to apprehend

The point of intersection of the timeless
With time, is an occupation for the saint—
No occupation either, but something given
And taken, in a lifetime's death in love,
Ardour and selflessness and self-surrender.
For most of us, there is only the unattended
Moment, the moment in and out of time,
The distraction fit, lost in a shaft of sunlight,
The wild thyme unseen, or the winter lightning
Or the waterfall, or music heard so deeply
That it is not heard at all, but you are the music
While the music lasts. These are only hints and guesses,
Hints followed by guesses; and the rest
Is prayer, observance, discipline, thought and action.
The hint half guessed, the gift half understood, is Incarnation.
Here the impossible union
Of spheres of existence is actual,
Here the past and future
Are conquered, and reconciled,
Where action were otherwise movement
Of that which is only moved
And has in it no source of movement—
Driven by dæmonic, chthonic
Powers. And right action is freedom
From past and future also.
For most of us, this is the aim
Never here to be realised;
Who are only undefeated
Because we have gone on trying;
We, content at the last
If our temporal reversion nourish
(Not too far from the yew-tree)
The life of significant soil.

WALTER JAMES TURNER (1889—1946)

Poetry and science

Night like a silver peacock in the sky
By Moon bewitched turns many thousand eyes
In vacancy. Flits past in fading mist
A Comet's tail, the Phoenix of the Sun,
Blown from her burning nest of whitened ash.

WALTER JAMES TURNER

If this be false it is illusion's gain
Since all we know is but a midday dream:
Sun Moon and Stars—are they not Fancy's names,
Products of human orbs which like these roll
In automatic frenzy, maddened by Light?

Light's blinding lust like an invisible worm
Hatched in the small, dark nucleus of the atom
Spies out a Dragon, which encyclopaedic seed
Sprouts wings thro' Natural History—red, blue, yellow!
Crocus, Auk, Griffin, Mandrake, Dandelion.

Latest begotten of Light's progeny,
Proton and Neotron have large unfound kin
Awaiting birth; some stay nameless heroes
Of stories not yet written, some—stars in films—
Lie, celluloid unremembered, packed in cans.

Man's endless Phantasy pours in procession:
Tyrannic Leaders, Kings and Presidents;
Phantoms of spiritual hunger—Christ and Buddha;
Construction vaguer still—Sin, Evolution—
Eggs of that Great Auk, human imagination.

But children, grown-up, take fairy tales for real
Yes, they are real, real stories of Hans Andersen
There is no other truth than purest fiction
But what it means let none pretend to say,
Or saying, at least say only, *This is my dream.*

This is my dream that all the world is one—
Stones, trees, birds, men, Light, Jesus and the Devil
Fret not on any rung of Change's spiral
For all is Change, yet all is One for ever—
Love, hate, crime, virtue fitting into one whole.

In short, these words are words and words are dreams
All words—the scientists' poets' philosophers' and priests'.
You like this dream? Methinks I like it not
Yet every thought is but a flower of Fancy
Beloved by someone even as every flower.

I like them all; some greatly, other less
To me ideas are fair as flowers or girls
(I cannot tell you why I find some silly
Yet still to like) others have such rare beauty
They fill me with new joy—this is my dream.

ISAAC ROSENBERG (1890—1918)

Break of day in the trenches

The darkness crumbles away—
It is the same old druid Time as ever.
Only a live thing leaps my hand—
A queer sardonic rat—
As I pull the parapet's poppy
To stick behind my ear.
Droll rat, they would shoot you if they knew
Your cosmopolitan sympathies
(And God knows what antipathies).
Now you have touched this English hand
You will do the same to a German—
Soon, no doubt, if it be your pleasure
To cross the sleeping green between.
It seems you inwardly grin as you pass
Strong eyes, fine limbs, haughty athletes
Less chanced than you for life,
Bonds to the whims of murder,
Sprawled in the bowels of the earth,
The torn fields of France.
What do you see in our eyes
At the shrieking iron and flame
Hurled through still heavens?
What quaver—what heart aghast?
Poppies whose roots are in man's veins
Drop, and are ever dropping;
But mine in my ear is safe,
Just a little white with the dust.

RICHARD ALDINGTON (b. 1892)

Evening

The chimneys, rank on rank,
Cut the clear sky;
The moon,
With a rag of gauze about her loins
Poses among them, an awkward Venus—
And here am I looking wantonly at her
Over the kitchen sink.

HUGH MACDIARMID (b. 1892)

Deep-sea fishing

I suddenly saw I was wrang when I felt
That the gapin' mooths and gogglin' een
O' the fish were no' what we should expect
Frae a sea sae infinite and serene.

I kent I'd be equally wrang if I wished
My nice concern wi' its beauty to be
Shared by the fishermen wha's coarser lives
Seemed proof to a' that appealed to me.

Aye, and I kent their animal forms
And primitave minds, like fish frae the sea,
Cam' faur mair naturally oot o' the bland
Omnipotence o' God than a fribble like me.

De profundis

I delight in this naethingness
Mair than ever I did
In the creation it yielded
And has aince mair hid.

Sae an ardent spirit
Should submerge a' its learned
And enjoy to the full
Whatna leisure it's earned.

For what is the end
O' a' labour but this?
—Earth's fruits to the flesh;
To the soul the Abyss.

Antenora

The stream is frozen hard. Going by
This wintry spectacle I descry
How even Edinburgh folk may be
In Scotland, not Antenora, yet,
Not traitors to their land, condemned
To a frore fate in Cocytus' pit,
But seasonably Scottish in their way,
And thaw, though hellish slow, some day!

SIR OSBERT SITWELL (b. 1892)

On the coast of Coromandel

On the coast of Coromandel
Dance they to the tunes of Handel;
Chorally, that coral coast
Correlates the bone to ghost,
Till word and limb and note seem one,
Blending, binding act to tone.

All day long they point the sandal
On the coast of Coromandel.
Lemon-yellow legs all bare
Pirouette to peruqued air
From the first green shoots of morn,
Cool as northern hunting-horn,
Till the nightly tropic wind
With its rough-tongued, grating rind
Shatters the frail spires of spice.
Imaged in the lawns of rice
(Mirror-flat and mirror green
Is that lovely water's sheen)
Saraband and rigadoon
Dance they through the purring noon,

SIR OSBERT SITWELL

While the lacquered waves expand
Golden dragons on the sand—
Dragons that must, steaming, die
From the hot sun's agony—
When elephants, of royal blood,
Plod to bed through lilied mud,
Then evening, sweet as any mango,
Bids them do a gay fandango,
Minuet, jig or gavotte,
How they hate the turkey-trot,
The nautch-dance and the highland fling,
Just as they will never sing
Any music save by Handel
On the coast of Coromandel!

WILFRED OWEN (1893—1918)

Anthem for doomed youth

What passing-bells for these who die as cattle?
Only the monstrous anger of the guns.
Only the stuttering rifles' rapid rattle
Can patter out their hasty orisons.
No mockeries for them; no prayers nor bells,
Nor any voice of mourning save the choirs,—
The shrill, demented choirs of wailing shells;
And bugles calling for them from sad shires.

What candles may be held to speed them all?
Not in the hands of boys, but in their eyes
Shall shine the holy glimmers of good-byes.
The pallor of girls' brows shall be their pall;
Their flowers the tenderness of patient minds,
And each slow dusk a drawing-down of blinds.

Futility

Move him in the sun—
Gently its touch awoke him once,
At home, whispering of fields unsown.
Always it woke him, even in France,
Until this morning and this snow.
If anything might rouse him now
The kind old sun will know.

Think how it wakes the seeds,—
Woke, once, the clays of a cold star.
Are limbs, so dear-achieved, are sides,
Full-nerved—still warm—too hard to stir?
Was it for this the clay grew tall?
—O what made fatuous sunbeams toil
To break earth's sleep at all?

SIR HERBERT READ (b. 1893)

A northern legion

Bugle calls coiling through the rocky valley
have found echoes in the eagles' cries:
an outrage is done on anguished men
now men die and death is no deedful glory.

Eleven days this legion forced the ruined fields, the
burnt homesteads and empty garths, the broken arches
of bridges: desolation moving like a shadow before them, a
rain of ashes. Endless anxiety

marching into a northern darkness: approaching
a narrow defile, the waters falling fearfully
the clotting menace of shadows and all the multiple
instruments of death in ambush against them.

The last of the vanguard sounds his doleful note.
The legion now is lost. None will follow.

The seven sleepers

The seven sleepers ere they left
the light and colour of the earth
the seven sleepers they did cry
(banishing their final fears):

'Beauty will not ever fade.
To our cavern we retire
doomed to sleep ten thousand years.
Roll the rock across the gap

Then forget us; we are quiet;
stiff and cold our bodies lie;
Earth itself shall stir ere we
visit Earth's mortality.

Beauty when we wake will be
a solitude on land and sea.'

ROBERT GRAVES (b. 1895)

Ogres and Pygmies

Those famous men of old, the Ogres—
They had long beards and stinking arm-pits.
They were wide-mouthed, long-yarded and great-bellied
Yet of not taller stature, Sirs, than you.
They lived on Ogre-Strand, which was no place
But the churl's terror of their proud extent,
Where every foot was three-and-thirty inches,
And every penny bought a whole sheep.
Now of their company none survive, not one,
The times being, thank God, unfavourable
To all but nightmare memory of them.
Their images stand howling in the waste,
(The winds enforced against their wide mouths)
Whose granite haunches king and priest must yearly
Buss, and their cold knobbed knees.

So many feats they did to admiration:
With their enormous lips they sang louder
Than ten cathedral choirs, and with their grand yards
Stormed the most rare and obstinate maidenheads,
With their strong-gutted and capacious bellies
Digested stones and glass like ostriches.
They dug great pits and heaped great cairns,
Deflected rivers, slew whole armies,
And hammered judgments for posterity—
For the sweet-cupid-lipped and tassel-yarded
Delicate-stomached dwellers
In Pygmy Alley, where with brooding on them
A foot is shrunk to seven inches
And twelve-pence will not buy a spare rib.

And who would choose between Ogres and Pygmies—
The thundering text, the snivelling commentary—
Reading between such covers he will likely
Prove his own disproportion and not laugh.

The bards

Their cheeks are blotched for shame, their running verse
Stumbles, with marrow-bones the drunken diners
Pelt them as they delay:
It is a something fearful in the song
Plagues them, an unknown grief that like a churl
Goes commonplace in cowskin
And bursts unheralded, crowing and coughing,
An unpilled holly-club twirled in his hand,
Into their many-shielded, samite-curtained
Jewel-bright hall where twelve kings sit at chess
Over the white-bronze pieces and the gold,
And by a gross enchantment
Flails down the rafters and leads off the queens—
The wild-swan-breasted, the rose-ruddy-cheeked
Raven-haired daughters of their admiration—
To stir his black pots and to bed on straw.

In the wilderness

Christ of His gentleness
Thirsting and hungering
Walked in the wilderness;
Soft words of grace He spoke
Unto lost desert-folk
That listened wondering.
He heard the bitterns call
From ruined palace-wall,
Answered them brotherly.
He held communion
With the she-pelican
Of lonely piety.
Basilisk, cockatrice,
Flocked to His homilies,
With mail of dread device,
With monstrous barbed stings.

With eager dragon-eyes;
Great rats on leather wings,
And poor blind broken things,
Foul in their miseries.
And ever with Him went,
Of all His wanderings
Comrade, with ragged coat,
Gaunt ribs—poor innocent—
Bleeding foot, burning throat,
The guileless old scape-goat;
For forty nights and days
Followed in Jesus' ways,
Sure guard behind Him kept,
Tears like a lover wept.

EDMUND BLUNDEN (b. 1896)

The barn

Rain-sunken roof, grown green and thin
For sparrows' nests and starlings' nests;
Dishevelled eaves; unwieldy doors,
Cracked rusty pump, and oaken floors,
And idly-pencilled names and jests
    Upon the posts within.

The light pales at the spider's lust,
The wind tangs through the shattered pane:
An empty hop-poke spreads across
The gaping frame to mend the loss
And keeps out sun as well as rain,
    Mildewed with clammy dust.

The smell of apples stored in hay
And homely cattle-cake is there.
Use and disuse have come to terms,
The walls are hollowed out by worms,
But men's feet keep the mid-floor bare
    And free from worse decay.

All merry noise of hens astir
Or sparrows squabbling on the roof
Comes to the barn's broad open door;
You hear upon the stable floor
Old hungry Dapple strike his hoof,
    And the blue fan-tail's whir.

The barn is old, and very old,
But not a place of spectral fear.
Cobwebs and dust and speckling sun
Come to old buildings every one.
Long since they made their dwelling here,
    And here you may behold

Nothing but simple wane and change;
Your tread will wake no ghost, your voice
Will fall on silence undeterred.
No phantom wailing will be heard,
Only the farm's blithe cheerful noise;
    The barn is old, not strange.

AUSTIN CLARKE (b. 1896)

The fair at Windgap

There was airy music and sport at the fair
And showers were tenting on the bare field,
Laughter had knotted a crowd where the horses
And mares were backing, when carts from the wheelwright
Were shafted: bargains on sale everywhere and the barmen
Glassing neat whiskey or pulling black porter
On draught—and O the red brandy, the oatmeal
And the whiteness of flour in the weighing scale!

Calico petticoats, cashmere and blouses,
Blankets of buttermilk, flannel on stalls there,
Caps of bright tweed and corduroy trousers
And green or yellow ribbon with a stripe;
The tanner was hiding, the saddler plied the bradawl;
Barrows had chinaware, knives and blue razors,
Black twisted tobacco to pare in the claypipe
And the ha'penny harp that is played on a finger.

Soft as rain slipping through rushes, the cattle
Came: dealers were brawling at seven-pound-ten,
On heifers in calf a bargain was clapped
When ewes, that are nearer the grass, had taken
Two guineas; the blacksmith was filing the horn in his lap
For the fillies called up more hands than their height,
Black goats were cheap; for a sow in the stock
O'Flaherty got but the half of her farrow.

Balladmen, beggarmen, trick o' the loop men
And cardmen, hiding Queen Maeve up their sleeve,
Were picking red pennies and soon a prizefighter
Enticed the young fellows and left them all grieving:
While the marriageable girls were walking up and down
And the folk were saying that the Frenchmen
Had taken the herring from the brown tide
And sailed at daybreak, they were saying.

Twenty-five tinkers that came from Glentartan,
Not counting the jennets and barefooted women,
Had a white crop of metal upon every cart;
The neighbours were buying, but a red-headed man
Of them, swearing no stranger could bottom a kettle,
Leaped over the droves going down to the ocean,
Glibbed with the sunlight: blows were around him
And so the commotion arose at the fair.

RUTH PITTER (b. 1897)

The stockdove

Close in the hollow bank she lies,
Soiling with clay her azure dress:
Then slowly lifts that head, whose eyes
Have given a name to gentleness.
O is she caught, and is she snared,
Or why so still, and perched so low?
She is not ruffled, is not scared,
And yet I watch, and cannot go.

And dumbly comes the hard reply;
Death shakes her like a winter storm;

Then her round head she would put by,
As she was wont, in feathers warm:
Half lifts the wing, half turns the bill,
Then leans more lowly on the clay,
Sighs, and at last is quiet and still,
Sits there, and yet is fled away.

The epoch will not suffer me
To weep above such humble dead,
Or I could mourn a century
For all such woe unmerited:
For the soft eye, the feathers blue,
The voice more gentle than the rain,
The feet that dabbled in the dew,
We strew the field with poisoned grain.

My questioned spirit's sidelong look
From her old fortress answers me,
From where she reads her secret book
On the tall rock Infinity;
From where the innocent dead to that
High spot is fled away from grief,
And whence as from an Ararat
She brings the silver olive-leaf.

SACHEVERELL SITWELL (b. 1897)

The Rio Grande

By the Rio Grande
They dance no sarabande
On level banks like lawns above the glassy, lolling tide;
Nor sing they forlorn madrigals
Whose sad note stirs the sleeping gales
Till they wake among the trees, and shake the boughs,
And fright the nightingales;

But they dance in the city, down the public squares,
On the marble pavers with each colour laid in shares,
At the open church doors loud with light within,
At the bell's huge tolling,
By the river, music gurgling, thin
Through the soft Brazilian air.

The Comendador and Alguacil are there
On horseback, hid with feathers, loud and shrill
Blowing orders on their trumpets like a bird's sharp bill
Through boughs, like a bitter wind, calling;
They shine like steady starlight while those other sparks are
    falling
In burnished armour, with their plumes of fire,
Tireless, while all others tire.
The noisy streets are empty and hushed is the town
To where, in the square, they dance and the band is playing;
Such a space of silence through the town to the river
That the water murmurs loud
Above the band and crowd together;
And the strains of the sarabande,
More lively than a madrigal,
Go hand in hand
Like the river and its waterfall
As the great Rio Grande rolls down to the sea.
Loud is the marimba's note
Above these half-salt waves,
And louder still the tympanum,
The plectrum, and the kettledrum,
Sullen and menacing
Do these brazen voices ring.
They ride outside,
Above the salt sea's tide,
Till the ships at anchor there
Hear this enchantment
Of the soft Brazilian air,
By those Southern winds wafted,
Slow and gentle,
Their fierceness tempered
By the air that flows between.

KENNETH SLESSOR (b. 1901)

Two chronometers

Two chronometers the captain had,
One by Arnold that ran like mad,
One by Kendal in a walnut case,
Poor devoted creature with a hangdog face.

Arnold always hurried with a crazed click-click
Dancing over Greenwich like a lunatic,
Kendal panted faithfully his watch-dog beat,
Climbing out of Yesterday with sticky little feet.

Arnold choked with appetite to wolf up time,
Madly round the numerals his hands would climb,
His cogs rushed over and his wheels ran miles,
Dragging Captain Cook to the Sandwich Isles.

But Kendal dawdled in the tombstone past,
With a sentimental prejudice to going fast,
And he thought very often of a haberdasher's door
And a yellow-haired boy who would knock no more.

All through the night-time, clock talked to clock,
In the captain's cabin, tock-tock-tock,
One ticked fast and one ticked slow,
And Time went over them a hundred years ago.

From *Five Visions of Captain Cook*

Five Bells

Time that is moved by little fidget wheels
Is not my Time, the flood that does not flow.
Between the double and the single bell
Of a ship's hour, between a round of bells
From the dark warship riding there below,
I have lived many lives, and this one life
Of Joe, long dead, who lives between five bells.

Deep and dissolving verticals of light
Ferry the falls of moonshine down. Five bells
Coldly rung out in a machine's voice. Night and water
Pour to one rip of darkness, the Harbour floats
In air, the Cross hangs upside-down in water.

Why do I think of you, dead man, why thieve
These profitless lodgings from the flukes of thought
Anchored in Time? You have gone from earth,
Gone even from the meaning of a name;

Yet something's there, yet something forms its lips
And hits and cries against the ports of space,
Beating their sides to make its fury heard.

Are you shouting at me, dead man, squeezing your face
In agonies of speech on speechless panes?
Cry louder, beat the windows, bawl your name!

But I hear nothing, nothing . . . only bells,
Five bells, the bumpkin calculus of Time.
Your echoes die, your voice is dowsed by Life,
There's not a mouth can fly the pygmy strait—
Nothing except the memory of some bones
Long shoved away, and sucked away, in mud;
And unimportant things you might have done,
Or once I thought you did; but you forgot,
And all have now forgotten—looks and words
And slops of beer; your coat with buttons off,
Your gaunt chin and pricked eye, and raging tales
Of Irish kings and English perfidy,
And dirtier perfidy of publicans
Groaning to God from Darlinghurst.

Five bells.

Then I saw the road, I heard the thunder
Tumble, and felt the talons of the rain
The night we came to Moorebank in slab-dark,
So dark you bore no body, had no face,
But a sheer voice that rattled out of air
(As now you'd cry if I could break the glass),
A voice that spoke beside me in the bush,
Loud for a breath or bitten off by wind,
Of Milton, melons and the Rights of Man,
And blowing flutes, and how Tahitian girls
Are brown and angry-tongued, and Sydney girls
Are white and angry-tongued, or so you'd found.
But all I heard was words that didn't join,
So Milton became melons, melons girls,
And fifty mouths, it seemed, were out that night,
And in each tree an Ear was bending down,
Or something had just run, gone behind grass,
When, blank and bone-white, like a maniac's thought,

The naphtha-flash of lightning slit the sky,
Knifing the dark with deadly photographs.
There's not so many with so poor a purse
Or fierce a need, must fare by night like that,
Five miles in darkness on a country track,
But when you do, that's what you think.

Five bells.

In Melbourne, your appetite had gone,
Your angers too; they had been leeched away
By the soft archery of summer rains
And the sponge-paws of wetness, the slow damp
That stuck the leaves of living, snailed the mind,
And showed your bones, that had been sharp with rage,
The sodden ecstasies of rectitude.
I thought of what you'd written in faint ink,
Your journal with the sawn-off lock, that stayed behind
With other things you left, all without use,
All without meaning now, except a sign
That someone had been living who now was dead:
'At Labassa. Room 6 x 8
On top of the tower; because of this, very dark
And cold in winter. Everything has been stowed
Into this room—500 books all shapes
And colours, dealt across the floor
And over sills and on the laps of chairs;
Guns, photoes of many differant things
And differant curioes that I obtained . . . .'

In Sydney, by the spent aquarium-flare
Of penny gaslight on pink wallpaper,
We argued about blowing up the world,
But you were living backward, so each night
You crept a moment closer to the breast,
And they were living, all of them, those frames
And shapes of flesh that had perplexed your youth,
And most your father, the old man gone blind,
With fingers always round a fiddle's neck,
That graveyard mason whose fair monuments
And tablets cut with dreams of piety
Rest on the bosoms of a thousand men

Staked bone by bone, in quiet astonishment
At cargoes they had never thought to bear,
These funeral-cakes of sweet and sculptured stone.

Where have you gone? The tide is over you,
The turn of midnight water's over you,
As Time is over you, and mystery,
And memory, the flood that does not flow.
You have no suburb, like those easier dead
In private berths of dissolution laid—
The tide goes over, the waves ride over you
And let their shadows down like shining hair,
But they are Water; and the sea-pinks bend
Like lilies in your teeth, but they are weed;
And you are only part of an Idea.
I felt the wet push its black thumb-balls in,
The night you died, I felt your eardrums crack,
And the short agony, the longer dream,
The Nothing that was neither long nor short;
But I was bound, and could not go that way,
But I was blind, and could not feel your hand.
If I could find an answer, could only find
Your meaning, or could say why you were here
Who now are gone, what purpose gave you breath
Or seized it back, might I not hear your voice?

I looked out of my window in the dark
At waves with diamond quills and combs of light
That arched their mackerel-backs and smacked the sand
In the moon's drench, that straight enormous glaze,
And ships far off asleep, and Harbour-buoys
Tossing their fireballs wearily each to each,
And tried to hear your voice, but all I heard
Was a boat's whistle, and the scraping squeal
Of seabirds' voices far away, and bells,
Five bells. Five bells coldly ringing out.

Five bells.

ROY CAMPBELL (1902—1957)

Horses on the Camargue

To A. F. Tschiffely

In the grey wastes of dread,
The haunt of shattered gulls where nothing moves
But in a shroud of silence like the dead,
I heard a sudden harmony of hooves,
And, turning, saw afar
A hundred snowy horses unconfined,
The silver runaways of Neptune's car
Racing, spray-curled, like waves before the wind.
Sons of the Mistral, fleet
As him with whose strong gusts they love to flee,
Who shod the flying thunders on their feet
And plumed them with the snortings of the sea;
Theirs is no earthly breed
Who only haunt the verges of the earth
And only on the sea's salt herbage feed—
Surely the great white breakers gave them birth.
For when for years a slave,
A horse of the Camargue, in alien lands,
Should catch some far-off fragrance of the wave
Carried far inland from his native sands,
Many have told the tale
Of how in fury, foaming at the rein,
He hurls his rider; and with lifted tail,
With coal-red eyes and cataracting mane,
Heading his course for home,
Though sixty foreign leagues before him sweep,
Will never rest until he breathes the foam
And hears the native thunder of the deep.
But when the great gusts rise
And lash their anger on these arid coasts,
When the scared gulls career with mournful cries
And whirl across the waste like driven ghosts:
When hail and fire converge,
The only souls to which they strike no pain
Are the white-crested fillies of the surge
And the white horses of the windy plain.

Then in their strength and pride
The stallions of the wilderness rejoice;
They feel their Master's trident in their side,
And high and shrill they answer to his voice.
With white tails smoking free,
Long streaming manes, and arching necks, they show
Their kinship to their sisters of the sea—
And forward hurl their thunderbolts of snow.
Still out of hardship bred,
Spirits of power and beauty and delight
Have ever on such frugal pastures fed
And loved to course with tempests through the night.

ARTHUR SEYMOUR JOHN TESSIMOND (b. 1902)

Daydream

One day people will touch and talk perhaps easily,
And loving be natural as breathing and warm as sunlight,
And people will untie themselves, as string is knotted
Unfold and yawn and stretch and spread their fingers,
Unfurl, uncurl like seaweed returned to the sea,
And work will be simple and swift as a seagull flying,
And play will be casual and quiet as a seagull settling,
And everyone will dance and drink red wine in the streets in the
    evening.
And everyone will sing, even in the winter, even in the rain.

WILLIAM PLOMER (b. 1903)

September evening, 1938

As the golden grass burns out
In a cooling ash of dew
The lovers disembrace
And face the evening view.

The long plain down
Shaped like a thigh
Slopes towards the sea,
And away up in the sky

Too small to be heard
A plane like a silver spark
Bright in the sun's last rays
Drifts eastward into the dark;

A single stack of hay
In the valley at their feet
Like a primitive small church
Looks simple, strong, and neat;

Inside a wattled fold
A flock of sheep
Stand, stir, or lie
Fleece against fleece asleep;

Lights in the bungalow,
A constant hum of cars;
Mallow flowers in the grass;
One or two stars.

With the fading day
All has grown clear:
That everything is vital
And infinitely dear.

Looking round, the girl thinks
'How precious to me
My home and my work and each thing
I can touch and can see,

George's navy-blue suit,
And my white linen dress,
And the way that his eyebrows grow—
This is my happiness!'

And he, clasping her hand,
More grave than before,
Says, 'Yes, I will fight
(If there is to be a war)

For all that has gone to make
Us, and this day.'
Then arm in arm along the path
Silent they saunter away.

C. DAY LEWIS (b. 1904)

Consider these
for we have condemned them

Consider these, for we have condemned them;
Leaders to no sure land, guides their bearings lost
Or in league with robbers have reversed the signposts,
Disrespectful to ancestors, irresponsible to heirs.
Born barren, a freak growth, root in rubble,
Fruitlessly blossoming, whose foliage suffocates,
Their sap is sluggish, they reject the sun.

The man with his tongue in his cheek, the woman
With her heart in the wrong place, unhandsome, unwholesome;
Have exposed the new-born to worse than weather,
Exiled the honest and sacked the seer.
These drowned the farms to form a pleasure-lake,
In time of drought they drain the reservoir
Through private pipes for baths and sprinklers.

Getters not begetters; gainers not beginners;
Whiners, no winners; no triers, betrayers;
Who steer by no star, whose moon means nothing.
Daily denying, unable to dig:
At bay in villas from blood relations,
Counters of spoons and content with cushions
They pray for peace, they hand down disaster.

They that take the bribe shall perish by the bribe,
Drying of dry rot, ending in asylums,
A curse to children, a charge on the state.
But still their fears and frenzies infect us;
Drug nor isolation will cure this cancer:
It is now or never, the hour of the knife,
The break with the past, the major operation.

On the sea wall

As I came to the sea wall that August day,
One out of all the bathers there
Beckoned my eye, a girl at play
With the surf-flowers. Was it the dark, dark hair
Falling Egyptian-wise, or the way
Her body curved to the spray?—

I know not. Only my heart was shaking
Within me, and then it stopped; as though
You were dead and your shape had returned to haunt me
On the very same spot where, five years ago,
You slipped from my arms and played in the breaking
Surges to tease and enchant me.

I could not call out. Had there been no more
Than those thickets of rusty wire to pen us
Apart, I'd have gone to that girl by the shore
Hoping she might be you. But between us
Lie tangled, severing, stronger far,
Barbed relics of love's old war.

NORMAN CAMERON (1905—1953)

The verdict

It was taken a long time ago,
The first pressure on the trigger.
Why complain that the verdict is so?
It was taken a long time ago.
And our grave will have many a digger,
The Mongol, the Yank and the nigger.
It was taken a long time ago,
The first pressure on the trigger.

JOHN BETJEMAN (b. 1906)

Before the Anæsthetic,
or
A Real Fright

Intolerably sad, profound
St. Giles's bells are ringing round,
They bring the slanting summer rain
To tap the chestnut boughs again
Whose shadowy cave of rainy leaves
The gusty belfry-song receives.
Intolerably sad and true,
Victorian red and jewel blue,
The mellow bells are ringing round
And charge the evening light with sound,
And I look motionless from bed
On heavy trees and purple red
And hear the midland bricks and tiles
Throw back the bells of stone St. Giles,
Bells, ancient now as castle walls,
Now hard and new as pitchpine stalls,
Now full with help from ages past,
Now dull with death and hell at last.
Swing up! and give me hope of life,
Swing down! and plunge the surgeon's knife.
I, breathing for a moment, see
Death wing himself away from me
And think, as on this bed I lie,
Is it distinction when I die?
I move my limbs and use my sight;
Not yet, thank God, not yet the Night.
Oh better far those echoing hells
Half-threatened in the pealing bells
Than that this 'I' should cease to be—
Come quickly, Lord, come quick to me.
St. Giles's bells are asking now
'And hast thou known the Lord, hast thou?'
St. Giles's bells they hear me call
I never knew the Lord at all.
Oh not in me your Saviour dwells
You ancient, rich St. Giles's bells.
Illuminated missals—spires—

Wide screens and decorated quires—
All these I loved, and on my knees
I thanked myself for knowing these
And watched the morning sunlight pass
Through richly stained Victorian glass
And in the colour-shafted air
I, kneeling, thought the Lord was there.
Now, lying in the gathering mist
I know that Lord did not exist;
Now, lest this 'I' should cease to be,
Come, real Lord, come quick to me.
With every gust the chestnut sighs,
With every breath, a mortal dies;
The man who smiled alone, alone,
And went his journey on his own
With 'Will you give my wife this letter,
In case, of course, I don't get better?'
Waits for his coffin lid to close
On waxen head and yellow toes.
Almighty Saviour, had I Faith
There'd be no fight with kindly Death.
Intolerably long and deep
St. Giles's bells swing on in sleep:
'But still you go from here alone'
Say all the bells about the Throne.

RONALD BOTTRALL (b. 1906)

Proserpine at Enna

When the black car came thundering from its pale
You, fairest flower, were gathering irises,
Marigold, toadflax, spurge, anemones,
In shades of prickly pear by the infernal well.
Gathered, too, his sinewy deft fingers
Denting your nesh skin, you faintly fell
From morning uplands to the Stygian quays
And shed your virgin petals deep in hell.

Derelict in the iron gorgon's train
The lipless skull sings of Plutonic rapes.
With spring your laughing mother re-assumes
Trinacria; you burgeon green, and green

Are the gangrenous bodies of our hopes
Composted in their fertile hecatombs.

WILLIAM EMPSON (b. 1906)

This last pain

This last pain for the damned the Fathers found:
'They knew the bliss with which they were not crowned.'
    Such, but on earth, let me foretell,
    Is all, of heaven or of hell.

Man, as the prying housemaid of the soul,
May know her happiness by eye to hole:
    He's safe; the key is lost; he knows
    Door will not open, nor hole close.

'What is conceivable can happen too,'
Said Wittgenstein, who had not dreamed of you;
    But wisely; if we worked it long
    We should forget where it was wrong:

Those thorns are crowns which, woven into knots,
Crackle under and soon boil fools' pots;
    And no man's watching, wise and long
    Would ever stare them into song.

Thorns burn to a consistent ash, like man;
A splendid cleanser for the frying-pan:
    And those who leap from pan to fire
    Should this brave opposite admire.

All those large dreams by which men long live well
Are magic-lanterned on the smoke of hell;
    This then is real, I have implied,
    A painted, small, transparent slide.

These the inventive can hand-paint at leisure,
Or most emporia would stock our measure;
    And feasting in their dappled shade
    We should forget how they were made.

Feign then what's by a decent tact believed
And act that state is only so conceived
    And build an edifice of form
    For house where phantoms may keep warm.

Imagine, then, by miracle, with me,
(Ambiguous gifts, as what gods give must be)
    What could not possibly be there,
    And learn a style from a despair.

WYSTAN HUGH AUDEN (b. 1907)

At last the secret is out

At last the secret is out, as it always must come in the end,
The delicious story is ripe to tell to the intimate friend;
Over the tea-cups and in the square the tongue has its desire;
Still waters run deep, my dear, there's never smoke without fire.

Behind the corpse in the reservoir, behind the ghost on the links,
Behind the lady who dances and the man who madly drinks,
Under the look of fatigue, the attack of migraine and the sigh,
There is always another story, there is more than meets the eye.

For the clear voice suddenly singing, high up in the convent wall,
The scent of the elder bushes, the sporting-prints in the hall,
The croquet matches in summer, the handshake, the cough, the kiss,
There is always a wicked secret, a private reason for this.

Musée des beaux arts

About suffering they were never wrong,
The Old Masters: how well they understood
Its human position; how it takes place
While someone else is eating or opening a window or just walking
    dully along;
How, when the aged are reverently, passionately waiting
For the miraculous birth, there always must be
Children, who did not specially want it to happen, skating
On a pond at the edge of the wood:
They never forgot

That even the dreadful martyrdom must run its course
Anyhow in a corner, some untidy spot
Where the dogs go on with their doggy life and the torturer's horse
Scratches its innocent behind on a tree.

In Brueghel's *Icarus*, for instance: how everything turns away
Quite leisurely from the disaster; the ploughman may
Have heard the splash, the forsaken cry,
But for him it was not an important failure; the sun shone
As it had to on the white legs disappearing into the green
Water; and the expensive delicate ship that must have seen
Something amazing, a boy falling out of the sky,
Had somewhere to get to and sailed calmly on.

Lay your sleeping head

Lay your sleeping head, my love,
Human on my faithless arm;
Time and fevers burn away
Individual beauty from
Thoughtful children, and the grave
Proves the child ephemeral:
But in my arms till break of day
Let the living creature lie,
Mortal, guilty, but to me
The entirely beautiful.

Soul and body have no bounds:
To lovers as they lie upon
Her tolerant enchanted slope
In their ordinary swoon,
Grave the vision Venus sends
Of supernatural sympathy,
Universal love and hope;
While an abstract insight wakes
Among the glaciers and the rocks
The hermit's sensual ecstacy.

Certainty, fidelity
On the stroke of midnight pass
Like vibrations of a bell,
And fashionable madmen raise

Their pedantic boring cry:
Every farthing of the cost,
All the dreaded cards foretell,
Shall be paid, but from this night
Not a whisper, not a thought,
Not a kiss nor look be lost.

Beauty, midnight, vision dies:
Let the winds of dawn that blow
Softly round your dreaming head
Such a day of sweetness show
Eye and knocking heart may bless,
Find the mortal world enough;
Noons of dryness see you fed
By the involuntary powers,
Nights of insult let you pass
Watched by every human love.

LOUIS MACNEICE (b. 1907)

The British Museum Reading Room

Under the hive-like dome the stooping haunted readers
Go up and down the alleys, tap the cells of knowledge—
   Honey and wax, the accumulation of years—
Some on commission, some for the love of learning,
Some because they have nothing better to do
Or because they hope these walls of books will deaden
   The drumming of the demon in their ears.

Cranks, hacks, poverty-stricken scholars,
In pince-nez, period hats or romantic beards
   And cherishing their hobby or their doom.
Some are too much alive and some are asleep
Hanging like bats in a world of inverted values,
Folded up in themselves in a world which is safe and silent:
   This is the British Museum Reading Room.

Out on the steps in the sun the pigeons are courting,
Puffing their ruffs and sweeping their tails or taking
   A sun-bath at their ease
And under the totem poles—the ancient terror—
Between the enormous fluted Ionic columns
There seeps from heavily jowled or hawk-like foreign faces
   The guttural sorrow of the refugees.

Among these turf-stacks

Among these turf-stacks graze no iron horses
Such as stalk such as champ in towns and the soul of crowds,
Here is no mass-production of neat thoughts,
No canvas shrouds for the mind nor any black hearses:
The peasant shambles on his boots like hooves
Without thinking at all or wanting to run in grooves.

But those who lack the peasant's conspirators
The tawny mountain, the unregarded buttress,
Will feel the need of a fortress against ideas and against the
Shuddering insidious shock of the theory-vendors
The little sardine men crammed in a monster toy
Who tilt their aggregate beast against our crumbling Troy.

For we are obsolete who like the lesser things,
Who play in corners with looking-glasses and beads;
It is better we should go quickly, go into Asia
Or any other tunnel where the world recedes,
Or turn blind wantons like the gulls who scream
And rip the edge off any ideal or dream.

Bagpipe music

It's no go the merry-go-round, it's no go the rickshaw,
All we want is a limousine and a ticket for the peepshow.
Their knickers are made of crepe-de-chine, their shoes are made of
  python.
Their halls are lined with tiger rugs and their walls with heads of
  bison.

John MacDonald found a corpse, put it under the sofa,
Waited till it came to life and hit it with a poker,
Sold its eyes for souvenirs, sold its blood for whiskey,
Kept its bones for dumb-bells to use when he was fifty.

It's no go the Yogi-Man, it's no go Blavatsky,
All we want is a bank balance and a bit of skirt in a taxi.

Annie MacDougall went to milk, caught her foot in the heather.
Woke to hear a dance record playing of Old Vienna.
It's no go your maidenheads, it's no go your culture,
All we want is a Dunlop tyre and the devil mend the puncture.

The Laird o' Phelps spent Hogmanay declaring he was sober,
Counted his feet to prove the fact and found he had one foot over.
Mrs. Carmichael had her fifth, looked at the job with repulsion,
Said to the midwife 'Take it away; I'm through with over-production.'

It's no go the gossip column, it's no go the Ceilidh,
All we want is a mother's help and a sugar-stick for the baby.

Willie Murray cut his thumb, couldn't count the damage,
Took the hide of an Ayrshire cow and used it for a bandage.
His brother caught three hundred cran when the seas were lavish,
Threw the bleeders back in the sea and went upon the parish.

It's no go the Herring Board, it's no go the Bible,
All we want is a packet of fags when our hands are idle.

It's no go the picture palace, it's no go the stadium,
It's no go the country cot with a pot of pink geraniums,
It's no go the Government grants, it's no go the elections,
Sit on your arse for fifty years and hang your hat on a pension.

It's no go my honey love, it's no go my poppet;
Work your hands from day to day, the winds will blow the profit.
The glass is falling hour by hour, the glass will fall forever,
But if you break the bloody glass you won't hold up the weather.

STEPHEN SPENDER (b. 1909)

Ultima ratio regum

The guns spell money's ultimate reason
In letters of lead on the spring hillside.
But the boy lying dead under the olive trees
Was too young and too silly
To have been notable to their important eye.
He was a better target for a kiss.

When he lived, tall factory hooters never summoned him.
Nor did restaurant plate-glass doors revolve to wave him in.
His name never appeared in the papers.
The world maintained its traditional wall
Round the dead with their gold sunk deep as a well,
Whilst his life, intangible as a Stock Exchange rumour,
    drifted outside.

O too lightly he threw down his cap
One day when the breeze threw petals from the trees.
The unflowering wall sprouted with guns,
Machine-gun anger quickly scythed the grasses;
Flags and leaves fell from hands and branches;
The tweed cap rotted in the nettles.

Consider his life which was valueless
In terms of employment, hotel ledgers, news files.
Consider. One bullet in ten thousand kills a man.
Ask. Was so much expenditure justified
On the death of one so young and so silly
Lying under the olive trees, O world, O death?

Ice

To M. M. B.

She came in from the snowing air
Where icicle-hung architecture
Strung white fleece round the baroque square.
I saw her face freeze in her fur
And my lips seemed to fetch quick fire
From the firelit corner of the room
Where I had waited in my chair.
I kissed this fire against her skin
And watched the warmth make her cheeks bloom
While at my care her smiling eyes
Shone with the health of the ice
Outside, whose brilliance they brought in.
That day, until this, I forgot,
How is it now I so remember,
Who, when she came indoors, saw not
The passion of her white December?

ROBERT FARREN (b. 1909)

The cool gold wines of Paradise

The God who had such heart for us
as made him leave His house
come down through archipelagoes
of stars and live with us
has such a store of joys laid down
their savours will not sour:
the cool gold wines of Paradise
the bread of heaven's flour.

He'll meet the soul which comes in love
and deal it joy on joy
as once he dealt out star on star
to garrison the sky
to stand there over rains and snows
and deck the dark of night
so God will deal the soul, like stars
delight upon delight.

Night skies have planet armies, still
the blue is never full;
rich massive stars have never bowed
one cloud's bed flock of wool;
red worlds of dreadful molten fire
have singed no speck of air:—
all is in place and, each to each,
God's creatures show His care.

The soul will take each joy he deals
as skies take star on star,
be never filled, be never bowed,
be airy, as clouds are,
burn with enlarging heat and shine
with ever-brightening ray
joyful and gathering thirst for joy
throughout unending Day.

WILLIAM ROBERT ROGERS (b. 1911)

White Christmas

Punctually at Christmas the soft plush
Of sentiment snows down, embosoms all
The sharp and pointed shapes of venom, shawls
The hills and hides the shocking holes of this
Uneven world of want and wealth, cushions
With cosy wish like cotton-wool the cool
Arm's-length interstices of caste and class,
And into obese folds subtracts from sight
All truculent acts, bleeding the world white.

Punctually that glib pair, Peace and Goodwill,
Emerges royally to take the air,
Collect the bows, assimilate the smiles,
Of waiting men. It is a genial time;
Angels, like stalactites, descend from heaven;
Bishops distribute their own weight in words,
Congratulate the poor on Christlike lack;
And the member for the constituency
Feeds the five thousand, and has plenty back.

Punctually, to-night, in old stone circles
Of set reunion, families stiffly sit
And listen: this is the night and this the happy time
When the tinned milk of human kindness is
Upheld and holed by radio-appeal:
Hushed are hurrying heels on hard roads,
And every parlour's a pink pond of light
To the cold and travelling man going by
In the dark, without a bark or a bite.

But punctually to-morrow you will see
All this silent and dissembling world
Of stilted sentiment suddenly melt
Into mush and watery welter of words
Beneath the warm and moving traffic of
Feet and actual fact. Over the stark plain
The silted mill-chimneys once again spread
Their sackcloth and ashes, a flowing mane
Of repentance for the false day that's fled.

ROY FULLER (b. 1912)

January 1940

Swift had pains in his head.
Johnson dying in bed
Tapped the dropsy himself.
Blake saw a flea and an elf.
Tennyson could hear the shriek
Of a bat. Pope was a freak.
Emily Dickinson stayed
Indoors for a decade.
Water inflated the belly
Of Hart Crane, and of Shelley.
Coleridge was a dope.
Southwell died on a rope.
Byron had a round white foot.
Smart and Cowper were put
Away. Lawrence was a fidget.
Keats was almost a midget.
Donne, alive in his shroud,
Shakespeare in the coil of a cloud
Saw death very well as he
Came crab-wise, dark and massy.
I envy not only their talents
And fertile lack of balance
But the appearance of choice
In their sad and fatal voice.

SEAN JENNETT (b. 1912)

The island

This island is the world's end. Beyond
the wide Atlantic drives its thunderous tides
backwards and forwards, beating on the land,
time out of mind, a hammer on the heart,
and the storms of the west race from the huge
infinity of sea, gathering anger,
and split their bellies and their fist of rage
against the island's shattered silent mountain.

The puffins and the rabbits own the land
and the gull and the circling ravenous eagle
and the seals bark on the edge of the sound
between the black rocks where the sea beats.
Where men trod once and wore the hard earth bare
the green illimitable grass
creeps back, over the garden and the gear
that fished the sea and farmed the ungenerous soil.

A lizard by a loosened door
peers into an abandoned room,
twisting his nostrils to the mummied air
that bore the shape of words, a cradle tale,
or some young girl's fresh, careless, idle song:
the sea wind and the subtle rain
break down all things at last, even the strong
stone of the wall, and the stubborn heart.

And yet they loved this island. Its hard rock
became their bone, its meagre earth their flesh,
the sea their tide of blood; and in the black
night they turned its sullenness to song.
The dancing foot that stirred the scattered sand
is quiet now or heavy overseas
and the singing voice has only songs that wound
with bitterness. The land is dead.

ANNE RIDLER (b. 1912)

For a child expected

Lovers whose lifted hands are candles in winter,
Whose gentle ways like streams in the easy summer,
Lying together
For secret setting of a child, love what they do,
Thinking they make that candle immortal, those streams
    forever flow,
And yet do better than they know.

So the first flutter of a baby felt in the womb,
Its little signal and promise of riches to come,
Is taken in its father's name;
Its life is the body of his love, like his caress,
First delicate and strange, that daily use
Makes dearer and priceless.

Our baby was to be the living sign of our joy,
Restore to each the other's lost infancy;
To a painter's pillaging eye
Poet's coiled hearing, add the heart we might earn
By help of love; all that our passion would yield
We put to planning our child.

The world flowed in; whatever we liked we took:
For its hair, the gold curls of the November oak
We saw on our walk;
Snowberries that make a Milky Way in the wood
For its tender hands, calm screen of the frozen flood
For our care of its childhood.

But the birth of a child is an uncontrollable glory;
Cat's cradle of hopes will hold no living baby,
Long though it lay quietly.
And when our baby stirs and struggles to be born
It compels humility: what we began
Is now its own.

For *as the sun that shines through glass*
So Jesus in His Mother was.
Therefore every human creature,
Since it shares in His nature,
In candle gold passion or white
Sharp star should show its own way of light.
May no parental dread or dream
Darken our darling's early beam:
May she grow to her right powers
Unperturbed by passion of ours.

O Love, answer

O Love, answer the hammering heart:
Only in love we live; then prove
That quickening good, take your own part,
Show us that all your modes are one.

Go where the frustrate lovers lie
On earth that gives back no caress,
Trying to calm in a chthonic pain ·
Their howling torment: raise and bless.

ANNE RIDLER

Appease with just and holy ends
Their tenderness; their need to give
Turn to some profit—what are their wounds
But mere irrelevance to Love?

To those whose inner wars forbade
The deed of love, grant a release.
The satisfied and then betrayed
Endure the greater torment, since
Love is not blind, but worships still
The glory in the mad and cruel.
Only the Cross can justify
Their folly and their agony.

Last, visit the lucky in love.
Make them as strangers, yet possessing
All the skill that use can give.
Let ecstacy convert the soul
At last, restore the mystery
Their raptures have burnt up, his ways
Instruct with spendthrift power and be
The light that leaps through all her house.

Then be their envoy to ask forgiveness
From the unsatisfied, a pardon
For their luck and for their ease.
O reconcile the twin directions
Not at the infinite point, but this.
We do not believe in the happy ending,
It must be now, for pain and peace
In present commerce, one perfection.

As, in poetry, rise and fall
Naming the measure, can exchange
Or take each other's semblance well,
Marked from a different point in time,
So might one measure hold us all:
All was in ecstacy begun,
Yet the poor heart beats pain for ever—
Prove that your terrible ways are one.

GEORGE BARKER (b. 1913)

Sonnet to my Mother

Most near, most dear, most loved and most far,
Under the window where I often found her
Sitting as huge as Asia, seismic with laughter,
Gin and chicken helpless in her Irish hand,
Irresistible as Rabelais but most tender for
The lame dogs and hurt birds that surround her,—
She is a procession no one can follow after
But be like a little dog following a brass band.

She will not glance up at the bomber or condescend
To drop her gin and scuttle to a cellar,
But lean on the mahogany table like a mountain
Whom only faith can move, and so I send
O all my faith and all my love to tell her
That she will move from mourning into morning.

Munich Elegy No. 1

Those occasions involving the veering of axles
When the wheel's bloody spikes like Arabian armaments
Release Passchendaele on us because it is time, bring
Also with blood to the breast the boon to the bosom:
I saw it happen, had near me the gun and the tear.
Those occasions are all elegiac. The wheel and the wish
Turn in a turtle the chaos of life. It is death,
Death like roulette turning our wish to its will.

I see a scene with a smother of snow over Love.
I know Spring will arise and later the swallow return;
I know, but my torso stands bogged in a load of time,
Like Love lying under the smother of our death and our
Dread. How soon shall the Spring bird arise and the
Summer bells hum with the murmur of our name?
  Soon, soon,
Soon the green room goes blue with the last autumn.

421

I sip at suicide in bedrooms or dare pessimistic stars,
Keep pigeons with messages or make tame apes
Commemorate in mime the master me who must go;
Or commit crimes of rage or rape to ease the ache:
I promise these cannot precipitate fate. No,
To-morrow it is not, it is not to-day, it is not
Wednesday or Thursday. It is the greatest day.

That morning not the rose shall rise or dog dance,
Kings with conscience and queens with child sleep long,
For duty is useless; the soldier and sailor glance
Down at their guns with a grin, but they are wrong.
The dodo shall rule for a moment, and the Thames
Remember. Invalids and paralytics shall sing
   'No more, no more!'
I shall hear the ceremony of heaven and God's roar.

What awaits is the veer of the lever and wheel
When the hands cross at midnight and noon, the future
Sweeps on with a sigh—but on this occasion Time
Swells like a wave at a wall and bursts to eternity.
I await when the engine of lilies and lakes and love
Reaching its peak of power blows me sky high, and I
   Come down to rest
On the shape I made in the ground where I used to lie.

O widow, do not weep, do not weep! Or wife
Cry in the corner of the window with a child by—
Look how Tottenham and the Cotswolds, with
More mass than a man, lie easy under the sky,
Also awaiting change they cannot understand,
'I have heaven a haven in my hand,' say,
   Like the boy
Cornering butterflies or nothing in cupped hands.

The tragedy is Time foreshadowing its climax.
Thus in the stage of time the minor moth is small
But prophesies the Fokker with marvellous wings
Mottled with my sun's gold and your son's blood.
The crazy anthropoid crawls on time's original

That casts his giant on the contemporary scene:
  That spreadeagled shadow
Covers with horror the green Abyssinian meadow.

Lovers on Sunday in the rear seats of cinemas
Kiss deep and dark, for is it the last kiss?
Children sailing on swings in municipal parks
Swing high, swing high into the reach of the sky,
Leave, leave the sad star that is about to die.
Laugh, my comedians, who may not laugh again—
  Soon, soon,
Soon Jeremiah Job will be walking among men.

DOUGLAS STEWART (b. 1913)

Rock carving

The lines grow slack in our hands at full high-water
The midnight rears in the sky; and beneath the boat
Another midnight, dwarfing the flare of a match
Or flare of a mind, expands and deepens. We float
Abandoned as driftwood on a tide that drowns all speech,
Where movement of hand or keel can make no mark
That will stand in space or endure one moment in time.
Flashing in shallows or hiding in murderous dark,

The fish live out their lives in weeds and silence;
And, locked like them in some alien struggle or peace,
No business of ours, from the moon to the water's edge,
Looming above us, tower the gigantic trees.
Among those rocks where time has ravaged the ridge,
In all that pattern cold and inhuman as the tide's,
Where shall the mind make camp? How in that darkness
Shall the mind ride tranquil with light as the high moon rides?

Shine the torch on the rock: we are not the first
Alone and lost in this world of water and stone.
See, though the maker's life has vanished like a leaf's,
The carvings living a hard strange life of their own
Above the water, beneath the tormented cliffs.
They glow with immortal being, as though the stone fish
May flap and slither to the tide, as though the great 'roo
May bound from the rock and crash away through the bush.

The moon lights a thousand candles upon the water,
But none for the carver of stone; and nobody comes
Of his own long-scattered tribe to remember him
With dance and song and firelight under the gums;
But he walks again for me at the water's rim
And works at his rock, and a light begins to glow
Clear for his sake among the dark of my mind
Where the branches reach and the silent waters flow.

I watch him working through a summer afternoon,
Patient as the stone itself while his tribesmen sleep;
The children jostle, the girls cry out in the sun,
And first the fish and then the great 'roo take shape.
The work is crude, and he knows it; but now it is done;
And whoever laughs is a little afraid in the end,
For here is a swimmer in stone, and a 'roo that leaps
Nowhere for ever, and both can be touched with the hand.

I could have sat down with that man and talked about fishing,
How the bream are fish of the night, and they take the bait
With a run before you are ready; of the fabulous catches
For which we always got there a week too late;
And of how a man in the lonely midnight watches
Becomes himself a part of night and the tide
And, lost in the blackness, has need of a wife or a dog
Or a blackfellow's ghost to sit in peace by his side.

Centuries dead perhaps. But night and the water,
And a 'roo and a fish on a rock have brought us together,
Fishermen both, and carvers both, old man.
I know as you how the work goes naked to the weather,
How we cut our thought into stone as best we can,
Laugh at our pain, and leave it to take its chance.
Maybe it's all for nothing, for the sky to look at,
Or maybe for us the distant candles dance.

The boat tugs at the kellick as it feels the ebb.
Good-bye, cld wraith, and good luck. You did what you could
To leave your mark on stone like a mark on time,
That the sky in the mind and the midnight sea in the blood
Should be less of a desolation for the men to come;
And who can do more than you? Gone, you are gone;
But, dark a moment in the moonlight, your hand hovers,
And moves like the shadow of a bird across the stone.

Mahony's mountain

If there's a fox, he said, I'll whistle the beggar;
And shrill the counterfeit cry of the rabbit's pain
Rang out in the misty clearing; so soon to be lost
In the stony spurs and candlebarks darker and huger
Where Mahony's mountain towers in drifts of rain.
No sharp wild face out of burrow or hollow stump,
No rustle shaking the raindrops from rushes or flowers
—Greenhood and bulbine lily lighting the swamp—
Nothing but bush and silence; so on and up
Tramping through moss where so many violets cluster
You cannot help but crush them; and still more steep
The sheep-track winds through the dripping leaves and the rocks,
And still no fox, no bandicoot's tiny fluster,
No flurry of green rosellas flashing past,
Nothing but the huge grey silence, the trees and—look,
There where the mountain breaks on its granite peak,
The doubletail orchid, O like some fairytale fox,
But whistled from earth by a wilder call than ours,
Pricks up its yellow ears and stares through the mist.

DOUGLAS YOUNG (b. 1913)

Ice-flumes owregie their lades

Gangan my lane amang the caulkstane alps
   That glower abune the Oetztal in Tirol
I wan awa heich up amang the scalps
   O snawy mountains where the wind blew cauld
Owre the reoch scarnoch and sparse jenepere,
   Wi soldanellas smoort aneath the snaw,
And purpie crocus whaur the grund was clear,
   Rinnan tae fleur in their brief simmer thaw,
   And auntran gairs o reid alproses, sweir tae blaw.

And syne I cam up til a braid ice-flume,
   Spelderan doun frae aff the Wildspitz shouther,
A frozen sea; crustit wi rigid spume,
   Owredichtit whiles wi sherp and skinklan pouther
Frae a licht yowden-drift o snaw or hail,
   Clortit by avalanche debris, gaigit deep
Wi oorie reoch crevasses, whaur the pale
   Draps o sun-heated ice ooze doun and dreep
   Intil the friction-bed, whaur drumlie horrors sleep.

They say ice-flumes maun aa owregie their lades,
  And corps o men win out ae day tae light.[1]
Warsslan remorseless doun reluctant grades
  They canny flumes hain their cauld victims ticht.
But nae for aye. Thretty or fowrty year
  A corse may ligg afore his weirdit tyde
And yet keep tryst. Whiles they reappear
  Gey carnwath-like the wey the glaciers glide,[2]
  Whiles an intact young man confronts a crineit bryde.[3]

A Lausanne pastor wi's Greek lexicon
  Vanished awa amang the Diablerets,
Syne eftir twenty years the Zanfleuron
  Owregya the baith o them til the licht o day,
Still at the Greekan o't.[4] Twa Tirolese,
  Faan doun a gaig, ate what they had til eat,
Scryveit their fowk at hame, and syne at ease
  Stertit piquet. Baith had the selfsame seat
  Saxteen year eftir, but their game was nae complete.[5]

In Norroway in 1792
  Frae fifty year liggan aneath the ice
A herd appeared, and syne beguid tae thaw
  And gaed about as souple, swack and wyce
As when he fall frae sicht i thon crevasse.[6]
  Sae sall it be wi Scotland. She was free,
Through aa the warld weel kent, a sonsy lass,
  Whill whummlet in Historie's flume. But sune we'll see
  Her livan bouk back i the licht. Juist byde a wee.

1. Professor Forbes o St. Andrews was the first prophet anent glacial deliveries. In 1858 he foretauld the reappearance about 1860 o three spielers tint i the Boissons flume o Mont Blanc in 1820. Frae 1861 till 1865 they appeared in three instalments, as calculate by Forbes, 9,000 feet frae the scene o the mishanter.

2. In 1914 Sydnye King disappearit on Mount Cook, New Zealand, and in 1939 cam out three inches thick.

3. At Grindelwald a Mr. Webster was engulphit on his hinnymune and eftir 21 year gien back til his widdaw.

4. In 1917 Pastor Schneider gaed aff amang the Diablerets; in 1938 the Zanfleuron glacier owregya him, and the fowk kent him by his dictionar.

5. In 1919 Peter Freuchen and anither chiel fell intil a crevasse in Tirol, and in 1935 were fand perfitly intact, ilk ane haudan a partie playit haund o the cairts.

6. This and the ither orra information I deriveit frae Mr. Frank Illingworth's article in *Chamber's Journal*, August, 1942. Gin it had been mair circumstantial my verses wald hae been mair circumstantial as weel.

DOUGLAS YOUNG

Last lauch

The Minister said it wald dee,
the cypress-buss I plantit.
But the buss grew til a tree
naething dauntit.

It's growan, stark and heich,
derk and straucht and sinister
kirkyairdielike and dreich.
But whaur's the Minister?

NORMAN NICHOLSON (b. 1914)

The Expanding Universe

The furthest stars recede
Faster than the earth moves,
Almost as fast as light;
The infinite
Adjusts itself to our need.

For far beyond the furthest, where
Light is snatched backward, no
Star leaves echo or shadow
To prove it has ever been there.

And if the universe
Reversed and showed
The colour of its money;
If now unobservable light
Flowed inward, and the skies snowed
A blizzard of galaxies,
The lens of night would burn
Brighter than the focused sun,
And man turn blinded
With white-hot darkness in his eyes.

The burning bush

When Moses, musing in the desert, found
The thorn bush spiking up from the hot ground,
And saw the branches on a sudden bear
The crackling yellow barberries of fire

He searched his learning and imagination
For any logical, neat explanation
And turned to go, but turned again and stayed
And faced the fire and knew it for his God.

I too have seen the briar alight like coal,
The love that burns, the flesh that's ever whole
And many times have turned and left it there,
Saying 'It's prophecy—but metaphor'.

But stinging tongues like John the Baptist shout:
'That this is metaphor is no way out.
It's dogma too, or you make God a liar;
The bush is still a bush, and fire is fire.'

HENRY REED (b. 1914)

Naming of parts

To Alan Mitchell *Vixi puellis nuper idoneus
Et militavi non sine gloria*

To-day we have naming of parts. Yesterday,
We had daily cleaning. And to-morrow morning,
We shall have what to do after firing. But to-day,
To-day we have naming of parts. Japonica
Glistens like coral in all of the neighbouring gardens,
    And to-day we have naming of parts.

This is the lower sling swivel. And this
Is the upper sling swivel, whose use you will see,
When you are given your slings. And this is the piling swivel,
Which in your case you have not got. The branches
Hold in the gardens their silent, eloquent gestures,
    Which in our case we have not got.

This is the safety-catch, which is always released
With an easy flick of the thumb. And please do not let me
See anyone using his finger. You can do it quite easy
If you have any strength in your thumb. The blossoms
Are fragile and motionless, never letting anyone see
   Any of them using their finger.

And this you can see is the bolt. The purpose of this
Is to open the breech, as you see. We can slide it
Rapidly backwards and forwards: we call this
Easing the spring. And rapidly backwards and forwards
The early bees are assaulting and fumbling the flowers:
   They call it easing the Spring.

They call it easing the Spring: it is perfectly easy
If you have any strength in your thumb: like the bolt,
And the breech, and the cocking-piece, and the point of balance,
Which in our case we have not got; and the almond-blossom
Silent in all of the gardens and the bees going backwards and forwards,
   For to-day we have naming of parts.

                From *Lessons Of The War*

DYLAN THOMAS (1914—1953)

And death shall have no dominion

And death shall have no dominion.
Dead men naked they shall be one
With the man in the wind and the west moon;
When their bones are picked clean and the clean bones gone,
They shall have stars at elbow and foot;
Though they go mad they shall be sane,
Though they sink through the sea they shall rise again;
Though lovers be lost love shall not;
And death shall have no dominion.

And death shall have no dominion.
Under the windings of the sea
They lying long shall not die windily;
Twisting on racks when sinews give way,
Strapped to a wheel, yet they shall not break;

Faith in their hands shall snap in two,
And the unicorn evils run them through;
Split all ends up they shan't crack;
And death shall have no dominion.

And death shall have no dominion.
No more may gulls cry at their ears
Or waves break loud on the seashores;
Where blew a flower may a flower no more
Lift its head to the blows of the rain;
Though they be mad and dead as nails,
Heads of the characters hammer through daisies;
Break in the sun till the sun breaks down
And death shall have no dominion.

The hand that signed the paper

The hand that signed the paper felled a city;
Five sovereign fingers taxed the breath,
Doubled the globe of dead and halved a country;
These five kings did a king to death.

The mighty hand leads to a sloping shoulder,
The finger joints are cramped with chalk;
A goose's quill has put an end to murder
That put an end to talk.

The hand that signed the treaty bred a fever,
And famine grew, and locusts came;
Great is the hand that holds dominion over
Man by a scribbled name.

The five kings count the dead but do not soften
The crusted wound nor stroke the brow;
A hand rules pity as a hand rules heaven;
Hands have no tears to flow.

A refusal to mourn the Death, by Fire, of a child in London

Never until the mankind making
Bird beast and flower
Fathering and all humbling darkness

Tells with silence the last light breaking
And the still hour
Is come of the sea tumbling in harness

And I must enter again the round
Zion of the water bead
And the synagogue of the ear of corn
Shall I let pray the shadow of a sound
Or sow my salt seed
In the least valley of sackcloth to mourn

The majesty and burning of the child's death.
I shall not murder
The mankind of her going with a grave truth
Nor blaspheme down the stations of the breath
With any further
Elegy of innocence and youth.

Deep with the first dead lies London's daughter,
Robed in the long friends,
The grains beyond age, the dark veins of her mother
Secret by the unmourning water
Of the riding Thames.
After the first death, there is no other.

When all my five and country senses see

When all my five and country senses see,
The fingers will forget green thumbs and mark
How, through the halfmoon's vegetable eye,
Husk of young stars and handful zodiac,
Love in the frost is pared and wintered by,
The whispering ears will watch love drummed away
Down breeze and shell to a discordant beach,
And, lashed to syllables, the lynx tongue cry
That her fond wounds are mended bitterly.
My nostrils see her breath burn like a bush.

My one and noble heart has witnesses
In all love's countries, that will grope awake;
And when blind sleep drops on the spying senses,
The heart is sensual, though five eyes break.

Light breaks where no sun shines

Light breaks where no sun shines;
Where no sea runs, the waters of the heart
Push in their tides;
And, broken ghosts with glow-worms in their heads,
The things of light
File through the flesh where no flesh decks the bones.

A candle in the thighs
Warms youth and seed and burns the seeds of age;
Where no seed stirs,
The fruit of man unwrinkles in the stars,
Bright as a fig;
Where no wax is, the candle shows its hairs.

Dawn breaks behind the eyes;
From poles of skull and toe the windy blood
Slides like a sea;
Nor fenced, nor staked, the gushers of the sky
Spout to the rod
Divining in a smile the oil of tears.

Night in the sockets rounds,
Like some pitch moon, the limit of the globes;
Day lights the bone;
Where no cold is, the skinning gales unpin
The winter's robes;
The film of spring is hanging from the lids.

Light breaks on secret lots,
On tips of thought where thoughts smell in the rain;
When logics die,
The secret of the soil grows through the eye,
And blood jumps in the sun;
Above the waste allotments the dawn halts.

Poem in October

It was my thirtieth year to heaven
Woke to my hearing from harbour and neighbour wood
And the mussel pooled and the heron
Priested shore
The morning beckon
With water praying and call of seagull and rook
And the knock of sailing boats on the net webbed wall
Myself to set foot
That second
In the still sleeping town and set forth.

My birthday began with the water-
Birds and the birds of the winged trees flying my name
Above the farms and the white horses
And I rose
In rainy autumn
And walked abroad in a shower of all my days.
High tide and the heron dived when I took the road
Over the border
And the gates
Of the town closed as the town awoke.

A springful of larks in a rolling
Cloud and the roadside bushes brimming with whistling
Blackbirds and the sun of October
Summery
On the hill's shoulder,
Here were fond climates and sweet singers suddenly
Come in the morning where I wandered and listened
To the rain wringing
Wind blow cold
In the wood faraway under me.

Pale rain over the dwindling harbour
And over the sea wet church the size of a snail
With its horns through mist and the castle
Brown as owls,
But all the gardens
Of spring and summer were blooming in the tall tales
Beyond the border and under the lark full cloud.

There could I marvel
My birthday
Away but the weather turned around.

It turned away from the blithe country
And down the other air and the blue altered sky
Streamed again a wonder of summer
With apples
Pears and red currants
And I saw in the turning so clearly a child's
Forgotten mornings when he walked with his mother
Through the parables
Of sun light
And the legends of the green chapels

And the twice told fields of infancy
That his tears burned my cheeks and his heart moved in mine.
These were the woods the river and sea
Where a boy
In the listening
Summertime of the dead whispered the truth of his joy
To the trees and the stones and the fish in the tide.
And the mystery
Sang alive
Still in the water and singingbirds.

And there could I marvel my birthday
Away but the weather turned around. And the true
Joy of the long dead child sang burning
In the sun.
It was my thirtieth
Year to heaven stood there then in the summer noon
Though the town below lay leaved with October blood.
O may my heart's truth
Still be sung
On this high hill in a year's turning.

RUTHVEN TODD (b. 1914)

Various ends

Sidney, according to report, was kindly hearted
When stretched upon the field of death;
And, in his gentleness, ignored the blood that spurted,
Expending the last gutter of his flickering breath.

Marlowe, whose raw temper used to rise
Like boiling milk, went on the booze;
A quick word and his half-startled eyes
Mirrored his guts flapping on his buckled shoes.

Swift went crazy in his lonely tower,
Where blasphemous obscenity paid the warders,
Who brought a string of visitors every hour
To see the wild beast, the Dean in holy orders.

And there were those coughed out their sweet soft lungs
Upon the mountains, or the clear green sea.
Owen found half an ounce of lead with wings;
And Tennyson died quietly, after tea.

Sam Johnson scissored at the surgeon's stitches
To drain more poison from his bloated body.
And Byron may have recalled the pretty bitches,
Nursing his fevered head in hands unsteady.

De Nerval finished swinging from a grid
And round his neck the Queen of Sheba's garter.
Swinburne died of boredom, doing as he was bid,
And Shelley bobbed lightly on the Mediterranean water.

Rimbaud, his leg grown blue and gross and round,
Lay sweating for these last weeks on his truckle-bed;
He could not die—the future was unbroken ground—
Only Paris, Verlaine and poetry were dead.

Blake had no doubts, his old fingers curled
Around dear Kate's frail and transparent hand;
Death merely meant a changing of his world,
A widening of experience, for him it marked no end.

ALUN LEWIS (1915—1944)

In hospital: Poona

Last night I did not fight for sleep
But lay awake from midnight while the world
Turned its slow features to the moving deep
Of darkness, till I knew that you were furled,

Beloved, in the same dark watch as I.
And sixty degrees of longitude beside
Vanished as though a swan in ecstacy
Had spanned the distance from your sleeping side.

And like to swan or moon the whole of Wales
Glided within the parish of my care:
I saw the green tide leap on Cardigan,
Your red yacht riding a legend there,

And the great mountains, Dafydd and Llewelyn,
Plynlimmon, Cader Idris and Eryri
Threshing the darkness back from head and fin,
And also the small nameless mining valley

Whose slopes are scratched with streets and sprawling graves
Dark in the lap of firwoods and great boulders
Where you lay waiting, listening to the waves—
My hot hands touched your white despondent shoulders
—And then ten thousand miles of daylight grew

Between us, and I heard the wild daws crake
In India's starving throat; whereat I knew
That Time upon the heart can break
But love survives the venom of the snake.

JUDITH WRIGHT (b. 1915)

Bullocky

Beside his heavy-shouldered team,
thirsty with drought and chilled with rain,
he weathered all the striding years
till they ran widdershins in his brain:

Till the long solitary tracks
etched deeper with each lurching load
were populous before his eyes,
and fiends and angels used his road.

All the long straining journey grew
a mad apocalyptic dream,
and he old Moses, and the slaves
his suffering and stubborn team.

Then in his evening camp beneath
the half-light pillars of the trees
he filled the steepled cone of night
with shouted prayers and prophecies.

While past the campfire's crimson ring
the star-struck darkness cupped him round,
and centuries of cattlebells
rang with their sweet uneasy sound.

Grass is across the waggon tracks,
and plough strikes bone beneath the grass,
and vineyards cover all the slopes
where the dead teams were used to pass.

O vine grow close upon that bone
and hold it with your rooted hand.
The prophet Moses feeds the grape,
and fruitful is the Promised Land.

The builders

Only those coral insects live
that work and endure under
the breakers' cold continual thunder.
They are the quick of the reef
that rots and crumbles in a calmer water.
Only those men survive
who dare to hold their love against the world;
who dare to live and doubt what they are told.
They are the quick of life;
their faith is insolence; joyful is their grief.

This is life's promise and accomplishment—
a fraction-foothold taken.
Where dark eroding seas had broken,
the quick, the sensitive, the lover,

the passionate touch and intergrowth of living.
Alive, alive, intent,
love rises on the crumbling shells it shed.
The strata of the dead
burst with the plumes and passions of the earth.
Seed falls there now, birds build, and life takes over.

Night and the child

In the morning the hawk and the sun flew up together;
the wildhaired sun and the wild bird of prey.
Now both are fallen out of the treacherous sky.
One holds a bullet as leaden as the lid of his eye
and one from the west's red beaches fell to the western water.
O hawk and sun of my morning, how far you are gone down.

The night comes up over you, faceless and forbidden,
over the hawk sunk in earth and the sun drunk by the sea;
and who can tell, the child said, no matter what they say—
who can be sure that the sun will rise on another day?
for he died in his blood on the water as the hawk died, and is hidden.
How far under the grey eyelid the yellow eye is gone.

Who can be sure, the child said, that there will be a waking?
Now I am given to the night and my soul is afraid.
I would people the dark with candles and friends to stay by my side
but the darkness said, Only in my heart can you hide.
I said to the dark, Be my friend; but the dark said, I am nothing,
and now I must turn my face to the sea of Nothing and drown.

And no one could reach me or save me out of that deadly dream
until deep under the sea I found the sleeping sun.
With the sun asleep in my arms I sank and was not and was gone
even as the hawk was gone after the noise of the gun.
I who run on the beach where the morning sun is warm
went under the black sea, and rose with the sun, and am born.

DAVID CAMPBELL (b. 1915)

Speak with the sun

From a wreck of tree in the wash of night
Glory, glory, sings the bird;
Across ten thousand years of light
His creative voice is heard.

Wide on a tide of wind are set
Warp and woof of silvered air;
But the song slips through the net
To where the myriad galaxies are.

And to the heartbeats of the light,
Now from the deepness of the glade
Well up the bubbles of delight:
Of such stuff the stars were made.

The end of exploring

See! down the red road by the brown tree
The gate leans wide like morning. Here's winter's green;
Here are summer's bleached affairs; and here between
Rain work and wind work, the road winds free.

The shed is slabbed with shimmer. Fence posts go
Hill-high for shadows. Ben's on his bright chain:
And it's the dog's limit, the green cock's strain;
And the road lies hard and open towards the snow.

But why go? The time waits deep for summer
With the grain, for the ringed shade and sheep
Cropping the silence while the swagmen sleep
Though on the height the ice-etched symbols glimmer.

And the road? Go then; and smothered in the snow,
Or on the violet ridge where the ice trees burn,
Trust to your lucky heart you may return
With love to dog-bark, gate and sweet cockcrow.

439

SYDNEY GOODSIR SMITH (b. 1915)

Can I forget?

Can I forget the sickle mune
Owre Largo throu the driven clouds,
The sea like bylan milk at our fuit?
Can I forget the snaw around
And the tent-flap like a gun boom
As the wind took it?

Can I forget the wolves' houl
Faimished rinnan throu the toun
O' haar[1] and wind and lamplicht?
Can I forget the staucheran news
As Christ received the Spainish doom
—And nocht to dae but drink o nichts?

Can I forget my black wound?
Kirkcudbright may ye be dung doun
And damned Dundrennan Rood!
Can I forget the splendant luve
Crottle[2] in my twa hands til stour[3],
The rose o my hert wormed wi grue?

Can I forget the Solway flows
Gray as daith, or the worm i the rose?
Whiles I micht, but it bydes its hour
And, thornit nou, hert's fanatic pouer
Strang as the skaith[4] it stranger flouers—
The skaith's a meisure o the luve.

Can I forget what the saul can pruve:
Luve is bricht as the skaith is dure,
And skaith as deep as the luve is hie?
Can I forget I'll neer can flee
Twa tyger een nae mair nor thae
Lang hochs like the heivan dunes o the sea?

Can I forget, my luve, my luve,
Havana thrang[5] wi drucken fules
And ye amang them, lauchan queen?

440

Can I forget, my luve, my luve,
Strathyre's muckle bed in a wee room,
White breists like hills i the mune's lily-leam[6]?

Can I forget the gifts o you,
The music that's the wine o luve,
The birds' wild sea-sang in your hair?
Can I forget, my pouter-dou[7],
Voar[8] and hairst[9] and winter are you,
Sun and mune and the world, my dear?

1. *haar* = sea-mist.   2. *crottle* = crumble.   3. *stour* = dust.
4. *skaith* = wound.   5. *thrang* = crowded.   6. *leam* = radiance.
7. *pouter-dou* = dove.   8. *voar* = spring.   9. *hairst* = autumn.

DAVID GASCOYNE (b. 1916)

On the Grand Canal

The palaces are sombre cliffs by night;
Some pierced with square-hewn caves,
Grottoes where chandeliers like stalactites
Frosted with electricity blaze dangling in the midst
Of sad high-ceilinged salons' tepid haze;
Or semi-concealed by casement shutter-slats
The twilit velvet cloister-cells of lives
Upon whose intimacy we may gaze
As we slide by, nor stir to any flutter
At solitary privacy intruded on
The page-perusing half-glimpsed inmates' eyes.
Others among these wave-lapped marble fortresses
Within which the patrician past lies passively beseiged,
Long before midnight look already left unoccupied
Except by somnolent and unseen soldiery,
As from their blank embrasures only blackness
Broods on the glimmering oracle of the tides
That slowly rise and fall about their feet.
One summer night a passenger upon a steamer, I
While we were floating past before them, tried
To read the mystery of the city's palaces
In the framed scenes and silhouettes displayed
To all that sail down the Canal, and when we paused

A minute at a *stazione* raft, looked up and saw
And seized on instantly, a young girl's head
In a near window, her sweet fresh-coloured face
Vividly lit with eagerness, whose aspect made
Me wonder what it was she held before her
And seemed to read from, what the text and page
Of Goldoni or Shakespeare she rehearsed.
But as the steamer stirred again I saw
It was a fan of playing-cards she held,
A lucky hand, as her expression showed . . .
I wished that lovely face good luck in love,
Though my excitement at that glimpse of her
Swiftly became an elegiac feeling
As the boat's motion swept her from my sight.

MAURICE JAMES CRAIG (b. 1919)

Ballad to a traditional refrain

Red bricks in the suburbs, white horse on the wall,
Eyetalian marbles in the City Hall:
O stranger from England, why stand so aghast?
May the Lord in His mercy be kind to Belfast.

This jewel that houses our hopes and our fears
Was knocked up from the swamp in the last hundred years;
But the last shall be first and the first shall be last:
May the Lord in His mercy be kind to Belfast.

We swore by King William there'd never be seen
An All-Irish Parliament at College Green,
So at Stormont we're nailing the flag to the mast:
May the Lord in His mercy be kind to Belfast.

O the bricks they will bleed and the rain it will weep,
And the damp Lagan fog lull the city to sleep;
It's to hell with the future and live on the past:
May the Lord in His mercy be kind to Belfast.

ALEX COMFORT (b. 1920)

Poem

One whom I knew, a student and a poet
Makes his way shoreward tonight, out of the sea,
Blown to a houseless coast near Bettystown
Where along sleeping miles the sea is laying
Printless meadows of sand, and beyond to seaward
Endless untrodden fields, louder than corn. These nets
Follow the long beaches. Tonight a guest
Noses his way to the shore. They wait for him
Where the sand meets the grass—and one unmarried holds
Her spine's long intricate necklace for his shoulders,
Pillows his broken face, his for another's
For she died waiting. He will learn much
Of roots and the way of stones and the small sand
And that the shoreward dead are friends to all
At whose heels yell the clock-faced citizens.
So like a ship the dead man comes to shore.

The atoll in the mind

Out of what calms and pools the cool shell grows
dumb teeth under clear waters, where no currents
fracture the coral's porous horn

Grows up the mind's stone tree, the honeycomb,
the plump brain coral breaking the pool's mirror,
the ebony antler, the cold sugared fan.

All these strange trees stand upward through the water,
the mind's grey candied points tend to the surface,
the greater part is out of sight below.

But when on the island's whaleback spring green blades
new land over water wavers, birds bring seeds
and tides plant slender trunks by the lagoon.

I find the image of the mind's two trees, cast downward,
one tilting leaves to catch the sun's bright pennies,
one dark as water, rooted among the bones.

Notes for my son

Remember when you hear them beginning to say Freedom
Look carefully—see who it is that they want you to butcher.

Remember, when you say that the old trick would not have
    fooled you for a moment,
that every time it is the trick which seems new.

Remember that you will have to put in irons
your better nature, if it will desert to them.

Remember, remember their faces—watch them carefully:
for every step you take is on somebody's body.

And every cherry you plant for them is a gibbet,
And every furrow you turn for them is a grave.

Remember, the smell of burning will not sicken you
if they persuade you that it will thaw the world.

Beware, the blood of a child does not smell so bitter
if you have shed it with a high moral purpose.

So that because a woodcutter disobeyed
they will not burn her today nor any day;

So that for lack of a joiner's obedience
the crucifiction will not now take place;

So that when they come to sell you their bloody corruption
You will gather the spit of your chest
And plant it in their faces.

SIDNEY KEYES (1922—1943)

William Wordsworth

No room for mourning: he's gone out
Into the noisy glen, or stands between the stones
Of the gaunt ridge, or you'll hear his shout
Rolling among the screes, he being a boy again.
He'll never fail nor die

And if they laid his bones
In the wet vaults or iron sarcophagi
Of fame, he'd rise at the first summer rain
And stride across the hills to seek
His rest among the broken lands and clouds.
He was a stormy day, a granite peak
Spearing the sky; and look, about its base
Words flower like crocuses in the hanging woods,
Blank through the dalehead and the bony face.

Time will not grant

Time will not grant the unlined page
Completion or the hand respite:
The Magi stray, the heaven's rage,
The careful pilgrim stumbles in the night.

Take pen, take eye and etch
Your vision on this unpropitious time;
Faces are fluid, actions never reach
Perfection but in reflex or in rhyme.

Take now, not soon; your lost
Minutes roost home like curses.
Nicolo, Martin, every unhoused ghost
Proclaims time's strange reverses.

Fear was Donne's peace; to him,
Charted between the minstrel cherubim,
Terror was decent. Rilke tenderly
Accepted autumn like a rooted tree.
But I am frightened after every good day
That all my life must change and fall away.

JAMES KIRKUP (b. 1923)

A correct compassion

*To Mr. Philip Allison, after watching him perform a Mitral Stenosis Valvulotomy
in the General Infirmary at Leeds*

Cleanly, sir, you went to the core of the matter.
Using the purest kind of wit, a balance of belief and art,
You with a curious nervous elegance laid bare
The root of life, and put your finger on its beating heart.

The glistening theatre swarms with eyes, and hands, and eyes.
On green-clothed tables, ranks of instruments transmit a sterile gleam.
The masks are on, and no unnecessary smile betrays
A certain tension, true concomitant of calm.

Here we communicate by looks, though words,
Too, are used, as in continuous historic present
You describe our observations and your deeds.
All gesture is reduced to its result, an instrument.

She who does not know she is a patient lies
Within a tent of green, and sleeps without a sound
Beneath the lamps, and the reflectors that devise
Illuminations probing the profoundest wound.

A calligraphic master, improvising, you invent
The first incision, and no poet's hesitation
Before his snow-blank page mars your intent:
The flowing stroke is drawn like an uncalculated inspiration.

A garland of flowers unfurls across the painted flesh.
With quick precision the arterial forceps click.
Yellow threads are knotted with a simple flourish.
Transfused, the blood preserves its rose, though it is sick.

Meters record the blood, measure heart-beats, control the breath.
Hieratic gesture: scalpel bares a creamy rib; with pincer knives
The bone quietly is clipped, and lifted out. Beneath,
The pink, black-mottled lung like a revolted creature heaves,

Collapses; as if by extra fingers is neatly held aside
By two ordinary egg-beaters, kitchen tools that curve
Like extraordinary hands. Heart, laid bare, silently beats. It can hide
No longer yet is not revealed.—'A local anaesthetic in the cardiac
    nerve.'

Now, in firm hands that quiver with a careful strength,
Your knife feels through the heart's transparent skin; at first,
Inside the pericardium, slit down half its length,
The heart, black-veined, swells like a fruit about to burst,

But goes on beating, love's poignant image bleeding at the dart
Of a more grievous passion, as a bird, dreaming of flight, sleeps on
Within its leafy cage.—'It generally upsets the heart
A bit, though not unduly, when I make the first injection.'

Still, still the patient sleeps, and still the speaking heart is dumb.
The watchers breathe an air far sweeter, rarer than the room's.
The cold walls listen. Each in his own blood hears the drum
She hears, tented in green, unfathomable calms.

'I make a purse-string suture here, with a reserve
Suture, which I must make first, and deeper,
As a safeguard, should the other burst. In the cardiac nerve
I inject again a local anaesthetic. Could we have fresh towels to cover

All these adventitious ones. Now can you all see.
When I put my finger inside the valve, there may be a lot
Of blood, and it may come with quite a bang. But I let it flow,
In case there are any clots, to give the heart a good clean-out.

Now can you give me every bit of light you've got.'
We stand on the benches, peering over his shoulder.
The lamp's intensest rays are concentrated on an inmost heart.
Someone coughs. 'If you have to cough, you will do it outside this
    theatre.'—'Yes, sir.'

'How's she breathing, Doug.? Do you feel quite happy?'—'Yes,
  fairly
Happy'—'Now. I am putting my finger in the opening of the valve.
I can only get the tip of my finger in.—It's gradually
Giving way.—I'm inside.—No clots.—I can feel the valve

Breathing freely now around my finger, and the heart working.
Not too much blood. It opened very nicely.
I should say that anatomically speaking
This is a perfect case.—Anatomically.

For of course, anatomy is not physiology.'
We find we breathe again, and hear the surgeon hum.
Outside, in the street, a car starts up. The heart regularly
Thunders.—'I do not stitch up the pericardium.

It is not necessary.'—For this is imagination's other place,
Where only necessary things are done, with the supreme and grave
Dexterity that ignores technique; with proper grace
Informing a correct compassion, that performs its love, and makes
  it live.

INDEX OF AUTHORS

INDEX OF FIRST LINES